TAKEN AT THE FLOOD

BOOKS BY JOHN GUNTHER

Taken at the Flood
Inside Russia Today
Inside Africa
Inside U.S.A.
Inside Latin America
Inside Asia
Inside Europe
The Riddle of MacArthur
Eisenhower
Roosevelt in Retrospect
Behind the Curtain
Death Be Not Proud
D Day
The Troubled Midnight
Days to Remember
(with Bernard Quint)
Meet North Africa
(with Sam and Beryl Epstein)
Meet South Africa
(with Sam and Beryl Epstein)
Meet the Congo
Alexander the Great
Julius Caesar
The Golden Fleece

John Gunther

TAKEN
AT THE FLOOD

The Story of Albert D. Lasker

H|B

HARPER & BROTHERS · PUBLISHERS · NEW YORK

Dedicated to all who loved Albert

There is a tide in the affairs of men,
Which, taken at the flood, leads on to fortune.
                    —*Julius Caesar*, iv, 3

CONTENTS

ILLUSTRATIONS

TAKEN AT THE FLOOD

Chapter 1

A GLIMPSE OF THINGS TO COME

When Albert Lasker, one of the most phenomenal Americans of his time, was sixteen years old he was already a veteran newspaperman, and had a part-time job as a reporter on the Galveston *News*. This was back in 1896, and Galveston in those days was the second-biggest city in Texas, with all of 30,000 people. (Dallas had a population of 18,000, and Houston was still a village with dust behind the ears.) Not only did young Lasker, who was packed with enterprise and zest, work on the *News;* he had a business of his own. This came about as a result of two circumstances. The first was that Galveston, where he grew up, was the largest cotton port in the world after Liverpool; second, the great press associations like the Associated Press did not, at that time, maintain regular correspondents in Galveston. All that they were interested in was the price of cotton—the daily quotations on the cotton exchange.

It happened that a somewhat shiftless, middle-aged reporter on the Galveston *News,* taking advantage of this situation, had been able to work up a tidy little business. He sat on the state desk of the *News,* where he had access to the cotton quotations, and, with the paper's consent but strictly on his own, formed a small syndicate and transmitted cotton news by wire to newspapers in Chicago, St. Louis, and New York. His revenue from this ingenious operation, although not large, was useful, and kept him plentifully supplied with drink. This, in turn, proved to be his ruin; he lost his job on the *News,* and, a drifter at heart, prepared to leave Galveston for a happier environment. Lasker, who was still in high school and who was working on the *News* in his spare time, the veriest cub, heard of this contretemps. Like an arrow shot from a stiff bow he went to his colleague, and offered to buy his syndicate for $100. The colleague did not believe that the young man could assemble any such majestic sum overnight, but he did so, and the deal was made.

Lasker was at this time a tall skinny boy with elbows sticking through his sleeves and the brightest of big brown eyes, which shone like buttons. He came from a prosperous Galveston family, and was well-known for his gifts of energy and push. But few Galvestonians of the day, no matter how keen their prescience, could have conceived in their wildest dreams what a rich, full, fruitful, and variegated career he was going to have.

One day young Lasker got a tip that Eugene V. Debs was in the city. Debs, the celebrated labor leader who later became Socialist candidate for the presidency of the United States no fewer than five times (in 1920 he got almost a million votes), had just spent a term in jail for organizing a strike of railway workers. He was a big story. Nobody had been able to find or interview him. Lasker heard that he had arrived secretly in Galveston to take part in the annual convention of the Brotherhood of Locomotive Firemen, and this would be his first public appearance since his experience in jail. But he was hiding out until the convention opened, in order to avoid publicity, and nobody knew his whereabouts. Albert scurried around, and found out that he was living in an obscure rooming house on the edge of town.

Albert waited until darkness fell, because he did not want to be seen, and then went to the local office of Western Union. He said to the manager, "Lend me a Western Union messenger boy's uniform and cap, and please give me some telegram forms and a receipt book." (In those days people had to sign for telegrams.)

The manager said, "I can't do that. It's strictly against regulations. I'd be fired if anybody ever heard about it."

The youthful Lasker said, "You'll be fired if you don't."

"How come?"

"I'll transfer my cotton quotations business to Postal, and that'll be the end of you."

Indeed, Postal had just entered Galveston, and was competing hotly with Western Union. Lasker was only a boy, but his account was substantial.

"Come on!" he urged amiably. "Be a good sport, and we'll do a lot more business together in the future."

Albert ducked down the street to the house of a friend, where he changed swiftly into the uniform and spent a few minutes at a typewriter. He rushed then to the house where Debs was hiding, strode nimbly up the steps, and knocked. A man opened the door, and asked him suspiciously what he wanted.

Now, young Lasker knew well this type of old frame house. It was built around a stairwell, and the walls were flimsy, so that a voice, if raised, could be heard throughout the building. Lasker yelled, making acoustics his ally, "I have a telegram for delivery to Mr. Eugene V. Debs."

The man said, "Give it to me. I'll give you a receipt."

Lasker had studied photographs of Debs, and knew that this man was not Debs. He shouted, "No. My instructions are to deliver this telegram into the hands of Mr. Debs, personally."

Debs appeared, having heard the loud voices. Eagerly Lasker handed over the telegram, and Debs opened it. This is what he read:

I AM NOT A MESSENGER BOY. I AM A YOUNG NEWSPAPER REPORTER. YOU HAVE TO GIVE A FIRST INTERVIEW TO SOME-BODY. WHY DON'T YOU GIVE IT TO ME? IT WILL START ME ON MY CAREER.

Debs was so amused by this that he invited the youth in and gave him a long interview, which reached newspapers all over the country—a real beat, Lasker's first scoop. The New York *Sun*, no less, offered the young man a job on the strength of it, but he turned the offer down because he was making more money in Galveston than the *Sun* offered. This little story tells a good deal about Albert Lasker. Even as a boy, he had imagination, initiative, persuasive power, and a clever sense of drama; he was tough, daring, and resourceful. The facets of this diamond were cut in childhood, and they stayed bright his whole life long.

Who Lasker Was

Before we go into Lasker's origins and tell the story of his career it may be well to pause briefly for purposes of identification. Who was Albert Lasker? First, a remarkable human being—a "character" in the full sense of that overworked word. Anecdotes clung to him like burrs to tweed. Second, for good or ill, the father of modern advertising. As such, few men have ever done more to change American social patterns and buying habits. Third, a very rich man who did fantastic things with money. Fourth, a person who impinged on an astonishingly varied number of elements on the American scene—politics, shipping, baseball, golf, government, show business, Jewish affairs, merchandising, public relations, aviation, civil liberties, art, philanthropy, and, above all, medical research.

Lasker went to work for Lord & Thomas, an advertising agency in Chicago, in 1898 for $10 a week, and left it in 1942, a multimillionaire. During most of these forty-four years he was its sole proprietor, and it became the biggest and most famous as well as the most prosperous advertising agency in the world. He took more money out of the advertising business than anybody who ever lived— more than $45,000,000—or anybody who ever will live. He made fabulous sums, spent fabulous sums, and lost fabulous sums. When he died he left only $11,500,000—a pleasant fortune certainly but a pittance compared to what, for example, contemporary oil men have. Most of the rest he gave away—to his family, friends, and multitudinous charities. But the most interesting thing about Lasker's money is that it all came out of his head. He made $45,000,000 by sheer brain power. His fortune did not come from inheritance (although his family was by no means poor), nor by the mass production and sale of some such commodity as automobiles, nor through speculation, nor by the lucky ownership of property bearing oil or some similar natural resource. He made the bulk of his fortune by communicating abstractions—by ideas.

Lasker, who was born in 1880 and who died in 1952, was extraordinarily generous—of time, of money, of himself. But he always retained a nice, down-to-earth attitude about money. Once in Florida a friend sought to persuade him to invest $300,000 in an enterprise. Albert refused. The friend, bitterly disappointed, kept pressing him, and, in a final plea, asked him what he had to lose.

Lasker replied dryly, "Three hundred thousand dollars."

As to philanthropy, he started to give money away for worthy purposes long before he was forty, and, in his later years, gave without stint to causes that interested him, particularly in the field of health and medicine. With the help of a few friends he remade the American Cancer Society, and, with his third wife, Mary Woodard Lasker, did much to awaken the federal government to the need for appropriating large sums every year for medical research. If a cure for cancer is discovered in the United States in this generation, it is not too much to say that some share of the credit should go to Albert Lasker.

But to return to advertising, the hard core of his business career. His contribution to advertising was prodigious, and some results of his pioneering are with us yet. Lucky Strike, Pepsodent, Kleenex, Palmolive, Studebaker, Sunkist, RCA, Frigidaire, were among the multitudinous products and trade-marks spawned or popularized by Lord & Thomas. His slogans, like "Keep That School Girl Complexion" and "Reach for a Lucky Instead of a Sweet," reverberated throughout the country. Lasker was an innovator in the merchandising of canned foodstuffs and evaporated milk, helped make citrus fruits something to drink as well as eat, helped encourage women to smoke, and introduced them to the miracle of Kotex. He was one of the first to foresee the power of radio in advertising, assembled the first soap operas, for which many will not thank him today, helped invent the radio commercial, for which ditto, and assisted in making broadcasting an overwhelming, irresistible national force.

Lasker was, however, not a huckster. He had clients who were hucksters and he employed hucksters, but he had no trace of hucksterism himself. He was not a cynic; he believed vehemently, passionately, in the products he advertised. He never belonged to an advertising club, avoided meeting his associates and competitors in the agency business, and would never dream of having a client in his home, unless the client happened to be close to him on a personal basis. He loved advertising with fervor for many years, but then turned against it, as we shall see, partly because it had become too "mechanical." After almost half a century he dissolved Lord & Thomas, his lifework, without a pang and on a moment's notice, as arbitrarily as a child, while he was still making a million a year or more out of it. Although he was proud of his accomplishments in advertising, he was appalled later by some of the bizarre phenomena that flew out of the Pandora's box he had inadvertently opened. He was a prime creator of Madison Avenue, and then moved far away; he was creator and repudiator both.

As a matter of fact, Lasker's life was a continual process of advance. Few men have ever changed more; the dimensions of his evolution are so extreme as to be hard to believe. He was a vociferous Republican for many years, and ended up voting for Franklin D. Roosevelt and Harry Truman. He was an ardent isolationist, and played a minor but effective role in keeping the United States from joining the old League of Nations, but he ended up as a vigorous disciple of Wendell Willkie, an advocate of One World, and a firm supporter of the United Nations. Consider his transformation on a different level. He disliked graphic art so much that for long years he even refused to have an art department at Lord & Thomas—and then, starting from scratch in his sixties, built up a highly personal collection of modern French painting which is one of the most notable in the world. He hated research in business, and then leaped wholeheartedly into research in medical fields. An idiosyncratic personality indeed!

He was not, however, unstable. He said once, "I have to be wrong a certain number of times in order to be right a certain number of times." He liked to say that it was not he who changed, but the times. He was always passionately interested in what was *new*. Not only was his life distinguished by a capacity for growth; he was one of the few people I have ever met who actually seemed to become younger every year. By the time he was seventy he had become forty-five.

One peculiar thing is that he was never particularly well known outside his own immediate circle. He never became a national figure, nor did he want to be one. He created publicity for others, but avoided it determinedly for himself. Lasker was never profiled by *The New Yorker*. He never had a cover story in *Time*. He was never written about by *Collier's* or the *Saturday Evening Post*. His listing in *Who's Who* was always brief. His name does not appear conspicuously in textbooks or histories of advertising. He never wrote anything for publication, and in fifty years made only half a dozen speeches. (One of these, it is true, lasted for three whole days.) Very little was ever written about him, even in the newspapers, and in this book I have had to rely, not on written records, but on the word-of-mouth testimony and memory of friends.

In fact, this book digs up a virgin field. Two documents of considerable interest do, however, exist. One is *The Lasker Story*, an eighty-six-page pamphlet put out by *Advertising Age* in 1953, following serial publication in 1952 and 1953, which is the verbatim record of a talk Lasker gave to his associates in Lord & Thomas in 1925; luckily, somebody had the foresight to have a stenographer in the room. Mostly it is about the theory and practice of advertising, and is an invaluable source for light on his business attitudes. The other, which has never been published in full, is the typescript of some reminiscences which he dictated to the Oral History Research Office of Columbia University in 1949-50; it includes some of his memories of the Shipping Board, early days in advertising, baseball, politics, Israel, and his relation with the American Tobacco Company. A summary of this transcript appeared in *American Heritage* (December, 1954). Unfortunately Lasker gave up dictating these memoirs after a few sessions, because to talk about himself in the past bored him, and large areas of his career are altogether untouched. It is a pity that he did not do more. The whole document is only eighty-one pages long, and some of it duplicates material in *The Lasker Story*.

Brushstrokes for a Portrait

I met Lasker for the first time in India in 1938, but did not get to know him well until 1942, when he was about to retire from business and was devoting himself to philanthropy and having fun. Then during the last decade of his life we became quite close.

Let me try to give a preliminary picture of his looks, mannerisms, attributes. He was a tall man, taut, very straight and slim; he never had a weight problem, because his nervous energy burned off surplus calories; he was constantly in motion, tense—almost vibrating. He was an extraordinarily warm person, with a passionate love of life, full of curiosity, as eager and enthusiastic as a child. He gave out a spark, a glow. You could almost see his face in the dark. One of his friends, a woman celebrated as a dress designer, testifies, "He could send a person out of a room *warmer*. People looked at him, and were no longer lonely." If you knew him well, it was impossible not to become actively involved with him.

He was one of those fortunate human beings who get better-looking as they mature. No one would have called him handsome in his youth, but, in his sixties and seventies, he became very good-looking, like a prophet out of Hebrew scripture. For years he struggled, as a result of some childish fear of being fancy, against a natural curl in his hair, and sought to paste it down; at last he let it grow out and it became two magnificent ridges of pure white foam, as white as coconut. But his eyebrows, which were commanding, stayed jet-black. His face was ruddy, with broad powerful bones under the eyes. His eyes were his best feature. They were large, of a deep bright brown, and they glittered with a liquid shine.

Once Lasker had an argument with Fairfax Cone, who was running his Chicago office, about the appearance of a colleague. Cone thought that this man was good-looking; Lasker thought not. Cone protested, "At least, Mr. Lasker, you'll have to admit that he's awfully pretty." Lasker transfixed Cone with a glare: "Mr. Cone, you and I have *strong* faces!"

This brings up an incidental point: Lasker seldom called his men by their first names, even if they had been with him for years. It was always "*Mister* Brown," "*Mister* Smith," or "*Mister* Jones." The camaraderie normal in an American business office was foreign to him. Nor, as a rule, did anybody ever call him anything but "Mr. Lasker," except a handful of close friends who said "A.D." Nobody ever called him "Al" or "Bert." He was Mr. Lasker. Even today, years after his death, his old associates still instinctively say "Mr." Lasker respectfully when they talk of him.

For years, he was somewhat careless about dress. He was far too busy to go shopping, and the legend is that he let his valet, who was approximately his own size and shape, go to the tailor for him. During the incumbency of one valet his friends noticed, with apprehension, that his wardrobe was gradually becoming more fiery— he was going in for suits with big checks and flamboyant stripes. The reason for this was, of course, that Lasker gave his discarded clothes to the valet, and this young man fell naturally into the habit of buying things that suited his own taste, which was exotic. When Lasker married Mary Reinhardt in 1940, she took him firmly in hand in the matter of dress, and enticed him to the lair of the best tailor in New York. Here, dutifully, he withstood the ordeal of trying on a new suit eight, nine, ten, a dozen times, until the shoulders were exactly broad enough, the lapels cut on precisely the proper slant. As a result he became well dressed at last, and in fact was several times listed as one of the ten best-dressed men in the United States. Incidentally, it was Lasker who in the early 1930's started the vogue, now more or less extinct, for blue shirts in daytime business wear.

Probably the most remarkable of his small personal traits was his manner of speech. This was unique. When he was interested in something, his mind went faster than his tongue, and he would continually hesitate, with little hems and haws, to let his voice catch up. "He talked," one of his friends puts it, "like a locomotive pulling a long freight train uphill." It is difficult to convey in print the force of this mannerism. He would interrupt himself to utter little nasal exclamations like "Unh . . . hunh!" These interjections were like question marks; he was saying, in effect, "Are you following me?" The sound was almost like the first syllable of the neigh of a really spirited horse. On the other hand, these eccentricities of speech never for a moment detracted from his dignity, which was marked.

If Lasker feared that people were not paying close enough attention to him, he would insert other phrases into the middle of sentences, like "Huh!—Ha!" or "Do you [understand]?" He was too hurried to add the word "understand" and would content himself with the simple "Do you." On the telephone (he hated the telephone) these peculiarities reached a major pitch. Between every other sentence he ejaculated some such exhortation as a staccato "Halloo!" "Hhhhaa!" "Um!" and "*Are* you [listening]?" Perhaps this was a carry-over from the early days of long-distance telephoning when communication was often interrupted by breakdowns in the line.

Lasker's mannerism in speech could not be called a stammer in the medical sense, and it was certainly not an impediment; on the contrary, he talked with the utmost fluency. Most people, after an hour or two with him, were exhausted. He liked contact when he talked; he fairly clutched you. Anna Rosenberg, the former Assistant Secretary of Defense, who was devoted to him, records that, in a crowded room on one occasion, he suddenly took advantage of a brief respite to seize the floor, with the indignant words, "Let *me* talk!" But he had been talking almost uninterruptedly for three hours. Once I called on him as member of an informal delegation requesting his advice on a political matter; Lasker listened to us with the utmost gravity, and then announced, "I will now talk for an hour, unh!" And he did—in a marvelously entertaining way.

Although he was something of a recluse so far as the public was concerned, he could not bear to be alone. He was intensely gregarious, and had hundreds of friends in a dozen different realms. He bathed himself in friendship. Moreover, he acted as a catalytic agent, and strove perpetually to bring people together, in particular young people. Also he had a nice talent for extracting power, luster, out of those close to him. He could be a tyrant on occasion, but as one of his doctors, trying to analyze his complex character, said to me once, "He could *squeeze* the good out of you!" Once he told Sheldon R. Coons, who was in charge of his New York office, "You know, Mr. Coons, I can get more out of people than they have in them!"

Core of the Character

Perhaps the most important thing to say about Lasker is that, although he was a multimillionaire he was not at all a typical multimillionaire. He was off-beat. He did not remotely resemble the conventional nabob or tycoon of his time—men hard as marbles, glacial, and rapacious. He was not at all a creature of the countinghouse (although he kept books with extreme accuracy). The mere acquisition of money did not interest him much once he was fairly well along in life. He said once, "I didn't want to make a great fortune; I wanted to show what I could do with my brains." Business was a kind of joust, a tournament, a duel. But the score was kept in money, and so he had to have it. Dollars were "frozen energy"— the essential chips.

Actually, as Dr. Alfred Frankfurter, the publisher and editor of *Art News* and one of his most intimate friends in his later years, has pointed out in a brief private memoir, Lasker's approach to almost everything, including money, was essentially romantic. This derived in part from his nineteenth-century German background. Neither Goethe nor Wagner ever meant anything to him, but touches of these weighty yeasts were in his heritage. He could not endure shopkeepers (although he helped revolutionize shopkeeping). He was continually bursting out with new enthusiasms, new enterprises; then getting bored with them and dropping them posthaste. He was romantic about everything from the movies to Israel, from how-to-sell-toothpaste to the institution of holy matrimony. Also, like most true romantics, he often seemed to be somewhat harassed.

He was emotional to a degree, and easily became upset.

All this helps to account for his impact on people, and why he was such fun to talk to. He was sensitive and perceptive, and forever interested, excited, by things he didn't know about. Many rich and successful men insulate themselves suspiciously from the infection of new people, new ideas; they are bored or blasé. But not Lasker. Time and time again, after his death, I would say to my wife, or she to me, in Moscow, Nairobi, or Greensboro, Vermont, when something fresh or compelling caught our attention, "How Albert would have loved to hear about this!" or "If Albert were alive what he could do with *that* idea!"

Then too Lasker was a showman, an impresario, and this too emphasized his romantic, unconventional quality. He dramatized everything; he was like Stanislavski, Guitry, or Belasco surveying audience response. Campaigns for Kleenex and Lucky Strikes were his Barnum & Bailey or Ballet Russe.

Finally in this realm, he was altogether nontypical of most wealthy men of his period because of his sense of humor, which was radiant. He certainly had a temper but mostly he was blithe—beguiling. He bubbled. If really angry, his first reaction would be to look deeply hurt, almost like a child puzzled by something not only wounding but inexplicable. But he smiled more than any man I ever met. Albert used humor as a device, a tool, with great effect. He had locked away in his mind a large fund of jokes, parables, anecdotes; these he could release with stunning effect when he needed them. He was a master of the art of relaxing tension in an argument by telling a story. Not only did he have a sense of humor; he had a sense of fun. He won with jokes.

*

Now some other factors. Lasker had a marked Judaic sense of righteousness, and, despite some mildly careless living in his youth, was an emphatic puritan. I never heard him tell an off-color story, and he had a formidable capacity for moral indignation. He had an almost clinical devotion to truth, inherited from his father. He respected women. He liked to drink, but I never saw him drunk. His vitality boiled the alcohol off. His only considerable vice was gambling in his early years—often for very large stakes. He would think nothing of losing—or winning— $5,000 at poker in an evening, and was quite capable of making side bets for $1,000 or so that he would be the first at the table to pick up a one-eyed jack—and usually was.

He had no manual dexterity whatever, and never learned to drive a car. Once or twice in the early Chicago days he dared to venture forth in an automobile alone, but a telephone call for succor would always come.

For many years, in spite of his effervescent vitality, Lasker was troubled by ill health. It was seldom possible for him to relax, and he had at least three prolonged nervous breakdowns. These did not, however, necessarily impede his activity. Ralph V. Sollitt, who was probably closer to him over a longer period than any other man at Lord & Thomas, records that, early in the 1930's, he left the hospital at Johns Hopkins, where he was a patient, to attend an urgent conference with officers of the American Tobacco Company in New York. Wrathful, he adjusted the difficulties that had arisen in his absence. Then he announced calmly, "Gentlemen, I have done all I can for you, uh. Good day, because I must return to Johns Hopkins now and continue my nervous breakdown."

Once he had a colloquy with Sam Goldwyn, the movie producer, at La Quinta, California. Lasker was complaining of various aches and pains.

"The trouble with you, Albert, is that you are a hypochondriac," said Goldwyn.

Lasker turned on him. "Do you affirm that, Sam?"

"Yes."

"Do you *attest* it?"

"Yes."

"Well! Humph! I would have you know that hypochondria is an extremely serious disease!"

Lasker was not, as a matter of blunt fact, very much of a hypochondriac; most of his illnesses were, unfortunately, real. In 1928 he and his wife gave $1,000,000 to the medical faculty of the University of Chicago specifically earmarked for the study of old age, geriatrics, and degenerative diseases. At this time, a gift of such dimensions was unusual, and the president of the University asked him why he had stipulated that the gift should be used for the study of old age. Lasker responded with his most winning smile, "Because if there are only two men left alive in the world I intend to be both!"

He was, of course, in a country where salesmanship is the first profession of the land, an unerringly good salesman. He could sell a horsecar to a railroad, or a straw hat to an Eskimo. He had to a commanding degree two of the prime essentials of a good salesman, resourcefulness and a sense of fundamentals. Also he had a signal gift for creating desires, and his powers of persuasion were unlimited. The greatest of his copy writers, Claude C. Hopkins, not a man easily taken in or given to exaggeration, wrote once, "No ordinary human being ever resisted Albert Lasker." Finally in this field, he not only loved to sell—he loved being sold.

The last possible remove from the conventional self-made executive, he could not endure what people nowadays call the "organization" mind. For instance, in the 1920's six or seven of his best men came to him to report, shamefacedly, that they had failed to get an important account, which went to a rival agency instead. "Why?" he demanded. The reason was that the client had been greatly impressed because the salesman from the rival agency was a vice president, whereas Lasker's men had no titles. Albert pondered for all of two seconds, and then announced to his six or seven men, "All of you are now vice presidents!"

He had an unexampled instinct for the public pulse and for gauging mass reactions, with the result that he helped revolutionize the marketing of goods and contributed substantially to the increase in the American standard of living that distinguished the first half of the twentieth century. His major objective was to get the most goods into the hands of as many people as possible in the easiest and cheapest way, so that mass production and mass consumption would intertwine. Doing so, he transformed advertising from a passive into an active force, and this was the most memorable of all his accomplishments.

Yet he steadily deprecated his talent by making remarks like, "I am nothing but an apostle of the obvious." His astuteness was based to an extent on a capacity to think in terms of the other person's thinking. He would never, on concluding a contract, dream of saying to a client, "Sign here." He would say, "Sign here, and now let us start doing business *together!*"

To be a success, he thought, a man had to have three things— energy, dedication, luck. Intelligence? "In *my* office," he said once, "we put the intelligence into 'em!"

His favorite maxim was, "The best way to keep out of trouble is not to get into it." Nothing could, at first glance, seem more banal, but Lasker added a subtle refinement to the concept. He said, "It's not what you do that gets you into trouble, but what you *start* to do." For instance, he wanted to visit Spain in the late 1940's, and made elaborate arrangements to take a trip there. Then it suddenly occurred to him that one of his good friends happened, at that time, to be the American Ambassador to Spain; he became convinced that the Ambassador would ask him, when he arrived in Madrid, to dinner to meet General Franco. This prospect filled him with horror. He did not relish at all the idea of breaking bread with a Fascist dictator. So, for this and other reasons, he called off the expedition. It was what he was *intending* to do that would get him into trouble. Misfortune has early roots, and foresight counts. In other words, think carefully about what temptation can get you into. Romance can go too far.

Probably, next to driving energy and intelligence, his greatest quality was his passionate desire for human contact at the fullest; he took everything at the flood. He was spontaneous, kindly, and fair. There were, of course, marked contradictions in his character, so much so that many people, even those who knew him well, had difficulty understanding him. He is not at all an easy person to write about. He was both sharp and winning. He had plenty of defects. He was not particularly elevated or sophisticated. He was often agitated and peremptory. He could be rude, arrogant, and intolerant.

Fortune smiled on this man, but demons pursued him too. All his life his enjoyments were checked by undefined anxieties and qualms of conscience in small personal affairs. In 1947 he testified before a Senate committee on the urgent need for federal support of a public health program. A Senator asked him, "But whom do you represent, Mr. Lasker?"

Lasker's reply was calm: "Forty million sufferers."

Chapter 2

OUT OF THE TEXAS FRONTIER

Albert Davis Lasker was born on May 1, 1880, of German Jewish stock; his father was an immigrant of liberal views who had settled in Galveston many years before. Albert, as it happened, was not born in Galveston but in Freiburg, Germany; this was a fluke, caused by the fact that his parents were taking a long trip abroad. At the age of six weeks he was transported back to Galveston, and lived there for the next eighteen years; the city meant a great deal to him, and he always thought of himself as Texas born.

In the 1880's Texas was still pretty much of a wilderness, boisterous and uncouth, but it had, even then, its special continental quality, its width of horizon and boundless zip. Needless to say, this was long before the discovery of the oil which turned Texas into a zoo of millionaires; the local economy depended on such prosaic items as cattle and cotton, and nobody even knew that oil existed under the hard, dusty cap of Texas earth.

Lasker's family was sound, intellectual in a peculiar Teutonic sort of way, and exceptionally civic-minded. His father owned a milling business, and was president of no fewer than three different banks—a national bank, a state savings bank, and a trust company; he got $5,000 a year salary from each bank and $3,000 from the trust company. These were excellent salaries for the time. The President of the United States got only $50,000 per year in this era, and members of Congress $5,000. The elder Lasker wore a silk hat on Sundays, the badge of the man who earned $5,000 a year or more, and was a substantial citizen.

The Lasker residence, on Broadway at the corner of Eighteenth

Street, looked like a castle—or prison—out of Grimm. In Albert's youth the neighborhood corresponded roughly to the East Sixties in New York City today, but now it is no longer fashionable. The Laskers lived in their crenelated, gabled house for more than forty years. It was four stories high, built of bright red sandstone, with sturdy masonry, a white window trim, round copings, and a magnificently Victorian roof bursting into steeples. It had iron balconies, Corinthian columns, triangular porches, and ornate glass bulges set at improbable angles behind clumps of palm—a remarkable hodgepodge indeed, but typical of the taste of the time.

Inside, a massive oak staircase led upward from a large somber hall, with intricately carved woodwork and dark oak furniture. In the library lines of books were heavily bound in tooled leather, and large sofas, hung with white lace squares, stood near tasseled lampshades made of fringed silk. A statue of Eduard Lasker, Albert's uncle, about whom more later, dominated a tall, deep niche in one room, and nearby were a marble Venus and some Imari chinaware. The dining room was large enough to hold forty guests; liquor was never served except when company was present.

The house had two bathrooms—an unprecedented number for the Galveston of the day—one for the family, the other for guests, if any. The story is that it was the first house in this part of Texas to have an indoor toilet, and legend even has it that, on one occasion, a guest from the open range took one look at this outlandish device next to his bedroom and fled to a hotel at once, on the grounds it was unsanitary to have an outhouse in the house.

Galveston itself was not an unpleasant city. Three seignorial families controlled it, and, to hold it within their grip, deliberately sought to keep it from expanding and competing with Houston, which presently began to grow rapidly. Today it has been described as "something like a fly in amber—not decayed, but arrested." Albert, with his usual talent for sniffing out the future, must have had some foretaste of this, because he left it in his teens and never came back. His family's house became a symbol of everything he wanted to get away from.

A Word About Morris Lasker

Morris Lasker, Albert's father, born in 1840, was a man of great force of character. All the Laskers derive originally from a village named Lask, in what was Germany (East Prussia) then but which is Poland now. Lask lies near Jarotschin (Jarocin today) in the province of Posen (Poznań). The area was, and still is, an ethnically confused borderland in which Teutons, Poles, and Jews mingle. The people of Poznań have always been electric in temperament, rebellious, and good fighters, combining Polish romanticism with Prussian dourness. In 1956 anti-Communist riots in Poznań led indirectly to the Hungarian uprising of the same year.

But to go back to the last century. The Laskers were merchants, moderately well off. Young Morris got a good education, learned Greek, and set out to be a classical scholar. Then, when he was sixteen, he decided to emigrate to the United States, as did thousands of young Germans in that era. One reason was lack of opportunity at home. Another was principle. Germans of the liberal tradition, whether young or old, fled the homeland wholesale after 1848. Moreover, an ugly wave of anti-Semitism, a foretaste of what happened under Hitler almost a century later, was making life difficult for German Jews and intellectuals.

So, in 1856, aged sixteen, Morris Lasker set sail for the United States. This was a conventional enough step to take, but Morris was not a conventional young man. The journey, on a clipper ship, took thirteen weeks from Hamburg to Fortress Monroe, Virginia. Young Lasker was penniless, and knew practically no English. He got a job as a clerk in a store in Portsmouth, Virginia, saved money, and learned fast. He decided to move on to Texas, which was open country and full of opportunity. But how to get there? He bought himself a horse, which had only one eye and was therefore cheap, and became a peddler. Covering half a dozen miles a day, offering his wares to housewives along the way, sleeping in ditches as often as not, he set out for Texas. It took him almost three years to make the trip. His packsaddle contained a number of books, mostly classics. Sitting alone by the roadside, the young man would amuse himself by reading Aristophanes aloud.

His knowledge of Greek, as well as the stamina of the one-eyed horse, served him well. He did his best business with slaves on the big plantations, who, like their African ancestors, liked beads and similar bright small trinkets. Sometimes friendly slaves gave him shelter. Near Atlanta, Georgia, young Morris begged a meal one evening, and a slave told him that he might stay the night in a small passageway between the kitchen and the master's dining hall. Here he overheard a quarrel. The daughter of the family had been sent off to a finishing school but, having flunked a course in Greek, had returned home in disgrace. Morris, overcome by impulse, propelled himself through the door to the master's dining room without warning, and stammered out that he would tutor the young lady in Greek, for six months, if the family, in return, would then help him proceed to Texas. The astonished father of the household accepted this offer. The young lady duly passed her course in Greek, and Morris eventually reached Texas. (Just to make this fairy tale complete, it may be added that, years later, the Atlanta family became impoverished, and Morris, now a prosperous man of affairs, gallantly came to its financial aid.)

Morris Lasker, settling down in Texas, had knowledge of three things—Latin, Greek, and peddling. The first two would not, he perceived soon enough, get him very far. But to become a merchant might make him successful. He was an experienced peddler, and, after all, a merchant was nothing more or less than a peddler without a horse.

His adventures for the next dozen years, from 1860 to 1872, make a real, if minor, frontier epic. First, he settled in a village near Fort Worth called Weatherford, which had been founded only four years before, and got a job as a clerk in a drygoods store. Then, restless, he wandered all over north central Texas. He came close to being murdered in one dramatic incident, and joined a band of Indian fighters, led by an illustrious guerrilla of the day, Colonel Baylor. From Weatherford (which was not served by any railroad) Lasker moved on to a town called Milliken, and then to Decatur. He discovered that he could always get a job by establishing residence, no matter how temporary, in any town which was on the projected path of a railroad before it got there. Everybody knew that, when the railroad arrived, business was bound to boom.

Came the Civil War. Lasker believed in union, and took the side of the North. But the town where he was living voted overwhelmingly for secession, and he was almost lynched. Then, a prudent young man, he promptly changed sides and joined the Confederate forces. He said to his fellow townsmen, "In a democracy, it is the majority that must count. I have registered my opinion. I believe that you are wrong. But you have won the decision, and so I will fight loyally on your side." He joined a company of Rangers (Company F2, Second Regiment, Texas Cavalry, C.S.A.), and saw service in Louisiana and in minor Texas battles which recovered Galveston and Sabine Pass from the Federals.

After the war, Morris Lasker was broke. He walked all the way from San Antonio to Waco looking for work. Then he became a peddler again. A comrade-at-arms in his regiment lent him a pair of mules and a jersey wagon. To his astonishment, he made money hand over fist. That is, he made $1,500 in gold in a few months. Lonely ranchers along the desolate trails needed merchandise. Lasker arrived back in Weatherford, set himself up in a shop (sleeping on the counter at night), and eventually became a partner in a trading company. Again he followed—or rather preceded—the iron trail of the railroads, by renting premises and establishing branch offices in communities being opened up. At last, in 1872, he was well enough off to join a firm of wholesale grocers in Galveston, and soon went into business for himself. He set up the Lasker Real Estate Company, and, in time, became owner of the Texas Star Flour and Corn Mill, one of the best known in the state. The immigrant peddler with his one-eyed horse had found the proverbial American pot of gold.

Morris Lasker was a magnificent-looking man as he grew older; to a degree he resembled Dr. Albert Schweitzer, another doughty

German full of acumen. He had piercing blue eyes and two swords of pure white mustache. When he smiled, his face took on a subtle, complacent air, and he looked like a stout cat full of cream, licking its chops. His manner was commanding, and his temper bad. When he laid down the law, he expected instant obedience. He was also an extremely good citizen, far in advance of his time. He went into the banking business partly because the existing banks in the city were untrustworthy, and his mill was the second in the United States to install an eight-hour day for labor, something unheard of in that period. He said, "I don't deserve a decent living if the people who work for me don't have a decent living." For expressing sentiments like these he was, of course, called "a traitor to his class," but he never yielded in his beliefs, and became more civic-minded year by year.

His children (after his death many years later) put out a brochure, "From Our Father," quoting some of his sayings, most of which are somewhat complacent and on the pious side. One was, "The Laskers are a different kind of family. Always stick together, and do what is good." Another: "To deserve success will be to attain it sooner or later." Still another: "I may not get it right, but I won't get it wrong. . . . I have reviewed my life and I am satisfied. I feel that I have done some good and there are at least fifty men in Texas whose characters I have helped to form."[1]

Uncle Eduard

Now we must have a word about Eduard Lasker, Morris' elder brother. He lived from 1829 to 1884, and is even more firmly fixed in the family hagiography than Morris. Eduard Lasker elected to remain in Germany after Morris emigrated, and became one of the best-known lawyers, publicists, and liberal politicians of his time. A member of the Reichstag, he was one of the first German Jews bold enough to take a strong public line against anti-Semitism. Several learned books have been written about Eduard Lasker, and

---

[1] The family also published a memoir, *Morris Lasker, Pioneer*, from which several of the foregoing details are drawn.

as recently as 1958 the University of Nuremburg published a definitive treatise on his contribution, which was considerable, to German law and parliamentary evolution.

The Laskers who remained in Germany, like Eduard, had no
idea of what happened to young Morris after his arrival in America,
and thought that he must be dead. The reason they had not heard
from him was that he did not wish to communicate until he was
successful. In 1866 Morris happened to run into a man who was
about to write to a friend in Berlin, and asked him to include a
message to Eduard in the letter, although he had no idea of Eduard's
whereabouts. The message was delivered, and from this time on the
brothers kept in touch.

Eduard Lasker supported Bismarck at first, because he too wanted
a strong, united Germany. Then after 1870 when the Iron Chan-
cellor turned to a policy of suppression of the Social Democrats and
other liberals, Lasker, an upright man, turned vigorously against
him. He uncovered a scandal (1873) in the railway administration
which gravely embarrassed one of Bismarck's principal underlings,
and thereby incurred the great man's ferocious enmity. It became
a major ambition of Bismarck's to break the hated Jew, Lasker,
and in the end he did so. Lasker lost his seat in the Reichstag in
1879.

Thereafter he took little part in public life. In 1883 he visited
the United States, partly in order to see Morris in Galveston, and
died unexpectedly of a heart attack in New York the next year.
The Congress of the United States, no less, passed a resolution
memorializing him. Part of this document reads:

Resolved, that this House has heard with deep regret of the death of
the eminent German Statesman

EDWARD LASKER

That his loss is not alone to be mourned by the people of his native
land, where his firm and constant exposition of, and devotion to, free
and liberal ideas have materially advanced the social, political, and eco-

nomic conditions of these people but by the lovers of liberty throughout the world. . . .

Members of the Lasker family have been proud of Uncle Eduard ever since, and an elaborate silver inkwell, a gift to him from the Reichstag, is a precious heirloom. For several generations, youthful Laskers have been steadily enjoined to remember Uncle Eduard's courage, liberalism, and devotion to civic duty. And, obviously, several of his traits, as well as those of Morris, come to the surface again in the personality of Albert Lasker. Dedication to principle and good works were bred deep in his bones, as well as German romanticism and a strong sense of Jewishness.

The Maternal Strain

In 1875, when Morris Lasker was well on his way to becoming a success, he met a young lady from New York named Nettie Heidenheimer Davis. He was thirty-five; she was seventeen. She was visiting friends in Galveston and he went east the next year to present himself to her family and pay court; they were married soon after. Nettie also came of German Jewish stock, but her people had arrived in America earlier than the Laskers; she was of the third generation born in the United States. The Davises lived in upper New York State, near Rochester. As a matter of fact, the family name was not Davis at all. Nettie Davis' father was named Schmul Schmulian. But he wanted to wipe out traces of the old country and became a "real" American, and so changed his name to Abraham Davis. He picked up the name "Davis" from the janitor of the rooming house where he lived. Albert Lasker, who was intensely proud of his ancestry, often talked with admiring affection about old Schmulian, and said that his own name should rightfully be Albert Schmulian Lasker. It particularly pleased him to announce grandly that his maternal grandfather was named Schmul Schmulian when he met somebody who was being stuffy or snobbish about Jews.[2]

Nettie Lasker, Albert's mother, was a beautiful young woman,

[2] Albert himself only narrowly missed being named Abraham after his grandfather.

who became stout in later years. She had brown eyes at once luminous and penetrating, which her son inherited, and a placid temperament, which he did not inherit. She was extravagant, and even in
the Galveston of the last century would pay $200 for a dress. She
was a neat housekeeper, tidy to the point of fussiness (as Albert
was). On the other hand, unlike Albert, she was inclined to be
somewhat lazy, spoiled, and not particularly affectionate or intelligent; her influence on Albert, although considerable, was never
anything like that of the ferocious Morris. He was never a mama's
boy. One peculiar small point is that she called him by the nickname "Bulldog," which he hated.

To Morris and Nettie Lasker were born eight children. Two boys
died at birth. The eldest surviving son was named Edward after
his renowned ancestor; he died at about sixty. After Edward came
Albert, born in 1880. Next came Harry, his mother's favorite, who
died of cancer at thirty-nine. Nettie, at the time of Harry's birth,
thought that she would never have the good luck to bear a daughter,
but then three girls came in quick succession, Florina, Henrietta
(Etta), and Loula. These sisters of Albert Lasker all led exceptionally
useful lives, and Albert was devoted to all three. He admired them
intensely, kept in close touch with them all his life, and enjoyed
their company. Florina, who died in 1949, left funds which established the well-known Florina Lasker Civil Liberties Award, given
annually to a deserving person in the field. Etta and Loula are still
outstanding members of their community. Florina and Loula never
married; Etta became the wife of a legal scholar, the late Samuel
Rosensohn, who was known as a "lawyer's lawyer."

The three Lasker girls, in the family tradition, set out to devote
large portions of their lives and funds to charity and good works;
after college, all went to the New York School of Philanthropy,
which is now known as the New York School of Social Work, on
East Ninety-first Street, and all became trained social workers.
Florina in particular had a brilliant career. She was founder of
the New York City Civil Liberties Committee, an executive for
many years of the Consumers League of New York, and a leading
member of the National Council of Jewish Women. Her special

interests were minimum wage legislation, migrant farm workers, and scholarships, which she endowed, for young Negro women in Northern universities.

Mrs. Rosensohn, who still clings nicely to her childhood Texas accent, was for years (and still is) a passionately dedicated Zionist. She has done much work in Israel, which she visits every year, and was once head of Hadassah. Loula has similarly devoted herself to Jewish affairs in general and Israel in particular. Also she was one of the editors of the *Survey Graphic,* one of the best liberal magazines in America for many years, and helped support it. She had a federal job for a time as a member of a commission dealing with welfare conditions of immigrants, became a specialist in urban housing, and was chairman of the Citizens Housing and Planning Council of New York.

＊

But we must return to Morris Lasker and the pungent early days in Galveston when Albert was growing up. Relations between father and son were bristly and complex, and marked Albert Lasker strongly all his life.

Chapter 3

A METEOR LET LOOSE

Brightness, like a coat of fresh paint, gleamed and sparkled all over Albert Lasker as a child. One photograph which survives portrays him at the age of three, wearing a lady-like white embroidered dress with eyeletting at the waist and scallops on the skirt, a wide black hat, and high-buttoned black shoes. His face, shining out of this fantastic costume, is attentive and aware; nobody is fooling him; his brown eyes, too big for the rest of him, glow like jellybeans. Nor, in the whole course of his life, did they ever lose their brightness, their dark glow.

He went to the public schools because, in those days, Galveston had extremely few private schools. All the Lasker children, despite the wealth of the family, were submitted as a matter of course to the rigors of a public education until they reached college age, and they developed a healthy sense of self-preservation as a result. The feeling against Jews in Texas, although neither aggressive nor virulent, was pervasive on social levels. The Laskers lived on the fringe of what was called "society" in the Galveston of the day; they were outsiders, thrown in on themselves and other Jewish families, until Morris became such a prominent citizen that he couldn't be ignored.

Within the home, the children were not—by contemporary standards—well brought up. They were neglected one day, spoiled the next. In the 1880's the functions of parents were more sharply defined than now; the father made the money, and the mother kept the home. Of course, this demarcation still exists today in most American families, but the frontiers between husband and wife overlap much more than they did in Albert's childhood. Nor were

27

the obligations of the parent as well understood then as now. The parents considered that children should get adequate schooling, but otherwise they were apt to pay comparatively little attention to them until they reached adolescence, and could prove themselves.

Morris Lasker thought that he had the most wonderful children in the world, but he was a complete tyrant, a dictator. He was proud of Albert and the others, but neither he nor his wife ever gave them anything like the amount of love they craved. All his life Albert Lasker had a painful inner feeling that he was not wanted enough, not loved enough. For a long time he had a recurrent dream, that he would do something outlandishly important someday, return to Galveston on a white horse, and then dance triumphantly on the kitchen table. He never got over the feeling that he had to prove himself worthy in his father's eyes, make good, and be accepted fully by his father, who, he felt, was forever standing suspiciously "behind the door." Thousands of boys have, of course, the same experience. To some it gives push and drive; to others, a sense of guilt and inferiority. To Albert it appears to have given both—an intense desire to outstrip his father, together with acute sensitivenesses which pursued him all his life.

School Days and the Youthful Newspaper Proprietor

Albert went through school like a flash, although his marks were never good. Mere study did not interest him. He was far too busy. Playmates taunted him with being "a rich man's son," and he was determined to prove himself.

At the age of twelve, astoundingly precocious, he became a successful independent businessman. He decided to go into the newspaper business, and, singlehanded, wrote, edited, and published a four-page weekly newspaper called the Galveston *Free Press*. The subscription price was $1.00 per year. I have seen a surviving copy of this publication, and it is remarkable. Probably it was greeted by the community as a curiosity, an aberration, but enough people bought it to give Lasker a profit of $15 a week, more than many adult Galvestonians were earning. Moreover, he managed to keep his paper alive for more than a year, which shows stick-to-it-iveness un-usual in a boy so young.

The copy I have of the Galveston *Free Press* is dated April 30, 1892. One column contains homely aphorisms under the title "Signs of Spring," which Lasker wrote with avid enthusiasm. Samples: "The first sign of spring is the feeling that your hat is shabby," and "The second is that your winter overcoat is getting heavy. If your overcoat is a particularly nice one, this sign will not be apparent." Also: "The dark shadow of the coming spring house cleaning broods like a bird of evil omen over your once happy home," and "Your landlord has discovered that things are going to boom, and booms your rent right away."

Even at twelve, Lasker was a great enthusiast for the theater, and one brief column is called "Theatrical Notes":

Next week Sarah Bernhardt returns to France.

Mrs. John Drew is 75 years old, and will not travel with Mr. Jefferson next season.

Maurice Barrymore will not be the leading man at Palmer's Theatre next season.

The divorce case of Leslie Carter and his wife is to have another re-hearing in the supreme court of Illinois soon.

Then jokes are picked up from the Harvard *Lampoon* and pub-lications like the old *Life:*

She: With what were you particularly struck when you first went on the stage?
He: Two bricks and a cabbage.

Social notes follow, in the manner of small-town newspapers to this day. There are notices of coming amusements at the opera house, and reports of activities at the Garten Verein. But the main feature of interest is the editor's own column, in which young Lasker expresses his personal views. Samples:

Where was the society that looks after cruelty to animals Thursday when two boxes of two-weeks old chickens chirped and yelled and died in front of the Wells Fargo express office? Packed tightly in a box they presented a sight, neglected in their distress, that melted many a kind heart.

There are alleys all over the city that are festering with filth, and yet the health department tells the people the city is clean.

The FREE PRESS is here to stay, why can't every business man in Galveston take an advertisement for a dollar or two. Every one complains of such dull business. "Advertise and make it good" is our motto.

As you ride homeward in the cars you hear talk of early peas.

The editor of the FREE PRESS is but a boy of thirteen years,[1] yet he has an opinion on the measures and merits of the respective candidates for governor. And it is that Judge George Clark should be nominated governor and the railroad commission be made selective. The office of governor already has enough power without being given that of the appointment of three railroad commissioners who are invested with authority to make and unmake the greatest corporations in the state. Such power held in the hands of the governor invites suspicion, favoritism, and, worst of all, corruption. . . . Judge Clark will add a spirit of tolerance and progressiveness foreign to the nature of the present executive. By all means let Judge Clark head the ticket and Texas will experience a change that will be "what she long has sought and mourned because she found it not."

Not bad for a boy of twelve!

Young Lasker got his first experience of advertising by means of this publication; he himself solicited the ads which kept it going. He would call on the local dentist, say, and get an ad. But, a revealing point, he would not collect the money from the dentist when the account came due, because he thought that this was beneath his dignity as owner of the newspaper. He would sell the space, but not collect the cash. As collector, he appointed an eleven-year-old Negro boy. He was very fond of Negroes. The Laskers had four servants, all of whom were Negroes except Nettie's maid, and from his earliest days Albert got along wtih Negroes on the basis of trust

[1] Actually on this date he was not quite twelve. His twelfth birthday was the next day.

and understanding. He never had the slightest taint of racial prejudice, which was unusual in somebody Texas-bred.

Lasker entered the Ball High School, and became a "big man" at once. For one thing he edited the magazine; there were only about twenty high school magazines in the whole of the United States at this time, and he was proud of this job and worked hard at it. However, he gave up the editorship after a year, so that it would rotate among his classmates; he thought that it was "undemocratic" for him to be editor for more than one school term. Albert's prowess in school activities was terrifying, and his precocity almost repellent. In his own words, "he organized the entire school." A photograph taken of him in this era shows him with the football squad; twenty tall young men in uniform stand in line, with Lasker, not uniformed, in the center—a puny youth compared to the husky athletes. But Lasker was the boss, because he was manager of the team.

*

Texas was virgin in those days, and boiling with opportunities for enterprise—also risks. Frontiersmen were paupers one day, millionaires the next. Morris Lasker went into various projects; he made money in some, and lost in others. Came the panic of 1893, and he was wiped out, largely because he had invested heavily in real estate. The market collapsed, his tenants could not pay their rent, and he, in turn, could not meet his obligations to the banks and mortgage companies. He owed a British syndicate more than a million dollars.

Morris sent his wife and several of the children to Germany for a year, on the ground that living there would be cheaper. Only Albert, thirteen years old, remained with him. The house was shut down except for Morris' bedroom; and here Albert slept on a cot. Morris wanted him in the room with him because, he told the boy, he was "so lonesome." Night after night, Albert was awakened by a strange sound. His father stretched an arm out of the bed and, as he slept fitfully, scratched the rug on the floor. Before many months passed, strands of the rug became loose; Morris had literally clawed it bare. The father was so frantically worried about failing in business and going further into debt that his anxieties burst out of his subconscious and found expression in this bizarre demonstration of tenseness and desire.

Albert never forgot this experience. Years later, in the 1940's, a friend in New York urged him to invest in a real estate venture. He refused: "I have not invested in urban real estate since 1893."[2]

Times got better in Galveston; Morris Lasker settled his affairs satisfactorily, and resumed his march to security and wealth. His milling business expanded to include properties in Wichita Falls and Waco, and he became an extremely shrewd buyer of grain; he spent much time in the Amarillo area, and was known as "Grandfather of the Panhandle." He served one term as a state senator, and was president of the Galveston Cotton Exchange.[3]

His relations with his son were sometimes good, sometimes bad. They quarreled frequently, and had violent scenes. Albert feared, loved, and at times hated him, and the acute ambivalence of his emotions toward his father was a powerful motivation in his own career. Morris once wrote down a curt opinion of him: "You can give out more, knowing little, than anyone I ever knew."

Meantime, approaching the ripe old age of thirteen, Albert dropped the Galveston *Free Press,* his own newspaper; there were broader worlds to conquer. While still in high school, he became (a) a bookkeeper in his father's office, in order to learn accounting, which was useful to him in later life, and (b) got a job on the principal daily of the town, the Galveston *Morning News.* He

---

[2] However, with his children he once went into a venture involving real estate in downstate Illinois and Chicago suburbs.

[3] Some years after this, in 1900, occurred the celebrated Galveston flood, in which 5,000 people lost their lives. The Lasker home lost 30 windows and 5 chimneys, but was otherwise undamaged, and 40 families took refuge there. Morris Lasker considered this flood, or tidal wave, to be a kind of insult delivered upon him by nature. He at once snubbed both Texas and the elements by packing most of the family off to Germany again, and he himself took a long trip to Egypt, to investigate the cotton business there.

covered sports, crime, theater, business, politics. It was at this time
that he bought the cotton quotations syndicate. Then, when he
was graduated from high school in 1896, he advanced to become a
regular member of the *News* staff at a salary of $40 a week, enormous
in those days for a beginner. He never went on to college or university, and never had any scholastic education after sixteen; he was
too busy earning money, and too entranced by the wacky world of
journalism. But it seems strange that his parents did not insist that
he get more education.

About this time he got his first practical experience in politics.
In 1896 William Jennings Bryan and William McKinley were rival
candidates for the presidency of the United States. In Texas the
Democratic party was badly split, because of the cleavage between
Bryan, a radical "Free Silver" man, and the dissident conservative
Democrats. The *News* assigned Lasker to cover the campaign for
Congress of a Republican named R. B. Hawley. He was a prosperous
Galveston sugar merchant, and, in spite of the rift in the Democratic
ranks, his cause seemed hopeless. Lasker had scarcely ever met a
Republican at this date. He records that his provincialism was
such that he thought "all Republicans and northerners wore horns."
The Laskers had been ardent Democrats since Morris arrived in
the state. Diligently, Albert studied Republican campaign pamphlets and inspected Republican horizons on a national level, while
accompanying Hawley throughout the district. Hawley liked him
so much that he hired him as his secretary and ghost writer, for
$15 per week. Young Albert, a full-fledged politician now as well
as a newspaperman, gave all his energies to the campaign. Hawley
won, and became the first Republican from below Mason and
Dixon's line to win a seat in Congress since the Civil War.

Hawley promptly offered Albert a job in Washington, but the
boy had to refuse—he was too young. This experience was, however,
a major turning point in his life, because, to his family's intense
discomfiture, he became an avowed Republican, and remained one
for more than forty years.

*

When he was seventeen Lasker got into the prize fight business, and, by a fluke, discovered Jack Johnson, the Negro fighter who was heavyweight champion of the world from 1908 to 1915. In his spare time, Albert had organized a boxing club. To have a successful boxing club he had to have boxers. Nothing interested him but heavyweights. He became the manager of one, whom he nicknamed the "Dixie Champ." The Dixie Champ was pretty good, and annihilated a series of local antagonists. Lasker, thirsting for bigger game, contrived to sign up a well-known fighter of the day, Joe Choinsky, and paid him $500 to travel from Philadelphia to Galveston to appear against the Dixie Champ. All the sport fans of the town, including Lasker and the Dixie Champ, congregated at the railway station to greet the formidable Choinsky when he arrived. The Dixie Champ took one look at Choinsky, who had hands like hams and was a real professional to boot, and promptly fled town on the same train that brought Choinsky in.

Lasker was in utter despair. He had invested most of his savings in this fight. Ticket-holders would demand their money back. He would lose every cent he had, and be disgraced as well. There might be a riot. Suddenly he had an idea. The Laskers had an uncle who lived nearby; through some extraordinary circumstance, he had met a Negro boy named Jack Johnson when he, Johnson, was serving a brief term in jail. Johnson then got a job in the uncle's house, helping with the laundry. Johnson was crazy about boxing. Albert Lasker picked him up, and used him as a sweep-boy in the ring. In spare moments, Johnson sparred with the Dixie Champ and other fighters on Lasker's string. Albert went to him and offered him $25 to step in the ring against Choinsky that night. At least he would have a fight. Johnson might be killed by the ferocious Choinsky, but Lasker calculated that he could escape from town before the police closed in. Johnson took the $25 with alacrity. Lasker pleaded with Choinsky, "Just let him stay a round or two— don't kill him the first moment." Actually, Johnson managed to

last four and a half rounds before being knocked out. This was
Jack Johnson's first fight, and it started him on his career. Whether
or not Lasker and Johnson ever saw one another thereafter I do
not know.[4]

An End to Journalism

At seventeen overconfidence and high spirits abruptly terminated
Albert's newspaper career. In those days a theatrical company headed
by James A. Hearn came to Galveston every year, and played *Shore
Acres* at the Opera House. Lasker was now dramatic critic of the
News; he had seen this ancient piece of fustian for several years
running, and knew it inch by inch. At this time he was courting
a girl in Houston, and had an engagement with her the night of the
opening. Knowing that he could review the play satisfactorily without seeing it, he wrote his review and arranged to have it delivered
to the newspaper at the proper time, and played hooky, going off
to Houston for the evening. Next morning, he discovered that the
Opera House had burned down just as *Shore Acres* was to go on the
stage: there had been no performance! Lasker, when he told this
story later, said that he did not wait to be fired. He knew that he
was finished, and added that he did not even bother to go to the
News office to pick up his paycheck. But surely his bosses would
have forgiven him. As a matter of fact, this experience, or experiences closely similar to it, are a legend in the newspaper business.
But it certainly happened to Lasker; others have carried the story
on.

In any case, Albert left Galveston but he did not give up the
idea of journalism as a career. He wanted above everything to be
a newspaperman. He went to New Orleans, and got a job on the
Times Democrat as a baseball reporter. Then he moved up to
Dallas, and worked briefly on the Dallas *News.*[5] Certainly the world
lost a wonderful reporter when Lasker left journalism. He could
have reached any height as a newspaperman; he would have been

[4] But a great many years later Johnson telephoned him from out of the blue
one day to ask for a loan.
[5] So far as I know the last assignment he ever had from a newspaper or magazine was from *Collier's*. This came later, in the early 1900's. Lasker, in Chicago

a masterful editor-proprietor, in the grand old tradition, if he had ever owned a big metropolitan daily. Nor did his reporter's instinct ever leave him. He always wanted to know the why and how of things, and he had an everlasting delight in news as well as a nose for it. In fact, it was he who first introduced a newspaper point of view into the advertising business, and this played a large role in the revolution in advertising he subsequently made.

Why did Albert leave journalism? The reason was his father. Albert wanted to go east and work his way up in the newspaper business, but Morris would not hear of this, largely because most of the newspapermen he knew were drunks. He did not think that journalism was a respectable profession, and insisted that Albert should turn to something else. Then, to make amends, he promised to buy the boy a small-town Texas newspaper later, and let him edit it. The promise was never fulfilled. Meantime, he suggested that he should go into something close to journalism, but sounder and more dignified—advertising. Albert was horrified. In his view, it was advertising that was disreputable, not journalism. He despised advertisers. He had the youthful reporter's traditional contempt for the advertising side of the publishing business. To be in advertising was, he thought, to live a life of shame. He himself records:

In those days, the separation of the business office and the editorial office was absolutely complete. A man in the editorial end just had a bowing acquaintance with a man on the business end of a paper. The editor edited the paper. The business men could make what money they could, but they couldn't affect anything in the paper whatever. . . . It may be that the change from this policy is one of the reasons why newspapers have so largely lost their influence in this country. An advertiser made no difference in those days. If an elevator (for instance one in a big department store) fell, the story got all over the front pages. If the advertiser didn't like it, it was just too bad.[6]

---

at the time, wanted an excuse to get back to Texas to see his family, and persuaded *Collier's* to send him to Texas to cover the discovery of oil there. He visited the new strikes at Sweetwater and Beaumont, but wrote little.

[6] From Lasker's reminiscences as recorded by the Columbia Oral Research History Center, hereafter to be called "Columbia."

But Morris Lasker would not budge in his determination to pry Albert out of journalism, and his son yielded, particularly when his father told him that, if he returned to newspaper work later, it would be of great advantage to him to have had experience of the business side. Then Morris said that he could get him a job with the Chicago advertising agency, Lord & Thomas, and proceeded to make the arrangements. He was able to do so for a curious reason.

In this era there were no effective bankruptcy laws in Texas. If a man failed, he could choose which of his creditors to favor; he could decide to settle with Creditor A and ignore Creditor B and so on. Naturally a debtor was tempted to favor his own friends, or family, and this led to much fraudulent bankruptcy. After the panic of 1893 a big development came in electric trolley cars. These were built in various Texas towns and created suburbs. A Northern syndicate came into Galveston, laid out trolley routes, and opened up tracts of land to home owners. Then it went broke. A considerable sum was found to be owing to Lord & Thomas in Chicago, which had handled the advertising for the project. The Galveston creditors, after long wrangling, suggested that Morris Lasker, whose reputation for fair dealing and independence of mind was impeccable, should be appointed as sole trustee to straighten the matter out.

Mr. D. M. Lord, of Lord & Thomas, came to Galveston from Chicago, a fifty-two-hour trip in those days, to lay his case before Morris Lasker, who listened to the facts and then insisted to his principals that Lord & Thomas, although it operated in faraway Chicago, should get exactly equal treatment with the other creditors. The sum involved was only about $30,000, but, at that time, this was equivalent to the total annual profit of the firm. Mr. Lord was grateful, and, when the matter was cleared up, told Morris Lasker that if he could ever do him a favor in return, he would be glad to do so.

So, a few years later, Morris Lasker asked Lord & Thomas to give Albert a job, and Lord agreed. Neither Morris—nor Albert—knew exactly what an advertising agency was. Albert records that he left Galveston for Chicago with a heavy heart. His father, he says, "never knew what a hurt he did me." He said to himself, "I'll go up to Chicago to please my father, but I won't stay more than a few weeks." This was in 1898, when Albert was eighteen. He stayed with Lord & Thomas for forty-four years, until 1942, and, except for occasional brief trips, never returned to Texas at all. But it should never be forgotten that he was a Texan, and sometimes a rough Texan at that. Texas gave him scope, vision, a sense of magnification and euphoria, a hard utilitarian point of view on most matters, and a vivid desire to be bigger than life-size.

*

Morris Lasker died in 1916, aged seventy-six. He was by this time a venerated figure in the community, and the city stopped all activity for five minutes when he was buried, as a gesture to his memory. He left a substantial fortune, and Albert was executor of his estate. Albert found that most of his father's holdings were in real estate, and, still smarting with memories of the panic of 1893, promptly sold them. That he did so has been a family legend ever since. The Lasker properties, it became clear later, included some of the richest oil land in the world near Galveston, and about a quarter of downtown Houston. If Albert had held on to these he would not have left a paltry $11,500,000 when he died, but probably several hundred million, maybe half a billion.

Nettie Lasker, Albert's mother, outlived her husband by fourteen years, and died at the Hotel Chatham in New York City, which was then her home, in 1930, aged seventy-two.

Chapter 4

EARLY YEARS AT LORD & THOMAS

Modern advertising was born largely because Albert Lasker, during his first month with Lord & Thomas in Chicago, lost $500 in a crap game. When he arrived and reported for work, he was given a salary of $10 a week, much less than what he had been earning in Galveston. Nobody paid a great deal of attention to him, and he was given little to do. Apparently the partners felt that he would quit in a month or two, and so why bother about him?—their obligation to Morris Lasker would soon be fulfilled. Albert fell into rough company, and some gamblers took him for $500. He did not, of course, have the money. His total capital was $75, which was all that his father had staked him with, and consequently he had to give the gamblers a due bill covering his debt.

Lasker did not dare communicate with his father, because this story would, he thought, "break his heart." Instead he threw himself on the mercy of Mr. Thomas, an understanding man. He records, "I had never before sold anything to anybody, but I did a salesmanship job that day. I talked Mr. Thomas into advancing me $500—which was a fortune in those days. He went with me, and we settled with the gambler. Both he and I were sure that the gambler had cheated me, but the gambler had the due bill, and so we settled with him for $500."[1]

So Lasker could not, as he had planned, leave Chicago after a brief interval and return to Texas to enter the newspaper business, his first love. He had to stay with Lord & Thomas until he paid off his debt. If he lived on $8 per week, which was not easy to do even in

---

[1] Columbia, p. 7.

those days, and paid what he owed at the rate of $2 per week, it would take him 250 weeks, or almost five years, before he was clear. He says in his reminiscences, "I had as big a problem as we have today with the national debt. I grew up and matured that day." (He was eighteen.) "Debt—and the circumstances under which I had gotten the debt—to me was a terrible thing. The day we paid the gambler, I grew up, and I never grew any older than I was that day."

Oddly enough, a genuine capacity to learn from experience is one of the rarest of all human traits; Lasker had it, and from that day till the day he died he was never in debt again.

*

Lord & Thomas, originally known as Lord & Brewster, was founded in 1873, and was thus a quarter of a century old when Lasker joined it. In its whole history, from 1873 until he liquidated it in 1942, it had only two changes in ownership and management. The biggest thing a business can have, he liked to say in later years, was historical background. "A business is like a river. People may settle on the river bank and move, but the river goes right on, and people will always live where there is a river." Businesses, however, like men, may change as they grow up; a business fifty years old can be as different from the same business at twenty-five as a man of fifty can differ from a youth of twenty-five. Still, the essential characteristics are likely to persist, and should be encouraged and maintained.

D. M. Lord, when Lasker joined the firm, was fifty-four. He had dark thin brows on a tall naked forehead, white mutton chop whiskers, and a narrow chin which jutted forward sharply. He looked like an orchestra conductor disturbed because his musicians were unaccountably out of control. Ambrose L. Thomas was a different type. He was stately and dignified, like a comfortably retired brewer or broker—victorious, but above the battle. He wore a high collar with slightly open wings. A pencil, like a quill, reposed behind his ear, and a heavy gold watch chain, with an elk-tooth fob, stretched across his capacious waistcoat. On his roll-top desk stood an upright telephone, and next to the high, narrow black radiator was a large brass cuspidor. Actually, one of Lasker's duties, as office boy, was to clean the cuspidors in the establishment every morning. This, in later years, led him to quote robustly from the Gilbert and Sullivan song in *Pinafore:*

> I cleaned the windows and I swept the floor,
> And I polished up the handle of the big front door.

Both Lord and Thomas, like many other early pioneers in advertising, were Yankees from Maine. Mr. Lord was the financial partner; Mr. Thomas ran the advertising side. Their office was on the corner of Wabash and Randolph, where Marshall Field's stands today. Their biggest account was Cascarets, a cathartic, which brought in about $300,000 a year. Others were Anheuser-Busch, the brewery, and Armour, the meat packers. Another was a distillery in Dayton, Ohio, named Haynor, which sold by mail order; an index of the times is that four quarts of bourbon cost $3.20, including tax.

Altogether, when Lasker joined Lord & Thomas in 1898, annual billings amounted to $800,000–$900,000.[2] By later standards this sum is so puny as to be laughable. In Lasker's heyday Lord & Thomas did $40,000,000 or even $50,000,000 worth of billings in a good year, and altogether during his tenure as head of the firm billings amounted to $750,000,000. Today, eighteen years after Lasker quit advertising, comparable figures are, of course, enormously magnified. In those days an advertiser like Cascarets, which spent $300,000 a year, was a major account; today a big account can be worth $25,000,000 a year or more, and there are scores, in fact

---

[2] "Billings" is a tricky word. It refers to the amount of money spent by clients to advertise their goods or services. This advertising space (or time on radio or television today) is made available at a 15 per cent discount to accredited advertising agencies by the newspapers, periodicals and broadcasting stations. The 15 per cent discount is not passed on by the agency to its clients but is kept as a fee or commission and constitutes the agency's gross income. The 15 per cent system was first worked out by N. W. Ayer of Philadelphia, but in Lasker's early days it had not yet become standard.

hundreds, of million-plus accounts. There were thirteen or fourteen advertising agencies of recognized standing in the country then; today, about 3,500, of which at least 70 have annual billings of $10 million or more. The total amount spent on advertising through agencies in the country was probably less than $20 million when Lasker reached Chicago; today, it approaches $10 billion, and is going up every minute.

Small as Lord & Thomas was in 1898, with its paltry $800,000 or $900,000 in billings, it was one of the three biggest agencies in the United States. The others were J. Walter Thompson and N. W. Ayer & Son, founded in 1864 and 1869 respectively. It is a striking fact that, when Lasker left the field in 1942, two of these same three agencies were still the leaders, after almost half a century. Advertising is supposed to be a wildly volatile business, but leadership has changed little. The three leading agencies today (figures for 1957) are J. Walter Thompson (total billings, $287,000,000), Mc-Cann-Erickson ($262,000,000), and Young & Rubicam, originally an Ayer offshoot ($230,000,000). Ayer itself is fifth, with $107,000,000. Foote, Cone & Belding, which succeeded to the Lord & Thomas business in 1942, is seventh with $96,000,000.

When Lasker started at Lord & Thomas in 1898 and for some time thereafter, most manufacturers looked at advertising with a frigid eye, and were often wary about buying space; bankers sometimes even refused to grant loans to new businesses for advertising appropriations. Wrigley's first appropriation for advertising was exactly $32.00; Borden's $513.75; Sunkist $7,500; Procter & Gamble $11,543. Today circumstances are, to put it mildly, different. General Motors spent $137,500,000 for advertising in 1958, Procter & Gamble $115,900,000, and General Foods $96,000,000. Space was cheap in the early days; you could get a page in a good magazine with a sizable circulation for $1,000. Today a four-color page in the *Saturday Evening Post* costs $37,695; in *Life* $39,500.

The whole tone, bent, and texture of advertising in Lasker's early days were altogether different from today. Magazine circulations were small by contemporary standards (although the *Ladies' Home*

Journal hit the million mark for the first time in 1902); newspapers hesitated to give space to big display ads; billboards were comparatively few, and, of course, radio and TV did not exist. Advertising agencies were, for the most part, mere brokers—space buyers for a product. Copy did little but describe merchandise perfunctorily; there was no story, no argument, no active salesmanship, no attempt to excite the customer and make him buy. Articles were listed as being available, with a brief text or inadequate illustration, and that was about all.

By far the biggest advertisers were patent medicines. Millions of citizens gulped down shady nostrums which they read about in inch-long, small-print ads. Most of these patent medicines were full of alcohol, and so it was natural that they should give people balm or stimulus. Some of the patent medicine people wrote ethical copy; some did not, and those who were most outrageous claimed to cure everything from heart disease to cataracts, from collapse of the womb to venereal disease. Other scandalous behavior had to do with railway advertising. The railways gave transportation, not cash, as payment to the agencies and newspapers; then these would, in turn, sell the railway tickets they had acquired for nothing to the public at cut rates. In Chicago, when Lasker got there, fifteen or twenty cut-rate ticket agencies existed on one short stretch of Clark Street, south of the Loop; here you could buy a rail ticket to California for roughly half what it would cost you at the railway station itself a block away.

Moreover, advertising was an indiscriminate gamble. (Much of it still is, of course.) But then, almost everything was hit or miss. An ad either succeeded or failed; no scientific study had ever been made of advertising. Mail-order business was important, but there were no checks or controls; no one knew why some copy pulled, some did not. The religious press was important, because, in an era which did not have cars or movies, the church was often the center of a community; but nobody knew just what made an ad in a religious paper pay, if it did. The same thing was true of farm journals, which were important too.

Finally, the agency business itself was chaotic. Most advertisers prepared their own copy, and used agencies merely to tend to the complicated business of buying space in newspapers, magazines, and other media. But few periodicals gave out honest circulation figures, which meant that nobody knew how many readers he was reaching per dollar spent. The agencies played one publication off against another, trying to get space at low rates. Today's system of a standard 15 per cent commission had just begun to evolve; the agency took what it could get, 10 per cent or even less. Agencies undercut one another unmercifully to get accounts, and the business as a whole, packed with chicanery, had no philosophy but dog eat dog.

All this Albert Lasker helped to change.

On the Road

When Lasker, aged nineteen, had been with Lord & Thomas about a year, the salesman who solicited accounts in Indiana, Ohio, and Michigan quit his job. He was a good man, and was paid $3,500 a year. At once, eager for opportunity, Lasker went to Mr. Thomas, and asked if he could take over the territory temporarily until a replacement was found. Lasker said he would ask for no more than the $10 a week he was still getting, and of which he was still paying $2 a week to settle his debt, because he wanted a chance to learn, to find out what he could do. Besides, he knew that he would never get a raise until he made good, and he would never get a chance to make good by sitting around the office filing bills and cleaning door handles.

He said to Mr. Thomas, "You keep looking to see if you can find a better man. But let me cover the territory to give you time. You have nothing to lose. The hotel expenses will be—at the outside— three dollars and a half a day, and we'll get the railroad fare for nothing. In the interim, the territory will be covered."[3]

Thomas agreed, and so Lasker became a solicitor, a traveling man. The first day he went out he got a $3,000 order. True, his predecessor had laid the ground for this, by building up confidence in Lord &

[3] Columbia, p. 12.

Thomas all over his territory; even so, it was Albert who brought the contract in. He credits this partly to the fact that he was so young—people were amused by this likable and enterprising boy—and partly to luck. "But," he says, "I had to know how to use the luck—and grab it." Within months, he brought in so much business—maybe $40,000-50,000—that "he was the talk of the line."

This was the era par excellence of the old-style traveling man. Slow dusty trains jerked their way across the meadows of the Middle West, dumping out salesmen at every wayside station—men who sold everything from tall tricycles to harness ware, from mandolins to big gold watches. Salesmen played pitch or penny-ante poker in reeking smokers, ate free lunch in robust saloons, or rocked on the porches of scaly boarding houses while waiting for the torpid, dirty, wheezing trains. For several years, young Lasker rode the trains. When no train served a destination, he used a horse and buggy, or, in winter, a sleigh. He records that, once in Indiana, he drove through snow for fifteen miles in order to sign up an account with a local school that was worth only $300 a year. "If I landed the account, we made 10 per cent on it—thirty dollars. It might take me the whole day to get there and hiring the sleigh might cost six dollars. However, there was no copy expense as the school prepared its own copy and twenty-four dollars net profit was twenty-four dollars."

Now (he was still nineteen) Lasker asked Mr. Thomas to turn over to him some old accounts, or new accounts that were not making much money, so that he could "practice on them" and learn about copy writing. An opportunity came quickly. Down in Louisville the Wilson Ear Drum Company made "Common Sense Ear Drums," small cardboard appliances ("invisible, comfortable, efficient") to aid people hard of hearing. Lord & Thomas handled its advertising, but it paid only 10 per cent commission. The ads were three inches long in small type, and the eardrums ($5) were sold by mail.

Lasker made a careful study of the mail-order market, and he became convinced that the Wilson ads could be much improved.

But he was uncertain of his own ability to write good copy. It happened that one of his friends in Chicago was a young newspaperman named Katz, who had worked with him in New Orleans covering baseball. Lasker was, even then, an eager manipulator. He got Katz to write some ads for him, and had him pose for a photograph showing a young man, "the deafest deaf man you ever saw," madly scratching his ear, distraught with agony at his deafness, trying vainly, desperately, to hear the conversation of his friends without the advantage that would be provided by the Wilson Common Sense Ear Drum. (Of course Katz's hearing was perfectly good.)

Lasker, without telling his superiors anything more than was strictly necessary, went down to Louisville, and showed the Wilson people the Katz ad. He said, "Look. Suppose Lord & Thomas could multiply your sales. We will write a new kind of copy for you, but you must pay us 15 per cent commission. If at the end of ninety days the results haven't increased, we'll give you back the money, and your account will still be on a 10 per cent basis. But as an earnest that you are interested, you will have to pay me a fee of $500."

The Wilson people agreed, and Lasker gave Katz the $500 as payment for writing and posing for the ad. The expenses to Lord & Thomas were nil (except for Lasker's salary) because he went to Louisville and back on a railway pass. Before this episode, Wilson had been spending $3,000 a month with Lord & Thomas. Within a year this rose to $20,000. So Lord & Thomas, instead of 10 per cent on $3,000 per month, or $300, was getting from the Wilson company 15 per cent on $20,000, or $3,000. Young Lasker had multiplied the yield of this account ten times!

In the same year, 1899, came another important coup. A Cincinnati firm named Rheinstrom Brothers, liquor manufacturers, wanted to advertise, and was willing to start out with a $10,000 appropriation. Lasker got wind of this, but also he heard that one of the best-known advertising men in the country, Charles Austin Bates of New York, had been promised the account. For Lasker to compete against Bates was like an unknown boy tenor competing with Caruso. At once the young man scooted down to Cincinnati. In those days everybody in an office worked from eight in the morning till six at night, six days a week. Also in those days a visitor could always identify the head of the firm if he got there early enough because it was the head of the firm who opened all the mail, in order to circumvent possible double-crossing or espionage by his employees, and this was the first business of the day. Lasker records, "In any private firm (even those run by intensely rich people) whoever you saw open the mail was the head of the firm. The head of the firm opened all the mail and signed all checks."

Lasker tells what happened as follows:

I went to Rheinstroms' straight from the train which arrived at 7:00 a.m. and waited in front of the establishment until the first man came to work. . . . At eight o'clock I entered. There was a man standing at a little raised desk opening the mail, and I knew that must be Mr. Abe Rheinstrom, the head of the firm.

He grunted at me and said, "What do you want?"

This greeting was frightening in itself, but I handed him my card and said I was with Lord & Thomas, that I had heard they were going to advertise, and that my firm had sent me down to solicit them. . . .

He said, "How dare your firm send a young boy like you down— disturbing me in my most important work of the day, early in the morning? Get out!"

There I was. I had induced my firm to send me, and I couldn't get an interview. I looked foolish.

I knew a good deal about the habits of the German population of that time. . . . Every German went home for lunch. You could always bet on that. You could also bet that after lunch, he took a nap. I knew that, so I went back and sat in the lobby of the hotel until about two o'clock, when I decided to take a chance to see whether Mr. Rheinstrom was up from his nap.

I called him at his home and . . . spoke so fast that he couldn't stop me. I remembered what had happened with Debs when I was a reporter, and I felt sure that it appealed to everyone to help a young man. Quick as I could, I said, "I'm-the-young-man-you-kicked-out-of-your-office-this-morning.-I-came-down-from-Lord-&-Thomas.-If-I-go-home-without-seeing-you-I'm-liable-to-lose-my-position.-What-difference-does-it-make-to-you-just-to-give-a-

few-minutes?-Maybe-it's-the-turning-point-in-the-career-of-a-young-man.-It-may-be-the-making-or-breaking-of-me.-Can't-I-come-to-see-you-for-a-few-minutes?"

He said, "Yes." I went. . . . That was about three o'clock. At six o'clock Lord & Thomas had the business.[4]

Obviously, Lasker was a young man going somewhere. He was full of heart, brains, and wile; even in the earliest days his solicitation of clients was masterful. He appealed to what, in that era, was called their "psychology." For instance, he went to Milwaukee to try to get a big candy account. But he did not tell the candy manufacturer this. Instead he said, "Mr. Stanley, I am a very young man, and I am thinking of going into the candy business. Is it a good business for a youngster? Will it grow? Tell me about your problems." Mr. Stanley did so. Lasker then said a polite thank you and good-by, not even mentioning Lord & Thomas. Then, a few months later, he returned to Milwaukee and called on Mr. Stanley again, saying, "I've decided not to go into the candy business, although it's a splendid business. Now, what I know about candy is thus-and-so." He would then tell Mr. Stanley all that Stanley had previously told *him*, with additions he had gleaned elsewhere which he knew would attract attention. Then the *coup de grâce*: "What I would like is to handle a good candy account for Lord & Thomas. Won't you give me yours?" The approach was almost irresistible.

Once, a little later, he went after a large account in St. Louis. No one had ever been able to persuade the St. Louis manufacturer to advertise; man after man from other agencies had sought to get the business, but without success. Albert went in, and came out two hours later with the contract in his pocket. He was asked how he had achieved this signal victory, and replied, "It could not have been simpler. I told the man the story of my life."

Years later a friend asked him his opinion of a businessman who had just taken a large job in government. Lasker replied, with his nostrils quivering, "Not a closer," i.e., not a man who, in the last

[4] Columbia, pp. 19-20.

analysis, got things *done*. Lasker himself, above everything, was a "closer."

*

Soon after the turn of the century, Battle Creek, Michigan, became a confused and violent arena for the advertising salesmen. Two immense properties in packaged cereal foods were born, Kellogg (corn flakes) and Post (grape nuts); the hatred and rivalry between them was that of Capulets and Montagus. Then other manufacturers sought to cash in on the bonanza of breakfast cereals; at one time there were twenty-four competing companies in what was known as the "Battle of Battle Creek." The atmosphere, Lasker mentions, was as frenzied as that of the oil boom towns in Texas. Stocks in various companies rose or fell crazily; companies that boasted of a brilliant future at noon were wiped out by nightfall. When it was all over, Kellogg and Post were the only big companies surviving, and they changed the breakfast habits of the nation forever. Oatmeal and hominy grits gave way to prepared cereals in packages.

Lasker visited Battle Creek scores of times, and the experience taught him much. He perceived how a good product, plus advertising, could literally revolutionize consumer patterns overnight. Also something else challenged his attention. One of the first of the great American trusts was formed, when several hundred cracker companies were put together to form the National Biscuit Company, and this became the first corporation in history to appropriate a million dollars for advertising in a single year. The agency was N. W. Ayer, and Ayer invented the name Uneeda Biscuit. Lasker always liked good names and slogans, but he was mystified by the trade-mark—a boy in a rubber storm suit. For months, he puzzled over it. A trade-mark ought to have a meaning; a picture ought to *add* something. But what on earth did a boy in slickers do for Uneeda Biscuit? Soon, however, Lasker saw that the Ayer campaign was triumphantly successful, and the example of Uneeda pointed out new empires. If Ayer could get a million-dollar contract (commission $150,000), so could he.

More and more, he devoted himself to studying copy. At this time Lord & Thomas, one of the three biggest agencies in the country, employed exactly *one* copy writer, who worked part time. His name was Case, and he got $30 a week; he worked for Lord & Thomas in the mornings for $15, and in the afternoons for Montgomery Ward for $15. Also the designing department of Lord & Thomas consisted of exactly one man, an artist named Doyle, who got $25 a week.[5] Lasker knew that expansion was bound to come soon. The heart of the advertising business had to be copy. He was so passionately excited and absorbed by advertising by this time that he gave up all thought of leaving Lord & Thomas and going back to journalism. "If someone had handed me the money to pay back my debt to Mr. Thomas, I couldn't have quit," he records. What fascinated him most was the mysterious power that good advertising could exert. But what were the constituents of this power? What exactly *was* advertising? He was obsessed by this question—a man driven. Meantime, he continued to ride the trains.

All traveling men like to tell tall tales about expense accounts, and Lasker was no exception. Once, he records, he included on his account the "cost" of a mythical lower berth from Minneapolis to St. Paul, and got away with it. When, on his day-to-day rounds by train, he signed up a new client he would immediately write the necessary copy. In order to do so comfortably he took to buying a seat in the chair car, for which he charged the company. The auditor at Lord & Thomas steadily disallowed such extravagant items, and argument became acrimonious. At last Lasker attached a memorandum to his expense account: "You will see that this does not include any item covering chair car space. Nevertheless this is included. But try to find it."

Mr. Lord and particularly Mr. Thomas became deeply attached to young Albert; he was, indeed, their white-haired boy. Morris

---

[5] Ayer, incidentally, never had a full-time copy writer till 1892, or an art man till 1898. Cf. *The Story of Advertising*, by James Playsted Wood, p. 245.

Lasker came up to Chicago from Galveston in 1900 to consult with the two chiefs of the firm and ask how his son was getting on. Thomas replied, "I don't know. He is either crazy or a genius." Albert, on his side, adored both Lord and Thomas, in particular the latter. Thomas was a character. He had a nice dry wit. On one occasion Lasker brought in a new contract which he had worked hard to get. Thomas wondered if the new client's credit was good enough, and the young man responded indignantly, "Why, the man's a millionaire!" Thomas said quietly, "I doubt that. One of the things you will learn in life is that is extremely difficult to hide a million dollars."

Thomas had an oblique approach. Later, when Lasker was a member of the firm, he wanted Thomas to hire a man but the latter refused. Albert asked why, and the reasons he gave did not seem satisfactory, since the man was a good man. Finally Thomas said, "I'll tell you the real reason. I don't like the way he wiggles a toothpick." This little story made a profound impression on Lasker. The lesson he derived from it was double: (a) nobody was better than his manners; (b) any employee in any company was at the mercy of a capricious boss. Once Thomas, in all seriousness, advised him not to protest about something unkind that had been said about him. "If you are ever accused of having murdered Abraham Lincoln, do *not* deny it," Thomas said. "Why?" asked Lasker. "Because," he replied, "people will then think that you *did* murder him. It is human nature for people to refuse to believe a denial."

Thomas warned him once never to discharge anybody unless a good replacement was available, and told this anecdote. His brother kept a hardware shop in Thomaston, Maine. He had a total staff of one clerk, to whom he was devoted. But, Thomas went on, his brother had one glaring idiosyncrasy—he could not stand the color red. Came Christmas, and the clerk arrived for work the next day wearing a bright red tie. The brother said, "You'll have to take off that tie. You know I can't stand the color red." But the tie had been given to the clerk by his daughter, and he was sentimental about it; a stubborn New Englander, he refused to take it off, and was fired.

Mr. Thomas went on: "In those days, every retailer had two institutions which guided him in everything he did. One was his bank, the other his jobber. The jobber really performed a function in those days. He educated the retailer.

"My brother phoned his jobber in Boston and told him that he'd lost his clerk. The jobber said, 'Don't worry. Tomorrow morning on the 9:10 there will be a man to see you. It just happens that we know a man who worked fifteen years for a customer of ours. The customer died, the business has been liquidated, and the man wants a job. You'll be *delighted* with him. He'll be just as good as the old man in two days.'

"My brother was elated, and the next day he went down to meet the train. Only one man got off the train, so he knew that that was his man. He went up to greet him, and then noticed that *the man was wearing a red vest!*"[6]

Flora

In 1901, visiting friends in Cincinnati, Albert Lasker met a young lady named Flora Warner. She was tiny. She weighed ninety-five pounds (he discovered later), and had a nineteen-inch waist. She was wearing (he never forgot) a blue silk dress with white polka dots; her jewelry was a string of coral beads. Her face was delicate, almost ethereal; she had perfect arched brows, like sickle moons, over large sherry-colored eyes, a long, slim, swelling throat, and heavy, glossy chestnut hair which she never cut. Lasker asked his host, "Who is that girl? I am going to marry her." One thing always characteristic of him was velocity.

Flora was Jewish, but, oddly enough, had been educated in a convent, which gave her a strong puritan streak. She lived in Buffalo. Her father was a dreamy, impractical man in the jewelry case business—a displaced intellectual. Her mother was Viennese, and had considerable force of character. One of her aunts was the author of a well-known Viennese cookbook (published in English under the title *A Thousand and One Recipes*) which is still treasured by connoisseurs of the kitchen.

[6] Columbia, p. 13.

Albert discovered immediately after meeting Flora that she was not only a most delightful person—gay, sophisticated, a belle, very popular—but that she was engaged to somebody else. He said calmly and with characteristic confidence, "You may be engaged, but you're not *married,* are you? Give me five days!"

Albert was twenty-one, Flora a year older. It embarrassed her greatly that she was his senior, and she made him promise never to tell this to anybody, not even the children subsequently born to them. At the beginning he was more in love with her than she with him. Obstacles were serious, even after she agreed to marry him. Both families opposed the match; the Laskers in Galveston thought that Albert was too young to marry; the Warners in Buffalo thought that he was too unstable, not assured enough of a sound future, and too much given to having a drink around the corner with the boys after the day's work was done. (Later they became devoted to him, and vice versa.) The young people managed, however, to have their way, and the marriage took place on June 9, 1902.

By this time Lasker had paid his debt to Lord & Thomas, and had been raised from $10 a week to $60, good money for a young man of twenty-two. He knew, however, that it would not be enough. He went to Mr. Thomas, told him that he was about to be married, and said, "I want $5,000 a year." Thomas's reply was unexpected— "Don't you want more?" Lasker knew well that he was worth a good deal more (as did Mr. Thomas) since he was now bringing in $250,000 worth of business a year, but he replied, "No. Five thousand will be enough. I want to work so cheaply for you that you will turn every opportunity that comes your way over to me to explore, and someday you will give me a partnership."

Flora Lasker liked to play the piano, and was a good cook; she wrote poetry, and played a nice game of tennis. She appreciated good clothes, and had a lively, original sense of decoration. Her taste was exceptional in several fields. Legend has it that she was the first woman in Chicago ever to use chintz curtains, and she was a pleasant hostess who made her guests comfortable. The youthful Laskers lived first at 5750 Woodlawn Avenue, on the South Side of Chicago near the Midway. This was a sound, pleasant, bourgeois neighborhood in those days with neat houses, most with wide porches, set close together on a leafy street. The house belongs to a University of Chicago fraternity today.

Catastrophe, in the form of serious illness, struck Flora Lasker almost immediately after her marriage. The medical details are obscure. Apparently she contracted a form of typhoid fever, which was followed by phlebitis. The joints of both legs were affected, and became frozen, as in a severe case of arthritis. She spent a year in a hospital bed. The bones of her toes and ankles had to be broken, one by one, reset, and locked in casts. She was one of the first patients in medical history to benefit from the modern orthopedic technique of traction; if this treatment had not been successful she might never have walked again. She became, in any case, a semi-invalid for the rest of her life. This hospital experience took place, not in Chicago, but in Buffalo where she had been stricken while on a visit home. Lasker, who was still spending three weeks of every month on the road, commuted back and forth to Buffalo. Doctor's bills were heavy, and presently he asked Lord & Thomas for a raise. He got it, and went up to $10,000 a year, an outlandish sum for a person of his age at the time. Even so, he was hard put to it to cope with the medical expenses Flora's illness entailed. His interest, many years later, in health insurance and making good medical care available to citizens at modest cost probably derived from this early struggle.

Within a silken cocoon, Flora had the strength of a steel bolt. She was never truly well again, because the phlebitis gave her a predisposition to embolism; exertion could be dangerous. Yet, when she left the hospital and returned to Chicago, she managed to partake fully in most aspects of her husband's life for more than thirty years, and bore him three children. Her doctor urged her to have the first child on the ground that this would "improve her circulation"; the others came in defiance of medical orders. Above all she wanted a boy to perpetuate the Lasker line, and who would be named after Uncle Eduard. Mary was born in 1904, Edward in 1912, and Frances (Francie) in 1916. All played a considerable role in Lasker's story, and we will mention them again.

As the years went on Albert and Flora built up an intricate relationship. Both had exceptionally strong wills; neither liked to
compromise; a most determined woman had married a most determined man. Flora was much more finely grained than Albert. She
gave him steadiness, and was an indispensable balance wheel.
Lasker's dependence on her lessened as time progressed, and in later
years they had fierce quarrels, but their relationship was predominantly tender and they never ceased loving one another. No matter
what happened, no matter how she disliked some of his business
associates (a major source of disputes between them), he knew that
she would always be on his side and he never lost his trust in her.
Night after night, year after year, he would wear her out by talking
to her till one, two, three in the morning, outlining deals and projects. In later life she told one of her children, "When I die, please
try to make your father marry again at once, because he has to have
somebody to talk to at all hours of the night." Of course, what
Lasker was doing in these nocturnal sessions was thinking aloud—
talking his ideas out—and she was an attentive and helpful
audience.

But Flora felt sometimes that Albert gave her everything except
himself. He was tempestuous, demanding, and often inconsiderate.
He was quite capable of losing heavily in an afternoon at the races,
and then of fidgeting furiously because the electric light bill was
too high. Yet there was a closeness between them, cemented slowly
during the years, that could not be broken.

Long after her death, he reminisced affectionately about her with
a friend. At this time he was maturely, radiantly happy with Mary
Reinhardt, whom he loved with every atom of his being. The friend
asked him what would have happened if he had met Mary before
Flora's death[7] and he replied, "Nothing. Flora made me unhappy
from time to time, but I would have never left her. I was committed."

But we have gone far ahead of our story.

[7] Flora died in 1936.

Chapter 5

SALESMANSHIP IN PRINT

More and more, Lasker became determined to find out exactly what advertising was. He continued to be amply aware of the magical, resounding effects it could have, but what, he asked himself again, gave it these effects? What, precisely, distinguished good, i.e., effective advertising, from bad? Why did advertising multiply enormously the sales of some products, but not others? Lasker's life became dedicated to a quest, a search, to find out the answer to such questions. He records—this was still in the early 1900's—that he felt like primitive man suddenly blessed by the gift of fire, or an engineer playing for the first time with electricity. In his hands was a new, untried form of energy, of power. What were its characteristics; what made it work; how could it be controlled?

Lasker, in his own reminiscences, describes his search virtually in terms of anguish. He was tortured. He was a man on a rack. It was not primarily desire to get ahead that stimulated him, nor greed for wealth; it was a burning interest in a concept, an idea—it was curiosity. He implored his elders, "Teach me!" But no one knew more than he did, or could give him answers that satisfied him. He decided after a time that advertising was "news." But, on further reflection, it became clear that this was not a good definition because advertising was obviously more than mere news. Why did some copy, which was full of news, pull in sales, whereas other copy, just as full of news, did not make a cent?

He addressed himself to various slogans in the advertising business. For instance Lord & Thomas, his own house, had a motto, "Advertise Judiciously." But when Lasker asked Mr. Lord or Mr.

Thomas what they meant by this phrase—did it mean spending more money, or writing better copy?—all that he could get out of them was that it meant to do "judicious" advertising, which did not carry him very far. Ayer, too, had a slogan—"Keeping Everlastingly At It Brings Success." Lasker went to a man with Ayer, and said, "Now, let me ask you this. Suppose I start wrong and I keep everlastingly at it. Where is that going to get me?"

"Well," the Ayer man replied, "what they mean is that keeping everlastingly at it *right* will achieve success."

"Well," Lasker said, "what is right? Can you define it for me?"

"Why," said the Ayer man, "keeping your name before the public."

Lasker said, "But suppose I don't live that long. Or suppose I go broke; then I won't be able to keep my name before the public. There must be something else to this thing!"[1]

Mr. Lord had always said that he would retire at sixty, and in 1903, on the stroke of reaching this age, he did so. Lasker, who had made a considerable amount of money on bonuses, was able to buy his share of the business, and become a partner. His salary was lifted to $52,000 per year, and there could have been few men of his age, twenty-three, in the United States at that time who earned so much money. Then, fortuitously, came the answer to his raging quest. In the spring of 1904 he was sitting with Mr. Thomas when a clerk came in and handed them a note. For years, Lasker remembered the peculiar expression on the senior partner's face as he glanced at the bit of paper and handed it over to him. It read: "I am downstairs in the saloon." (The building which housed the Lord & Thomas offices did indeed have a saloon on the first floor.) "I am in the saloon downstairs, and I can tell you what advertising is. I know that you don't know. It will mean much to me to have you know what it is and it will mean much to you. If you wish to know what advertising is, send the word 'Yes' down by messenger." Signed—John E. Kennedy.

Thomas said, "Have you ever heard of this man?"

[1] *The Lasker Story*, p. 4. Copyright 1952, 1953 by *Advertising Age*.

Lasker had not.

Thomas said, "The man must be crazy. I won't waste any time on him."

Lasker said, "Let me see him. What have we got to lose?"

Word went down to Kennedy, who then appeared in Lasker's office. After an hour they went down to the saloon together, and emerged at midnight. From that time on, Lasker knew what advertising was. First Kennedy asked him what his own ideas were, and Lasker mentioned news. Kennedy said, "No. News is a technique of presentation, but advertising is a very different thing. I can give it to you in three words." Lasker said, "I am hungry. What are those three words?"

Kennedy said, *"Salesmanship in print."*

This may seem to be the height of obviousness now, but no one had ever put the concept, the definition, into such simple terms before. And these three words have defined advertising ever since, although of course "print" includes nowadays the radio and the television screen. All of Lasker's groping, his striving for terms of reference, his search for knowledge of the potentialities of the weapon he was handling, were crystalized by Kennedy's three simple words. He grasped the implications at once—advertising must be positive, not negative—it must attack. Now he knew what he was about, and today, half a century later, most of the art and practice of advertising is still based on those same three words.

Out of the "Salesmanship in Print" formula came a second vital concept. What, Lasker demanded, was the mysterious element, compound, essence, which made salesmanship in print *work*—what made sales, what made people purchase goods? Kennedy answered, "That too is simple. You have to give them a *reason why.*" If, for instance, the proprietor of a grocery store should simply invite people to come in and buy, for no definite reason, he would get nowhere. But if he explained *why* his products were better, or sold at a cheaper price and were still just as good as the other fellow's, if he presented a convincing argument to prove his superiority, then the chances were, like as not, that people would flock to him. So

"Reason Why" advertising, pioneered by Lord & Thomas, was born. This concept that the consumer must be actively wooed may also seem obvious today, but nobody had ever put it into concrete, effective practice before.

Kennedy was, of all things, a former member of the Canadian Mounted Police. He was accustomed to getting his man. Lasker has recounted that he was the handsomest man he ever met—tall, stalwart, calmly muscular. He had a forehead like a beveled dome, and twirling upturned mustachios. He was extremely vain. He was moody, silent for long periods, and morose. He liked to be alone, and was a very slow worker, easily fatigued. Lasker's considered opinion was that, next to Claude Hopkins, whom we will meet soon, he was the greatest advertising copy writer who ever lived, and he has called his association with him "the most memorable thing" in his whole lifetime.

At the time of their first meeting Kennedy had a job writing ads for a patent medicine known as Dr. Shoop's Restorative. Lasker had seen and admired these ads, but had not known who the author was. One was headlined, "What Tea Does to Rheumatics." He records, "I wasn't a rheumatic, but it sounded to me most interesting. What *would* tea do to rheumatics? Someday I might get rheumatism."

From Dr. Shoop, Kennedy got a fantastic salary for a copy writer, $28,000 a year. Lasker determined to hire him for Lord & Thomas, and found that he could buy his contract for a modest sum; he took the matter up with Mr. Thomas, who, however, had taken a pronounced, bitter aversion to him. Still, Thomas realized that Kennedy might, after all, be worth his keep, although Lord & Thomas had never paid a copy writer more than $30 a week before. At last he said, "All right, go ahead and hire him, but on one condition." Lasker said, "What is that?" Thomas said, "That I don't ever have to see the fellow." At once, like crazed children (although Kennedy was in his late forties), Lasker and Kennedy got to work. Albert said, "Teach me." Kennedy said, "After work every night, I will write you out a lesson," and for months they spent every evening together, planning campaigns and experimenting with copy.

Lasker heard that a washing machine company in Binghamton, New York, which sold the "1900 Ball Bearing Family Washer," was flirting with the idea of getting a new agency and might come to Lord & Thomas. With Kennedy, he examined carefully one of its best-known ads, which portrayed a woman chained to a washtub. Kennedy said: "Well, there just isn't one thing about this advertisement that isn't wrong if you want to sell goods. First the headline, 'Don't be chained to the washtub.' You are speaking negatively. Every woman doesn't feel chained to the washtub; lots of women might enjoy it. You miss her entirely.

"Second, the average woman is put in the position of a drudge, and slavery ended in '65. She won't know it consciously, but subconsciously she won't admit that she has been reduced to such bestial servility.

"Third, it makes it an installment plan proposition, and people do not like to buy a trade-marked article on the installment plan because, when it is in the house, everybody who comes in and sees that 1900 washer says, 'Un huh! Two dollars down and two dollars forever!'

"And the worst crime of all, it has . . . no news interest. Otherwise, it is all right!"[2]

Lasker went to Binghamton, presented these views, and got the account. Kennedy wrote a new series of ads for the company, and within four months it had doubled its advertising appropriation; within six it was one of the three or four largest advertisers in the country, and before a year it had trebled its output and built a new plant. The reason was largely the first Kennedy-Lasker campaign. Their first ad, a miracle of calm persuasiveness, bore the headline, "Let This Machine Do Your Washing Free," and the illustration, instead of showing a woman chained to a tub, portrayed one in a rocking chair, reading a book without a care in the world while casually turning the handle of the ball-bearing machine, which appeared to be working by itself!

[2] *The Lasker Story*, p. 12.

One thing Lasker and Kennedy did in their spare time was revamp the Lord & Thomas house organ, *Judicious Advertising*. (Lasker no longer believed in the "judicious advertising" concept, but the name of the magazine was retained.) Files of this publication, which appeared regularly for more than thirty years, make fascinating reading even today. It contained reports of progress, homilies, notes on campaigns, and reflections embodying the new Lasker-Kennedy concepts. One article is headlined, " 'I,' cried John Consumer, 'I Pay for Advertising!' " Editorials suggest that Abraham Lincoln was "the greatest copy writer of all time," and jokes interlard the pages.[3]

> Copywriter: Johnny, give me a sentence using the word "diadem."
> Office boy: People who drink moonshine diadem sight quicker than those who don't.

Within two years Lord & Thomas was paying Kennedy $75,000 a year, but he still maintained his night sessions with Lasker, as if he were a schoolmaster, and kept on drumming into the younger man his major precept, that what counted in an ad was copy—the way it was *written*. (Incidentally he was preceded in this discovery by Addison and Steele in the *Tatler*, who wrote in 1710 that "the great art in writing advertisements is . . . to catch the reader's eye.") Soon Lasker, the $1000-a-week boy wonder, realized that Lord & Thomas must have a full-dress copy-writing department. But there were, in his words, "no such things as copy-writers" in those days. He sounded out Mr. Thomas, and came up with an idea. "I have been upstairs," he proffered, "and I have measured that we can take out all the files against half of the west windows and we can make nine offices eight by ten each. It will cost about $2,000 to build the partitions. I want you to let me put up nine offices there . . . and advertise for nine young newspapermen. Kennedy and I will start training them, because out of the nine we might only get three or four."[4]

---

[3] Also Kennedy prepared a brochure, *The Book of Advertising Tests*, which sought to define, chart, and put down once for all the results of his experiments, and which still makes instructive reading.
[4] *The Lasker Story*, p. 18.

Thomas agreed, nine candidates were duly found, and the training sessions began. Lasker, with burning enthusiasm, held regular classes after hours, twice a week for four or five hours each time. Kennedy was incapable of teaching groups, because he could not talk to more than one person at a time, but he superintended what went on. This was the origin of modern copy writing in the United States; Lord & Thomas was the first agency in America to set up a systematically trained copy staff. Then Kennedy had a fit of temperament, quit, and moved on to New York, where he set up a business of his own. What happened to him thereafter I do not know. This is a pattern which we will come across elsewhere in this story. Lasker himself, a great innovator of techniques, had an unexampled gift of finding creative people and getting them to work for him. Nobody ever hired talent better. Then his men drifted away or progressed elsewhere.

By 1905 all activity on copy at Lord & Thomas was in the precocious Lasker's charge. But, interestingly enough, he himself gave up writing copy soon after this; he was perpetually inventive in suggesting copy ideas, but seldom wrote anything. This was because he wanted to retain a free position as a *critic* of the work of his own agency. If he participated, he felt that he would not be sufficiently free of subjective emotion to be a good editor. He could not, he decided, be a satisfactory critic of anything he himself had written, but this made him all the more acute as an editor. Once, hiring a man, he greeted him with the words, "You are supposed to be the best copy writer in the country. Please remember that I am the best copy editor . . . or at least I think I am!"

About this time young Lasker became a pioneer in the public relations business, which he later gave up because it bored and irritated him. The difference between advertising and public relations is that advertising depends on space paid for in a publication or elsewhere, whereas public relations is what produces material in the editorial or news columns; it is unacknowledged advertising. Of course, as Lasker was quick to realize, good public relations work depended largely on good private relations, and these he cultivated everywhere. One of his first public relations stunts was to organize a beauty contest on behalf of a Chicago newspaper, the first beauty contest ever held in the United States for promotion purposes. He always loved new ideas.

In 1906 Mr. Thomas died suddenly. He was walking down the street with Lasker, and had a heart attack; he collapsed in the young man's arms. Together with a veteran colleague, Charles R. Erwin, who was later to become a member of a well-known advertising agency of his own, Erwin, Wasey & Company, Lasker bought up the Thomas interest, and they became owners of the firm. Yet Albert was still only twenty-six. The years, as he put it later, "shot by like bullets." In 1912 he bought Erwin out and became sole owner, although the latter stayed with the company until 1918.

Year by year business got better, but success was beginning to take a toll out of Lasker. He hardened. Almost everything had to be sacrificed—private life, human relationships, opportunity for leisure, cultivation of other than commercial values—to the stern scramble to get ahead. He was an intense competitor and seized every advantage that could legitimately be seized; he was full of tricks and played the game hard, but, on the other hand, he played it within the rules.

*

From first to last Albert was extraordinarily sensitive to any business upset. Once in the early days he came back from a trip, and Flora met him at the Twelfth Street Station. He was always a person who, to understate the case, painted a large picture. Depending on his mood, he could deal in the most glowing exaggerations. If things were black, they were black indeed; they were blacker than a coffin or a top hat. He gave way to emotion easily. This particular morning Lasker emerged from the Pullman with his face shattered by strain. A big account had failed him. He told Flora, "I am ruined. We are poor." Nervously he said that he must hurry to the office. She said, "Well, if we're ruined, I don't see any reason for you to go to the office at all. Now we have plenty of time. Come home and have some breakfast." She was often able to make him tranquil, smooth down his sharp-pointed nerves, by her own calmness and common sense.

When they quarreled, trivial household affairs or the petty worries common to youthful marriages were usually the reason. She was a good housewife, but was lax about paying bills; he went crazy if bills were not paid by the tenth of every month. She was an accomplished cook, but often he was too busy to come home to dinner. Also his sheer animal energy was too much for her; she felt frustrated and even guilty because her physical disabilities made it impossible for her to keep fully up with him. So snarls and discomfitures were inevitable. If he wanted black, she wanted white. When she was really hurt, she sometimes lost her temper and struck at his most vulnerable spot by snapping, "You're just a salesman!"

Yet they loved one another fiercely, and got on well most of the time. They moved from the house on Woodlawn Avenue to another in the same neighborhood, extended the web of their friendships, saved money, and were devoted to their daughter Mary, who had been born in 1904.

The Remarkable Mr. Hopkins

In 1908 one of the most extraordinary advertising men of his day, Claude C. Hopkins, entered Lasker's life, and for many years their careers were intertwined. Each taught the other much. The contribution he made to Lasker cannot be overestimated. We must have a word or two about Hopkins, who was born in a small town in Michigan in 1866. He came of a long line of clergymen and wanted to go into the ministry, but could not afford to go to college; in fact, he worked for a living from the age of nine, and spent some years as a janitor in a church. His mother, a Scot, taught him from the earliest age that a dime was as big as a dollar, a maxim he never forgot. Like Lasker, he was a ferociously hard worker and, for years, seldom left his office till two in the morning; Sunday was his favorite day, because he could work all day without interruption. Then, when he became successful, he did most of his writing in an isolated shack out in the country; he never had a clerk, researcher, or secretary. He calculated that, after thirty-five years of work, he had already spent seventy years in the advertising business because he did two years' work every year.

Hopkins was a mouse of a man, but with a brain full of electricity. He was shy, but a daring go-getter. He had gentle doe's eyes and his nickname was "Thee-thee," because he spoke with a lisp. "Thee-thee" was his own pronunciation of "C.C.," his initials. Seldom has a man of such mild exterior possessed more explosive internal force.

He became a very rich man indeed, but he records that he never paid more than $6.50 for a pair of shoes. He was penurious to the bone, but until the advent of the income tax, kept no record of his earnings; his wife paid the bills, and he never signed a check. He had no idea what his own house cost. At the end Lasker was paying him more than $200,000 a year, which Hopkins thought was too much, not too little. Eventually an arrangement was worked out whereby he drew up his own contract each year, which Lasker then signed without reading.

Hopkins drifted into advertising when he was still in his teens (many years before meeting Lasker), and got a job with the Bissell Carpet Sweeper Company. He revolutionized the business by offering sweepers in a variety of different colors of wood, and then contriving to get retailers to maintain full stocks in each flamboyant color. Hopkins was a firm believer in safety first, but his character contained an almost berserk note of enterprise. Consider what happened when, soon after the turn of the century, he became advertising manager of Swift & Company, the Chicago packers. Swift did little advertising in those days, and several members of the Swift family resented Hopkins bitterly, because they thought that he would "waste" money. One Swift product was Cotosuet, an inexpensive substitute for butter and lard made out of cottonseed oil and beef suet. But Cotosuet had a rival, Cottolene, manufactured by a competing company and better established than Cotosuet. It was Hopkins' job to vanquish Cottolene. This was as if he had been asked to launch a new white soap to beat Ivory. Hopkins paced the hot Chicago streets, thinking, and laid out several principles. He never sought to *sell* anything; instead he offered people "the privilege of buying." He did not say, "Buy my brand, not the other fellow's"; instead he said, "I will show you *why* it is better to buy from me, because I am doing you a favor." (John Kennedy, at about the same time, was experimenting with identical theories of salesmanship.) He thought that the most easily exploitable of all emotions was curiosity. His favorite maxim was: "No argument can compete with one dramatic demonstration."[5]

He learned that a well-known Chicago department store, Rothschild & Company, was about to open new premises, and would celebrate this event by appropriate festivities. The grocery department was on the fifth floor, and had a large bay window. Hopkins asked the Rothschild advertising manager if he could borrow the window for the occasion, saying that he would put the Rothschild name on every lip. What Hopkins did then was to order from a baker *the largest cake in the world,* made out of Cotosuet instead of butter. The cake filled the entire alcove, and, magnificently decorated, was almost as high as the room. Hopkins then advertised the advent of this stupendous monster among cakes in the daily newspapers. His copy conveyed the idea that, if Cotosuet was good enough a substitute for butter to make a cake, it was certainly a good enough substitute for lard as well. The cake caused a sensation when Rothschild's held their opening. Police had to hold back excited mobs. In the next few days, 105,000 people climbed four flights of stairs to see the fabulous cake; the elevators would not hold them. Hopkins organized a contest—prizes went to those visitors who guessed nearest to the cake's correct enormous weight. But every guesser, in order to be qualified, had to buy a pail of Cotosuet first. Cotosuet was made overnight, and so was Hopkins.

Presently Hopkins left Swift and entered the field of patent

[5] For much of this I have drawn on Hopkins' own record, *My Life in Advertising* (Harper & Brothers, 1936).

medicine. He got a job in Racine, Wisconsin, with Dr. Shoop's Restorative, the same company which spawned Kennedy. Patent medicines, even those flooded with alcohol, were still thought to be perfectly respectable by most advertising media; the argument was that they helped people who could not afford regular medical care, and gave relief for simple complaints at low cost. Hopkins went to work on a cough syrup, and developed a proposal whereby the local druggist signed a warranty guaranteeing the customer his money back if the syrup didn't work. The ads read, "Try this remedy; watch the benefits it brings. It cannot harm, for no opiates are in it. If it succeeds, the cough will stop. If it fails, it is free. Your own druggist signs the warrant." The catch was that the druggist gave the guaranty only if the customer bought more than one bottle, and sales multiplied fantastically. Next Hopkins moved on to another patent medicine company, founded by a typewriter manufacturer, which made "Powley's Liquefied Ozone"; later the name was changed to Liquozone. The company was going broke, but the diabolically clever Hopkins had confidence in it and thought that he could save it; as an indication of his faith, he bought a quarter interest in it. He proceeded then to do for Liquozone what he had done for Dr. Shoop, even more successfully, by working out a scheme whereby the customer got a fifty-cent bottle free if he bought six. "Consider how irresistible was such a proposition," Hopkins wrote later. "A fifty cent bottle free. Then a five dollar lot under warrant. 'Just say to your druggist that you are dissatisfied, and your money will be returned without argument.' I had a proposition which no reasonable person could refuse. My offer was impregnable." And Liquozone swept the country. The profits were $1,800,-000 the first year after Hopkins took over (his share being 25 per cent of this) and soon Liquozone was being advertised and sold all over the world. Hopkins himself came to believe fervently in its medicinal properties, and even said that it saved his own daughter from certain death when she became seriously ill.

Meantime, he organized a campaign for Schlitz beer ("The Beer That Made Milwaukee Famous"). First he went to a technical school to learn about brewing, and then spent dutiful days going through the Schlitz brewery inch by inch. All beers concentrated on purity as their big selling point in those days, and Hopkins sought doggedly for a way to dramatize how pure Schlitz beer was. Something suddenly caught his imagination. He discovered that Schlitz purified its bottles by live steam. Nobody in the brewery thought that this was of any particular interest, but Hopkins was like a bright newspaper man who, covering a story, unexpectedly sees a feature angle; this gave him exactly what he wanted. He based his whole Schlitz campaign on the idea that the use of live steam to clean bottles prevented the beer from fermenting, and thus guaranteed its purity. Of course *all* breweries cleaned their bottles with live steam, but no one had ever thought before of exploiting this for advertising purposes. Hopkins' ads were perfectly honest; he did not say that other breweries did *not* use live steam, but the implication was that it was a Schlitz exclusive. His campaign was a raging success, and Schlitz rose from fifth place in national beer sales to neck-and-neck for first in a few months. Rival beers were chagrined, but caught in a trap. They could not imitate Hopkins and say that they too used live steam, which they did, because then they would fall under the charge of basely imitating Schlitz.[6]

*

Lasker was traveling to Philadelphia, and on the train met by accident Cyrus H. K. Curtis, founder of the Curtis Publishing Company, proprietor of the *Saturday Evening Post* and *Ladies' Home Journal,* and incomparably the most important magazine publisher in America. Curtis said, "Lasker, I am just about to order a bottle of Schlitz beer as a result of an advertisement that I read, and you ought to go and get the man who wrote that advertisement."

Albert pricked up his ears. He was more than normally interested because Curtis, as was well known, never allowed a line of advertising of alcoholic beverages in any of his publications, and seldom,

[6] Wood, *op. cit.,* p. 289.

Poor Beer *vs.* Pure Beer

Both cost you alike, yet one costs the maker twice as much as the other. One is good, and good for you; the other is harmful. Let us tell you where the difference lies.

POOR BEER	PURE BEER
Is easy to brew.	calls for the best materials—the best that money can buy.
The materials are cheap. The brewing may be done under any sort of surroundings.	The brewery must be as clean as your kitchen; the utensils as clean.
Cleanliness is not important, for the users never see it brewed.	The cooling must be done in filtered air, in a plate glass room.
Any water will do. No air is too impure for the cooling.	The product must be aged for months, until thoroughly fermented, else it causes biliousness.
No filtering, no sterilizing; almost no ageing, for ageing ties up money.	The beer must be filtered, then sterilized in the bottle.
What is the use of expense and care when there is no reputation to defend?—	You're always welcome to that brewery for the owners are proud of it.
When few people who drink it know even the name of the maker.	And the size of it proves the eventual success of worth.

Schlitz is a pure beer, famous for fifty years. To maintain its standard, we double the necessary cost of our brewing. Don't you prefer a pure beer, a good beer, a healthful beer, when it costs no more than the common?

Ask for the brewery bottling.

Schlitz

The Beer That Made Milwaukee Famous

if ever, touched a drop to drink. But now he was tasting beer because an ad emphasized its purity! Moreover, this beer was the deadly rival of a beer which Lord & Thomas itself represented, Anheuser-Busch of St. Louis. At once Lasker got a copy of the Schlitz ad. It was headlined "Poor Beer vs. Pure Beer," and told all about live steam and fermentation.

Lasker records, "Well, that appealed to me, by golly—beer that wouldn't ferment. I didn't stop to think that I had never heard of beer fermenting. . . . But when the writer put the thought in that the bottles were cleaned in live steam, that was interesting!" He found out that the Schlitz writer was Claude C. Hopkins, and then discovered that Hopkins was also the author of the Liquozone campaign, which he had admired extravagantly. Instantly he determined to find and hire this man. But how to get him? Hopkins was rich, a lone wolf, and tired of working. Lasker went to a friend, the head of a drugstore chain, who knew him well. The friend said, "You'll never get Hopkins by offering him money. He can buy and sell you. But you could get him by offering to buy his wife an electric automobile."

Lasker said, "What?"

The friend said that Mrs. Hopkins' dream was to have an electric car, but that Hopkins, a notoriously stingy man, refused to buy her one. Electrics, driven by storage batteries, were widely popular at this time; gasoline-driven cars were still comparatively rare.

The drugstore man, Lasker, and Hopkins met for lunch. The two advertising sharks sounded each other out warily. Albert asked if, as a token of his admiration for Hopkins, he might present his wife with an electric car. Hopkins said, "Delighted—now what do you want of *me?*" Before the afternoon was out Lasker had hired him as his chief copy writer at $185,000 a year, not including bonuses and commissions. Hopkins stayed with him for eighteen years until his retirement in 1924. Twice he served terms as president of Lord & Thomas, and once was chairman of the board. (Lasker continually made and unmade presidents; the post was largely titular but in the case of Hopkins it was he, not Lasker, who actually did sit on the throne for long periods, because Lasker spent a great deal of time away from business in the next few years.)

Lasker and Hopkins became, so to speak, blood brothers, although Albert was fourteen years younger. One thing Lasker, a swift man himself, liked most about him was his swiftness. Unlike Kennedy, he was an extraordinarily quick as well as hard worker. He would visit a client, and, as a rule, could within twenty-four hours design or outline a campaign that would quadruple earnings;

within forty-eight, he could sketch out enough actual copy for a whole year's advertising. After Hopkins saw a client Lasker would usually hold up his recommendations for at least six weeks. Otherwise the client was apt to feel that Hopkins worked too fast and that he was being cheated. Then too Lasker admired his colossal industry. For one mail-order campaign he assembled a list of every head of family in the United States, classified by 86,000 post offices.

Lasker and Hopkins worked so well together mainly because they shared the same fundamental concepts. They both felt deeply that the ultimate object of business was profit and to create a demand for goods, but at the same time they loved advertising because it was a game—full of wackiness, danger, joy, and adventure. They were in the pit, fighting. What they tried to do, of course, was make the game more scientific as they went along, but the element of improvisation never ceased to fascinate them both. Then too they believed in sound goods and both were convinced that no advertising campaign could be successful which did not offer service. You had to give people something in order to get something, but the important thing was to get the something. As Lasker put it, "I had no desire to make money and not render service, but I certainly had no desire to render service and not make money."

Hopkins taught Albert a good deal about the value of testing (for instance, by trying out a campaign in miniature in a small town), and about coupons as a device for tracing results. He devised what was probably the first use in America of the monthly club idea— later to be immortalized by the Book-of-the-Month Club and similar organizations—by selling a brand of shoes at greatly reduced rates to people who joined a shoe "club" in Racine. He was full of maxims, like "Don't boast" and "All advertising disasters are due to rashness," to which Lasker listened attentively. He thought that copy should consist of the shortest possible sentences, and that headlines should have a personal quality, with "the impact of a bell-boy paging a man in a crowded room." He did not like to use capital letters because the reader is more used to lower case, and for the same reason he avoided both abnormally small and large type. Not everybody reads every ad in a series, and so his ideal was that every ad should tell the whole story. Above all, he hated fancy language, jokes, and tricks. The function of advertising was, he held, not to amuse, but to sell. "Spending money is a serious business, and people do not buy from clowns."

All of these ideas and principles Lasker incorporated into Lord & Thomas, to a fruitful end, because it soon passed Ayer and Thompson to become the biggest advertising agency in the world.

Some Early Accounts

One of these was Sunkist. The California Fruit Growers Exchange, later called Sunkist Growers, Inc., was always one of Lasker's pet accounts. The origin of his interest in California citrus is curious. Oddly enough, there was at this time a superabundance of citrus production on the West Coast. More oranges were grown than could be sold, and trees were deliberately cut down in order to limit the output—a foretaste of what happened to many crops in the United States years later. Lasker thought that to kill orange trees was a crime. It wounded him deeply that natural resources should be wasted. He got the Sunkist account, and an innovator always, conceived the idea of encouraging people to drink orange *juice*. This was a novelty at the time. Oranges were eaten by millions, yes, but comparatively few citizens had learned to drink them. Sunkist sales advanced considerably as orange juice became more and more popular, and the growers no longer had to sacrifice their trees. This is a good example of how, in the early days, a single idea put forward in an advertising campaign could not only help to rescue a failing industry, but could change consumer habits. Moreover, oranges contain Vitamin C, and Lasker felt that by stimulating the taste for orange juice he was contributing substantially to improvement of the public's health. To make sure that his theory was correct that Vitamin C was a vital element in diet he financed a research project at the University of Chicago, and his views, much in advance of the time, were fully confirmed.[7]

---

[7] Sunkist, years later, provided an illustration of his uncanny capacity to estimate public response to a product. Sugar was short after World War I, and

Next, Lasker sought to make people interested not merely in oranges in general, but in California oranges in particular as against rivals from Florida. To get citizens at large to be Sunkist-conscious he had to make them California-conscious as well. Shrewdly, to this end, he tried out his first campaign in Iowa, with the slogan "Oranges For Health, California For Wealth," and the effect was beyond belief. It would be too much to say that Lord & Thomas was the instigator of the great mass migrations of Iowans to California that presently took place, but it contributed a spark. As to oranges, their sale climbed from 35 to 72 per capita per year in twenty-eight years, and few things in his career made Lasker prouder than that he helped to double American orange consumption. Meantime he went into other California products—olives, prunes, walnuts, peaches. A final touch is that railway business went up sharply in California as a result of the increasing sales of food products, and Lasker got into railway advertising—Southern Pacific became one of his most lucrative accounts. New fields create new fields.

In 1911 another exceptionally important client came to Lord & Thomas—Palmolive—and so did the Van Camp Packing Company. Hopkins had a great deal to do with both. It is a pity to have to abbreviate the Palmolive story. A Milwaukee soap manufacturer, B. P. Johnson & Company, approached Lord & Thomas for help in selling one of its products, Galvanic Laundry Soap. The sales manager, Charles Pearce, argued the case, but Lasker-Hopkins said No. They didn't think they could advertise Galvanic to advantage. Then, however, they asked Pearce if he had any other product, and he replied that his company made a toilet soap called Palmolive, the first soap in the world to be colored green, but that its sales were so slight that it was not worth pushing.

Lasker-Hopkins became attentive. Why was it green? Why was it called Palmolive? Because, said Pearce, palm and olive oil went into it. This gave Lasker-Hopkins the idea of advertising it on a basis quite new (and revolutionary) in the soap business—to stress

everybody yearned for sweets; Lasker thought up the idea of a Sunkist marmalade to help assuage the hunger of people for chocolate, candy, and so forth. Officers of the company calculated that they would sell about a million gallons of this in a year; he said 600,000. He was right, the legend says, within a gallon.

its exotic appeal, not merely its cleansing power. "Women like Cleopatra," Hopkins reasoned, "must have sat under palm trees and used olive oil." Palmolive would be the soap to make contemporary women beautiful. Hopkins suggested a test campaign, which was performed in Benton Harbor, Michigan, and cost $700.[8] The rest is history. "Beauty" advertising was born, the account made millions, and within a few years Palmolive was the leading toilet soap in the world, which it still is.[9]

In their first Palmolive campaigns Lasker-Hopkins used coupons with sensational success. They blanketed the country with ads containing coupons good at any drugstore for a ten-cent miniature cake; the coupon authorized the dealer to deliver a cake to the custtomer and charge the Palmolive company for it. This, as both Lasker and Hopkins have recorded, was much better than a "free" offer.[10] No longer did the astute Hopkins believe in giving away commodities for nothing. People instinctively thought that there must be something spurious about products—even samples—given away free. So he emphasized that the company was *paying* for the ten-cent cake, to show its supreme confidence in its product. The customer got the sample free, but it was *paid for*. This technique was startlingly novel at the time. It stunned and outraged Palmolive's competitors, and scared the Palmolive people themselves half to death —they thought that they would go broke paying out dimes. Instead, their business soared.

One well-known Palmolive slogan was "Keep That School Girl Complexion." About this time Lasker saw a J. Walter Thompson ad for a competing soap, Woodbury's, which had an even more enticing headline, "The Skin You Love To Touch." This was one of the major shocks of his life. He saw to the heart of the matter in a second. His brain rocked. He was consumed with a mixture of

---

[8] A test in a slightly bigger city would have cost $1,000, which was considered too much to gamble.

[9] "SOAP FROM TREES—NATURE'S GIFT TO BEAUTY" was the headline of one famous early Palmolive ad. Another for Palmolive shaving cream was "WE TRIED 130 TIMES BEFORE WE PERFECTED A SHAVING CREAM LIKE THIS."

[10] Hopkins, *op. cit.*, p. 133.

envy, admiration, and indignation. He pointed out to his staff, "You see what Thompson has done. They have gone us one better and put *sex* into soap advertising." He snorted, "Sex . . . SEX!" Years later it was his considered opinion that this Thompson ad was one of the three greatest landmarks in the entire history of American advertising, the others being the standard 15 per cent contract first worked out by Ayer and his own Lord & Thomas formula, "Salesmanship in Print."[11]

Van Camp was an Indianapolis canning company, the first in the world to put soup and spaghetti into cans. The potentialities of this fascinated Lasker. Canning of foodstuffs was in its infancy, and the subsequent enormous expansion in the use of canned foods all over the country derived, at least in part, from the early Lord & Thomas campaigns for Van Camp. One product was pork and beans, and Lasker-Hopkins dove into this with brisk and joyful energy. They discovered that 94 per cent of American housewives baked their own pork and beans; the problem was to persuade them to buy canned beans instead. Hopkins outdid himself emphasizing the quality of the beans Van Camp used, the softness of the water, the efficiency of the automatic steam ovens in which the mixture was baked "scientifically," and the superlative flavor of the pork. He told them that home-cooked beans could never be made really digestible, and pounded on the theme that housewives wasted untold hours in producing inedible beans "too crisp on the top, too mushy below," whereas Van Camp beans were *uniform right through the can.*

As a next step, Hopkins had to contrive to make the Van Camp product seem more attractive than competing brands. To prove this he put on a demonstration lunch, serving six or seven different kinds of pork and beans to a jury. No one, not even the Van Camp executives who were present, could tell which was which! Hopkins, a subtle man, instantly took advantage of this contretemps. He put out ads saying, "TRY OUR RIVALS TOO."[12] He actively urged people to

[11] Wood, *op. cit.,* p. 295, quoting from *The Diary of an Ad Man,* by James Webb Young.
[12] Martin Mayer, *Madison Avenue, U. S. A.,* p. 53.

buy other pork and beans than Van Camp's, and compare them. This, strange as it may seem, turned out to be a cardinal feat of salesmanship, because customers reasoned that if Van Camp was so sure of its superiority that it could invite business for its rivals it must indeed be superior.

Presently Van Camp went into canned milk; this was the origin of today's great condensed milk industry. But people thought at first that canned milk tasted "scalded." Now Lasker came forward with an idea to counteract this. What was a pleasant taste universally liked? Almonds! This might influence people to forget about scalding. So Van Camp milk became the milk with the almond flavor, although, of course, it did not contain any actual almond at all. Lasker relied simply on the power of suggestion. "Be sure and taste the milk and see if it has the Almond Flavor," he had Hopkins write with complacent vigor. "If it has not the Almond Flavor, it is not the genuine!"

Van Camp was unknown in New York, and Lasker-Hopkins determined to invade this large market. They put out a coupon ad, similar to the one for Palmolive, and in one day got 1,460,000 returns. They paid out $146,000 to the grocers to redeem the ten-cent coupons, and were content: Van Camp was now installed in 1,460,-000 New York City homes. This ad was one of the most celebrated, as well as successful, in the history of advertising. The illustration showed a cow made of tin cans, with a spoon for the tail and can openers for horns, under the vibrant headline, "YOU CAN HAVE A COW RIGHT IN YOUR KITCHEN."

Van Camp was one of the first companies in which the youthful Lasker had a direct financial interest aside from advertising. As a rule he was chary of going into business with a client; in fact, he did so with no more than three or four companies in his whole experience.[13] There was a peculiar reason for this, similar to why

[13] Pepsodent and Kotex-Kleenex were others; see Chapter Ten below. Also Lasker had at one time or other holdings in such companies as Quaker Oats and Schenley (after Prohibition), but never to such an extent as to give him anything to do with management. Sometimes—a curious point—he bought into businesses run by competitors. (*The Lasker Story*, p. 41.)

he did not like to write copy himself. He wanted to retain his free, independent position as a critic; he wanted to be able to disagree with the management of any business, and tell any client to go to hell. (Which he did, often.) Also he didn't want to risk money. If Lasker had taken advantage of stock options or otherwise bought into some of the giant businesses with which he was intimately associated for many years, he would have become a much richer man than he ever was, but his sense of duty to his own profession, plus a curious kind of idealism, plus caution, plus his fixed delight in always being an umpire, an arbiter, restrained him. Often, however, he lent money to businesses in order to help them finance advertising appropriations or to show his confidence in them. He would say to a prospective client, "I am so certain that I can multiply your business that Lord & Thomas will advance you credit for a year on what you spend with us." In other words, he lent the client the money with which the client advertised. Sometimes this process did not work out and, in fact, Lasker got into Van Camp because the company found itself in financial difficulties, and could not pay Lord & Thomas what it owed. So Albert and four other large creditors, whom he had not met before, took over and found themselves partners in the canning business, about which they knew nothing. One of the four was an Indiana banker, William G. Irwin, who later became Republican National Committeeman from Indiana, and, later still, a conspicuous actor in Wendell Willkie's campaign for President. Lasker, as we shall see in a subsequent chapter, was brought into national politics by a letter from Irwin. Pork and beans and a cow in the kitchen led straight to Will H. Hays, Warren G. Harding, and the Shipping Board.

Van Camp also led to a nice little scene between Albert and Flora. He thought that Van Camp soups were so good (they had to be, since he advertised them) that he saw no point in his wife's cooking her own. She could not, he said, possibly manage to compete against canned soups made by trained chefs with "scientific" methods, and ordered her to put the matter to a test. She prepared a certain soup on the kitchen stove while he heated a Van Camp can of the same variety. Both were then served at the table, but a servant brought them in so that neither knew which was which. Excited beyond measure, smiling his wide smile confidently, Lasker took careful tastes of each. "This," he announced, "is the best, and must be Van Camp's!"

But it was Flora's.

＊

One more Hopkins masterpiece (1913) deserves mention. A very important client was Quaker Oats, which had come to Lord & Thomas in 1908. Quaker Oats itself was doing well, but two other cereal products made by the company, "Wheat Berries" and "Puffed Berries," were faltering. First, to stimulate sales, Lasker changed their names so that they could be better advertised as twins and gave them a uniform price; they became what they still are today, Puffed Rice and Puffed Wheat. Then Hopkins, in his mild, seemingly absent-minded way, set out to visit several Quaker Oats plants. His experience at the Schlitz brewery miraculously duplicated itself. Something that was being taken altogether for granted in the Quaker Oats factory caught his alert, artful eye for a feature. He saw a mechanism, an instrument like a drum or blunt cannon, in which the wheat and rice grains were subjected to pressure; then they were exploded upward, puffed out to eight times their natural size. This was all that Hopkins needed. Puffed Wheat and Puffed Rice instantly became "THE GRAINS THAT ARE SHOT FROM GUNS." Sales of both went up ten, twenty, thirty times, when dramatic advertisements appeared showing millions of tiny wheat and rice kernels exploding out of projectiles and hitting the ceiling with mad, macabre frenzy. This was probably the single most effective campaign Lord & Thomas ever launched.

Chapter 6

CHICAGO DAYS

In 1912 the Laskers built a house in Glencoe, on the property of the Lake Shore Country Club. Glencoe was, and is, a pleasant suburban community on the shore of Lake Michigan north of Chicago. Lasker's architect, one of the most sophisticated in the Middle West, was Samuel A. Marx, who had studied in Paris; he is a salty old veteran, and has in Chicago today one of the most exquisite small collections of modern French art in the world. Marx had a hard time with Lasker, who was a demanding client. A few days after the Laskers moved in there came a savage rainstorm, and Albert telephoned Marx in the middle of the night, saying that water was pouring into the house from a floorboard hole. "How big is the hole?" Marx asked. "Big enough to put a pencil in," Lasker replied with fierce indignation. "Well, put a pencil in it," Marx said, and rang off. This was *lèse majesté*. Not for months did he forgive Marx, a devoted friend, for his refusal to drive out to Glencoe at once and repair the leak himself.

Lasker chose Glencoe instead of communities like Winnetka or Hubbard Woods for several reasons. First, he had become fond of golf, although no man could have been less fitted temperamentally to be a golfer—everything that a golfer should be, he wasn't—and the club links were only a stone's throw away. Second, several of his cronies, like Louis Eckstein, the publisher and patron of the Ravinia Opera, also had houses on the club's property, and he liked his friends to be within instant call. Third and most important, the Lake Shore Country Club was Jewish—in fact, the leading Jewish

79

country club (it still is) in the area. This was important to Lasker, who had become a serious anti-anti-Semite. For instance, he made it a rule never, under normal circumstances, to accept hospitality in a club of which he himself or any Jew could not be a member. He would not set foot in any club which barred Jews. (It pleased him, however, to break this rule once a year or so as a gesture to one man, James Douglas, the head of Quaker Oats; he liked him so much that he would play golf with him occasionally at his thoroughly gentile club, Old Elm in Lake Forest.) One must remember, in this context, how virulently anti-Semitic most Chicago clubs were in those days, particularly country clubs. Lasker would have no part in this kind of thing. The steel in his character never wavered on this point, even though he was being widely courted in non-Jewish business circles.

He had a keen, good-humored appreciation of Jewish characteristics. One anecdote of the period survives. A beginner on his staff at Lord & Thomas, whom he liked extremely, was Merrill C. ("Babe") Meigs, a tall blond youth out of the Iowa cornfields, as goy as goy could be, who years later became publisher of the Chicago *American*. Lasker and Meigs had an argument about copy one morning, and Meigs started to gesticulate violently with his hands. Lasker, whose own hands were tightly clenched, shouted out, "Mr. Meigs! Mr. Meigs! Please remember that this is a *Jewish* agency, and nobody in this office is allowed to use his hands that way except *me!*"

Lasker was always a good Jew, but he never carried a chip on his shoulder about Jewishness and was never in the least self-conscious about being Jewish. Actually, in a curious way he was not particularly pro-Jewish; but he detested anti-Semitism. His attitude was based not so much on race or religion, but on standards of behavior. He hated to be pushed around; he hated to take second place. Here again may be seen an example of his romantic approach. Anti-Semitism was a personal plot against *him*.

The Lake Shore Country Club, which had come into being because prosperous Jews, excluded from gentile clubs, founded country clubs of their own in the fashionable Chicago suburbs, had a pro named George O'Neill, who was also a well-known golf architect. He could not do much to improve Lasker's eccentric game, but the two men liked each other. O'Neill fell ill of pernicious anemia, and would have died except that, just in time to save him, the use of liver as cure for this ailment was discovered.[1] For months, Flora Lasker cooked special food for O'Neill. He recovered and then Albert, who always had a regal way with men he liked and who created executives out of whim and then endowed them with his own qualities, put him in charge of the Studebaker account at Lord & Thomas. O'Neill knew little about automobiles and nothing whatever about the advertising business, but did quite well.

Golf aside, Lasker's chief relaxation at this time was poker. I have done a good deal of research on this subject and am unable to say positively whether Albert was a good poker player or not. Testimony is conflicting. He loved to bluff, he would do anything for a laugh, and his game differed radically from day to day. "The trouble with A.D.'s poker," Sam Marx has told me, "was that it was somewhat emotional." Out of golf and poker came the Partridge Club. It rained steadily one weekend at the Lake Shore Country Club, and Lasker and a group of cronies, unable to play golf, started a poker game. It lasted seventeen hours, and one man won $11,000. This was such fun that the decision was taken then and there to create an organization, known as the Partridges, to be devoted to golf on weekend afternoons, poker at night. There were nine members, Lasker was perpetual president, and the group held together for more than thirty years. All members were self-made, and all were— and had to be—rich, because chips went up to $500, it was an extremely tricky game, and it was quite possible to lose $20,000 in an evening. The usual game was draw poker, no limit, with deuces wild. One Partridge (all members, in the good old American way, wore small golden partridges in their lapels, more precious than the

[1] Lasker heard about this new cure by chance in a hospital corridor, and instantly got on the long-distance telephone to its discoverers and made use of it. Years later he often thought of this story, which taught him how medical research could be made to pay off.

red ribbon of the Legion of Honor) was the well-known lawyer, Samuel O. ("Sol") Levinson, who originated the Kellogg-Briand peace pact; others were David B. Stern of the stockbroking house A. G. Becker & Company, another Stern (David L.), and, the comedian of the group (there had to be a comedian), a shoe merchant named Abe K. Selz, who was a character straight out of Sinclair Lewis. Of the nine only two survive today.

At about this period Lasker developed a minor idiosyncrasy which clung to him all his life, a passion for being shaved so close that the blood almost ran. He liked barbers and held that they knew more about what was going on in the world than members of any other trade. His various barbers loved him, but he terrified them. An extremely restless man, he would wriggle while in the chair, use the telephone, or dictate correspondence, muttering the while to the barber, "Closer! Closer!" He kept barber chairs in his office, in his house on the South Side, in Glencoe, and, later, in Lake Forest and Miami. Sometimes he took a folding barber chair with him when he traveled. Once he telephoned his Beverly Hills barber from a place far out in the California desert, instructing him to drop everything and come to him at once. The barber arrived, to find him being shaved in a perfectly satisfactory manner by a man on the spot. Lasker said, "Oh, I just wanted to talk to you, and find out what's going on." If he traveled beyond the reach of his own barbers, he would search out the best local talent available, and offer $10 for a shave. "That's too much," one recruit said. Albert replied: "Wait. It isn't too much for shaving *me!*"

Lasker played golf and poker; also he worked. Few men have ever worked harder. Usually in the Chicago days he got to the office at 7:30 in the morning, and often did not leave till midnight. Late in 1912 he had a serious physical collapse. He records that he could not talk to anybody for five minutes without "bursting into tears." He went to Europe with Flora for five months, recuperating in various spas; another breakdown followed, also marked by fits of uncontrollable weeping, and he spent some time in Mexico. Then his health cleared up to a degree, and for some years he was able to resume working fourteen or fifteen hours a day without worry or impediment.

His incessant interest in things new helped to keep him going. One of his associates asked him when he came back from Mexico what was the best asset a man could have. Lasker replied, "Humility in the presence of a good idea."

Adventures with Automobiles

Lord & Thomas had some large early automobile accounts, but Lasker, unlike most of his contemporaries, never had an obsession about automobiles. For various reasons, he preferred to handle light consumer goods—soaps, cigarettes, household ware, and so on—rather than heavy industry. For one thing, there was a bigger turnover in articles that were used quickly and had to be replaced soon, and consequently a bigger profit. For another, he tended to avoid commodities which depended for their sale on new models every year; this, he thought, made advertising campaigns difficult and complicated. But the automobile age was now coming into full fancy flower, and he could not ignore it. Incidentally, one of his own early cars was a pale lemon yellow Rolls-Royce. It rode the muddy tracks around Chicago like a fairy chariot, a luminous metal wasp, skimming over a morass.

Actually, even if automobiles baffled him on occasion, and even though the early automobile manufacturers themselves strenuously resisted advertising for a time (they thought that it was useless and too expensive), Lord & Thomas was a highly successful pioneer in automobile advertising. It put out, in fact, the first automobile ads ever printed in America, the first tire ads, and the first ads for automobile accessories. Lasker's first automobile client was John N. Willys, a bicycle salesman in Elmira, New York, who created the Willys-Overland. Willys, in Lasker's words, "didn't have a cent." Albert told him that he would advance him $200,000 to prove that advertising could sell a car; Willys agreed ("He didn't have any money, therefore he didn't have anything to lose") and Lasker went to the *Saturday Evening Post* with an elaborate piece of copy, which became the first double-page ad—other than a center spread—ever to appear in an American magazine. And such was the instantaneous effect of Lord & Thomas copy that Willys sales shot up at once.

In those days, people still had to be convinced that automobiles were practicable, and would run; when cars lurched and slithered along streets full of bumps and yawning holes, pedestrians shouted out with hilarious contempt, "Get a horse!" It is one of the most amazing of American statistics that in 1900 there were only ten miles of concrete road in the entire United States, and in 1910 probably not more than a thousand miles.[2] The advertising man's first task was to make people *believe* in automobiles. After Willys, Lord & Thomas worked on campaigns for Chalmers, Hudson, and, above all, Reo. Here Hopkins played a piquant role. He boiled with ideas for Reo, which was named for the initials of its manufacturer, the celebrated R. E. Olds, for whom the Oldsmobile was also named. Hopkins not only succeeded in persuading Olds to call his new model "Reo the Fifth," thus emphasizing the factor of continuity and reliability, but in getting him to state that this model would be his *last* car, his positively farewell appearance in the realm of automobiles. Olds had no intention at all of retiring, but the tricky Hopkins observed sagely that Sarah Bernhardt had "retired" half a dozen times, and so could he if this would make people think that their final chance for an Olds car would be lost if they did not buy a Reo that very moment.

Lasker-Hopkins then turned their cunning, agile minds to tires, and helped create an immense new industry. Goodyear became an important client, and remained so for many years. It started out spending $40,000 a year with Lord & Thomas, and soon was spending $2,000,000. First, Hopkins discovered that Goodyear had an innovation—"straight-side" tires instead of the older clincher-type. The advantage of the straight-side tire was that, in the event of a puncture, the rim was not cut. So Hopkins coined the phrase, "No-Rim-Cut-Tires," which became a sensation; customers bought by droves. One result was that competing tire companies had to turn

[2] Mark Sullivan, *Our Times*, Vol. I, p. 379.

to straight-side tires, which meant that Goodyear no longer had a novelty. So Hopkins dropped his first slogan, and put all his emphasis instead on the name "Goodyear," in order to build up company identity. Then came the anti-skid tire. Hopkins put it over by giving it a catchy name—"All-Weather." Finally, he went after the dealers. He did not want people to ask for Goodyear in a tire store or garage and find no Goodyears, and so Lord & Thomas issued local ads all over the country offering to *name* individually every dealer who would stock $250 of their product. No dealer likes to see a large ad appear in his community which names his competitors and not himself, and 30,000 dealers promptly joined the Goodyear ranks. Hopkins wrote, "This naming of dealers in local advertising is an almost irresistible inducement to stock . . . I have often secured on new products almost universal distribution in this way."[3]

Lasker took several beatings in the automobile business; for instance, he invested almost a million dollars in a car called the Mitchell, and lost it in a year. Later he had an opportunity to buy Maxwell. He let it slip, because his basic interest was not production, but selling, and the Maxwell car was taken over instead by a rising young man, Walter P. Chrysler. The Maxwell was renamed Chrysler, and history was made. Lasker cudgeled himself for years about this, but with good humor. He was convinced that he could have done for Maxwell what Chrysler did. He would say, "There goes Walter Chrysler. He doesn't even know that, except for an accident, unh, I would be him." Meantime, he made one interesting contribution to the business by being co-inventor, if automobile folklore is to be believed, of the four-door car. Early cars had only two doors, which were placed high in the back, and you walked down a small stubby aisle to the front seat. (In open models, of course, the front seat was reached directly; there was no door at all.) Lasker and a man named Albert Russell Erskine, the head of Studebaker, put their heads together to try to find something startling, and *a car with four doors* was what came out. This, to automobile specialists of the day, was the dawn of a new world.

[3] Hopkins, *op. cit.*, pp. 126-7.

Paul G. Hoffman was a bright young man on Erskine's staff at this date. Lasker could not have known that Hoffman, another superlative salesman, smooth as glass and as sharp if need be, but unbreakable, would rise to become president of Studebaker, president of the Committee for Economic Development, administrator of the Marshall Plan and ECA, president of the Ford Foundation, head of an important UN agency, and, in all, one of the most liberal, useful, and public-spirited of contemporary Americans. He was the first man Lasker ever met who became a national figure. Hoffman, an inconspicuous junior in those days, remembers that he was so impressed by the design for the four-door car that he muttered to himself, in positive awe, "This is the end! There will never need to be anything new in automobiles again!"

Lasker in those days would go to almost any length to get an account. Erskine was a pathological gambler, and to keep him content Albert had to play cards with him; he, too, fancied himself as a gambler, but he had never met anybody who gambled like Erskine before. Stakes were enormous, and bets fantastic. Hoffman sometimes watched these games, goggle-eyed, but did not play himself; he couldn't afford it, and besides was a cautious man. But Erskine's gambling led to a severe crisis in his relations with Lasker before many years passed, as we shall see.

The Frank Case

This marked Lasker's first entrance into public affairs. The case interested him passionately not merely because it involved anti-Semitism but because it had to do with basic injustice; he was not the nephew of Eduard Lasker for nothing, and wanted to pitch in to help right a wrong.

On Saturday, April 26, 1913, a youthful Jew named Leo M. Frank sat alone in his office in a pencil factory, of which he was superintendent, in Atlanta, Georgia. He was twenty-nine years old, was well educated, and had an excellent reputation in the community. Married, he lived in Atlanta with his parents-in-law; he was a somewhat frail young man, almost aesthetic in appearance. He was a prominent member of B'nai B'rith, and no breath of scandal or irregularity had ever touched him.

Frank's factory was empty, because April 26 was Memorial Day for Confederate veterans. In the afternoon a fourteen-year-old girl named Mary Phagan, a factory worker, who was dressed up for the holiday parade in a lavender dress trimmed with lace and a blue hat, came to collect some back pay. Frank gave her $1.20, and she left his office. She was never seen alive again, and, to this day, nobody knows who murdered her. The resulting case was the most notorious of its kind in American history until Sacco-Vanzetti, although it is largely forgotten now.

Mary's body was found in the factory basement at 3 A.M. Sunday morning by a Negro night watchman. Her head was bashed in, and she had been strangled with a cord. There was no evidence of rape. Two notes were found near the body. One accused a "tall, sleam [slim], black Negro" of the crime. Frank and the night watchman were both arrested, but the watchman was freed after prolonged questioning. Frank was indicted for murder on May 24, largely on the evidence of a Negro worker at the factory, Jim Conley. He testified in an incoherent way that he had heard a woman's screams in Frank's office that afternoon, that he had helped Frank carry the body to the basement, that Frank had offered him $200 to shut up, and had then dictated the two notes to him, to cast suspicion on someone else. Frank flatly denied all these charges, and the defense insisted that it was Conley, a "shiftless degenerate," who was the murderer.

We have not the space to go into what happened later. There was no evidence whatever against Frank except Conley's statement, but he was convicted of murder on August 25, and sentenced to hang. But the turmoil incited by the crime had made a fair trial impossible; mobs bent on lynching Frank surrounded the courthouse, and even pushed into the court. A large part of the feeling against Frank was based on anti-Semitism, which was acute in

Atlanta at the time. The case aroused national attention, and the verdict was appealed. The United States Supreme Court, after repeated hearings, confirmed the original verdict, with Justices Charles Evans Hughes and Oliver Wendell Holmes dissenting. The case dragged on, through 1914 and into 1915, and in all the miserable Frank was sentenced to die four different times.

Lasker first heard about all this from his sister Etta, who had friends in Atlanta, and from his father Morris, who urged him to do something for Frank. He responded at once. Every instinct he had for justice and fair play, for racial tolerance, for dignity in the courts and good citizenship, was aroused. He set about establishing committees and working out methods by which public opinion might be influenced, and got Jane Addams, Thomas A. Edison, Billie Sunday, and Rabbi Stephen A. Wise to participate in his campaign. He helped organize mass meetings, and tried to get Senators and Congressmen to intervene. He marshaled the services of three powerful journalists—Arthur Brisbane, Mark Sullivan, and Adolph Ochs—and spent $100,000 on legal fees for Frank. In fact, he suspended for the time being all interest in his own business, and it was his calculation that he spent a solid year working on the Frank case to the exclusion of very nearly everything else.

He would have won, had not mob rule and lynch law been too strong. In June, 1915, the governor of Georgia at last commuted Frank's sentence to life imprisonment. So at least Frank, who still steadfastly declared his innocence, was saved from the gallows. But passion rose so violently in Atlanta that martial law was invoked, and a regiment of the Georgia National Guard had to be used to protect the governor. Then a month later a mob broke into the prison where Frank was held, drove him 125 miles to Marietta, where Mary Phagan was buried, and hanged him to a tree.

Father and Son

The following excerpts are from a letter from Morris Lasker, who was now in his seventy-fifth year, to Albert during the middle of the Frank case. Morris urgently wanted him to do something for a rabbi named Krauskopf, who was about to found a "farm school" for indigent boys.

And now, my dear son, I want to approach a subject that I hope you will not misunderstand me in, or think me perhaps a little too urgent about; but it is close to my heart, so that I do not want to fail in impressing you thoroughly just how I feel about it—and that is, the subject of your future mission. On various occasions, as you know, I felt deeply impressed, by conversations that we had with each other with regard to yourself, that you were destined to carry out some mission in this life of importance to the world, and that your mere business career, great as it started out, and has continued so far—was but a trifle compared with what you were destined to accomplish to humanity at large. I have felt, from your earliest youth, as if the mantle of Uncle Eduord (*sic*) was to fall, some future day upon you—and with your practical genius would, no doubt, add to the great lustre that he bestowed upon the name of Lasker.

Morris then describes the Krauskopf project and his own willingness to contribute. Next:

By all means, I would impress upon you—go into the investigation calmly and deliberately—do not undertake it simply because you think it would please me that you would do so. If you feel inspired about the matter after you go into it, then I know that you will recognize it as important enough to make it your life's mission. . . .

My dear Flora, I intend this letter for both of you—read it carefully; no one can have a greater interest in Albert than yourself. It is my firm idea that the undertaking about which this letter treats will give Albert a greater opportunity to carry out the ambitions that you have so often expressed for him, than could a United States senatorship.

Excerpts from Albert's reply, dated December 26, 1915, are revealing, if only because they show how he was pressing himself.

Yesterday was Christmas. Our office is closed today, but as I am leaving the city tomorrow night, to be gone for several days, I came down this morning to clean up my desk, and find on same your letter of December 23rd. I hasten to dictate a reply to same, even though I will not be able to remain at the office to sign it.

I am very deeply in earnest in my desire to not stay in commercial pursuits too long, but to devote myself to other and more altruistic activities.

I cannot remember a time when I did not have this desire. I was impelled to stay in business not only because I wanted to make material success, for my own sake, but because I realized that the possession of money would help me in many ways to overcome my shortcomings in any other work that I would undertake.

What I mean is, that I am keenly alive to both my intellectual limitation and my lack of profound information. . . . I do not feel that I will ever accomplish anything out of the ordinary. . . . All I have proved, thus far is, that I can make money. I know that I desire to do better things with my life. . . .

Whether or no Doctor Krauskopf's venture offers . . . attraction to me, I cannot tell. . . . I shall give him every opportunity to place all the facts before me, as he sees them, and then shall make exhausted (*sic*) investigation of my own. . . .

Further, I am very doubtful whether I will be at all able to go into the matter, in any event, before my return from California. First, the Frank case is taking practically all my time, and leaves me sorely pressed to even keep up with my business in a most superficial way. Second, resultant from the pressure of the Frank case, and keeping up with my other work, I am mentally so tired that it would be unfair to Dr. Krauskopf, or to myself, to undertake, even superficially, to enlighten myself on his programme . . .

I am leaving the city tonight, to be gone until New Year's Day. I have to cover a different town each day. Pleasant holiday week, is it not?

How formal, how serious, how courtly Morris and Albert were with each other, and what a good son Albert sought to be!

Morris died the next year. Albert presently gave $50,000 to the National Farm School and Junior College in Bucks County, Pennsylvania, to encourage the interest of Jewish students in agriculture, and as a salute to his father's memory.

Chicago Moods and Scenes

Flora Lasker, if they had been poor, would have been perfectly willing to live in a log cabin for the rest of her life, but, since she and Albert were rich, she saw no reason why they should not be rich right, and she was ambitious for her husband. She wanted to move. Of course, they had Glencoe for the summer, but during the rest of the year they still lived in a modest, old-fashioned house on the South Side. Lasker, however, did not want to move. He felt that he belonged to the South Side near the University, where many prosperous and intensely respectable families lived. The North Side was terra incognita. That was Astor Street; that was the Gold Coast; that was the territory of McCormicks, Swifts, and Potter Palmers. He would have none of it. One evening in 1915 when he came home from work (it must have been one of the rare evenings when he did come home from work at a reasonable hour) Flora commanded, "Come for a drive with me. I have something to show you." They went north, crossed the river, and entered the Gold Coast fastness. Flora stopped their car before a house at 15 West Burton Place, in the best residential district of the city (it still is), and announced calmly, "I have just bought this house, and we are going to live in it."

Lasker was horrified. It took Flora six months to put the house (nineteen rooms, seven baths) into shape and decorate it, during which time, amazingly enough, he never once set foot in it! He snubbed it. His attitude was that this was all her doing, and let her do it. Moving in then, he came to love it, and this remained the Lasker town house for more than twenty years.

Albert and Flora were still close these days. She was expanding his horizons steadily by teaching him something of the difficult art of living. When he was not traveling he came home to lunch every day, walking from his office and back. At night the two played backgammon or some similar game. A careful score was kept, but this was only settled once a year—on Christmas. Albert was always ahead, and one of his Christmas presents to Flora every year was to tear up the score sheets and cancel the debt.

Mary, their daughter, was now eleven, and Edward, born in 1912, was three. One of Mary's earliest memories is of a spanking. Her father caught her in a minor lie, and whacked her till it hurt. She sobbed in protest, and he replied, "If I whip you and don't hurt you, you won't remember it. What I want you to remember is that it is more *trouble* to lie than to tell the truth. If you had *remembered* your lie, I would never have caught you in it." This brisk Laskerism passed into family folklore. So did a little epigram in the cracker-barrel style, which he communicated to Mary once: "Life is like a bank. You get out of it what you put into it."

Christmas, which was always celebrated at Burton Place, was a splendid event. Flora would bake a large Jack Horner pie, which she stuffed with jokes, favors, and bits of paper with verses, and hang copiously filled stockings which she made herself. The great moment was not Christmas Eve, but one o'clock in the afternoon on Christmas Day. Everybody had to wait until then, because Albert always played poker with the Partridges on Christmas Eve, and was apt to be up all night. At last he would arrive in the cozy living room, lit by a blazing tree, and would open his stocking first. No one was permitted to budge until he did so. One of the children remembers the methodical way in which he then proceeded to unwrap his presents, which were laid out in majestic ranks. "These are the things I will keep," he would say in an authoritative voice, putting them carefully aside, "and these are the things that I will return." He was tyrant, child, and doting father all at once.

End of the First Phase at Lord & Thomas

This is not, I should interject at this point, a book about the advertising business. It is a book about a man, a human being, a personality, whose story follows a classic pattern of prodigious success and bitter disillusion—and then contains an additional offbeat element of fruitful rebirth.

However, forty-four years of Lasker's life were taken up by advertising, and Lord & Thomas was the bedrock of his existence for almost half a century. So we must not only continue to describe his career in advertising, but from time to time summarize his attitude to it, which changed radically with the years, and estimate his contribution to it, which, as we know already, was immense.

Lord & Thomas continued to take in more and more business in the years before World War I; its prestige was unassailable; it had offices in Los Angeles, San Francisco, Toronto, New York, London, and Paris, all of them complete self-sustaining agencies; clients had to be turned away; for a manufacturer to be accepted by Lord & Thomas was like getting his daughter into Vassar. By 1906 billings had risen to $3,000,000; in 1912, when Lasker became sole owner, they were $6,000,000; in 1918, about $10,000,000. These figures may seem small by the standards of today, but, again, we must measure them against the background of the times. Media were limited and a number of products which we take for granted today and which have huge advertising appropriations did not even exist. In 1908 the circulation of the *Saturday Evening Post* was only 805,000; the *Literary Digest* had 160,000, *Leslie's Weekly* 100,000, *Judge* 60,000, and *Vogue* 30,000. The magazine with the biggest sale in America was *Woman's World* (2,250,000). A magazine called *Grit,* published in Williamsport, Pennsylvania, had 200,000. The leading farm paper was *Wallace's Farmer* ("Has an Actual Paid Circulation; Doesn't Carry Delinquents").

As to commodities, there were of course no such things in those days as an electric dishwasher or air conditioner. Automobiles and movies were coming in, but nobody so much as dreamed of radio, a deep-freeze, plastics, high-octane gas, waterproof watches, caterpillar tractors, or aircraft carrying passengers in their long silver bellies. A potent factor in Lasker's spectacular success was that his own life span coincided with the era of mass production, mass entertainment, and mass use of consumer goods, which he helped so vividly to stimulate. Automobiles, movies, aviation, radio arrived in turn to transform utterly the face of the nation just at he himself was rising to the peak of his formidable powers and could take full advantage of the illimitable possibilities in these new fields of endeavor. He rode a new national tide.

All his good qualities—ingeniousness, fertility, magnetism, drive—were paying off. His mind still glistened. It had edge, intuitive grasp, and extraordinary swiftness. A friend of the period writes,

"His brain worked like a highly complex modern electronic computing machine. He would instantaneously organize, analyze and tabulate all variables, reach a conclusion and deliver a clear and concise opinion which invariably made sense. Working with him was a blessing."

As to Lasker's contribution to advertising, we may recapitulate some items already indicated, and, projecting ourselves into the future, mention others. First and foremost, he gave advertising motive force, motive power. He was an "open" persuader, not hidden. Every agency in the world adopted the "Salesmanship in Print" and "Reason Why" formulae, because they would have gone out of business if they had not done so. The days of passive advertising, "reminder" advertising, were no more. This was a real revolution. Out of it has come much that is deplorable and repellent, right up to such contemporary items as "subliminal effects," dishonest commercials, crooked disc jockeys, concealed plugs, and phony quiz shows. On the other hand, A. D. contributed substantially to the universal use of products which make the ordinary process of living easier for the average citizen, lowered the price of products by making them available in greater quantity, and assisted considerably in the general expansion of business in the United States.

Lasker was like Henry Ford in one respect—he helped new businesses flower, created employment, and stimulated industrial advance by urging on his clients the maxim "Cut your price, and you will sell more." His advertising methods made his clients wealthy, but he stood firmly on the consumer's side. Rather, he thought of himself as a kind of middleman between producer and consumer, which, as a matter of fact, is exactly what a good advertising man should be. His business was to promote business, and thus lift the purchasing power of the masses. Not only did he help make the country rich by raising its standard of living—no mean accomplishment—but he gave a new power of initiative to business by creating industries and opening up virgin fields for exploration and endeavor.

Second, Lasker was certainly a master of the hard sell, but he could sell soft too. Lord & Thomas used all sorts of tricks and employed sensational devices, but it was always a dignified agency—even staid. One of Lasker's main sources of power was his ability to cloak inflammatory ideas with the most primly decorous presentation. Lord & Thomas was, in fact, nicknamed the "Cheltenham Bold" agency because it seldom utilized anything but this old-fashioned headline type. Neither in substance nor in form did it ever go in for "yellow" advertising, which is the more remarkable because this was the era par excellence of yellow journalism in the newspapers.

But, third, Lasker believed in live, burning, creative copy, no matter how calmly it was presented. With Kennedy, he invented the modern art, or craft, of copy writing. Lord & Thomas was the first agency ever to have a copy staff.

Fourth, Lord & Thomas was, if not the actual founder, a principal practitioner of "scientific" advertising. Testing was born, and so was sampling. The technique was evolved of trying out a campaign in miniature (as in the case of Palmolive) in a small, carefully chosen community, under strict controls. Before this there had been no way at all of forecasting in advance what the result of advertising a given product in a certain area might be. Even today, forecasts cannot be altogether accurate, as every advertising man well knows, but as a result of pioneering by Lasker and others the framework was laid for market surveys, polling, and the like.

Fifth, he spawned all manner of technical innovations. There have been few basic changes in advertising methods since Lasker. "He was responsible," one authority says, "for almost every new development that came to advertising for twenty-five years."

Sixth, Lord & Thomas played a large role in training men who went to other agencies, or founded agencies of their own. It became a kind of school. The joke was that if a man was *fired* from Lord & Thomas this was enough to get him a job anywhere else. At one time, around 1916, nine major agencies in the country were headed by Lasker graduates. More on this topic later.

Seventh, Lord & Thomas (other good agencies assisted in this, of course) helped to give ethics to the advertising business. The trade was full of outrageous scamps and charlatans, with ragpicker morals, when Lasker entered the field, and as much as any man he took a stand against corrupt and dishonest advertising. He thought that false advertising was "heresy."

Eighth, Lord & Thomas helped build up (as did other leading agencies) a new type of relationship between agency and client. The agency became a partner, not merely in writing copy but in packaging, marketing, and the philosophy of selling.

Finally, his personality dominated an entire epoch. Several competing agencies gave Lord & Thomas the hottest kind of run for its money, but Lasker himself, as a character, an individual, never had a rival.

He had two blind spots, art and research. He thought (1) that art should never be more than a kind of illustration, subordinate to copy, and (2) that elaborate, intensive, prolonged research was a waste of money. "Research," he said, "is something that tells you that a jackass has two ears." He would tolerate research only if it agreed with him. The organization of a big contemporary agency, in which literally several thousand highly expert men and women may be employed exclusively on research in all its various bewildering ramifications, would have appalled him. But, as a matter of fact, he was soon forced to open large art and research establishments in Lord & Thomas, because the competition of other agencies made them indispensable. One reason why Lasker held out so long against building up extensive art and research departments was simple; it was to save money. Not having them made his agency cheaper to run. As a result, Lord & Thomas outdid every other agency for a good many years in the amount of profit it kept out of its basic revenue, the 15 per cent commission. The average agency kept around 3 per cent of its 15; Lord & Thomas kept 7 or even 8.

In any case, to summarize, by 1917 Lord & Thomas was the most celebrated and prosperous advertising agency in the world. Lasker, not yet forty and sole owner, was taking out of it a cool million-dollars-a-year income. The boy wonder from Galveston, the tense ambitious prodigy from the Texas frontier, was made. No wonder he began to show touches of megalomania on occasion. Inevitably, his ego grew. He told one astounded would-be customer, "*I* am the chief client of this agency!"

Chapter 7

FIRST TASTE OF POLITICS

Politics laid its mottled hand on Lasker, for the first time since his boyhood, in June, 1918, when he met a man who was to have substantial influence on his life for a good many years—Will H. Hays.[1] At this time Hays, an Indiana lawyer, had just been elected chairman of the Republican National Committee, and was scouting around for talent. Hays was an operator, a mender of broken fences, a man who did not knock heads together but pasted them together, a plausible Hoosier with energy, humor, and imagination, and a fixer par excellence.

Hays called on Lasker in Chicago with an introduction from William G. Irwin, who, as has been recounted in a previous chapter, was one of his partners in the Van Camp Packing Company. Lasker had never heard of Hays, but he regarded Irwin highly, and thus received him cordially. World War I was still, of course, going on at this time and it worried Lasker that he had contributed so little to the American war effort. Hays, he felt, might get him a worthy job, or even put him into uniform. But all that Hays would talk about was politics. Hays explained that the off-year elections for Congress in the coming autumn would be vitally important, but that the Republican party, which had been split between Theodore Roosevelt and William Howard Taft in 1912, was still disintegrated; it had been beaten in 1916, and faced catastrophe now, if only be-

[1] During the previous year (1917) Lasker had, however, served as a dollar-a-year man in the Woodrow Wilson administration, as an assistant to the Secretary of Agriculture. His knowledge of food marketing made him valuable and he worked on projects to stimulate home canning of foodstuffs, but he did not stay in Washington long and this was hardly a political experience.

cause it had no money. Thereupon he proceeded to offer Lasker a job as his assistant. Albert records that he was "about as interested as if Hays had asked him to become a ballet dancer with the Russians." He asked him, "Why do you come to me?" and Hays replied winningly, "Because you are a man who can make sick businesses get well."

Not only did Hays want money; he wanted propaganda, and thought that Lasker would be the best man available to provide it. Albert was flattered, and said that he would think the matter over. Hays said, "Very good. Now I want you to come to New York with me and meet Colonel Roosevelt." No bait could have attracted Lasker more, because he was a passionate admirer of T.R.

He records: "I went down. Will Hays got me in a machine and drove me out to Oyster Bay for lunch. We got there and I will always remember Col. Roosevelt waiting for us on the front porch. He was dressed in khaki, with khaki shirt, khaki pants and boots and no hat, and as I came up he put his arm around me and he said, 'I am glad to meet you, Lasker.' Hays had tipped off to him who he was bringing. He had studied the name."[2]

Roosevelt went on, "They tell me you are America's greatest advertising man." Lasker was not wanting for a quick reply. Graciously bowing, and smiling to his ears as T.R. did, he responded, "Colonel, no man can claim that distinction as long as you are alive!"

The old Rough Rider appreciated this lively riposte. Lasker said that he wanted to go into the Army, but Roosevelt dissuaded him, on the ground that he could be more useful in other ways; such absolution, coming from a former President of the United States who was, moreover, a military man, comforted him greatly. Then T.R. won him over to the idea of working for the Republican National Committee. Lasker records: "By golly, with no more idea at the start [of this conversation] about working for the Republican party than going home and murdering my wife and children . . . I

2 *The Lasker Story*, p. 31.

left Oyster Bay and only saw Chicago in the next five months for three days."

Interestingly enough, T.R. captured him by stressing international affairs, not national politics—moreover, by asserting menacingly that Wilson would drag the United States into the disaster of permanent European entanglements. Lasker did not, as a matter of fact, need much persuasion on this point, because he was a fanatic isolationist already. His own father, he told Roosevelt, had come to America as an immigrant to get away from the European system that was "grinding down individualism." He recounts, in typical accents of the time: "I had been trained with the Anglo-Saxon viewpoint of individualism, and I thought that Europe was so blighted by the centuries preceding . . . that America could only help Europe by staying independent. Deeply burned in me then . . . were the precepts of Washington's Farewell Address. And that is how Teddy Roosevelt got me."

A Man Named Sollitt

Hays set Lasker up in an office in midtown Manhattan, and here he worked for most of a year. Hays had two principal assistants—Lasker, in charge of publicity and propaganda, and Ralph V. Sollitt, on the executive side. Lasker met Sollitt for the first time on a summer morning in 1918, and they scarcely had a day apart for the next fifteen years. Sollitt became Lasker's right arm. He was his traveling companion, consultant in family affairs, confessor, messenger boy, secretary, ghost writer, alarm clock, and hair shirt. It was a wonder he did not become his valet as well, or even barber. His devotion was utter and absolute. Lasker had a notoriously bad memory for names, or, rather, he failed often to attach the right name to the right face. One legend is that, for years, he never entered a crowded room except with Sollitt close at his side. As celebrated persons, whom he was supposed to know, appeared at a party it was Sollitt's duty to murmur, before he could speak and make some monstrous *faux pas* based on mistaken identity, "Al Jolson, Mr.

Lasker—not Irving Berlin," or "Katharine Cornell, Mr. Lasker—not Lynn Fontanne!"

Lasker even taught Sollitt to imitate his handwriting, and the two men had a secret code; when Sollitt, for instance, signed a check with Lasker's name, he put a tiny dot over one letter, so that Lasker would know later (if he was curious) that it was Sollitt who had signed it. Sometimes Sollitt wrote longhand notes to members of the family, or cards with gifts, in Lasker's handwriting and with his signature; even Flora could not tell if they were genuine.

Sollitt, like Hays, was a Hoosier lawyer, patient, adroit, and good-humored. He was as temperate as Lasker was agitated, as relaxed as his boss was high-strung. The attraction between them was of opposites. Lasker made him his executive assistant in Washington when he became chairman of the Shipping Board, and then brought him into Lord & Thomas, where he rose to be president when Lasker himself was chairman of the board. He retired in the mid-thirties and lives today near Westport, Connecticut, with his accomplished wife (of whom Lasker was also very fond); he collects china and glass, and maintains a printing press on which he produces exquisite small pamphlets. When he talks about Lasker now, his eyes still glisten.

Isolationism and the Fight Against the League

Hays, Lasker, Sollitt and a staff of twelve started work. None of them, Lasker records, had any real idea of what they were about. It was all a confused heap of fun; he had not had such a good time since the apprentice days at Lord & Thomas. In a pattern that repeated itself several times in his life, he flung himself with full ardor into the mysteries and excitements of a new world. He was a romantic still.

One thing that fascinated him was Hays's way with campaign contributions. The committee was being financed largely by a loan from a renowned mining magnate of the day, Colonel Thompson. But this could not be revealed freely because, if it were known, other contributors would feel that they were doing nothing but bail out Thompson, a multimillionaire. Hays established a rule that the Republicans would not accept individual contributions of more than $1,000 for the rest of the campaign. Since it was difficult, if not impossible, to get gifts as big as this from anybody except a handful of rich men, Hays was being very shrewd—he improved his public relations by making it seem that the Republicans welcomed modest contributions, whereas in reality he was doing nothing more than make the best of a tight financial situation. Next came an astonishing coincidence. Hays rang the buzzer in his office, asked Albert to come in, and said, "Lasker, I want you to meet our first thousand-dollar contributor, Mr. Hawley." And it was none other than the Hawley who had run for Congress in Texas twenty-two years before, whom Lasker had worked for as a ghost writer and who had turned him into a Republican.

It was now the early autumn of 1918; Wilson was President, and World War I was almost won. The mid-term election approaching in November was, as Hays had explained to Lasker, critical. The Republican aim was to gain control of Congress. This would cripple Wilson. The presidency was not at stake in November, 1918; but Wilson's future was. The heart of the campaign was the issue of American participation in the peace to come. Wilson had (on January 8, 1918) announced his Fourteen Points, the last of which laid down plans for "a general association of nations," with American adherence. Naturally, this was a red rag to the extreme isolationists. But the Republican party was divided on the isolationist issue; a good many eminent Republicans stood for some sort of league or other international organization to secure peace, with participation by the United States. For instance, William Howard Taft, no less, was head of an influential League to Enforce Peace which envisaged co-operation with Europe. Even Henry Cabot Lodge, Senator from Massachusetts, who later became the most obstinate of all enemies to Wilson's League, and who killed American participation in it, favored some kind of league at this time.[3]

[3] Henry Bamford Parkes, *Recent America*, p. 349.

But even if many good Republicans were not extremists on the isolation issue, Lasker was. The mark of Teddy Roosevelt lay heavily on him. He was convinced that "the party did not know its own mind," and that Republicans who were flirting with internationalist ideas and wanted to "enter the European lion's den" were traitors. So, with his customary initiative, he set out to "educate" the party. As always, he used money to transform ideas into action. He records that he spent "thirty or forty thousand dollars" of his own money to issue several million copies of a pamphlet called *After the Peace, What?* This summarized the extreme isolationist view, and was distributed to all Republican party workers during the campaign; it was the first organized effort, he says, to sway opinion *within* the party.

When it became clear that the peace treaty to come would include Wilson's League, the Republican anti-Leaguers redoubled their efforts. Wilson, piqued by Republican attacks on his high-mindedness, made a grievous blunder on October 24—he appealed to the country to elect a Democratic Congress so that the peace treaty would pass the Senate. Nowadays it is a routine matter for a President to appeal to the people for partisan support; but then it was not, and for Wilson to have asked citizens to vote for a straight party ticket with the supreme issues of peace and the League covenant at stake aroused the bitterest dismay and indignation. The Hays organization instantly took advantage of this. Hays said that the President had cast a slur on Republican patriotism, and that he was "ungracious . . . wanton . . . mendacious."[4] Whether or not Lasker wrote this Hays manifesto is unknown. It is quite possible that he did.

Wilson's October 24 statement, together with the advantage taken of it by the Republican publicity machine, was probably what beat him in the November elections. These took place November 3; the Republicans captured the Senate by 49 to 47, the House by 239 to 194. This meant among other things that the fierce, frosty Lodge would become chairman of the Senate Foreign

4 Oscar Theodore Barck, Jr., and Nelson Manfred Blake, *Since 1900*, p. 240.

Relations Committee. Meantime, Germany capitulated on November 11, and the war was over. Wilson had won the war, but even so was repudiated.

We must return to Lasker. These pages are not, and do not remotely pretend to be, a sketch of the long harassing fight over the League. All they aim to do is give enough background to explain Lasker's own career during a stormy and controversial period. Incidentally, he had the most profound admiration for Wilson personally. He thought that he was the "loftiest" man he had ever known. But he disagreed with him hotly on the League issue at that time, and would have fought him to the death on it. One should not, however, exaggerate Lasker's role in the months that followed. He was active, yes, but he was still a cub, a junior, in big-time politics. His chief contribution was to organize an informal "lay group" of Republican workers against the League, which worked mostly behind the scenes. Meantime, he was tempted strongly to return to Chicago, where Hopkins was holding the fort at Lord & Thomas. But Hays persuaded him to stay on in New York, and he was elevated to be assistant chairman of the Republican National Committee.

Wilson, recoiling from the November rebuff, went to Paris, and, unalterably fixed in his determination to make a decent peace, came to disastrous grips with Lloyd George and Clemenceau. He neglected to mend his fences at home, because he was still stubbornly, narrowly sure that he could force ratification of the treaty through the Senate. The kernel of the League covenant, which was embraced in the treaty, was Article X, and this, providing for collective defense against aggression or threatened aggression on a member state, infuriated the isolationists. Prolonged, subtle maneuvering went on in the Senate, which was divided between (a) Democratic supporters of the treaty, (b) "reservationists" in the Republican ranks who were willing to accept some of it, and (c) the "small wilful band" of last-hurdle irreconcilables, like Borah of Idaho and Hiram Johnson of California, who were determined to fight it to the end. Lodge now joined this third camp, but played an astute delaying game. He had to be cautious because a large sector of public opinion still stood firmly for the League.

Lasker records:

I remember that I thought the fight against the League in the Senate was going much slower than it should. With all the time and work our lay group had put in, I felt that we should have some say, and I went to Mr. Hays very indignantly. I said that I thought the Senators on our side were not as aggressive and constructive in the fight as they should be.

Mr. Hays said, "All right, if you feel that way, I'll phone down and see if we can't get some of them together tonight."

We had dinner at the Shoreham Hotel that night. I don't remember who else was there, but I do remember Senator Lodge, Frank Brandegee, James Watson of Indiana, Moses [New Hampshire] and McCormick [Illinois] were there. The whole purpose of the dinner was for the Senators to hear what their lay co-workers felt about the way things were going. Senator Lodge had never seen me—nor even knew that I was born. As you know, he was very much of an aristocrat, and I was a midwestern advertising man. Quite a contrast.

I presented my views, and when I finished, Lodge traced with fine logic what they had been doing. Although later, when I went into the Administration in Washington, Lodge and I became very good friends, I shall never forget the sarcasm and contempt he put into his remarks as he addressed me. The contempt was for an outside young whippersnapper like myself coming down to criticize. I don't think he meant to belittle me. He was just unconscious that he was displaying his superiority in his annoyance that I couldn't see the obvious. He said, "I want the progress to be faster, just as you do, but there are only fourteen of us, and we've got to bring along a lot more if we are to have the necessary one-third vote to defeat the League proposal. We have to do it very gradually." Then he said something I'll never forget—"Remember, a general who gets ahead of his army, loses the battle. I can't go any faster than I can get my army to follow." . . . I left that night feeling that I hadn't grasped what was going on behind the scenes. Senator Lodge was working patiently for complete defeat and using the strategy he felt was necessary.[5]

[5] Columbia, pp. 58-59. Incidentally, it was characteristic of Lasker that he should reveal details of his isolationist past so candidly when he was dictating his memoirs years later in a period when isolationism was fiercely unpopular. He was never one to cover up.

The fight went on. Wilson was cut down by a stroke in September, 1919, and could no longer actively lead his supporters. Lodge, after skirmishes, marshaled his forces for the final battle on March 19, 1920. The result was 49 to 35 for the covenant and treaty, which was seven votes short of the two-thirds necessary for ratification. So the isolationists won, and an incidental result was that the United States, seventeen months after the armistice, was still, ridiculously enough, technically at war with Germany.

This did not, however, by any means finish the League struggle, because it was still a prime, burning issue throughout the country. Republican moderates and reservationists were unhappy at Lodge's victory, and the Democrats refused to concede defeat. Thus the League, knocked on the head but not yet dead, became the major factor in the 1920 presidential campaign which soon got under way.

•

The question may well be asked by persons who did not live through the 1920's how it could have been possible for a man of Lasker's acumen to have been such an extreme, adamant isolationist. Today, isolationists of this category seem faintly grotesque, like a Don Juan with false teeth. But there were plenty of perfectly respectable isolationists in those days; moreover, many of these were authentic liberals, like Norris of Nebraska and LaFollette of Wisconsin. Men who were progressives on domestic issues were, in fact, particularly apt to be reactionaries on foreign policy, because they thought that an active foreign policy would impede reforms at home. There were four chief reasons for isolationism in the early 1920's, all quite valid in the light of the times: (1) fear; (2) selfishness; (3) naïveté; (4) tradition. Isolationists did not want to be taken in by the European city slickers, hated to prejudice American "security," and were unwilling to spend money. Finally, geographical considerations played a role. Lasker, as an example, was much influenced by his Illinois background and by the fact that he was a close friend of Medill McCormick, whose family owned the *Chicago Tribune*. Nobody who did not grow up in the Chicago of those days can possibly appreciate the gross provincialism and insularity that distinguished most (but not all) Middle Western opinion.

Old Hiram

Now for some secret history. Theodore Roosevelt hoped and planned to be Republican candidate for President in 1920. Possibly he would have got the nomination, and been elected. However, an untoward event cut off his hopes: he died. On January 6, 1919, the incomparable, the magnificent T.R. was killed by a tooth infection. Had antibiotics existed in those days, he would almost certainly have recovered from what was, in its inception, a minor ailment, as Lasker points out in his Columbia reminiscences. He was only sixty-one.

This left the Republican convention (June, 1920) wide-open. The two principal contestants were mediocrities—General Leonard Wood, a well-known military man of the time, and Governor Frank Lowden of Illinois. By every normal calculation, Lasker should have been a Lowden man. Instead he broke away from orthodox party considerations to give his support to an off-beat runner, Hiram Johnson. Few people today remember Hiram Johnson of California. A good biography should be written of this refractory, able and grumpy man. Johnson was a kind of T.R. in miniature, a mixture of bully and idealist. He was a rugged people's man, who broke up the corrupt party machine in California, annihilated the railroad lobby, cleaned up San Francisco, and was probably the best governor California ever had, all of which made Lasker like him. The chief defect of his character was a colossal vanity. His chief blind spot was foreign policy, and, of course, like so many Western liberals of the time, he was a deep-dyed isolationist.

Lasker, who was always a creature of enthusiasms, became passionately devoted to Johnson. He met him first through Harold Ickes, the valiant old curmudgeon who became Secretary of the Interior under F.D.R. years later, and who was a neighbor in Winnetka. Johnson and Ickes were both Bull Moosers, T.R. men. (So, strange as it may seem today, were Felix Frankfurter, Gifford Pinchot, Norman Thomas, Alfred M. Landon, Francis Biddle, Dean Acheson, and John G. Winant—a mixed bag if there ever was one.)[6] Johnson did not have much of a chance of getting the nomination—everybody agreed on that. He, Ickes, William Allen White, and Lasker met in the latter's house in Glencoe to talk things over. Johnson had no organization support and it was too late to enter most primaries. But Lasker, who was a novice no longer and who was beginning to have serious influence, thought that, even if the effort was hopeless, some out-and-out, last-ditch isolationist should be among the Republican candidates for the nomination, in order to keep the fight against the League fiercely alive. He would have preferred Borah as a candidate. Borah would have none of it, and Lasker settled for Johnson, the stiff, squat, moody Californian. Then, as usual, leaping from thought to practical action, he set about raising money—the first thing necessary—for the Johnson campaign. He contributed a substantial sum himself, and got more from his intimate friend William Wrigley, the Chicago chewing gum tycoon.

Then Lasker went to Hays, and offered to resign his position on the National Committee on the ground that his backing of Johnson might embarrass the Committee, which was supposed to be neutral vis-à-vis the various Republican candidates. Hays would not let him resign, but gave him a leave of absence. So Lasker took formal charge of the Johnson movement, and gave everything he had to it. The result was that, although Johnson started late, he went into the convention with no fewer than 136 votes, a respectable number. Old Hiram began to take his candidacy seriously for the first time, and, as Lasker puts it, "we found ourselves with a serious candidate on hand."

The 1920 Republican convention took place in Chicago. Lasker got a suite for Johnson at the Blackstone Hotel, directly underneath the notorious "smoke-filled room" where, a few days later,

[6] Arthur M. Schlesinger, Jr., *The Crisis of the Old Order*, p. 26.

the party bosses engineered the nomination of Senator Warren G. Harding of Ohio. The leading candidates, Wood and Lowden, knocked each other off, and a deadlock ensued, which opened the way to the choice of the preposterous, infantile Harding. Johnson, despite the dogged efforts of Lasker, Ickes, and others, was squeezed out. But there is more to tell.

The oligarchs of the party, like Senator Boies Penrose of Pennsylvania, decided to back Johnson, not as President, but as Vice President, when they discovered that he had a good deal of popular support, thanks to Lasker's work. He was too radical and too much of a lone wolf for the first place on the ticket, but they thought that he would be admirable for the second, because of his prestige and vote-getting power. They sounded out Senator Philander C. Knox of Pennsylvania, asking him if he would run for President with Johnson as vice presidential candidate. Knox agreed. Then they went to Johnson. Old Hiram said, "The ticket should be Johnson and Knox, not Knox and Johnson." This the bosses would not have, and the movement for Knox collapsed. *If* Knox had been nominated and elected with Johnson as his running mate, Lasker's man Johnson would have been President of the United States within a short time, because Knox died a few months after the new administration took office.

Johnson missed out on the possibility of being President not once, but twice, at this convention. With Knox eliminated, the plug-uglies in the smoke-filled room decided on Harding. Lasker recounts:

About three or four of us were in his suite with Senator Johnson about two o'clock the morning of the day the nomination was made, when Senator Harding came to the suite. That was the first time I met Harding.

The suite consisted of a sitting room and a bedroom. Harding said he wanted to talk to Johnson alone, and they went into the bedroom. They talked for five or ten minutes, and when Harding left, Johnson was *livid* with anger. He said, "*I* like Harding. I like him very much, but I can't conceive of his being President of the United States. He's done nothing to deserve it. He tells me they have just agreed upstairs to make him President, and *he* came down here to ask *me*, wouldn't I run as Vice President. Of course I indignantly refused."

Had Johnson accepted Harding's proposal, he would have been President in a little over two years, at Harding's death. That's how fate decides, more than men, the direction of a nation. I don't think this has ever been published, because I don't think there's anyone living except myself who knows it. The other two men in the room—I remember who they were— are dead, and Johnson's dead. Harding's dead. I never wanted to tell this until both men were dead.[7]

Harding, as big a blob of butter as has even been President of the United States, was duly nominated by the convention in the course of that day. The running mate finally chosen for him was, all of us should remember, a Massachusetts personage almost unknown on the national scene, Calvin Coolidge. This ticket disappointed Lasker bitterly. He, Alice Roosevelt Longworth, and Ruth Hanna McCormick met together, and all three, Lasker says, felt that "the end of the world had come." This was not out of personal dislike of Harding, nor, in Lasker's case, mere disappointment over Johnson. It was because they felt that Harding was not isolationist enough! They thought that, deep in his heart, he would be soft on the League of Nations issue. Lasker determined to leave politics forever. But Hays telephoned him from Marion, Ohio, Harding's home town, the next evening. Harding had asked Hays to stay on as chairman of the National Committee, an unusual thing to do because normally a presidential nominee chooses a man of his own for this post, and Hays wanted Lasker to stay on too. Lasker went down to Marion, and Harding received him promptly. Albert says:

He asked me to remain on the job, in the same capacity as I had occupied before the convention. I said, "Well, Senator, I'm glad to remain, because there's a major issue involved in which I'm deeply interested— that is, the defeat of the League of Nations. I don't want you to have me continue without knowing that I am very ardent on this subject. I was one of the main backers, both financial and otherwise, of Senator Johnson,

[7] Columbia, pp. 59-60.

and while I can assure you that you can absolutely trust me, so long as you're against the League, I want to tell you—in fairness to both of us—don't trust me at all, if I ever feel you are no longer wholly against it. I might then use my position to embarrass you."

Mr. Harding was a kindly man. . . . That was his weakness. Senator Harding revealed his whole character at our first meeting. After my declaration he put his arms around me and looked me square in the eyes. He said, "Lasker, let's at the start agree on one thing—that we'll never fall out because we disagree." That was the key to him. Of course one must fall out on vital issues when there is major disagreement. But Mr. Harding, once he gave his friendship, would forgive anything in a friend.[8]

Lasker was an important money raiser for the Harding campaign that followed, and gave substantial sums himself, including $2,000 to the general party fund and $25,000 earmarked specifically for the fight against the League. Some years later he underwent mild examination by a subcommittee of the Senate, which was investigating campaign contributions in the 1920 race, in regard to these gifts. The Senators were curious to know exactly how the $25,000 contribution was paid. Lasker said he made out a personal check to Fred W. Upham, the treasurer of the Republican National Committee, intending that this should be cashed at Lord & Thomas. But there was not that much cash in the Lord & Thomas till, and Lasker made the check over to the Foreman Bank in Chicago, with which he had close affiliations. Then, perhaps oddly, he walked over to the Foreman Bank himself, cashed the check, and gave the cash to Upham. The testimony reads:

Senator Walsh: What was the particular purpose of making payment in cash?

Mr. Lasker: It is possible that Mr. Upham asked for cash. Secondly, I made most of my political contributions in cash. Most of the politicians like to get it that way.

Senator Walsh: The politicians in Chicago like it that way. (Laughter)

Mr. Lasker: Universally I should say.

Later in this hearing a further contribution of $5,000, made to

[8] Columbia, pp. 60-61.

help defray a party deficit, was mentioned as having come from
Lasker. He denied that he had ever made this payment, saying that
Upham must have received it from somebody else and used his
name as the donor without even bothering to tell him he had done
so. Lasker went on, "If Mr. Upham should have gotten a subscription from some man who did not want to have the Democrats
know about it, I would not be surprised if he had used my name."⁹
Such were the airy methods of those days!

But the most interesting contribution Lasker made to the 1920
campaign did not have to do with money at all: it had to do with
advertising. This was the first presidential election in American
history in which the modern techniques of advertising were applied
on a comprehensive scale, and for this Lasker was largely responsible.
The seeds were thus sown, far back in 1920, for such piquant
phenomena as the "Spots for Ike" in Eisenhower's campaign thirty-
two years later. Lasker was in charge of all publicity that came
from Marion, Ohio, in 1920, and, since Harding fought a front-
porch campaign and did not leave Marion often, this meant that
he played an extremely cogent role. He sat with Harding at the
fountainhead, and sprayed its water where he willed. One feature
was the massive use of billboard advertising. Another was a public
relations job "humanizing" Harding as an old-fashioned, sage,
honest-to-the-core Middle Westerner who could be trusted never
to rock the boat.

The Democratic team opposing Harding-Coolidge in 1920 was,
of course, composed of Governor James A. Cox of Ohio and a rising
young politician named Franklin Delano Roosevelt, who had been
Wilson's Assistant Secretary of the Navy. Cox and Roosevelt cam-
paigned mainly on the League. They promised, if the Democrats
came in and gained control of Congress, to submit the peace treaty
to the Senate once more, and bring the United States into active
participation in European affairs after all. The Republicans were
still split on the League; many (like Herbert Hoover and Charles

⁹ Chicago *Daily News*, March 24, 1928.

Evans Hughes) still favored American adherence with reservations. But Harding was steadily forced into taking more and more of an isolationist position. The Republicans won by a landslide, as Lasker had predicted; Harding-Coolidge got more than 16,000,000 votes as against 9,100,000 for Cox-Roosevelt. Not only was Republican control of both houses of Congress made secure, but the isolationist wing of the party became dominant. This finally put the quietus on the League fight, and the United States set out on an isolationist course which it did not leave for the next dozen years.

Once Harding and Coolidge won, Lasker dropped politics, at least for the time being. He resigned his position on the National Committee, and did not even bother to attend Harding's inauguration. He had become involved in a crisis over baseball, and was far too busy.

*

In the personal realm this story has one curious postscript. Cox had never met Lasker, and told people during the campaign that he "hated" him. He was, he thought, the most powerful, "sinister" force in the entire Republican machine. The morning after the election Cox telephoned him, and opened the conversation with the dramatic words, "I'm Jim Cox—remember me?" Lasker was astounded. Cox went on to say that he had expected to be defeated, but not crushed, and that he considered this result to be due largely to Lasker's work in publicity. "I think we ought to meet," Cox said. "I'd like to salvage something out of this defeat, and perhaps we could be friends." Lasker, who could scarcely believe his ears, but who could never resist an off-beat challenge, accepted at once Cox's invitation to visit him. In fact, he gave up a meeting scheduled for the next day with Harding, no less, to spend it instead with Cox, his detested pro-League opponent—a nice example of his outgoingness and spontaneity. He and Cox became friends at once.

For many years they met regularly; they were inseparable companions in Florida, and every year Lasker gave a grandiose party to honor Cox on his birthday. This is an almost bewildering demonstration of the way personal values can cut across political affiliations in twentieth-century America—no doubt in other countries too.

International Opinions in General

In spite of his position on the League, Lasker was much more liberal on foreign policy than many of his colleagues; flashes of enlightenment were beginning to illuminate his political attitudes. For instance, he firmly supported the Washington Disarmament Conference which was soon to meet, and was one of the first Republican leaders to advocate forgiveness by the United States of the war debts. For an isolationist Republican from Chicago to urge that Britain, France, and the other Allies be let off their debt was most unorthodox—in fact, sensational. This was the era when people, echoing Coolidge, said acidly, "They hired the money, didn't they?" But Lasker always looked ahead. He wanted business to be good everywhere, and knew that the war debts impeded trade.

He took a brief trip abroad after the elections, and an interview he gave to Edward Price Bell of the Chicago *Daily News* in London gives insight into his thinking. He was sound on some issues, and on others merely echoed the platitudes of the time: "We should refuse even to negotiate with the Europeans until they agree not to disagree. . . . Europe is best let alone with its troubles; peace will come soonest in that way. . . . No American statesman knows his way about in the labyrinth of Europe."

But some of his observations had pith:

Europe's economic restraints are astounding. . . . I was at Basle, Switzerland, and wanted to see some customers of mine across the border in Germany. I wired my friends to meet me in an automobile at the Swiss frontier, six miles from Basle. They were to pay $20 for the car for the day and might just as well have come straight to Basle, to see me, but they were stopped at the frontier, and I was compelled to pay $2.80 for a taxicab to drive me out to them.

When I reached the dividing line I found it closed with a gate fence such as we see at railroad crossings. My German friends were there. They had got out of their car and were leaning on the barrier that kept them out of Switzerland.

Such are the handicaps that lame all the intercourse of the European peoples. These customs barricades almost fatally constrict the arteries of European economic life, and behind them develop and harden national-istic ambitions, prejudices, apprehensions, and antagonisms adverse to general understanding and dangerous to peace.

Clearly, the European Common Market of today derives from thoughts like these.

Lasker had one fanciful idea at this time, and he persuaded his friend William Hard, the well-known journalist, to write an article in *Collier's* presenting it. It was a spoof, but he made a point. He suggested that an international agreement be reached whereby every king, on ascending a European throne, and every prime minister, on assuming office, must forthwith appoint a substitute, an alter ego, for his job. Then, in the event of war, the real king or head of state or prime minister would be obliged to go to the front at once as a private, with the substitute staying behind to do his work in safety. Lasker always believed that responsibilities should be direct. In another William Hard interview published in *Collier's* about this time Lasker made a mild sensation by urging that income taxes should be lowered but that inheritance taxes ought to be steeply raised—a proposal which was nothing less than treason in the eyes of the propertied class. Several of his wealthy friends cut Lasker off their books. They refused to have social contact with him—liter-ally. He didn't mind. Again, instincts toward enlightenment which he had always had were breaking out to the surface.

In the 1940's, when he was traveling the Vandenberg-Willkie road and had given up almost all his early isolationist principles, his daughter Frances asked him if he had changed his mind about the League and regretted his crusade against it. He said No, on the ground that the League could never have been made to operate successfully, even if the United States had been a member.[10] Somebody else asked him why he himself had become a Willkie man, a One-Worlder. His reply was double: first, aviation had shrunk the world to new dimensions; second, isolation simply had not worked, and so why not try something else, even if it was the opposite! Maybe he was a romantic, but he never ceased being practical.

[10] But David Noyes, one of his closest associates at Lord & Thomas for a decade, gives different testimony. Noyes visited Lasker in Arizona during the early forties, when he was trying to "add up" his life, and says that he continually gave expression to remorse for his League stand.

Chapter 8

BASEBALL

For long years Lasker had been a rabid baseball fan, and his favorite team was the Chicago Cubs. He went to baseball games even if he had to work additional hours at night to make up the lost time; baseball relaxed and refreshed him. In that day baseball had a position in the public consciousness which no other sport has ever reached in America. It really was the national game. Lasker's interest in the Cubs began when he was a boy, because the team, known then as Anson's Cubs, did its spring training in Galveston, and he picked up odd dollars by telegraphing news of practice games up to Chicago. He became fascinated in baseball not only as a game, but as a business. The mechanics of running a big league team, with all its complexities and involvements, enthralled him.

In 1916 a man who had an option to buy the Cubs needed $150,000 to put through the deal, and asked him to help him raise it. Lasker was the only baseball enthusiast in Chicago rich enough to be able to produce $150,000 cash overnight. He went home, and talked the matter over with Flora. He records that this was the only occasion in their marriage when she insisted on his going into an investment. She had no interest in baseball herself and had, in fact, probably never seen a game, but she felt that her husband needed baseball if only to take his mind off his other work. Merely seeing games and rooting for the home team was not enough. If he had a serious financial stake in baseball (so Flora argued) he would give more time to it and this would remove some of the merciless pressures that came from advertising.

The next morning, Lasker agreed to put up a large sum of money. The baseball situation in Chicago was complicated in the extreme (for instance, there were three Chicago clubs, one belonging to the old Federal League) but the details are of little interest nowadays except to baseball historians, who would be well advised to consult the Lasker archives. As protection for his new position as an important stockholder in the Cubs, Albert demanded the right to approve the board of directors, or to appoint new directors. Two men joined him with $50,000 each, J. Ogden Armour, of the packing family, and William Wrigley. Lasker knew both well, and he insisted that both must sit on the new board. Wrigley, at that time, had no interest in baseball at all. He did not even know (Lasker records) that three strikes meant out, or what a single was. All that he lived for was chewing gum.[1] This was the age of businessmen who really did dedicate themselves to business. In those days, few self-made millionaires dared to relax until they retired.

Presently Wrigley bought out the man who had originally invited Lasker to purchase into the Cubs, but Albert, through manipulations too complicated to go into this space, remained the largest stockholder in the team and its controlling owner. However, he did not want this to be known. Years later Albert said ironically to Robert M. Hutchins, president of the University of Chicago, "You never heard of a *respectable* citizen being owner of a baseball team, did you?"

Three items of interest to baseball *aficionados* occurred early in the Lasker period with the Cubs. (1) He, Wrigley, and William L.

[1] Originally Wrigley had been in the baking powder business. To stimulate sales, he gave away chewing gum as a premium. Then chewing gum became fantastically popular and soon the tail wagged the dog. The original baking powder business was lost sight of and all the Wrigley energies, which were considerable, went into gum. Oddly enough, although Lasker and Wrigley were intimate for many years, Lord & Thomas never handled the Wrigley account, which was worth millions. This was a notable instance (Yellow Cab under John Hertz was another) of Lasker's resolute determination to keep business and friendship separated. He did not want to imperil his relations with Wrigley or Hertz by having them as clients. On a different level I know a distinguished author today whose best friend is a publisher. But he won't under any circumstances let his friend publish him, for fear that they may quarrel.

Veeck, a sports writer whom he made president of the club, purchased Grover Cleveland Alexander, one of the greatest pitchers
who ever lived, together with William Killifer, Jr., a prominent
catcher of the time, from Philadelphia and brought them to Chicago. They paid $50,000 for the pair, and this was the first big-money
purchase in the history of baseball. There had never been a sale
before for more than about $10,000. Players and fans were stunned
alike. Obviously, Lasker-Wrigley were prepared to go any financial
length to make the Cubs a winning team. (2) Lasker changed the
name of Cub Park in Chicago to Wrigley Field. "This will do your
chewing gum business a lot of good," he told Wrigley sapiently.
(3) Lasker got wind of a scandal, which gave a foretaste of much
worse to come. Veeck came to him and said that he had discovered
that a player, a second baseman whom they had recently bought
from Cincinnati, was a crook. The previous owners of this player,
who was bribed by professional gamblers to throw games, had
known that he was crooked, which was why they got rid of him to
Chicago, but of course they did not tell Chicago this and Lasker-
Wrigley bought him innocently.

Lasker was struck dumb with outrage. He determined to get rid
of this second baseman at once, and ordered Veeck to fire him. The
player then filed suit for breach of contract. The big moguls of
baseball, the potentates who controlled the other teams, tried to
call off or at least hush up the suit, because they knew that it would
injure the game as well as their reputations. But Lasker recounts
that he said, "By gum! I will fight this thing out, if it busts up
baseball!" The suit was at last heard openly in a Cincinnati court;
Lasker won it, and the offending second baseman was forced out of
baseball, never to return. Lasker said later, "I went into that thing
because my innocence had been abused. It is a good thing for a
man to be naïve."

From Black Sox to Czar

Then in 1919-1920 came the notorious Black Sox affair, the most
sensational scandal in the annals of American sport. The Chicago

White Sox won the American League pennant in 1919, and were thought to be invincible. They were one of the greatest teams in baseball history. But the Cincinnati Reds of the National League beat them in the 1919 World's Series five games to three.[2] Gamblers who had bet against the White Sox, the overwhelming favorites, cleaned up. Nobody could understand how the magnificent White Sox had collapsed against the puny Cincinnati opposition. Then during the winter, after the Series, the sordid, unbelievable truth began to leak out—professional gamblers had bribed several White Sox stars to toss the series to the Reds. The turmoil was resounding. It was as if Mr. Justice Holmes had been found out to be a cocaine addict who set orphanages afire, or a blackmailer who went in for counterfeiting on the side. Idealism and trust were shattered. The White Sox promptly became nicknamed the "Black Sox" and stout citizens everywhere, hearing the appalling news that baseball, the most precious of all games, was crooked, that the integrity of the foremost of American sports had been debauched, cried out in bewildered anguish and despair.

Lasker had nothing to do with the Chicago Sox, White or Black. His team, the Cubs, was in the National League, not the American. Nevertheless, as a public-spirited citizen as well as baseball owner, he took it on himself to do something to wipe the stain clean and restore the game to its former chaste, honorable place. It wasn't, he says in his reminiscences, a question of saving the baseball business. It was a question of saving the ideals of American youth. Youngsters all over the nation had to be cleansed of their disillusion, or American morale (Lasker believed this quite seriously) would be irretrievably ruined. Baseball *had* to be put back on the level. One is reminded of the TV networks, payola, and quiz-show scandals twenty-nine years later.

Lasker, almost singlehanded, performed the feat of cleaning up baseball, and this was a salubrious accomplishment. To tell the story in detail would take a book. Lasker felt that the nut of the

---

[2] In those days the World's Series was decided by the winner of a possible five out of nine games, not four out of seven.

problem was that the commission which was then at the top of organized baseball consisted of men who were heads of the leagues or owners or part owners of important clubs. Hence they had a vested interest in the game. They might be honest, but they could not be relentlessly impartial when their own clubs were involved in trouble. So he conceived the idea of getting some outside authority of irreproachable reputation, composed of men who had never had any connection with baseball, financially or otherwise, and who could not possibly be mixed up with the fate of any club or player, to run the game. In a word, he wanted to reorganize baseball so that it would be operated by people who were outside baseball.

His first thought was to set up a commission of three men, who would represent the American, National, and minor leagues, and he proceeded to draw up a scheme whereby this supervisory board would regulate every aspect of the game in the national interest. This over-all proposal revolutionized baseball, and has dominated it ever since; Lasker's document, four pages long, is still the charter of organized baseball in the United States. But it took almost a year of internecine struggle before the plan was accepted by the clubs. Several owners did not want to give up their privileges. Lasker had to threaten to draw the two New York and two Chicago clubs (the source of most of the big money) out of the existing leagues, and found a new twelve-team league of his own, which would have wrecked the existing structure, before the obdurate owners came around and agreed to accept his terms. Later he described this as "the bitterest, most complex, and most fatiguing struggle" of his life. At last he won, and the wrangling clubs agreed to give up their autonomy.

Meantime, Lasker reached the conclusion that one man, a "czar," could do the job better than a three-man commission. But how to find one? His first candidate was General John J. Pershing, who had commanded the American overseas armies in France and whose reputation was unassailable. Pershing, however, would not be approached. Time was pressing. One of Lasker's lawyers in Chicago was Alfred S. Austrian, an astute and highly regarded leader of the bar. A meeting was summoned to put into final shape the agreement between Lasker and his fellow owners and, if possible, settle on a czar. Austrian telephoned Lasker an hour before the meeting to say, "I've found your man. In fact, I have engaged him." Lasker spluttered to the effect that Austrian had no right to go so far and then asked, "Who is the man?" Austrian replied, "The man I have engaged is Judge Landis." Lasker almost dropped dead with shock and delight. Kenesaw Mountain Landis, a judge on the federal bench in Chicago, was a character of almost mythological renown. He was tough as a railway tie, incorruptible, bold, and, above all, a fighter. Not long before he had fined the Standard Oil Company *twenty-nine million dollars!*—for a matter having to do with rebates to railways, the largest fine ever imposed in American history; it made him a national figure. This was a man who meted out justice with a sinewy hand. Lasker, gulping, asked Austrian what salary he had offered Landis. The lawyer answered, "The only figure I could get him for. He loves to be a judge, and I had to name a good figure." "What?" Lasker cried. "Fifty thousand dollars a year," said Austrian. "I would have gone up to a hundred, but Landis would have thought that there was something wrong with us if we offered that much. Fifty thousand was exactly right."

Some days later Lasker and Austrian met for lunch quietly, and Lasker asked him how he happened to think of Landis for the baseball job in the nick of time. Austrian answered amiably, "For two reasons. He will do a tremendously good job, and will serve the country well. Second, I wanted to get him off the bench in Chicago!"

A sad little addendum attends this tale. Years later, in New York, several guests suddenly descended on Lasker while a World Series was in progress, and asked for seats, which were unobtainable. Lasker picked up the phone, called Landis, and asked him to send him a pair of tickets. The judge refused to do so and, moreover, rebuked him soundly for having made the request. Albert was bitterly hurt. The revenge he took was, however, characteristically subtle and indirect. He inserted a new line in his biography in

Who's Who to the effect that he was the man responsible for Landis' position in organized baseball. (But Lasker, although resentful of the judge's bad manners, understood perfectly well on reflection why he had not given him the tickets. It was *because* Lasker had put him in baseball. Landis did not want to be in the position of doing a return favor, no matter how minor, to anybody who had been associated with him in any way, for fear that this might compromise his position in baseball, which was to be free of all "influence" of any kind.)

Lasker's basic concept in all this—that of getting an outsider to be the impartial boss of a game full of conflicting private interests—has been interestingly followed in other fields. The movies got a czar, and various labor unions and other organizations set up "impartial arbiters." In fact, Lasker's idea was a contribution not merely to baseball itself but to American business as a whole. Of course the czar idea had been subject to severe criticism, if only because it provides an easy method for an industry involved in something disreputable to clean house without having to face up to any public accounting. It seals the front door, inhibits external regulation, and promotes hush-hush solutions. But as to baseball it is only fair to state that the game has never had a scandal since Lasker-Austrian made Landis czar.

Once Landis was in charge of baseball Lasker, a volatile man, got tired of it. In 1925 he sold his control of the Cubs to Wrigley, and, although he stayed on as a director and trustee, his days of active participation in the club were over. He had severe difficulties and differences with Wrigley about Cubs policy. But he valued Wrigley's friendship highly, and looked for a way out that would leave no hard feeling. The method he chose was characteristically original. He said to Wrigley, "I will buy all your stock at $200 a share, or you buy all mine at $150, whichever you prefer." He knew that this sporting offer would appeal to the chewing gum magnate, and Wrigley, as he had anticipated, chose to buy him out.[3]

[3] Chicago *Tribune,* June 6, 1925.

Golf Greens and the Movies

In 1919, the year of the Black Sox World Series, Lasker spent part of the winter in Pasadena, California, and noticed that few golf courses had grass greens. This was because grass was expensive, difficult to maintain, and, in some California areas, impossible to grow. He decided forthwith that something should be done about this. He knew that grass greens, to replace gravel, clay, sand, or just plain dirt, would improve the game immensely, not merely by eliminating dust and making courses more attractive to look at, but by making putting much more accurate and scientific. The fact that leading golf experts said that grass was impossible to grow merely stimulated him. He brought in an agronomist from Chicago, and set up a greenhouse for experimenting in types of grass that would survive conditions in California. As a result, the first eighteen-hole public golf course with grass greens on the West Coast was soon built near Pasadena. The effect was magical. In 1919 California had exactly seven public golf courses. In 1925 there were 140. Lasker did not like to boast about this, but he always considered himself, with reason, to be the father of popular golf in the Western states.

This experience led him to golf architecture as a hobby, and he became a knowledgeable expert on grass. The United States Golf Association maintained its experimental grass station on property he subsequently bought near Lake Forest, Illinois, and here he built one of the most extraordinary golf courses in America, as we shall soon see.

Presently he found another hobby—movies. Movies, like automobiles, were still in a primitive stage, but he became movie mad. Not only was he crazy about good movies; he was so crazy about movies in general that he loved bad movies too. His behavior at movies became notorious. He was shameless. He wept copiously at sentimental scenes, hissed villains aloud, and would even shout out some such interjection as "Look out!" when the hero in a Western was about to fall into a trap, much to the astonishment of other members of the audience. He insisted, however, that his movie-going served a useful purpose. "I spend too much time with the rich," he told one associate. "The movies tell me what the common people are thinking, and *what they want*."

His eyes would gleam, and off he would bounce to drown himself ecstatically in such favorites of the masses as Lillian Gish, Norma Talmadge, and Clara Kimball Young.

Chapter 9

WASHINGTON AND THE
SHIPPING BOARD

Politics kept beckoning, and twice Lasker just missed becoming
Harding's Secretary of Commerce. This would, of course, have
given him important cabinet rank, and his whole later career might
have been different. The story is tied in, to an extent, with that
ponderous character, Herbert Hoover. Lasker and Hoover had met,
but were not good friends. (They did become good friends later.)
Lasker thought that there was something odd about Hoover if only
because, when he called on him in Washington once, he was kept
waiting for forty minutes. Impatient, he asked the butler what his
master was doing, and the servant replied, "He is in the library
alone, thinking."

Shortly before Harding's inauguration in March, 1921, Will Hays
asked Lasker if he would like a job in the administration. Hays was
about to become Postmaster General in the new cabinet. Lasker replied frankly that he would like very much to be Secretary of Commerce. Hays replied just as frankly that this was impossible because
he, Hays, (not Harding) had committed himself to Hoover for this
post. There the matter ended, and Lasker forgot about it. Two years
later Harding told him that, as a matter of fact, he almost *did* get
the Commerce appointment, because Hoover was torn between
Commerce and the Secretaryship of the Interior. But Harding had
promised Interior to Albert B. Fall. Fall, as everybody knows, later
became implicated in the Teapot Dome scandal, and was eventually
disgraced and went to jail. If Hoover had been Secretary of the
Interior there would certainly have been no scandals over the oil

reserves at Teapot Dome, or anywhere else, and the whole history of the Harding administration might have been quite different. Lasker tells the story thus:

The last time I saw President Harding, which was late in June, 1923, he said to me, "I never tell men of things I wanted to do for them and didn't do. I have never done that, but I do want to tell you. On the night of March 2, 1921 [two days before the inauguration] I had not heard from Mr. Hoover accepting Commerce although I had telegraphed him (he was in Florida) that he *must* give me his answer. When he didn't, I prepared a telegram to you, tendering you the job. Just as I was about to send it, came word from Hoover that he would accept."[1]

Fall resigned in 1923, and again Lasker narrowly missed getting Commerce. Harding, bewildered by what was going on in his administration and tortured by his own inadequacy, sent for Hoover and asked him to quit Commerce and take Interior instead. Hoover asked who, in that case, would be his successor at Commerce, and the President replied that he planned to give it to Lasker, who was then chairman of the Shipping Board. Hoover said that he would have to think it over, and the next day refused to make the change. This was not because Hoover had any animus against Lasker, but because he felt (Lasker says) that he had brought so many people out of private life into the Commerce Department that he could not leave them with another boss, and, anyway, he felt morally bound to dedicate himself to Commerce until his job there was concluded. "So," Harding told Lasker, "You missed being Secretary of Commerce twice."

More Secret History

But to return to 1921. After Harding was inaugurated Hays came to Lasker and said that the President wanted him to be a member of the United States Shipping Board; appointments had to reflect geography and a man from the Middle West was needed. Lasker records: "I can remember, although I don't think Mr. Hays knows

[1] Columbia, p. 63.

it to this day, the hurt I felt at being tendered what I felt to be a very minor position." He told Hays coldly not to pursue the matter. Then in June, 1921, Harding invited him to the White House and offered him something better—the chairmanship of the Shipping Board. Harding's words, according to Lasker, were the following:

> I have to appoint a Shipping Board. I have not done so because I could not get a proper chairman. It's gone undone all too long. Because of circumstances, it's been running without any proper supervision for some eighteen months or so. There's so much money involved there, and so many unliquidated assets that if it runs longer without a head there is liable to be a great scandal. . . .
>
> It just happens that the thing that interests me most in being President of the United States is the Merchant Marine.[2]

Lasker asked him how this could possibly be so, since he came from landlocked Ohio. The President replied that, as a young man, he had worshiped Senator Mark Hanna, his "mentor," and that Hanna, in the early 1900's, worked for legislation to improve the American merchant fleet. Hanna's ship-subsidy bill to this end fell through, and Harding thought it was his duty, both to history and the memory of Hanna, to revive it. Then he went on to say frankly that Lasker was not his first choice for the chairmanship of the Shipping Board, but his fourth. The first was James A. Farrell, the head of the U.S. Steel Corporation, which operated a fleet of tankers; the second was P. A. S. Franklin, who ran a line of American ships, which, however, sailed under the British flag; the third was Walter Teagle of the Standard Oil Company of New Jersey, which had large shipping interests. But Farrell had declined the post; it was doubtful if the Senate would confirm Franklin because of his British connections; and Teagle had told Harding that to put in a Standard Oil man as head of the Shipping Board would create a storm of hostile comment. So, Harding got down to Lasker. Albert said that he was totally uninformed about shipping, and had little interest in it. He urged Harding to push on with Teagle, and said that his affiliation with Standard Oil didn't matter. Andrew Mellon

[2] Columbia, pp. 63-64.

was a member of the cabinet; if the public would swallow *him,* Lasker said, they would swallow Teagle without a gulp. Moreover, he volunteered to stay on in Washington a month or two and help Teagle with publicity (he said he could easily counteract any bad publicity that might arise out of the Standard Oil connection), if Teagle could be persuaded to accept the post.

This was arranged; Lasker and Teagle met and liked each other; then the illness of an important executive in Standard Oil made it impossible for Teagle to carry on with the agreement. Lasker, back in Chicago, got a long telegram from Harding offering him the job again and ending with the words, "As the President of your country I call upon you in the distressful position I find myself, [and] with time pressing, to wire me your acceptance."

Lasker, desperate, did not know what to do, and turned to Flora. She said, "I could never live happily with a man who would say No to an appeal like that from the President of the United States."

Chairman of the Shipping Board

So, aged forty-one, Albert Lasker became chairman of the United States Shipping Board; he turned Lord & Thomas over to Claude Hopkins once again, and moved his family bag and baggage to Washington. Accepting the post, he told Harding that he would hold it only for two years, and his tenure did in fact last two years to a day, from the summer of 1921 to the summer of 1923. When his two years were up, he left, and that was that.

The gist of the shipping problem, and Lasker's job, was that the United States had built an immense amount of merchant tonnage during World War I, to assist the Allies and transport troops and supplies overseas; this was a vital part of the war effort, but, with the war over, such a weight of tonnage was not only useless but a colossal expense. Some 2,200 ships were lying at anchor or rotting away in harbors. The cost of maintaining this derelict fleet, including depreciation, was estimated at $500,000,000 a year, which was approximately one-tenth of the entire federal budget at that time; in all, it was Lasker's job to liquidate an investment valued at $3,500,-

000,000 and build a new merchant marine out of what could be salvaged. Moreover, he had to pare down to size an enormously swollen office staff, which was being run so badly that it was called "the worst mess in Washington." (There have been other "worst messes" since.) When Lasker assumed office he found, to his consternation, that his organization had 3,000 bookkeepers, and, believe it or not, 750 lawyers. But, in spite of this fat profusion of personnel, work had come almost to a standstill. Books were not kept accurately, and nobody knew what the inventory was. No one knew with precision what property the Board controlled, nor what was due the Board, nor what it owed. Lasker took grip of the situation, and did a first-rate job. On the day he was sworn in, the fleet (that part of it which still sailed the seas) was losing more than $150,-000,000 a year and the Shipping Board's account at the Treasury stood at $4,000,000. By June, 1923, operating losses had been cut to $50,000,000, and the Board had $425,000,000 in the bank.[3]

The first thing he did was to get Ralph Sollitt to work with him; next, he hired a man named Jim Sloane, who wore a six-shooter and had been the personal bodyguard of President Taft a decade before, to be his receptionist and handy man. Mr. Sloane, picturesquely armed, made Lasker's office colorful. Lasker was an impresario now —something of a showman. Then he proceeded to produce as department heads the best experts on shipping he could find, and paid them unprecedented salaries for government servants at that period —$25,000 a year. He himself took only $10,000, as did Sollitt. Some wonderful stories may still be heard among Washington veterans about the way Lasker (with Sollitt running interference) managed to get salaries like $25,000 through Congress. Then Lasker decided to cut down on his existing payroll. He concluded that the only possible way to do this was, as he put it grimly, by "decimation." In those days, a carry-over from the war, the Board worked all night, with three shifts of employees. Lasker and Sollitt paid an unexpected call on the premises at midnight soon after their regime

[3] Chicago *Daily News,* October 4, 1921, and June 11, 1923.

began, and found hundreds of men sleeping on their desks. The next morning came one of the most drastic purges in the history of Washington bureaucracy—621 men were fired. On another occasion A. D. had to jettison two or three hundred others and, since it was all but impossible to do this on a personal basis, he chose the draconian method of arbitrarily firing all men on certain floors who had desks next to windows!

Lasker got rid of useless ships, including a fleet of worthless wooden craft, at an average price of $30 a ton. This was, of course, much less than they had cost, and he was severely criticized in Congress and elsewhere for "throwing our ships away." Meantime, another task was to fulfill Harding's ambition and set up a reformed American merchant marine. One thing that crippled him in regard to passenger traffic was Prohibition, which had come into force in January, 1920. People simply would not travel readily on dry boats, which American boats had to be.[4] Lasker, attempting to win passengers over to American liners against stiff and deeply entrenched British and other foreign competition, had some bright ideas. Vacationers, he reasoned, liked to play golf, but nobody had ever worked out a way to play on a ship. So he set up tees on the sports deck, and provided unlimited balls free for golfers to drive into the ocean. This practice had to be given up, however, after one passenger used more than 500 balls on a voyage; it was too expensive. To assuage the agony of passengers who could not get a drink legally he resorted to several devices; one was putting first-run movies on ships, an innovation at the time, and another was the provision of superior night club entertainment. Paul Whiteman, the orchestra leader, was an early contributor to this end, and so was the singer Morton Downey. To this day, following Lasker's lead, American ships make a big point of having name bands on board, like the

---

[4] Actually it was thought at first that the Eighteenth Amendment would not apply to ships at sea, but Congress passed legislation to make it do so. Lasker blamed one of the big Midwestern brewers for this. The brewery was eager to promote the sale of near-beer and hence set up a powerful lobby in Washington to make Prohibition even more extensive than was first envisaged.

Meyer Davis unit on the S.S. *United States*. Also it was Lasker who originated ship-to-shore telephone service.[5] In how many fields, major and minor, was he a lively innovator!—from paying high prices for baseball players to promoting beauty contests, from creating a demand for orange juice to wearing blue shirts and working out ways for people to have fun on ships.

Before his first year at the Shipping Board was up Lasker realized that his new merchant marine could not survive without help. There were two alternatives. The government itself would have to operate the American merchant fleet, or the private owners would have to be assisted by a large government subsidy. Without financial aid from the government, private shipping interests could not live in the face of foreign competition. Lasker chose the second alternative. He was (at this time) a fervent believer in private enterprise, and wanted firmly to get the government out of the shipping business. Hence, a subsidy was the only solution, if the American merchant marine, essential to national defense, was to survive. But "subsidy" was an ugly word in the 1920's. It meant, in this instance, that the American taxpayer would be footing the bill for the private shipping operators. Lasker fought for his solution—a subsidy—in and out of Congress for a year, and was beaten by one vote in the Senate. His act failed to pass even though the subsidy would not have cost more than $30,000,000 a year. He was heartbroken. He took the defeat in an acutely personal manner, and from that day until he died always had a subconscious resentment against Washington, and even avoided visiting the city if he could. One correspondent wrote, "Lasker is made of a foundation of molybdenum wrapped with piano wire and catgut, but he is tired." In fact he had a physical collapse, and turned gray overnight, although he was only forty-two.[6]

[5] He was also the first shipping man to provide unlimited caviar for first-class passengers. This, again, was to make up for the absence of liquor. Other lines were obliged to follow suit, and any time you eat caviar plentifully on a transatlantic crossing today, thank Albert Lasker.

[6] Lasker's views on shipping were at last vindicated, but not until years later. Under Franklin D. Roosevelt (1936) a Maritime Commission was set up embodying the subsidy idea. Lasker records dryly the ironic fact that a measure

A Trial Cruise

The best-known episode connected with Lasker's tenure on the Shipping Board was the trial run of the S.S. *Leviathan*. This mighty ship (59,597 tons) was the old German *Vaterland*, which had come to the United States as an item in war reparations. Lasker reconditioned it (all its internal decoration was done by Gimbel's of New York) and genuinely thought that it was the finest as well as largest ship afloat, superior even to such glittering British mistresses of the seas as the old *Aquitania* or *Olympic*. Presently he decided that, since he had to have a shakedown cruise anyway, he might take advantage of this to make a mild little junket, and give his friends a ride. The party was strictly stag. The only woman aboard was a nurse. Some six hundred male guests were invited, including members of the cabinet, Senators, Congressmen, business associates, newspaper proprietors, figures in the world of sport, celebrities at large, and, of course, the poker-playing Partridges. Lasker never forgot his friends, and seldom—unlike most successful men—shed them. The Partridges came first.

Hopes were high, but then came the threat of trouble. Public protests sounded against the impending junket. People asked, "Would liquor be provided?" (It was not—guests brought their own.) Congressman (later Senator) Cordell Hull said that the expense of the trip was not justified, and Herbert Bayard Swope, the incandescent editor of the New York *World,* which was bitterly anti-administration, let loose with all his thunder against the project. For a time it seemed that an injunction might prevent the *Leviathan* from sailing. As a result it set sail from Boston instead of New York in surreptitious circumstances—if the word "surreptitious" may be used in connection with anything as big as the *Leviathan*. It steamed in the general direction of the West Indies, circled around grandly in tropical waters for several days, and returned to New York without untoward incident. One passenger was Ring Lardner.

---

first proposed by such an arch-Republican as Mark Hanna and later espoused by Harding (and himself) finally became law under the New Deal.

He went to bed the minute he arrived on board the ship, and was not seen again until it docked. Another was a well-known sports writer who never went to bed at all.

This trip was notable in Lasker's life, if for no other reason, because it was the foundation of his long friendship with David Sarnoff, who was then around thirty and was a rising executive in the Radio Corporation of America. Sarnoff shared a cabin with Congressman Sol Bloom. A large radio traffic developed between ship and shore, partly because newspapermen aboard filed voluminous dispatches describing the festivities that went on, and the *Leviathan*'s radio operator was swamped. Sarnoff had been an expert wireless operator since his boyhood. Back in 1912 it was he, working for the Marconi Company in New York, who picked up the first despairing S.O.S. signals from the S.S. *Titanic,* and then for long hours was the only link between the sinking liner and the mainland. Now he volunteered to help Lasker, and spent most of the next three or four days tapping out messages. Moreover, he worked out a way to evade the static which was the curse of all dot-and-dash radio-telegraphic communication at that time, improved reception, and served as a kind of tinkerer-superintendent for all communications on the voyage. Sarnoff was much amused by all this, and Lasker, rapt in admiration for this man who could apparently harness the secret forces of the universe, decided that he must be a friend for life.

Anyway, the trip was a grand success. It served a useful purpose in giving the crew shakedown training, and gained more in publicity than the million or so it cost. Lasker had it to his credit that he was the host of what was probably, as of that date, the most stunning party ever given by anybody since Heliogabalus or Louis Seize.

The Harding Scandals

Lasker had nothing whatever to do with these; yet some mention of them is necessary. There were two camps around the President. One was beyond reproach. Corruption in the Harding regime has become so notorious that people nowadays are apt to forget that some extremely respectable men sat in the cabinet. Charles Evans Hughes, than whom no man could have been more correct, was Secretary of State; Hoover had Commerce and Henry C. Wallace, the father of Henry A. Wallace, was the able Secretary of Agriculture. Others in lesser posts were similarly incorruptible.

In the other camp were a fancy lot of crooks, grafters, shysters, and malfeasors. The worst was Harry M. Daugherty, the Attorney General, who had been Harding's campaign manager and who, years before, had undertaken the task of building Harding up from nothing. Now he demanded his reward. Daugherty was leader of the "Ohio Gang," the headquarters of which was the "Little Green House on K Street." "This place," one observer relates, "was a port of call for big liquor operators, office buyers, jobbers in bribery, and all the sorry, furtive drift of the political underworld."[7] One flourishing business was the wholesale sale of federal judgeships, no less. Some members of the gang met lugubrious fates. Daugherty never went to jail, but he was forced out of office (by Coolidge after Harding's death) and was indicted twice; he set a contemporary pattern by refusing to testify on the grounds that he might incriminate himself, and was saved from prison by two hung juries.

Jess Smith was Daugherty's chief hatchet man. He killed himself to avoid arrest. One felon on a really big scale was Charles R. Forbes, head of the Veteran's Bureau, who looted millions. He went to jail eventually, and his principal accomplice, Charles F. Cramer, shot himself. The picturesque Gaston B. Means, who did much of Daugherty's gumshoe work, got a jail sentence. And there were others. Thomas W. Miller, the Alien Property Custodian, was a creature of the gang, and its principal bootlegger was Elias H. Mortimer, one of Harding's intimates. Miller went to jail, and Mortimer was a suicide. Above all, there was Albert Fall.

Lasker, at this time, did not have much discrimination in personal relationships; his tendency was to be naïve about people rather than sophisticated; he wanted to be liked, and to be liked he had to like; *Babbitt* had not yet made the country self-conscious about the

[7] Samuel Hopkins Adams, *Incredible Era*, p. 235.

provincialism of most American businessmen; everybody slapped everybody else's back, and to be a good fellow was the end of all. It is therefore the more remarkable that a subterranean intuition kept him from close relations with the worst miscreants of the Harding era. He had no more than a speaking relationship with Daugherty (who distrusted him if only because he knew that he, Lasker, was spotlessly honest) , and never, so far as the record shows, even met Jess Smith. He had nothing to do with K Street, although he played cards with Harding in the White House, and stood firmly on the Hughes-Mellon-Hoover side of the administration.

The Teapot Dome story may be summarized briefly. The scandal revolved around oil resources on public land. Certain reserves of rich oil-bearing territory had been set aside for the permanent use of the U.S. Navy, in case oil for naval use ever became short. But, in 1921, soon after he assumed office, Harding secretly transferred control of these reserves from the Navy to the Department of the Interior, headed by Albert Fall. One big field, Teapot Dome, was situated in Wyoming; another, Elk Hills, lay in California near Bakersfield. Oil magnates became hungry for these lucrative properties. Their claim was that precious oil was seeping steadily off the reserves, and that they could save it by putting wells into production. What they wanted, of course, was to get hold of the reserves themselves for vast private gain. In 1922 Fall leased Teapot Dome to Harry F. Sinclair of the Sinclair oil interests, and Elk Hills to Edward L. Doheny, a large-scale California oil operator, without competitive bidding and in circumstances of total secrecy.

But rumors of corruption began to creep out even before the leases were signed. The oil business is competitive, and has loose tongues. So have politicians. Lasker records that Walter Teagle, head of Standard Oil of New Jersey, burst into his office at the Shipping Board one morning, and spoke as follows:

"I've come down just to see you, and my cab is waiting outside. I'm taking the next train back in thirty minutes. I understand the Interior Department is just about to close a contract to lease Teapot Dome, and all through the industry it smells. I'm not interested in Teapot Dome. It has *no* interest whatsoever for Standard Oil of New Jersey, but I *do* feel that you should tell the President that it *smells*—that he *must* not permit it to go through."

I said, "Now look. You go tell the President. I have nothing to do with any other department but this."

When I accepted the Shipping Board job, I did make *one* condition to President Harding—that no department head have a right to interfere with me. No one else was to have any say excepting himself. Whenever the way I ran it didn't suit him, he could let me go. He should never ask me to do anything for anyone. He kept the faith throughout.

I said, "You go see the President."

He said, "But I told the President that when I wanted to communicate with him, I would do it through you. I've discharged my duty."

I really didn't intend to go, but it bothered me all during the day, and so that evening I went over to see the President and told him what Mr. Teagle had said.

The President paced up and down in back of his desk as I disclosed the matter to him. He turned to me and said, "Albert, this isn't the first time that this rumor has come to me, but if Albert Fall isn't an honest man, I'm not fit to be President of the United States."

It shows his great trust in people he believed in—a fatal trust. He had been warned, and he still believed.[8]

The scandal did not break all the way open until 1923, after Harding's death. Then Senator Walsh of Montana and others set up a Senatorial committee to investigate, and for years Teapot Dome and Elk Hills made smeary headlines. Fall, it became known, had received $100,000 from Doheny in a "little black satchel," and $260,000 from Sinclair. He was forced to resign from the cabinet; so was Edwin Denby, Secretary of the Navy. Fall managed to avoid trial for years, but in 1929 was convicted of receiving bribes and was sentenced to a year in jail and fined $100,000. Sinclair went to jail as well, but on a different charge, contempt of the Senate, and, of all things, "for hiring detectives to shadow members of the jury appointed to try him."[9] The storm finally died down, and in the

[8] Columbia, pp. 66-67.
[9] Parkes, *op. cit.*, p. 424.

end the oil reserves went back to the government.

Why did not the respectable members of the Harding cabinet, like Hughes and Hoover, do something about the scandals when they first came to light, or, at least, resign office in protest? If Lasker knew what was happening, others must have known. The answer is, of course, that nobody wanted to stick his neck out and take responsibility; nobody wanted to embarrass the President, or deface the "normalcy" façade; nobody wanted to attack colleagues or lose his job. As to Lasker, he had specifically told Harding that he was going to quit in two years, and his time was nearly up; moreover, he felt removed from the scandal and impervious to it if only because his own record was so impregnable. Indeed, it was a matter of pride to him for many years that no shadow of taint ever touched the Shipping Board during his administration, although he was surrounded by corruption and his Board could have been peculiarly vulnerable, because it handled such enormous sums. For Lasker to have achieved this record proves not merely that he was an honest man, which goes without saying, but also that he was tough, perspicacious, and full of savvy. Still, the atmosphere of the period left its mark on him. Years later he was apt to be sensitive if the Harding scandals were brought up, and once he threatened to sue for libel a writer who called him a "member" of the Ohio gang. His affection for Harding himself, however, was always undimmed. He defended him loyally and felt that he was a good, kindly man who had been duped.

Life in Washington

During the Washington years the Laskers lived in a pretty rented house at 1706 Eighteenth Street. The children still remember it as a "divine" house with a lovely garden. Flora was intermittently ill, and their daughter Mary, now in her late teens, sometimes served as hostess for the family. (Later, Flora recovered and was even able to play golf regularly.)

Albert made new associations, and his social world became wider. He had never known anything beyond a Chicago and New York business milieu, and now he entered that segment of society known as "high." One friend was Mrs. Nicholas Longworth, the daughter of T.R. and wife of the Speaker of the House; another was the publisher Edward B. McLean, whose wife entertained at a house called Friendship and owned the Hope diamond. Of course, Lasker had considerable prestige because he was on such intimate terms with the President; the Hardings came to dinner with the Laskers a good many times, and he was often at the White House. Harding got into the habit of calling Albert at all hours, asking him to drop in for a game of poker. This practice played havoc with his engagements, and could be a nuisance; still, when the President of the United States asked him to the White House, he had to go. He never—a curious point—played poker with Harding in his own house. He liked poker and liked Harding but, puritanically, he did not think that it was proper for him to gamble with the Chief Executive of the nation in a private home, even his own.

Another point is that Lasker would not provide alcohol to guests in his own house. He hated Prohibition but he felt that, as an important government official, he must scrupulously obey the law, even if nobody else (including Harding) did. Guests were, however, permitted to bring their own liquor on the hip. Andrew Mellon came several times with a bottle of beer in his pocket.

Lasker paid practically no attention to Lord & Thomas or affairs in Chicago during this time. Claude Hopkins was running the company. Lasker did nothing to solicit accounts, but, when a very important client happened to be in Washington, he would contrive, in the good old American way, to take him over to the White House and introduce him to the President. Nothing, of course, could have been better calculated to impress the client. Incidentally, Lord & Thomas never did so well under Hopkins as under Lasker, and in fact during these years business fell off; which seems to indicate that Hopkins, for all his genius, and to whom Lasker owed so much, came nowhere near having the over-all business capacity that he had, and worked best when he was immediately under Albert's thumb. No matter how many brilliant people contributed ideas, it was Lasker who *was* Lord & Thomas, first, last, and all the time.

Lasker's chief pleasure during this period came from his children. Edward was now ten, and Frances, who had been born in 1916, was six. He was obsessed with love for the children, bullied them, worried about them, and spoiled them. He played baseball with Edward, and took them all to the Rock Creek Park Zoo every Sunday morning.

In the Washington years, young Francie was mostly in the hands of a governess of German origin, who believed in keeping children clean. Once Lasker protested to Francie, who was a sedate and well-behaved little girl, "For heaven's sake, don't you ever get dirty? Now go out and play and come back DIRTY!" Children, even the best, can exasperate a parent as demanding and quixotic as Lasker. Once he told his friend Leonard Lyons, the columnist, "I have made only two mistakes with my children. Whenever I said Yes, I should have said No. Whenever I said No, I should have said Yes."

Edward entered St. Albans, the best-known boys school in Washington, did well there, and stayed on for a period after the family moved back to Chicago. The teacher most closely associated with him was named Parke Dolan. For several years Lasker peppered Dolan with letters—at least one a week. Here are excerpts which show his fatherly concern, pride, and zeal:

October 10, 1923

I do not want him [Edward] to feel that I am complaining, but I am very firm in the belief that failure for him to write us at least once a week at length . . . will mean a great loss to him—in fact, more than to us, for if he is to keep alive those ties of love and devotion which in the ultimate will react to make his own character more sturdy, it is necessary that he have the desire to communicate at length at least once a week with his parents; that he may express to them all that he thinks and lives.

. . . I am sure it is only because of the excitement of the change in his life that he isn't writing more regularly.

October 18, 1923

Indeed, Edward is a boy with whom you can reason out anything, when he knows that correction is inspired by loving interest. All one has to do is to lay before him the reasons for the correction; he is quick to grasp the right and wrong, and quick to respond to the right. . . .

December 21, 1923

We are, of course, delighted with your letter, which reached Mrs. Lasker during my absence, as to how Edward came out in the play. . . . Nothing could make parents happier than to receive a report such as you sent us. His home-coming has, of course, brought the greatest possible happiness to our household. . . . I feel much of the credit for bringing out the best in his character is due to your example and inspiration, and I can only repeat the sense of unliquidated obligation I have so often expressed to you.

Lasker *père* is told that Edward is given to occasional boasting and bluffing. So:

. . . He has such a fine character that I don't like to feel our boy ever bluffs but that which he starts he is determined, in advance, to see through to conclusion with credit to himself and while I know it is normal and boylike to tease, still it seems to me that it is possible to build up a viewpoint that such action is unworthy. . . .

April 2, 1924

One of the fine points about Edward is—and it is an unusual trait to find in a boy—that not only he does not resent criticism from those who love him, but seeks it. I remember the day he left we were walking on Michigan Avenue. I was making many suggestions to him; feeling that possibly I had covered too much ground, I said to him—"Edward, I don't want you to feel that I am giving you too many admonitions." I was much touched by his reply—"No, indeed, Father, I am very grateful to you for them."

May 5, 1924

In fact, I am sure our minds meet when I say, where he stands in his class really means little. One boy can stand first and another can stand sixth and still the boy who stands sixth got more out of it than the boy who stands first. . . .

Many years later, in December, 1959, Edward Lasker and Mr. Dolan had some correspondence. Dolan wrote that he thought that

Albert Lasker had the "profound sympathy and a humility and simplicity that only great men have." Also:

Because of your father's make-up and temper, his Dombey and Son attitude toward you was a fascinating study— . . . He was able to classify people and the way he moved us all about—he used to remind me of a chess player—he understood Mary and Francie perfectly—but where you were concerned he went completely off-balance—You—his *son*—were the delight of his life and the association was one of the beautiful situations that make the world go round. Your mother was amused by it all—realizing that you had a good brain—were normal and healthy and good looking—everything a mother—or father—could ask for—(Your mother and I struck up a warm friendship from the first—and her wit and charm are often in my thoughts). Your father used to arrange conferences and we'd spend hours and hours discussing you and planning for your welfare— He was so deeply interested—he used to go over not only all *your* grades but the grades of my other nineteen boys as well, for detailed comparison. . . . This constant auditing of my records kept me on my toes. . . . Your father was a stimulating companion and I believe he influenced my life more than my own dear father did. . . . He was one of the fairest people alive.

Lasker Leaves Washington

Although devoted to Harding personally, Lasker was still a Hiram Johnson man. Johnson thought that he might have a chance for the Republican nomination in 1924, when Harding's term would expire, and asked Lasker to sound out the President about this. Presumably Johnson thought that Harding, because of the imminent threat of scandal, might not wish to run for a second term, but he was quite wrong. The President replied not merely that he did intend firmly to run again, but hoped to be renominated by acclamation! Lasker tried to work out an arrangement whereby Johnson, still a powerful insurgent force in the party, would call off his opposition to Harding in 1924, if Harding on his side would support Johnson in 1928, when he (Harding) would be out of the picture. The President, according to Lasker's recollection, was impressed by this suggestion, but would not commit himself at the moment.

At last Lasker's two years at the Shipping Board were concluded, and he resigned office. He was glad to get out, and left at once for a European holiday on his creation, the S.S. *Leviathan*. Looking back, he said that this Washington interlude was the "unhappiest" of his life. One reason for this was that he disliked violently being in the public eye. He was fond of power, but preferred to wield it unseen; he was more comfortable off the throne than on. Does this mean that he feared public responsibility? Not necessarily. What he liked was the mobility that came with being anonymous. In any case he did an admirable job, and had the satisfaction, if he ever wanted it, of knowing that he had created the modern American merchant marine.

President Harding died suddenly, in circumstances that have never been fully explained to the satisfaction of everybody, in San Francisco on August 2, 1923, while Lasker was still in Europe. He was supposed to have had an attack of ptomaine poisoning, and then suffered a stroke. One rumor was that he was poisoned, possibly by his wife, the formidable "Duchess"; another was that he killed himself, because he knew that the Teapot Dome scandal was about to burst open. No autopsy was performed. Lasker may (or may not) have thought that Harding was murdered; no record exists. But he was certain that he did not commit suicide. This was because Mrs. Harding telephoned Flora Lasker in Chicago shortly before the President's death asking her when Albert would return from Europe, because her husband had decided to go along with him on the 1924-1928 Hiram Johnson deal. Lasker felt that Harding could not possibly have killed himself if, a few days before his death, he was worrying about the 1924 nomination.

Coolidge became President, and offered Lasker a job in the new administration; he refused. He was desperately eager now to return to Chicago and resume control of Lord & Thomas.

Lasker knew that Coolidge's accession meant that any further effort for Johnson was useless; Coolidge was bound to be the 1924 nominee. Harold Ickes and a few last-ditch Johnsonites tried to make him change his view, but without success. Nevertheless he gave a minor sum—$15,000—to Johnson's campaign, which got nowhere. Another man had seized Lasker's restless attention now. This was the Chicago banker, Charles Gates Dawes, who became Coolidge's running mate (1924) and Vice President. Lasker did more than any single person, except Dawes himself, to promote the Dawes candidacy; he was manager of his campaign, and contributed heavily to his funds.

Again Movies

Sam Goldwyn, the motion picture producer, asked Lasker if he would consider a job in the movie industry. The Hollywood moguls, beset by fierce tribal warfare, were searching around for a czar, like Landis in baseball, to end their fratricidal infighting, and Lasker was an obvious possibility for the post. Goldwyn offered to sound out his fellow producers, and used all his persuasive powers, which are considerable, to interest him in the idea. Lasker's answer was simple. "I could never control those movie fellows. They haven't grown up."

However, this led to his getting the job for someone else. His good friend Will Hays had resigned from the Harding cabinet, and was looking around for a new post.[10] Lasker thought that he would be a perfect man for Hollywood, and talked Goldwyn and the movie people into accepting him. So Hays, thanks to Lasker, became czar of the movies, and retained this fragrant position for more than twenty years, until 1945. Hays was grateful to him, and this in turn led later to something else—Lasker's second marriage, which we will come to in due course.

[10] Hays was never directly implicated in the Harding scandals, but it came out much later, in 1928, that he had accepted large campaign contributions from Sinclair, the oil man, on behalf of the Republican party, during the early days of the administration.

There Were Two Laskers

By the mid-twenties it was clear that there were two Laskers, who might be called Lasker A and Lasker B. This anomaly should not be stressed unduly; Lasker was certainly not a Jekyll-Hyde. But in every human being, even the simplest, both a player and a counter-player exist; every man (and Albert was not simple) contains some elements of bipolarity. His bipolarity was, in fact, so extreme at times that it all but tore him apart. Lasker A was the hard-driving, on-the-go businessman, relentless, a ruthless competitor, still raw, rough, and often rude and inconsiderate. Like most of his contemporaries he exalted commercial values. Lasker B was the person who gave up a year of his life to the Frank case, the devoted son, the loving paterfamilias, a man gay, warm, and generous, the apostle of civic pride and duty, and the Hebraic puritan who increasingly sought to become a high-minded man of affairs. There were two Laskers. Could both be contained in the same bodily integument? Which would win?

Chapter 10

BACK TO ADVERTISING—THE
GREAT ACCOUNTS

Lasker returned to Chicago to resume active charge of Lord &
Thomas in September, 1923, after five years away. He was now
forty-three. The family settled back into residence on Burton Place
and in Glencoe. During his long absence business had gone down-
hill a bit, and new agencies, upstarts, were snapping at his heels.
He took prompt and energetic measures to restore his leadership
and retrieve his position as king without peer of the advertising
world; he testifies that he did the equivalent of three or four years
of work in the next sixteen months. So the great Lasker years, the
tremendous years, began.

First he persuaded Ralph Sollitt to come to Chicago to be his
executive assistant. Sollitt protested, "What do I know about advertising?" Lasker replied winningly, "What did either of us know
about shipping?" Then in 1924 Hopkins retired. No man ever did
more for Lasker, and the parting was affectionate: but Albert was
glad to see him go. He did not want a viceroy in the kingdom now
that he was running it himself.

In 1925 came a celebrated pep talk to his staff; he summoned his
key men around him, and said that he would talk "for a few minutes." The only notes he had were a few scribbles on the back of an
envelope. The talk lasted for three days, with brief interruptions,
and it is the transcript of this which is the text of *The Lasker Story.*
Pep talk? That is not quite a correct description. Lasker was appealing for more effort, yes, but he was not merely a cheer leader; rather

146

Is Advertising Read?

Three examples that bring out the answer

THE word *halitosis* lay buried in the widely "read" dictionary of the English language scores of years until set in ordinary type in an advertisement it became a by-word of the millions.

As a result, a product 40 years on the market with moderate sale became a world leader. Bad breath became almost a fashion.

On the other hand, yeast was something merely to make bread with—until Fleischmann advertisements said otherwise.

Now we gain fair skins, robust health, cure ourselves of many of the common ills of mankind, and even look forward hopefully to Eternal Youth because of it.

For centuries women used makeshift hygienic pads. The subject itself was admittedly a forbidden one. A subject no one spoke about, much less wrote about, except in medical practice.

Then came Kotex. A sanitary pad. A product no woman had ever heard about. A product that admitted no definitely descriptive words in headlines to describe it.

Thus to learn what Kotex was intended for, the reader had to go *deep into the text*

of the ads. Kotex headlines perforce had to be more or less indirect. No person could get the import of a Kotex ad *without reading virtually every word of the ad itself.*

That women did, everyone who follows advertising knows. Over 80% of the better class of women in America today employ Kotex. The makers of this product would be quick to answer whether or not advertising is read.

Thus Listerine, Fleischmann's Yeast and Kotex—at least three of the most notably successful products of the day—must be regarded as Simon Pure Advertising successes.

All had their basic selling stories, not in the headlines, but in the text of their ads. And readers had to read that text to be "sold." All stand as indisputable answers to the question, "Is Advertising Read?"

If people didn't read ads as carefully as news or feature matter, most of the successful concerns whose names are household words would be virtually unknown to the reading millions.

Men who have made money through advertising know how true that is.

Number 37 of a series . . . from Foote, Cone & Belding's file of Lord & Thomas originals.
Published April 21, 1927.

he assumed the role of the benevolent head of a family who, at long last, has returned to his flock; he told (for the benefit of newcomers) the story of his life and the detailed story of Lord & Thomas, a noble organization, from its beginnings, and then set forth precepts and injunctions for his staff to follow, so that the organization would once again be the biggest, most glittering, and grandest advertising agency on earth.

About this time came a series of house advertisements for Lord & Thomas. Seeking new clients, Lasker decided to advertise for them; he was, so to speak, putting his own profession to the test.[1] Of course other agencies had advertised themselves before (many still do) , but they never used copy quite like this. The Lord & Thomas ads were plausible, modest, and of extreme sobriety. There was no beating of the tom-tom or jangling of bells. It was always Lasker's theory that there could never be enough advertising; the better business was for his agency, the better it would be for all. One ad that startled people bore the heading "WHY WE CLAIM NO MAJOR PART IN THE SUCCESSES POINTED TO AS OURS." His argument was that no business could succeed only by virtue of advertising, no matter how freely money was spent. The best advertising campaign in the world could not, he was convinced, sell a poor product. All the advertising agency could do was help, but its help would be fruitless if the product was not good, i.e., salable.[2]

He liked strong competitors, but he didn't want them to be too strong. He said once, "When I hear that a rival is going around town telling everybody that I'm a fine fellow, I know I must be slipping. When other agencies say that I am a God-damned cut-throat, then I know I'm doing all right."

[1] This was not the first time he had done this. While he was away in Washington Lord & Thomas had issued a series of small advertisements about itself. Written by Hopkins, they were in the form of editorial homilies, under brief headlines like "Exaggeration," "Good Nature," "Vanity," and "Good Name." They were part of Lasker's continuing incessant effort to make advertising more respectable, give it a code of ethics, and establish standards.

[2] Many years later Foote, Cone, & Belding, the company which succeeded Lord & Thomas in 1942, repeated this whole series of ads verbatim, without a word changed—an unusual thing to do. Lasker's copy proved to be just as effective in the 1940's as it had been twenty years before.

Psychology

This is the twenty-first of a series of
business creeds by

LORD & THOMAS

NGUIDED by psychology, salesmanship is crude. Good advertising must recognize facts like these:

People are dilatory. Without
some incentive to prompt action or
decision they will usually delay and forget.

It is natural to follow others. Impress folks
with the crowd that goes your way.

It is natural to obey. A direct command is
more effective than request.

People don't like problems. Present them
only the worked-out solutions.

Too evident desire to sell puts men on guard
against you.

Curiosity incites men more than fact. Half-
told tales have interest which completed tales
have not.

Men covet an advantage. Things they can
get which others can't are things they want the
most.

Folks are not impressed by boasting.

When you quote others to confirm your state-
ments you indict your own veracity.

Evident bias kills influence. Praise of an
article is made doubly effective by a touch of
criticism.

One's honesty can never be impressed save
by some evident self-denial.

Masterful advertising has to consider a
thousand such basic axioms.

That's one reason for its rarity.

Once he told Edward, his son, that he had never failed to get an account so long as he was actively afraid that he would *not* get it. As soon as complacency set in, results were not so good. One thing that gave him confidence was that, in Washington, he had become accustomed to dealing in large sums—amounts much larger than any that normally entered the advertising business. He could talk in terms of millions more familiarly than his competitors. He records: "From the very vastness of the responsibilities that came to me,

dealing with sums that made Ford look like a pauper . . . I came
to an understanding of what motivates and activates industrial
life."[3] Also business flowed in by reason of valuable contacts he had
made at the Shipping Board.

But, consumed as he was with the business end of the business, he
never lost his avid interest in advertising *per se*. He was still an
artist. He loved copy. Some of the principles he inherited from
Kennedy and Hopkins became even more firmly fixed. This was an
adventurous, gaudy era in advertising—the era of Mr. Addison
Sims of Seattle, halitosis, and Jesus Christ presented as a businessman devoted to "service"—but Lord & Thomas kept carefully on
the conservative side of the road. Lasker continued to deplore fancy
layouts. He had an obsession against "reverses"—that is, ads printed
in white ink on black. He would say, "If it was natural to read that
way, the *New York Times* would be printed that way." Humor was
outlawed, as it was under Hopkins. So was anything esoteric. "Sell
your product, not yourself," was one principle. Above all, he still
refused to countenance anything ornamental or "clever." "Beware
of 'clever' ads," he enjoined his staff. "Ads that *are* clever don't
show it." He wanted people to think of the product, not the ad.
Everything had to be fixed to a single, all-embracing key—what
would best sell goods.

One thing that still fascinated him to this end was the news
element in ads. "Discover the *news* in your product; then play it
up." Another continued to be headlines. "You must stop a streetcar
before you get on it." Another was the shrewd use of long and short
copy. Copy should be cut to fit commodities. Nobody, he reasoned,
was willing to read a thousand words about a box of matches: but for
an automobile a thousand words might not be enough. Above all, he
sought good prose, and to give copy an edge, a point. He knew that
he was mixing metaphors when he said that copy should be "eu-
phonious to the eye," but this conveyed his meaning exactly. "Make
copy sing" became a famous Lasker watchword. A jingle com-
memorated it as follows:

[3] *The Lasker Story*, p. 44.

"Make it sing," says L. & T.
Step up your ads with sound.
Keep one ear tuned for harmony,
Another to the ground.

Give the prospect "Reasons why,"
But do it with a song.
Beware of slogans "cut and dry";
They'll only get the gong.

And when you talk of homey things
Like bedsocks, say, for gramma,
Be sure that every sentence rings
With music and with drama.

Pack your headlines with a thrill
And load them down with news,
And don't forget the lyric trill
If baby needs some shoes.

And if you just can't sing in key,
We earnestly beseech you,
Just drop a line to L. & T.
And they'll be glad to teach you.[4]

What, to summarize, brought so many new and valuable clients to Lasker in these turbulent years? The gist of it, aside from his personality, his showmanship, was that he continued to unite daring originality in conception with extreme conservatism in execution, an unbeatable combination.

The Kotex-Kleenex Saga

One of the prime accounts which came to Lasker in the 1920's was Kotex and, later, Kleenex. This story has a double root. Back in 1872 four enterprising young men set up a paper mill in Neenah, Wisconsin, in the heart of the Menominee Indian Reservation, and

[4] By Richard C. Francis. *Advertising & Selling*, February 27, 1926.

established the Kimberly & Clark Company, manufacturers of paper.
One was John A. Kimberly, part owner of Neenah's general store;
another was Charles B. Clark, a youngster from New York, newly
arrived on the raw Wisconsin frontier. Their mill prospered, and
the business eventually became the Kimberly-Clark Corporation,
well-known paper manufacturers today; it makes paper for the
New York Times and *The New Yorker,* among many other publications. Another important personage in the story was F. J. Sensenbrenner, the son of a blacksmith in Neenah, who never went to
school after fourteen, became a bookkeeper in the company in 1889,
and rose to be its president.

The other root in the Kotex-Kleenex story goes back to Vienna.
A man named Ernst Mahler was born there in 1887. His father
owned a paper mill. Young Mahler decided to go into the family
business, studied cellulose chemistry at the Darmstadt Technical
University, which is still one of the foremost institutions in the
world for the scientific study of paper products, got a job with the
great German chemical combine known today as I. G. Farben (the
name was different then), and came to the United States. He went
out to Neenah, which was still very much in the backwoods, in 1913,
to give technical advice on dyes for paper used in magazines; people
at Kimberly-Clark (which employed only one chemist at the time)
were much impressed with him, and offered him a job. Thus began
an association which lasts to this day. Mahler has retired from active
participation in the company, but is still a member of the executive
committee. The present president of the company is John R. Kimberly, a grandson of one of the founders. Sensenbrenner died some
years ago.

Mahler, a big ruddy-faced man with gray-blond hair whose voice
still holds a gritty trace of Viennese accent, has a place nowadays in
Tryon, North Carolina. He likes to ride, is fond of Viennese cooking, has a good rough sense of humor, and is a formidable con-
noisseur of glass, mostly German and Bohemian.

During World War I Mahler invented the substance which subsequently became Kotex. At this time, although he had only been
with Kimberly-Clark a few years, he had risen to be general super-

intendent. There was a serious shortage of cotton in the United States at this time, and a substitute for it was desperately needed, in particular for bandages and surgical supplies for American troops overseas. Working with cellulose, Mahler succeeded in producing a fluffy wadding which proved to be satisfactory, and Kimberly-Clark trade-marked this under the name "Cellucotton." Large quantities were shipped to the Army, the Red Cross, and military hospitals. Then word began to filter back that nurses were using this new substance not merely for bandages but for sanitary napkins—it was perfect for the purpose. Mahler had never dreamed that his invention would have this use. But he and his associates at Kimberly-Clark were quick to take advantage of the idea, and the new product was named Kotex and put on the market. This was around 1921. But, although it filled an obvious need and might pleasantly revolutionize personal habits and save untold millions in laundry bills, Kotex did not sell well. The subject of menstruation was so wrapped in taboos at that time that it could not be talked about. Women were shy of going into shops and asking frankly for Kotex, so that it had to be sold under the counter. Kotex hired an advertising agency, but this made slow progress. Its copy was good, but indirect; it did no more than hint at what the function of Kotex was. Indeed, its task was difficult, because no magazine would accept an advertisement which used such a term as "sanitary napkins."[5]

At this point Lasker entered the picture. Kotex let it be known that it was in the market for a new agency, and a Lord & Thomas salesman called on Mahler. Negotiations began, and then Lasker himself (breaking all the rules, because he seldom solicited accounts personally these days) went to see the Kotex people. He did not, however, want to seem to be too eager, and his first words to Mahler were, "Mind you, I'm not here to solicit any business." Mahler wondered why, in that case, he was sitting there in his office, but he restrained any crude impulse to say so. Instead, politely, he out-

[5] One early sketch for an ad showed a nurse talking to a wounded soldier, and indicating that she used a kind of "bandage" too. The illustration contained some flowers, and the magazine insisted these be cut out, on the theory that flowers connoted scent, and that this would make the covert reference to menstruation too "strong."

lined his problem, and Lasker made a bid for the account. He told Mahler that he was convinced that Kotex could be the greatest boon to women in a thousand years, and he wanted to be part of the effort to make it succeed. Indeed women of today who have never been without Kotex can scarcely conceive the discomfort and misery of having to use something that was not disposable. Mahler asked him if hygiene was the only reason he was interested and Lasker, beaming like a boy, replied cozily, "The products that I like to advertise most are those *that are only used once!*" Lasker the idealist was speaking, and Lasker the money-maker too. Not knowing for certain how shrewd Mahler was, he thought for a moment that he had not caught on to his meaning, and he added, "I don't go in for grand pianos!"[6] But Mahler did not need any explanation. He had understood.

Lasker, Mahler, and Sensenbrenner became the warmest of friends from this time on, although three years passed before Mahler dared to call Lasker "A.D." instead of "Mr. Lasker." Mahler thought that he was "a fearless genius," to whom he owed "the greatest inspiration" of his life, and "the finest man he ever met."

Attacking the Kotex problem, Lasker acted with his usual vivacity. First, he insisted that his advertisements be straightforward as well as tactful; he cut through the hush-hush screen, and made magazines accept them. Then, on several fronts, he set himself to overcome further obstacles. To make women purchasers less shy he worked out a campaign whereby advertisements in newspapers told them that Kotex, in a wrapped package which gave no clue to its identity, would be available in shops and did not even have to be asked for by name; the customer could put fifty cents in a box near the pile of packages, take one, and walk out without having to say a word to a clerk or anybody. Meantime, he educated dealers by sending out thousands of circulars. Then, much as he hated public relations, he did a big public relations job with the magazines. He persuaded the *Ladies' Home Journal,* no less, to print an article about menstruation, and systematically organized a campaign to inform school boards and other organizations all over the country about the new

---

[6] But actually Lord & Thomas had a big piano account at this time.

product, and to explain how teachers could perform a valuable public service by instructing girl students about elements of feminine hygiene.

Nothing in Lasker's career ever satisfied him more than his success with Kotex. Kimberly-Clark made millions, and Lord & Thomas did extremely well out of the account; but this was not all. What Lasker liked was that he was developing a smash-hit business and doing good for humanity at the same time; it always pleased him to make money out of benevolence, and confirm his position as an off-beat kind of millionaire.

Around 1924 came Kleenex. This too was a Mahler invention, although he claims no credit for it. He was afflicted by hay fever, and played around with developing a soft creped tissue that might be used instead of a handkerchief. At first the new tissue was called "Celluwipes," and then "Kleenex 'Kerchiefs." Mahler took it to Lasker, who, for some strange reason, had little faith in it at first; he said that it might go as a cosmetics remover, but would be useless as a handkerchief. Mahler said, *"A.D., do you enjoy putting germs in your pocket?"* This remark instantly challenged Lasker's imagination, and he inaugurated a campaign for Kleenex as the "handkerchief you can throw away." A dirty cloth handkerchief, he implied, was a menace to society. The entire handkerchief industry rose in wrath, but to no avail. Kleenex was launched with a whoop, and has been a solid success ever since. Lasker, whose genius for merchandising devices was not ebbing, gave it a large push forward by changing its size. The early Kleenex sheets measured six by seven inches; Lasker was sure that these were too small, and had them enlarged. But the new size was, he found, untidy for loose sheets on a lady's dressing table, and so his men at Lord & Thomas worked out a new type of box, which Kleenex uses to this day.

After a year Mahler asked him how he thought Kleenex was going. Lasker replied, "Fine. Women are beginning to waste it. Once you can afford to *waste* a product, it's bound to be a success!"

Kleenex was first organized as a company of its own, but the Cellucotton products made by Kimberly-Clark (Kleenex, Kotex, and Cellucotton itself, for use in hospitals) became such a flourishing business that a new organization was formed, the International Cellucotton Products Company, to include all three. Kimberly-Clark had, of course, a large holding in this, but it was an independent corporation. A peculiar incident occurred in Philadelphia in 1926, at the time of the Dempsey-Tunney fight. Lasker invited Mahler, Sensenbrenner, and other friends to attend this event, and engaged a private railway car for the trip. After the fight Albert suddenly announced that he was going to "buy" International Cellucotton. He had had a drink or two, and, as he explained apologetically later, his ego became "inflamed." Sensenbrenner was astonished, but raised no objections. Lasker asked him belligerently what he would take for his share in the company, and Sensenbrenner replied calmly, "Nine million dollars." Lasker said, "Agreed." Then, he records, he became in one second "the soberest man in Philadelphia," because he was not sure that he *had* nine million dollars readily available. The next morning, when all heads were cooler, an arrangement was worked out, and he bought, with Sensenbrenner's consent, a million and a half dollars' worth of stock for himself and more for his associates; he held on to this investment zealously, and it repaid him well. To the end of his days, he was proud to be part of this company the products of which, to say the least, have been a considerable convenience to contemporary humankind.

Adventures in Toothpaste

Another account which mattered profoundly to Lasker was Pepsodent, the toothpaste. He became fascinated by it partly because it occurred to him, during World War I, that hundreds of thousands of American boys from poor urban families or remote hillbilly farms, who had never seen a toothbrush in their lives before, were being taught by the Army to clean their teeth. Obviously, he calculated, there ought to be a terrific market for a good inexpensive toothpaste after the war. Lord & Thomas would make money, and, as with Kotex, be contributing at the same time to better hygienic standards, and even raising the level of the nation's health. Once again, he was hitting on a combination that served both his own and the public good.

The story behind Pepsodent is somewhat complex. It was launched by a man named Douglas Smith, who had been the principal owner of Liquozone, the magic cure-all for which Claude Hopkins wrote the first ads, and of which he was part owner. But patent medicines were going out of fashion. *Collier's* put on a brisk, inflammatory campaign attacking Liquozone and similar products, and both Smith and Hopkins felt that they should give up a product which was subject to such attacks, although they believed in it devoutly and although it was making large amounts of money. So Smith searched about for something else. He had a toothache one day, and went to his dentist. The dentist told him casually that he had just worked out a formula for a new kind of toothpaste, which would remove mucin plaques from teeth. Smith bought the formula, and out of this Pepsodent was born.

One of Smith's partners and backers was a person whom all Chicagoans of the day will remember, Louis Eckstein. He had large interests in publishing, real estate, and the drug business, and, as a hobby, financed the Ravinia Opera. This, a summer opera house in a lake shore suburb, gave out-of-door performances in an exquisite rustic setting. Eckstein managed to procure opera stars of major rank, like Tito Schipa and Lucrezia Bori, for Ravinia, and it became a mecca for music lovers all over the Middle West, a minor Glyndebourne. Now, Eckstein, who was something of a man of mystery, lived next door to Lasker on the Glencoe property, which was close to Ravinia, and the two men were good friends. So, when Eckstein became interested in Pepsodent, it was natural that Lasker should become interested too.[7]

Actually, Pepsodent first went to Lord & Thomas as far back as November, 1916, but it did not become important until the 1920's. It was no more than a nice little toothpaste company. Then Lasker made it boom and sing. One of the first things he did, when the product was explained to him, was to abolish the word "plaque"

[7] Later they quarreled bitterly when Lasker accused him of copying the shutters on his house, and they were not reconciled for some little time. Flora gave a lunch to celebrate the end of the quarrel, with fourteen guests. Lasker and Eckstein were put alone together at a card table decorated with hearts and flowers.

in Pepsodent advertising. Nobody, he said, would know what "plaque" meant, and so Pepsodent became the toothpaste that removed *film* from teeth. Later a minute quantity of a harmless detergent substance was added to the Pepsodent formula. In this era, detergents were little known except in chemical laboratories; Lasker was fascinated by this new factor, and asked what the detergent was. He scowled when he got the answer—sodium alkyl sulphate. That would never do in a Lord & Thomas ad! So he told his men to dig up a new name for it, and said that he wanted a word with three vowels and two consonants; this was the only specification he gave. His copy writers came up with "irium," and this single word made Pepsodent world-famous; the company still uses it. But, to his dying day, Lasker never had the faintest idea what irium was, or anything about it except that it helped clean teeth. He loved to joke about this. "I invented irium," he would chuckle with his eyes burning. "Tell me what it is!"

Lasker liked catchy words and phrases, and had a remarkable talent for finding them although he seldom created them himself. One of his basic principles in advertising was what he called "exclusivity." He wanted his products, above all else, to have something that automatically distinguished them from competitors. For instance he did wonders with the phrase "water-level route" for the New York Central.

Another reason why Pepsodent fascinated Lasker was that it had no sales force; he was setting out on an experiment unprecedented for the time, to see if he could achieve mass sales for a product without any salesmen whatever; he wanted to prove, once and for all, the brute power and force of advertising. He said frankly, "Let us think of this as a pie in three equal slices. One-third of our money goes to manufacturing, one-third to advertising, and one-third to profit."

Douglas Smith died in 1927, and the Pepsodent business was taken over by his son, Kenneth. Lasker had a close relationship with him for many years, in a pattern that became familiar. He was still a comparatively young man, under fifty, but most of the manufacturers he dealt with, and whom he had first encountered in his youth, were older. So, when they died and were succeeded by their sons, Lasker became a kind of protector-mentor for the new generation. Meantime, he acquired a good deal of Pepsodent stock. The company did not have money enough (at that time) to finance the imsense advertising drive it was promoting, and so Lasker himself provided the capital and in return took shares in the company; soon he was its second-largest stockholder, and was thus not only making money by getting 15 per cent of what it spent on advertising, but sharing in its profits as well. Both sides of the coin were lucrative in the extreme, particularly as Pepsodent soon became the biggest-selling toothpaste in the world. But, as we shall see, it gave Lasker a good deal of misery before its course with him was run.

*

Studebaker was still an important client at this time, and so was Sunkist. So were Bissell carpet sweepers, Todd protectographs, and Union Oil of California. The Beverly Hills Hotel of Beverly Hills, California, came to Lord & Thomas, and so did the Auto Strop Razor Company, the California Redwood Association, the First National Bank of Chicago, and Holeproof Hosiery. Even so (about 1925) Lasker had only thirty-six accounts in all, whereas J. Walter Thompson had sixty-five and Ayer many more than that. Lord & Thomas was doing about $14,000,000 a year in total billings, Ayer $17,000,000, and Thompson around $22,000,000. Lasker, in a word, still had not regained his prewar position as Number One. Also he had several failures. He turned down an ice-cream account which made a fortune later for another agency, because he did not think that ice cream could be advertised nationally, and he lost a million dollars or more on a cold-cream project. Such defeats he regarded as honorable—but unfortunate—wounds of battle.

Paul G. Hoffman remembers an encounter he had with Lasker at a Studebaker conference at about this time; Lasker made a remark which he thought—and still thinks—was a semantic masterpiece, to the effect that there was "no mystery to mastery" of the market. What Lasker meant was that merchandise had to be actively pushed before it could make money. It was no longer true that, if a man built the best mousetrap in the world, customers would automatically, instinctively, beat a path to his doorstep. Instead, the customer had to be aggressively enticed, his resistance deliberately broken down. Again, we see the genesis of today's hard sell. Lasker added, "All that advertising gives you is what is rightfully yours." Then he defined what, in his view, successful merchandising depended upon—knowledge of people. "The whole art of salesmanship," he concluded benignly, "is simple as ABC."

The Master and His Flock

The man closest to Lasker during these years was Sollitt; he was a brother, but also a slave. Now other important executives were coming up. One was Don Francisco, whom Lasker loved like a son, and who eventually became closer to him than anybody in the office. Another, Sheldon R. Coons, was never so intimate with him personally, but played a large role in his business affairs for many years. A third, David M. Noyes, did not join the organization until later, but it is convenient to include him here. For a decade or longer the triumvirate that ran Lord & Thomas for Lasker consisted of Francisco, Coons, and Noyes.

Francisco was, and is, an altogether different type from such eccentric individualists as Kennedy and Hopkins—bland, cheerful, outgoing, and a good executive. In all the time he was with Lord & Thomas, nineteen years, he lost only one account. Francisco started life in Michigan as a student of horticulture, and moved on to California, where he got a job with Sunkist. While working for the Fruit Growers Exchange he devised the system whereby citrus fruit could be stamped with a name, like Sunkist, without damaging it. No one, in that era, had ever dreamed of identifying fresh fruit with a trade-mark in this manner, and he performed his first experiments at home by heating a fly swatter and burning an impression into the orange. Lasker picked him up in 1921, and by 1924 he was in charge of the California operations of Lord & Thomas. One of his functions was to counteract the California impression (in those days) that "all the money went back to a fellow named Lasker in Chicago." The best way to do this, he records, "was to live a full community life," in other words to respectabilize Lord & Thomas by becoming a pillar of the local society.

An anecdote nicely illustrating Lasker's gift for supersalesmanship has to do with Francisco. It dates from later years. Francisco loved California, and was happy there, but Lasker, setting out to effect a thorough reorganization of Lord & Thomas (maybe for the tenth time in ten years), decided to transfer him to New York and put him in charge in the East. Francisco refused to come because he felt certain that, if he left the West Coast, disaster would follow. He said to A.D. frankly, "You know we always work better apart." His chief doggedly kept on pursuing him, until at last he agreed to work in New York for a stated interval strictly as an experiment. This period came to an end, and, after consulting with his wife on the long-distance phone, he gave his final answer; he absolutely would *not* succumb to A.D.'s blandishments and stay east permanently. Lasker intercepted him on his way back to California. He said, "I have just made a will. I have designated you to succeed me as head of the business. This means, of course, that you will have to leave California when the time comes. Do you agree?"

"Yes," replied Francisco.

"You accept to do this for me?"

"Yes."

"You will do it for me dead?"

"Yes," Francisco repeated.

Out of the mouth of the cannon came the charge. *"Then why not do it for me alive?"*

Francisco capitulated, and wearily telephoned his wife again, this time to tell her to pack up and move.

Coons, the second triumvir and an exceptionally able, discerning man, came to Lord & Thomas through Gimbel Brothers, of which he had been a vice president. Lasker, tired out, needed executive help; Coons stayed with him for ten years, during most of which time he was vice president in charge of New York. His relations with Lasker were complex. After years, he and his boss still seemed to be warily feeling each other out.

David M. Noyes was also close. Noyes, who has a subtle gift for language, creative warmth, and alert brown eyes set widely apart and rather like those of Mr. Macmillan, the British Prime Minister (they seem faintly hooded at the edges), was a small-town newspaper publisher in the Chicago environs, and had waged an interesting little war on local crooks and racketeers which brought him to Lasker's attention. Noyes's chief characteristic was his independence. He was the only man in the office who dared talk back to A.D. Also he was unique in being the only Democrat. Years later he became one of Harry Truman's closest advisers. Lasker walked into Noyes's office at Lord & Thomas one day and asked him if he would not like to have an autographed photograph of himself for his wall. Noyes said No. A.D. was bitterly hurt. Noyes explained that he did not go in for photographs and did not even have any of his own family on display. Then, embarrassed, he saw that Lasker had actually brought the photograph into the room with him, and was holding it under his arm. The boss walked out after an uncomfortable silence, but his words were, "You are good for me, Mr. Noyes. More people in this office should say No to me."

Noyes could not stand the pressure of Lord & Thomas after a while, and announced that he was leaving. Albert's reaction was characteristic. He pinioned Noyes, had him hustled into a taxicab, and delivered him—before you could say one, two, three—into the arms of a psychiatrist. If a man wanted to quit, Lasker thought, he must be crazy.

*

I have asked several of Lasker's old associates what they thought his greatest quality was, and the answers make a small anthology. One was sense of detail. He would spend weeks on end arguing with an artist on the precise color to be given to the cheeks of the girl on Palmolive ads ("Keep That School Girl Complexion"). Concurrently he had a marked gift for surmounting detail and grasping at once the "big" picture. Then too, although his executive methods were eccentric (as we shall see soon), he was a masterful leader of a group: he could amalgamate people into a unit, and draw out the best of each. But most testimony centers on two other factors: (1) he was a sublimely good editorial judge of copy; (2) he had a fantastically accurate sense of what consumer reaction would be, the alpha and omega of success in advertising.

Nobody on the staff, even the highest executives, knew from one hour to the next what to expect from Lasker; he oscillated continually between being eagle and dove. One of his men told me, "I'm not at all certain that I ever liked him, but I sure did *love* him!"

Lucky Strike and George Washington Hill

By far the greatest Lord & Thomas account, at this or any other time, was the American Tobacco Company, that is, Lucky Strike. By the end of the 1920's Lucky Strike brought in more business than all other Lasker clients combined; 58 per cent of the total billings of the company came from this cigarette. Lord & Thomas' revenue was doubled, merely by reason of this single account, and then almost tripled. Lucky Strike dominated Lasker's life for the next fifteen years; he fell in love with it, and it made him really rich.

It was World War I which made manufactured cigarettes a universal craze. Before that many smokers thought that they were vaguely effeminate; men who were men chewed tobacco, smoked pipes or cigars, or rolled their own. Then, as cigarettes became acceptable, the great tobacco companies experimented with formulae to make them more attractive, and the first blends (mixtures of domestic Virginia and Turkish tobaccos) were produced. Such blends are, of course, still the overwhelming leaders in the cigarette business today, but they were a novelty then. Reynolds had Camel, and Liggett & Myers had Chesterfield. The American Tobacco Company was late getting into the race with blends, and its business suffered accordingly. According to Lasker's own reminiscences, it had been hurt so badly that it "was on the way out" as a leader in the industry.

Moreover, the American Tobacco Company did not concentrate on one product. It was selling fifty or more brands of smoking tobaccos, plug tobaccos, cigars, and cigarettes. Each had its own small advertising appropriation; none was outstanding. Lucky Strike was not, at this time, a cigarette at all, but a chewing tobacco. To compete with Camel and Chesterfield the company composed a blend, and decided to give it the Lucky Strike name, which had a good reputation. Even the package for the new cigarette was the same as that of the chew—green and red. The slogan was "It's Toasted." It did moderately well, but not sensationally. Then, late in 1923, Lasker—by a series of flukes—entered the picture, and an overwhelming boom for Lucky Strikes began.

The New York office of Lord & Thomas had done substantial business before the war, but was much reduced in strength. Now a man named Lou Hartman, who has a prosperous agency of his own in New York today, came to Lord & Thomas in New York and brought with him a small American Tobacco account for one of its cigarettes known as Blue Boar. Hartman worked out a complicated and ingenious scheme whereby the manufacturer, in order to attract sales, made up to the dealer the amount of federal tax on each pack of cigarettes. Blue Boar business rose steeply in consequence, and the American Tobacco people wondered if the same process could not be extended to Lucky Strike.

The president of the American Tobacco Company was Percival Hill. His son, George Washington Hill, was in charge of advertising for the company. Hartman knew both well. Lasker, eager for the Lucky Strike account, came to New York, and Hartman asked him to lunch at the Hotel Vanderbilt (which had just been opened) to meet the Hills. A.D. at once opened up on them by saying that they must stop frittering away their advertising on a variety of small accounts—all their minor brands—and throw everything into one gigantic effort to build up Lucky Strikes. Otherwise, they would be drowned by Chesterfield and Camel. The Hills were much impressed by Lasker's line of thought, and before lunch was over proffered him the Lucky Strike account.

Lasker said to Percival Hill, "Do you handle this advertising yourself? Do we deal with you, or somebody else? Before I can accept your offer I must know who exactly I am dealing with, and know that he will have complete confidence in us."

The elder Hill replied, "My son, George, here, looks after the advertising, but I make the decisions. It'll be time enough for him to make the decisions when I'm dead."

Lasker said, "That's fine, Mr. Hill. But if I'm to deal with George, and not you, I cannot accept your account unless George and I get to know each other better. If he'll come out to Chicago for a week, watches us work, and then decides that he likes what we do and *he* asks us to take the account, I'll take it."[8]

This was agreed upon; George Hill spent some days in Chicago as Lasker's guest, and Lucky Strike went to Lord & Thomas. Percival Hill died two years later, in 1925. Thereafter for long years the lives of Lasker and George Washington Hill were inextricably intertwined.

Hill was about forty at this time, younger than Lasker. He was, in the full sense of the word, a personality. With a man like Ernst Mahler, Lasker had a relationship based on trust and esteem; his relationship with Hill was almost wrecked time and again by an explosive conflict of rival egos. One theory to account for Hill's almost insane bumptiousness was that he had been kicked around by his father for many years, and now enjoyed the chance to assert himself untrammeled. He was a rawboned, smallish man, who looked like a cowboy; he wore a big tilted sombrero, and, as a rule, kept it on while at work in his office. The hat was a symbol—his crown. He liked fishing, and usually had fishhooks or flies stuck in the hat. As business grew, so did his idiosyncrasies. He liked to drive down Fifth Avenue in an open Cadillac, with a bodyguard prominently on show; the windshield of the car was festooned with packages of Lucky Strikes.

He had a house on a fashionable East Side street in Manhattan, but lived most of the time secluded in a castle at Irvington, New York. Here he kept Japanese deer, black and white swans, and two dachshunds, Mr. Lucky and Mrs. Strike.[9] He was an extremely tough, able businessman. He ran American Tobacco Company sales from

[8] Columbia, p. 47.
[9] *Time*, September 23, 1946.

$153,000,000 a year to $558,000,000 in twenty years. Not only did he run the company, singlehanded, with a fist of iron; he ran it capriciously. Like most moguls of the period, he was full of tricks. Once he hired two rival public relations consultants without telling either that he had employed the other. His ingenious theory was that if he hired both, his competitors would be able to get neither. *"Le roi, c'est moi."*

He paid himself an enormous salary, and paid his executives well too. Lasker records: "He really liked to pay his head men big money. Therefore, he had to get more money than they did to prove that he was on top of them. It wasn't the reverse—that he paid them big money to justify *his* money." He was not, to put it mildly, as generous about labor. In 1932, the worst year of the depression, Hill paid himself $825,607, but the average annual wage of a full-time worker in the tobacco industry was—$614.12!

Hill always acted as if he had a chip on his shoulder, waiting to have it knocked off, but, maddeningly, would never fight. One of his odd characteristics was his handwriting; he must have used a quill pen. His signature was like a broad stab, with the letter "G" of Herculean size; then the letters sloped upward in a diminishing triangle like a pennant. Hill, incidentally, is supposed to have been the prototype of one of the more unpleasant characters in a novel by Frederick Wakeman, *The Hucksters,* and indeed his personality contained some startling vulgarities. There was only one fixed line in Hill's life—Lucky Strikes. A true megalomaniac, he ate, slept, and lived for one purpose only—to sell more Lucky Strikes. He had no interest in the manufacture of cigarettes, but only in selling. Nor was his primary interest money. He would destroy a $4,000 set of plates to change one word in an ad.

Naturally, when Lasker and Hill came into contact, sparks flew. There are few rooms big enough to hold two Napoleons, especially if both insist on talking all the time, and seldom listen. But Albert handled him with the utmost skill, humoring him and giving way to his vanity. He said once, "It isn't hard to work with Hill. All I have to do is let him be the agency, and pretend that I'm the client." Lasker was content to take Hill's 15 per cent, and let Hill have credit for all the ideas. In later years he felt that 15 per cent did not represent a fair return for the work he put in for Hill, and it was certainly Lasker, as much as Hill, who made Lucky Strikes sell. When Lord & Thomas took the account Camels were selling 80,000,000 to 100,000,000 cigarettes a day, Chesterfields 60,000,000, and Lucky Strikes a poor 25,000,000 Within three years, Lucky was up to 150,000,000 a day, led the entire field, and held its position as a pacemaker for two decades.

Lasker's devices in handling Hill were several. He had a first-class man, Coons, on the firing line in New York, and under Coons were various minor executives, who, as it has been coarsely put, "took the ulcers." Deliberately A.D. sought to arrange matters so that Hill would be in contact with underlings, because he knew that this would make him happy by stimulating his already monstrously swollen ego. At the same time, he was careful to keep supreme control of the account in the *Chicago* office of Lord & Thomas, not the New York office. Thus there was always a physical distance —space—between himself and Hill. Of course, Lasker visited New York regularly, but the fact that Lord & Thomas was nine hundred miles away from the American Tobacco Company in New York played a major role in the Lasker-Hill relationship.

*

Lasker's first coup with Lucky Strike was his greatest. In those days it was comparatively rare for women to smoke, and almost unknown for them to smoke in public. The nearest anybody dared to get to the subject—in advertising—was to portray a woman in a picture in which a man was smoking; the woman says, "I love the smell of a good cigarette." Paul Hoffman of Studebaker said casually to Lasker one day, "Get women to smoke, and you'll double your market." Lasker replied, "We've given it a lot of thought." Then Albert had lunch at a well-known Chicago restaurant, the Tip Top Inn, with Flora. She had put on a good deal of weight, and, on medical advice, had taken to smoking a cigarette before meals; it soothed her nerves, and made her digestion better. Flora lit a cigarette, and the manager of the establishment, who knew Lasker well, came up to them apologetically, and said that she could not be permitted to smoke in public; he suggested that they withdraw to a private dining room. Albert went into a rage. It seemed to him intolerable that his wife should be forbidden to smoke in a restaurant. He determined, then and there, to *make* it possible for women to smoke in public, no matter what.

Things moved fast. European women, Lasker reasoned, did smoke in public; this might be a clue to breaking down the taboo. Moreover, *foreign* women were much admired in the United States, particularly actresses and opera stars. So he conceived the idea of getting a series of celebrated singers to give testimonials for Lucky Strike, with slogans like "Cigarettes Are Kind To Your Throat," and "I Protect My Precious Voice With Lucky Strikes." Before long, almost the entire roster of the Metropolitan Opera had provided testimonials—for nothing! The stars were glad to do it for the publicity. Now talking movies were beginning to come in at this time, and Lasker instantly thought of extending his campaign to include movie stars who would dare to appear in advertisements which showed women smoking and enjoying it. The effect was beyond belief. No campaign in the entire history of advertising has ever made such an impact. The results were far beyond anything that Lasker, Hill, or anybody had so much as dreamed of. Women started to smoke all over the nation, and the sale of Lucky Strikes—other cigarettes too—rose almost overnight to a spectacular degree. As Hoffman had predicted, Lasker *doubled* his market with one stroke.

An odd coincidence attends what happened next. Lasker, in Pittsburgh, happened to see in a newspaper that a group of candy manufacturers was meeting there to prepare a campaign against cigarette advertising. They had nothing against cigarettes *per se;* it was simply that people were spending more money for cigarettes, so that less pocket money was available for candy. The candy people appropriated $150,000 for an advertising campaign; it was to be based on the idea that, if you ate a piece of candy, it "fixed" your saliva so that the impulse to smoke was lessened. This gave Lasker a startling, almost diabolical idea. He determined to beat the candy men at their own game by reversing the equation. Everybody, he reasoned, has a fear of getting fat, and candy was certainly fat-making; why not put on a campaign telling people to avoid candy, and smoke cigarettes instead, with the word that this was an easy change to make because smoking lessened the desire for sweets. Lasker rushed to New York at once to present this dazzling concept to Hill. But, before he could open his mouth, Hill presented him with the identical idea, which he had picked up from a woman he had met in Paris, who said that, although seventy, she looked forty because she smoked cigarettes all the time, but did not touch candy. So Hill said that Luckys should inaugurate a new campaign based on the slogan "Reach For a Lucky Instead of a Bonbon." Lasker, recovering from his astonishment that both he and Hill had, independently, arrived at precisely the same idea at precisely the same time, said that he agreed fully with Hill, but that one word must be changed. He thought that "bonbon" was too foreign a locution, which people would not understand. He said, "Make it, 'Reach For a Lucky Instead of a *Sweet*.'" He added happily, "Why should we limit it to candy, which is just one form of sweet? By using 'sweet' instead of 'bonbon,' we can kill the taste of people for cakes and pies as well!" Hill agreed, and the most famous of all Lucky Strike slogans, "Reach For a Lucky Instead of a Sweet," was born. Again, results were dazzling, and Lucky Strikes sales rose 312 per cent within a year. The candy people made acrid protests, but their voice was like the feeble trickle of raindrops into the sea.

All told, Luckys spent $180,000,000 with Lord & Thomas over the years; its appropriation rose from $400,000 at the beginning to not less than $19,000,000 in 1931. Lucky Strike made Lasker, but, like Pepsodent, it was to cause him agony before the years were done. Also it continued to add substantially to his ego. He told one friend, "I made Lucky; I could unmake it too!" and said to another boyishly, "There is no advertising man in the world but me!"

Politics Again

Lasker was still profoundly, passionately interested in politics, and still a black Republican. Always (in this period) he voted the straight ticket. His reason for this was that, in any showdown, he felt that the party was bound to control the man, so why not vote for the party in the first place. One small anecdote survives, preserved by Leonard Lyons. An idealistic young lawyer, trying to fight the machine in a Chicago primary campaign, asked Lasker for help. The young man averred that, even if he was unknown, he was sure that, with a little support, he could beat the organization's candidate. Lasker replied: "Maybe so. David beat Goliath. But you had better remember that David's victory over Goliath was such an exceptional event that people are still talking about it two thousand years later."

The 1924 presidential campaign (Coolidge-Dawes versus Davis-Bryan) occupied him closely, because he was Dawes's campaign manager. Dawes was a man of the utmost conventionality, who, to conceal inner bleakness, liked raucous and unconventional behavior, but this did not bother Lasker. He liked Dawes, and was sometimes given to raucous and unconventional behavior himself.

In 1928 (Hoover-Curtis versus Smith-Robinson) Lasker did not play much of a role: he was too busy with Lord & Thomas. But he maintained his position as an important member of the Illinois delegation to the convention, and became a devoted friend of Charles Curtis, the Vice President. Curtis, an Indian of Kaw origin, was an amiable person, much given to gregariousness; he was no great thinker but he had a certain air, and Lasker found his company engaging.

After the arid and timorous Coolidge left the White House Lasker sent an emissary to Northampton, Massachusetts, with a check for $50,000 made out to Mrs. Coolidge, which was hers if she would give a testimonial to Lucky Strikes and say that they protected her voice. Coolidge said to the emissary, rejecting the offer, "I don't think Grace would be interested in this." She never saw the emissary, or the check. Lasker was astounded.

Lord & Thomas Becomes Lord & Thomas and Logan

During this period Lasker and David Sarnoff, of the Radio Corporation of America, became steadily closer. Sarnoff, who was born in

Minsk, Russia, and than whom no one can be more self-made, was now well up in the RCA hierarchy; he was, and is, not merely a businessman and engineer, but a poet of a kind. His rhymes were symbols in electronics, and he had imagination. He was the first genius Lasker ever met. Conversely, Lasker was the first man of real wealth Sarnoff ever met. Often they did not understand one another. Sarnoff, talking about radio tubes, might as well have been speaking Chinese. Sarnoff was interested in science; Lasker was interested in business; but the art of communication absorbed them both. Sarnoff found him "insular," but fascinating. When Albert visited New York they would take walks together around the reservoir in Central Park. Sarnoff would say, "If I had to make my living selling a fifteen-cent package of cigarettes, I'd cut my throat." Lasker would say, "Until you learn to think in terms of fifteen-cent packages you'll never make a success of RCA."

RCA was a pygmy then, compared to the giant it became. Its advertising was handled by a youthful ex-newspaperman, Thomas F. Logan, who was on intimate terms with Sarnoff. The Logan agency was small, compared to the behemoths, but it had some excellent accounts—General Electric, Anaconda Copper, the New York Central, Cities Service, RCA—and was bigger than the Lord & Thomas office in New York. Sarnoff talked about Logan with enthusiasm, and Lasker asked to meet him. Then an astounding thing happened. Lasker invited Logan to consolidate with Lord & Thomas. There were three main reasons for this. First, Lasker was worn out, and wanted a partner to take some of the general load off and relieve him of office routine.[10] Second, he felt that Lord & Thomas had become too personal, too much a concentrated reflection of his own personality. Third, he wanted deeper roots in New York.

Logan, as a condition for merging his agency with Lord & Thomas, asked that the name be changed, and so, on July 1, 1926, Lord & Thomas became Lord & Thomas and Logan. Interestingly enough, Lasker had never dreamed of putting his own name into the agency.

[10] He several times told members of his family that he was so tired that "he did not expect to live to be fifty."

Lord & Thomas was a splendid old name, and it had never occurred to him to modify it in any way. Everybody knew that he *was* Lord & Thomas, and that was all that mattered to him. But Logan felt that his name must go into the firm, and Lasker agreed. Of course, Albert continued to own the company, but Logan and several of his men were given small amounts of stock. Lasker elevated himself to be chairman of the board of the new firm, and Logan became president.

Lasker and Logan got on well, and the merger was a success. The mild witticism was heard that Logan was "A.D's Irish Rose." Then suddenly in 1928 Logan died of a heart attack. Lasker did not know what to do about Logan's widow. Technically there was no obligation to make a settlement with her, beyond turning over to her Logan's small interest in the firm, but he felt impelled to do something. Sarnoff was the intermediary. First, he found out from Mrs. Logan exactly what she had in the world; then he demanded that Lasker produce the same information about himself. He did so, and Sarnoff then recommended that he pay her a flat $1,000,000 although he owed her nothing like this amount. Albert was stunned by the magnitude of the sum and he protested loudly at first, but Sarnoff insisted that this was a fair settlement and that it would be good business for him to be generous, and he paid it.

Lasker found himself alone in the saddle again, and presently the name of the company was changed back to Lord & Thomas. The most significant thing about all this was that his relations with RCA became entrenched, and this was to become of marked importance on account of the National Broadcasting Company, the child of RCA which soon opened up to him new and brightly fertile fields.

Note in a Different Field

On May 20-21, 1927, a slim youthful falcon, Charles A. Lindbergh, flew the Atlantic solo for the first time. Lasker heard the news, and was probably the only American out of the total population of the United States at that time, around 120,000,000, who not only was not impressed and who did not respond to the unique glory of this adventure, but who took a distinctly negative view of it.   •

He said to his daughter Mary, "The boy's no good."

"No *good*? Why?"

"He must be devoid of imagination; therefore he's no good. Nobody would do anything so foolhardy if he had a mind worth paying attention to."

A Love for His Own

What drives advertising men to drink to the grave, gives them ulcers, sends them shrieking their neuroses out into the night, and makes a bad joke of many of the procedures of Madison Avenue, is very simple—so many of them devote their professional lives to pushing products which they despise, do not believe in, or regard with cynical indifference. They are hucksters. This, as I mentioned in the first chapter of this book, is something that Albert Lasker never was. On the contrary, his devotion to the articles he advertised was unmitigated—almost an obsession. Hill was a maniac about Lucky Strikes; but Lasker was a maniac about *all* his products. So it was natural that he should make a point of using them religiously and conspicuously.

In fact, everybody in the Lasker establishment, not just the master, was obliged to use Lord & Thomas goods, at least in theory. To do otherwise was treason. All hands at Burton Place, Glencoe, and the Lord & Thomas offices in the Wrigley Building (later the Palmolive Building), and subsequently in New York, Miami, and Lake Forest, were supposed to smoke Lucky Strikes, use Pepsodent, and buy Cities Service gas. They had to listen to RCA radios, travel on the New York Central (*never* the Pennsylvania!), drink Schenley whisky, go to RKO movies, buy Armour meat, ride on Goodyear tires, use Chanel perfume, and even eat Quaker Oats for breakfast. One morning Lasker came across a new employee smoking a Chesterfield. He did not fire the wretched miscreant at once, but fixed him with his eye and uttered the icy warning, "Mr. Smith, I presume your *wife*, hunh, has an independent income!"

Chapter 11

MORE CHICAGO DAYS

Now Lasker, approaching fifty, became a grand seigneur—but in his own special way. He bought a property a few miles west of Lake Forest, Illinois, the most luxurious of the Chicago suburbs, in the mid-1920's, and built a sumptuous house there. His property at Glencoe compared to this as a postage stamp compares to a really big Rubens. The Lake Forest place, called Mill Road Farm, and as a rule referred to by the family simply as "the Farm," covered 480 acres, contained 27 buildings, and cost $3,500,000, which was a pretty penny to spend on a property, no matter how elaborate, even in the 1920's when dollars were really dollars, and the businessman was king.

Lasker's estate was probably the most impressive place of its kind in the United States between the Atlantic Seaboard and California; once it was aptly characterized as an "American Chantilly." On the other hand, it was not overtly palatial; it was a comfortable country house rather than a full-dress château, with the emphasis on simplicity and ease rather than formality. Flora had a good deal to do with the decoration, and did it with her accustomed expert and unpretentious taste.

The main structure, designed by the architect David Adler, was in the style of a seventeenth-century French provincial manor house; wide white gates, swinging on square pillars, led to a spacious courtyard, and the fifty-room house itself rose behind a screen of greenery. About 250 acres, more than half the total, were landscaped. Both the architecture and the landscaping were perfectly proportioned in a design far in advance of the time, and the gardens, covering ninety-seven acres, were superb. Lasker himself did not know (at this period) the difference between a tulip and a begonia, but he had people serving him who did. Flora superintended much of the planting. There were six *miles* of clipped hedges, trees planted symmetrically in careful relation to the landscape, acres of grass manicured to the roots, a frostproof "snow-blooming" chrysanthemum that became the special glory of the annual chrysanthemum show in the fall, and a topiary garden of Chinese dwarf elms such as had never been seen in the Middle West before. The greenhouses were, to understate the case, well stocked. Norman K. Winston, the real estate magnate who was a friend of Lasker's, testifies, "For twenty-five years I have never tasted a grape without thinking of Albert's greenhouses. He grew a special variety of Belgian grape; I can still smell them." Another curiosity was a particularly succulent variety of nectarine.

The swimming pool measured 100 feet by 40, and rested placidly at the end of a landscaped vista; the guest house, decorated by Flora, was done in early American, and near it were a twelve-car garage and a theater. This was Lasker's special pride, and held fifty people; each seat was in the form of a large armchair. Private theaters of this type are commonplace today, but were a luxurious novelty then. Jokingly, Lasker said that he built it so that nobody could object if, in the middle of a movie, he cried out at the villain, or yelled encouragement to a harassed hero.

Also on the estate were a barbecue pit, a sundial with fifty-seven faces which told the time in fifty-seven cities, a herd of prize Guernseys, an ice-cream soda fountain (adjacent to the swimming pool), chicken houses, stables, and a paddock. The principal buildings in the establishment, including the guest house and the theater, were air-conditioned, which was also something unusual for the day.

The most unusual feature of this enticing establishment was, however, its private eighteen-hole golf course, one of the few private courses in America at this time. It cost $1,000,000, and Bobby Jones, no less, said that it was one of the three best courses in the United States of any kind. It was, first of all, delicious to the eye. The fairways, a combination of Kentucky bluegrass, redtop, and fescue, shone and sparkled, and were green as parrots; the greens, made of a grass known as "Virginia bent," made velvet seem coarse; the traps were landscaped with a consummate eye for the aesthetic. More than fifty experimental greens were built, with grasses from all over the world, before a final choice of grass was made; if, in spite of incessant care, a patch of brown ever showed on a green, this was at once sprayed with a bright green dye.

Second, the course was fascinatingly difficult. But it was an honest course—tough, yes, but not tricky. Par was 70. The best pros and amateurs in the nation tried to break 70 time and again, without success. Finally Lasker posted a prize ($500) to go to any golfer who did do it in 70, playing from the back tees, with the qualification that no pro could try more than three times a year; not till 1934 was the feat achieved, when Tommy Armour, the winner of the U.S. Open in 1927, shot a 69. He took forty minutes to play the last hole. Lasker himself, if he were at the top of his game, generally did between 95 and 120. This golf course was so remarkable, and it has become so firmly embedded in American golfing history, that the temptation is considerable to write more about it. Lasker had to build it twice. A perfectionist always, he wanted it to be exactly right, and the first effort produced by his golf architects was a course (around 7,100 yards) that was *too* difficult. The traps and bunkers were made easier (by a shade) in the second effort, and the length reduced to 6,557 yards.[1]

To maintain the farm Lasker had to have a substantial staff; it numbered no less than fifty, including the gardeners and golf course attendants. One of these, armed with a twenty-foot bamboo pole, had as his chief duty the task of *brushing* the dew back into the bent

---

[1] The problem of traps perplexed Lasker mightily. He was still exuberantly interested in making golf a universal game for the populace at large, and his friend Charles G. Dawes suggested that he might take a step in this direction by eliminating sand traps and substituting something else on his own course. Dawes's point was that a man had to have extra clubs to play difficult sand traps, which made the game more expensive, and that if Albert took the lead in getting rid of sand other courses would follow. But in the end he did not do so.

grass each morning; this kept it from being waterlogged. Some of the help slept in dormitories; some commuted back and forth to the nearby village of Highwood in buses which Lasker provided. He was the largest employer of labor in the Lake Forest area. What his labor bill must have been can be imagined. When he was asked one day how he could run such an establishment so smoothly, his reply was, "It's simple. You have a good steward and a good butler, and it's *their* problem." When he hired a new butler he would say straight off, "You need keep only one thing in mind—be prepared to handle ten guests or two hundred for dinner, on an hour's notice." His general manager, who rendered him matchless service, was C. A. Tregillus, a British agronomist who had spent a lifetime studying grass in Canada. The quality of Mr. Tregillus may be judged by the fact that, years afterward, he became manager of the installation on Stagg Field, at the University of Chicago, where the first nuclear chain reaction in history occurred.

Lasker, learning from Tregillus, became an expert not only on grass but also on trees and shrubbery. One of his sons-in-law asked him years later for advice about trees for a small garden he was setting up. Albert replied cheerfully, "You've come to the right man. In my life I have bought more than a million trees."

Lasker entertained widely on the farm, and people poured in upon him. The Vice President of the United States, Mr. Curtis, was a frequent guest; so were the New York merchant, Bernard Gimbel, and John D. Hertz, the taxicab tycoon; so were athletes like Gene Tunney, who had just retired as heavyweight champion of the world (boxing), and Gene Sarazen, the American Open champion (golf) in 1922 and 1932. Lasker loved having athletes around. One favorite guest was Governor Cox. No other Democrats—literally—were allowed. Once a year, in June or July, a house party was held which would last four or five days. These, like the cruise on the *Leviathan,* were stag affairs; Flora and the women of the household retired into Chicago; the farm took on the atmosphere of a kasbah in Morocco, with females excluded or invisible. Business talk was, in general, taboo during these festivals; guests played golf during the day, and went to the movies (a first-run double feature started at 8:30 every evening) or played poker or bridge at night. At dinner, members of the company took turns making short informative speeches; in particular Lasker liked Cox to speak. The guests at one of these weekends early in the thirties made an interesting mixed bag: Theodore Roosevelt, the son of the old Colonel; John N. Wheeler of the North American Newspaper Alliance; Grantland Rice, the sports writer; Joseph C. Grew, a career diplomat who later became United States Ambassador to Japan; W. Alton Jones, the head of Cities Service; Clarence Budington Kelland, author and political zealot; the cartoonist Rube Goldberg; several NBC executives; and a silvering of Chicago fat cats and men of affairs.

About this time Lasker met John Golden, the theatrical producer. They took to one another immediately, and Golden cried out, "Let's not waste ten years. Let's be *best* friends at once!" No approach could have been better calculated to please Albert. For years, they loved to play jokes on one another. Once, in the middle of a golf game, Lasker was suddenly called away. "Play for me," he asked Golden, "one ball for you, one ball for me." Golden telegraphed him that evening. "You played very badly, and owe me $270."

Lasker never begrudged a cent of what Mill Road Farm cost him. Expenditure so grandiose on what was, after all, no more than a place to live in and play in may seem grotesque today, or even obnoxious (some years later, he came to think so too); but it must be measured against the spirit of the time. Anyway, thousands of hours of planning and limitless love went into the project, and it served a useful purpose. Finally, as a matter of fact, the house cost him comparatively little in actual outlay; he had bought a large amount of RCA stock, which rose fantastically and paid for most of the Lake Forest investment.[2]

This, we should remember, was still the age of the nabobs. Not only were plutocrats respected—they were vociferously admired.

2 Radio rose from 94½ on March 3, 1928, to 505 on September 3, 1929, and later reached 549. Back in 1923 it had been 25. Frederick Lewis Allen, *Only Yesterday*, pp. 166 and 318.

Photo: Dorothy Wilding

Albert D. Lasker

Nettie Davis Lasker

Morris Lasker

Albert D. Lasker
at the age of three

The Morris Lasker residence in Galveston, Texas

D. M. Lord

A. L. Thomas

Claude Hopkins

John E. Kennedy

Flora Lasker

The house at Mill Road Farm, Lake Forest, Illinois

Some of the gardens

Photo: *Walter Sanders*

The topiary garden at Mill Road Farm

Gardener brushing dew
off the grass

Albert D. Lasker as a young man

Doris Kenyon

Photo: Daniel Berns

Albert D. Lasker with George Washington Hill

Albert D. Lasker and John Golden

Photo: Ann Rosener

Frances Lasker Brody with her husband, Sidney Brody,
and their children, Susan and Christopher

Mary Lasker Block
dancing with her father

Photo: Harcourt-Harris

Photo: Cecil Beaton

Mary Lasker

Mary and Albert D. Lasker

Albert D. Lasker and his son Edward

Let this Machine do your Washing Free.

Here are Motor Springs beneath the tub.

These springs do nearly all the hard work, when once you start them going. And this washing machine works as easy as a bicycle wheel does.

There are slats on the inside bottom of the tub. These slats act as paddles, to swing the water in the same direction you revolve the tub.

You throw the soiled clothes into the tub first. Then you throw enough water over the clothes to flow....

twenty garments, or five large bed-sheets, can be washed at one time with this "1900" Washer.

A child can do this in six to twelve minutes better than any able washer-woman could do the same clothes in TWICE the time, with three times the wear and tear from the washboard. [Continued.]

This is what we SAY, now how do we PROVE it? We send.... ....you....

Courtesy, *Advertising Age*

Are You Chained To The Wash Tub

Whether a housekeeper does her own washing or not, the worry and work connected with "Blue Monday" literally chain her to the Wash Tub. *We can sever the chain.* Let us send you the

"1900" Ball Bearing Family Washer

FREE TRIAL Freight prepaid. No money or promise of any kind is required. Use it for 30 days; then if you do not wish to purchase return it at our expense. We pay the Freight both ways. Unlike all other washers, the "1900" sends the water through the clothes and washes them absolutely clean in six minutes with no wear or tear on the garments or the operator. Perfectly adjusted Ball-Bearings do the same for it as for the bicycle—make it work with little effort. IT IS ABSOLUTELY FREE TO YOU FOR THIRTY DAYS Write to-day for full information and Free Catalogue.

"1900" Washer Co., 22 Henry St., Binghamton, N. Y.

Courtesy, *Advertising Age*

On left a 1900 ad and which did not sell washing machines and, right, the first of a series of successful ads in the Kennedy-Lasker campaign for the same washer.

When the Telephone has a Bad Breath

THAT'S the time to take a Cascaret.
—When your Tongue is coated—
—When you have Heartburn, Belching, Acid Risings in Throat.
—When Pimples begin to peep out.
—When your Stomach Gnaws and Burns.
—That's the time to check coming Constipation, Indigestion and Dyspepsia.

One single Candy Cascaret will do it, if taken at the right minute, just when you first feel the need of it.

A "Cascaret in time is worth 'nine'" later on.

Cascarets don't Purge, nor Weaken, nor waste Digestive Juices in flooding out the Bowels, like Salts, Castor Oil, Cathartics.

But,—they act like Exercise on the Muscles that shrink and expand the Intestines, thus pushing the Food on naturally to its Finish.

The little thin, flat, Ten Cent Box is for your Vest Pocket or "My Lady's" Purse. Carry it constantly, like your Watch.

Warranted to Cure
—Constipation
—Indigestion
or Money Refunded

They act like Exercise.

Cascarets
-for the Bowels

10¢   10¢   10¢ &z

This Cascarets ad emphasizes Mr. Lasker's insistence that "art" should be simple and not distract from the sales message.

You Hear!
when you use
Wilson's Common Ear Drums
sense

The only scientific sound conductors. Invisible, comfortable, efficient. They fit in the ear. Doctors recommend them. Thousands testify to their perfection and to benefit derived.

Information and book of letters from many users, free

WILSON EAR DRUM CO.

103 Trust Building   Louisville, Ky.

Wilson Ear Drum ad shortly after the turn of the century features "the deafest deaf man you ever saw."

The WINTON *of* 1905.

Model C (Shown Above) . . . . 16—20 Horse-power . . $1800
Model B . . . . 24—30 Horse-power . . $2500
Model A . . . . 40—50 Horse-power . . $3500
Model A, SPECIAL, same as Model A, but with
                    Special Limousine Body, ... $4500

EASIEST controlled car in existence! Can be run by a Youth, after one hour's coaching. Automatic "Fool-proof" Motor. Does its own work infallibly, without "tinkering" or adjusting.

Four upright cylinders, fed by one single Gas-mixer (Carburetor), and fired by one single Magneto (Electric Sparker).

Simplest and best system we ever used. No Dry Cell Batteries. No Storage Battery. No Multiple Vibrator Coils. No Irregular Ignition. No Gauges to Watch. No Lever-moving necessary, to vary speed in regular running.

No getting under seats, nor craning below car, to inspect or repair working parts.

Motor instantly accessible, by merely lifting hinged top of hood, which is forward of dashboard. Crank-shaft, Connecting Rods and Pistons, exposed by turning a hand screw.

Transmission Gear exposed, in five seconds, by simply lifting one board, under driver's foot, turning a handle, and lifting off cover of Aluminum Casing.

New patented Steering Gear.

No "worm" to wear into "lost motion," nor to wedge, (when worn) in dangerous places.

Safest, surest, simplest Speed-control.

All speeds, graduating from 4 miles an hour, to 40 miles an hour, available by merely pressing right foot on pedal.

The $1,800 Winton is shown in above picture. Same Power as last years' $2,500 Winton, but lighter Car.

Note it's dashing Style,—it's long, graceful, lines, and its sidedoor entrance.

Note its new patented Twin Springs, that adjust themselves automatically to light or heavy loads, adding ease to the Car, protection to Motor, and longer Life to the Tires.

Write today for Catalog, and book on *How to Choose an Automobile.*

Address The Winton Motor Carriage Co., Dept. C., Cleveland, Ohio.

Courtesy, Advertising Age

An example of "real advertising" showing that even in 1905 Lord & Thomas was not mincing words

Wealth was not merely the indispensable index of prestige and power; it was the moral equivalent of righteousness, and to have money proved not only that a man was successful but also that he must be a pillar of the community. Lasker wasn't particularly interested in money as such any longer, but recognized that it was the easiest way to measure success. Once, in a discussion with a stuffy client whose judgments about advertising were often faulty, he stopped the talk abruptly with the words, "Mr. Blank, how much money have you?" The reply being given, Albert responded perfectly seriously, "I have twice that much, *so I must be right.*" No longer did he win clients by telling them the story of his life. He would say instead, "Come to Lord & Thomas, and I will make you *rich!*"

*

Lasker and John D. Hertz, the creator of Yellow Cab, the Hertz Rent-a-Car system, and much else, who had become friends some years before, were by this time almost inseparable. Hertz had an estate at Cary, Illinois, not far from Mill Road Farm. Lasker and Hertz were so close that they even had a joint stock account, on which either could give orders for both. They were in and out of one another's houses all the time, and Hertz, reminiscing about Albert, says with nostalgic emotion, "We lived together for twenty years." Also he was extremely fond of Edward Lasker, and Edward warmly reciprocated this feeling. Edward was about seventeen now. He was crazy about horses, as he still is. Hertz was a big figure on the turf; his Anita Peabody was the best two-year-old filly of 1927, and his celebrated Reigh Count won the Kentucky Derby in 1928. Edward, who was at Exeter and who had a marked will of his own, loved to play around the Hertz stables during the holidays, and his father bought him several of Hertz's brood mares.

This was partly because he wanted to tempt Edward to spend more time in Lake Forest. He felt that his son might be growing away from him, although Edward loved and admired him profoundly.

One revealing point is that, during all the years that Edward was
away at school and later, Albert wrote him a letter *every* business
day. He also wrote Flora without fail every day if they were separated, even when a rift came between them in the twenties.

Hertz was a quite different type from Lasker. Born in Czechoslo-
vakia, Hertz worked as a newspaper reporter in Chicago, and became a prize fight manager. In 1915 he founded the Yellow Cab
Company. The taxicab business was, in the Chicago of those days,
full of thugs and gangsters and very rough. Hertz did not do things
with a limp hand. But he fascinated Lasker, because he had vision,
magnetism, and a miraculously good eye for money.

Hertz bought a house on Miami Beach, which was just beginning
to be developed, in the 1920's, and persuaded Lasker to join him
there. Lasker bought 200 feet of ocean frontage at 4925 Collins
Avenue next door to Hertz, and proceeded to build. From this time
on, he spent most of each winter in Florida; he and Hertz were
known as the "Miamese Twins."

One of Hertz's associates and a close friend of Lasker's, Charles
A. McCulloch, the president of the Parmalee Company in Chicago,
a transportation agency, also had a house on Miami Beach. Florida
was suddenly invaded by gangsters, members of the Chicago mob
run by Al Capone; one of these, the notorious "Machine Gun Jack"
McGurn, bought a house in Miami for Capone. This was too much
for Lasker and other law-abiding, upright citizens, and they rose
in outrage. They could do nothing against Capone and his brood
in Chicago, but Florida was something else again, a holiday spot
not yet polluted, and where gangsters might be kept out if decisive
action were taken. So Lasker sent a blazing telegram to the Chief of
Police in Chicago, and signed it with Hertz's name, also McCulloch's,
as well as his own, demanding that he take steps to extradite McGurn
back to Illinois. Hertz and McCulloch, away on a fishing trip, did
not know what had happened until they saw the headlines. They
were terrified. They were convinced that Capone would take revenge
on them. Capone was in a position to do a lot to the taxicab business.
Capone, however, behaved in a most gentlemanly manner. *He* com-

municated with the Chicago Chief of Police, forgiving Hertz and Lasker magnanimously for their intervention in his affairs, and instructing the *police* to pass word down to Florida that Hertz, McCulloch, and Lasker, when they returned to Chicago, would not be harmed. Such was public morality in Chicago in the 1920's.

After many years of friendship Lasker and Hertz fell out, and never patched up their differences. Albert left Florida eventually, and sold the Miami Beach house contemptuously for a song.

University of Chicago, Philanthropy, and the Crash

In the 1920's Lasker became interested in the University of Chicago, and in 1928 gave it a million dollars, a large sum for the time, in his name and Flora's to set up the Lasker Foundation for Medical Research; this was to further research in the causes, nature, prevention, and cure of degenerative diseases, those which strike people in old age. He followed this the next year with a gift of $125,000 (Julius Rosenwald and Max Epstein, an outstanding Chicago industrialist, gave similar sums) for corollary studies at clinics associated with the University.

In 1929 Robert M. Hutchins, the boy wonder of Yale, became president of the University of Chicago, one of the foremost institutions of learning in the world, at the age of thirty; before this, he had been dean of the Yale Law School at twenty-eight. Hutchins, like Lasker, was vigorous, enlivening, and an original. The two men took to one another at once, and spent a dozen years in warm association, although their temperaments differed totally and although Hutchins was much younger. Hutchins was certainly a far cry from Hertz. Lasker was always notable for the catholicity of his friendships. Hutchins found A.D. both stimulating and refreshing. Reminiscing affectionately about him today, he compares him to Old Faithful, the geyser in Yellowstone National Park; he was like some bizarre and overwhelming, but predictable, force of nature.

Hutchins had then, and still has, the habit of getting up every morning at 5:30 A.M., and he liked to go to bed early at night. Sleep was, however, difficult for him if Lasker was in a conversational mood, because the older man would call him at all hours of the night, posing innumerable questions and soliciting advice. Once a call came from New Haven; Lasker was visiting Edward, who had entered Yale. Hutchins picked up the phone sleepily, and heard Albert's impassioned voice asking, without preface or explanation, "Should Edward have polo ponies?" Hutchins replied, "Certainly!" and rang off.

*

Lasker's views on philanthropy were, at this time, mildly eccentric. One rule, although it was not applied rigorously, was never to give money to anybody who asked for it. His theory was that, if an organization appealed for funds, it was certain to find donors if it was worthy enough; more interesting was the adventure of giving to organizations relatively unknown. Another theory had to do with "seed money"; he liked to give to a cause if this would, in turn, entice other people to give more. He was willing to be the spark plug, but not the engine. One of his early gifts—they were scattered in those days—was a $50,000 grant to the Hebrew Union College; another was a contribution to the Youth Aliyah Fund of Hadassah, the women's Zionist organization.

Lasker was now a member or director of the American Jewish Committee, the American Council of Christians and Jews, the Associated Jewish Charities of Chicago, the Mobilization for Human Needs Committee, and the Anti-Defamation League, and was generally regarded as the most effective money-raiser for charitable drives in Chicago. One day, however, he came a cropper. He and Philip D. Block, the head of the Inland Steel Company and a close friend, took a day off from business to solicit funds for a Jewish charity. They approached a prosperous banker, who had already made one contribution, but who refused to add to it. He would not give an additional cent. Lasker, the supersalesman, said quietly, "Of course, Mr. Cohen, you certainly do not owe it to us to give money just because we call on you, but, after all, we are busy men, and if it's important enough for us to take a day off from our businesses just in order to see you, surely you have the duty to give us a *reason* for your refusal."

Mr. Cohen replied, "The reason is that I don't like mince pie."

"What kind of a reason is that?" asked Lasker, astonished.

Mr. Cohen said, "Listen, Lasker, if you don't want to do a thing one reason is as good as any other."

Mince pie promptly entered the family folklore.

In the autumn of 1929 came Black Tuesday and the great Wall Street crash. First Lasker thought that "business was just taking a little rest." Then unemployment increased, suffering spread swiftly, and the depression got fully under way. Albert himself was not much hurt by the crash—at first. This was largely because John Hertz, with stunning intuition, guessed what was going to happen and sold some of their holdings just before the market collapsed. He was in the nick of time. Lasker, in truth, did not want to sell; Hertz overrode him and in fact went to his comptroller in the Lord & Thomas offices and arranged to liquidate some of his holdings without even letting him know. But, even though Lasker escaped at this time, a round dozen of his closest friends came near to being wiped out. He did his best to rescue them, and in all, before the depression ran its course, lent three *million* dollars to friends to help bail them out—hardly a cent of which he ever got back.

As the depression spread remorselessly A.D. plunged into emergency relief work for the community at large, and this had the incidental effect of enlarging considerably his field of social vision. In early 1931 federal aid to the unemployed had not yet come into force, and a good many rich Chicagoans gave generously, if only because they thought that, by so doing, they might stave off the "embarrassment" of federal aid. Lasker organized a special gifts committee for relief, with Hutchins as chairman; he himself gave $50,000, and got ten of his wealthy friends to give $100,000 each—a big sum, but still a drop in the bucket compared to the total civic need. A little later he gave $300,000 (and the Pepsodent Company $100,000) for further aid, and became head of a citizens' committee to raise

$1,695,000 for 75,000 destitute Jews. The New Deal was, of course, anathema to him at this time. But presently it became clear to him that the broadest possible federal intervention, not merely to avert disaster but to reconstruct the entire economy of the nation, was not only inevitable, an absolute necessity, in order to save the country, but might be a good thing to boot. Before many years passed he progressed further, and at the end of his life there was no more fervent advocate of government controls where they were necessary than Albert D. Lasker, the onetime anarchic individualist and soloist tycoon.

Some of the Partridges thought that, because of the misery all around them, they should suspend their poker games.

Lasker: "Certainly not. But from now on ten-dollar chips are five cents."

In 1931 the great Foreman Bank in Chicago got into severe difficulties. Lasker was intimately connected with this institution; several members of the Foreman family were his cronies, he had $2,000,000 on deposit there, and, above all, his daughter Mary had married Gerhard Foreman, a youthful member of the clan, in 1927.[3] This was a very good match. Albert was enormously fond of young Foreman, and proud as could be of him. Now it appeared that the Foreman Bank, caught in the devouring suction of the depression, was in such critical shape that it would go under. To help save it, Lasker made his whole $2,000,000 account available to the family; the attempt at salvage failed, and he lost every nickel of the two million. He had other losses too, as the market continued to collapse. His attitude varied between stormy indignation and philosophic calm. Walking down Park Avenue one morning with Edward, he muttered, "I'm seventeen million dollars poorer than two years ago." Edward looked startled, and his father grunted amiably, "But I don't feel any different!"

Lasker, Hertz, McCulloch, and William Wrigley, Jr., were all directors of Foreman. If this bank should close its doors (it was the third largest in the city) thousands of men and women would

[3] Lasker's wedding present to them was the Glencoe house.

be ruined and there would certainly be a panic in Chicago, and perhaps throughout the nation. At the last minute it was taken over by the First National Bank of Chicago and catastrophe was averted. The directors of the First National attempted to drive what seemed to Lasker to be an unnecessarily hard bargain during the eleventh-hour negotiations. He said grimly, with his wonderful gift of reaching down to raw fundamentals and expressing them to his own advantage, "Very well, gentlemen. You can force us to close the Foreman Bank tomorrow morning, but that will make a run on every other bank in Illinois. *We* will be out of the banking business, but you will still be in it!" This was hard talk. Also it made sense, and First National modified its terms and absorbed the Foreman Bank. Stockholders like Lasker lost everything, but no Foreman depositor lost a cent. Lasker then became a director of First National, and had a cordial relationship with it for many years.

Once More an Old Subject

Lasker, it seems, was more sensitive about Jewishness during this period than at any time in his life. The atmosphere of Chicago, heavily spotted with anti-Semitism, contributed profoundly to this. His Jewishness was one reason why Albert—particularly in the environment of North Shore Chicago—found it agreeable to be rich. Only by wealth could he establish standing. Also, a curious item, he had been blackballed by a *Jewish* club, one of the downtown businessmen's clubs, and this wounded him a good deal; but it had the paradoxical effect of making him more Jewish than before. Jews could do no wrong, even if they did wrong to him! Meantime, being a proud Jew, he continued to loathe apostate Jews and, above all, those whom he called "scared" or "ashamed" Jews. Once, in later years, he told one of his sons-in-law good-humoredly, "The trouble with you is that you are not Jewish *enough!*"

Once at a Lord & Thomas conference some figures were being discussed. Grabbing a balance sheet and working out details in his head instantly, Lasker said that one figure must be wrong—a percentage that was given as 19 per cent of something should be 21. His accountant remonstrated, "No, Mr. Lasker, 19 per cent is correct." A.D.'s eyes almost popped out of his head with wrath. "Mr. Williams," he intoned, "*I* have been calculating percentages for two thousand years!"

Lasker never attended services in a temple, but he sent a substantial contribution to one of the leading synagogues in Chicago every year, and was a good friend of its rabbi. The rabbi came to see him one day, saying, "You are my most generous supporter. But rather than have any more gifts from you I would like to have you come to our services, and be a member of our congregation." Lasker said No. The rabbi persisted, with the words that, if he attended services, it would vastly increase the prestige of the synagogue and make it easier for him, the rabbi, to do a better job—an argument which he thought would appeal to him. Again Lasker refused, and the rabbi asked him why. Albert answered with benevolence, "I don't want any middleman between myself and God."

His daughter Mary asked him once, "What is my religion, father?" He replied in the accents of his own father, "Your religion is to be able to say to yourself, at the close of every day, as if God were listening and watching you, 'I have done nothing wrong today, nothing of which to be ashamed.' "

Two Rosenwald Anecdotes

The most distinguished Jewish citizen of Chicago in this period was Julius Rosenwald, the philanthropist and head of Sears Roebuck. Lasker was second; but Rosenwald was first. He was twenty, thirty, forty times richer than Lasker. He lived in Highland Park nearby, and Lasker, in a large and imposing automobile, came upon him one day on a narrow lane driving an old Ford runabout. Lasker said amiably, "Mr. Rosenwald, it's a disgrace for a man in your position to drive so small a car." Rosenwald, who was fond of him, replied dryly, "I can afford to drive this kind of car."

In these days Lasker kept an apartment in New York, at the

Ritz, and perpetually commuted between Chicago and New York; he practically lived on the Twentieth Century Limited. Traveling back and forth, he affected a certain style; he had, of course, a drawing room on the train, and Flora another; other quarters usually held his valet, a maid, and Ralph Sollitt. On one trip Rosenwald happened to be on the same train in much less commodious space. Lasker smiled jokingly, "Mr. Rosenwald, can I put you up?" He disapproved of men who had worked hard for money being too hard on themselves. But Rosenwald wouldn't budge.

Politics; Aviation; More Anecdotes

The 1932 presidential campaign (Hoover-Curtis versus Roosevelt-Garner) came along presently; it interested Lasker, but he played little role in it. For political advice he still leaned heavily on Cox, who, although Roosevelt had run with him in 1920, was now bitterly anti-Roosevelt; Lasker, when asked about F.D.R.'s chances in 1932, answered, "He has about as much chance of getting nominated as Bernie Gimbel has of becoming Pope." Then after the nomination, gritting his teeth at his mistake, he began to take Roosevelt very seriously indeed. Hoover invited him to Rapidan, the President's fishing camp, during the campaign, and asked him for advice on publicity; Lasker said that he would be delighted to help but must, as he did with all his clients, tell the truth bluntly as he saw it. Hoover asked him what he meant and he replied, "You haven't got a dog's chance of getting elected." This time he was right, and this was the last he saw of Hoover for some little time.[4]

In 1936 (Roosevelt-Wallace versus Landon-Knox) Lasker was much more active, largely because he had a new political hero now —Frank Knox. Knox, a ruddy-faced extrovert with teeth which literally snapped when he talked, and who played golf with blunt fury, had become publisher of the Chicago *Daily News,* and was one of Lasker's intimates. Lasker, assisted by Colonel William J.

---

[4] As to F.D.R., Lasker never met him until 1937 in circumstances to be recounted later.

("Wild Bill") Donovan, played a considerable role in getting Knox the vice presidential nomination, and then managed his campaign. He was also, of course, a leading member of the Illinois delegation at the convention. After the nominations Lasker called a meeting of a dozen Republican bigwigs, and asked for money to support Landon-Knox. He said, in his most winning impresario manner, "I am putting up $50,000. I will judge whether you are better or worse off than I am by what you put in." The only man to give more was Colonel Robert R. McCormick of the Chicago *Tribune,* but in half an hour the meeting produced $600,000. So were campaign funds raised in those happy days, before the Hatch Act limited contributions to a miserable $5,000.

*

About this time Lasker became much interested in aviation. He had not quite acknowledged the existence of airplanes before; they were not for him, and hence not real. His attitude underwent transformation, characteristically enough, by reason of something personal, which dramatized the fact that men really could fly. Merrill C. Meigs, who had worked for him before the war and who was now an important Chicago publisher, had his own airplane, a single-engine Stinson, and flew it everywhere. One of Lasker's executives in this era was the late Steve Hannagan, whose exploits in public relations are well known. Meigs happened to run into Hannagan in Detroit one day, and discovered that he had just missed a train and was late for an urgent appointment with Lasker in Lake Forest. So Meigs volunteered to fly him there. Without warning, he landed the Stinson on Lasker's fairway near the sixth green, fifty feet from the house, and he and Hannagan climbed out of the cockpit and walked in. Lasker was overwhelmed with amazement, curiosity, and delight.

Later, Meigs had flaps and adjustable propellers put on his plane, so that he could put it down in any small place in a hurry, and sometimes, as a stunt, he would take up a party of fellow golfers and play three holes on each of six courses in Chicago on the same afternoon, flying from course to course. Mill Road Farm was the usual take-off point, and Lasker thought that this was the most exhilarating thing he had ever heard of in his life.[5]

One day in the mid-thirties Lasker called on Charles G. Dawes, who pointed proudly to a newspaper cartoon which he had framed and put on his office wall; this portrayed him as a circus rider handling four horses at once, under the headline, "How Can a Man Ride Them All?" Dawes was, at the time, president of a large corporation, head of the Chicago World's Fair, president of an important bank, and had other big jobs as well. Lasker studied the cartoon with some care, noted the headline, and turned to Dawes with the words, "No man can." Dawes was annoyed. A week or two later, the Dawes bank came close to failing, and had to be bailed out.

Meantime, Lasker gave up one of his most cherished and valuable accounts, Studebaker. The reason is piquant. Albert R. Erskine, the head of Studebaker and a pathological gambler, came to visit him in Florida, and the two men dropped in one evening at Bradley's, a celebrated Palm Beach gambling club of the day. Lasker did not feel like playing, but Erskine did. A.D. said, "Play for me. I'll put up half the stakes, and take half of what you win or share the loss fifty-fifty." An hour later he wandered into the gaming rooms and discovered that Erskine had lost $150,000. Lasker said, "I'm out. You're on your own now, win or lose." Back in Chicago he sent Erskine a check for $75,000 to cover his losses up to the moment he had intervened, and then abruptly canceled the Studebaker account—"resigned" it, in the jargon of the advertising trade. Lasker seldom took a holier-than-thou attitude, but Erskine's excesses made him apprehensive. He hated to be associated with failure of any kind, and he told his friends, "Any man who gambles like that will die broke, and I won't do business

---

[5] Meigs, at seventy-four, is still flying, and has done thousands of solo hours. He is (so far as records go) the only civilian pilot ever to be hit in flight by a jet who survived.

with him." As a matter of fact Erskine did go broke, and subsequently killed himself.

Flora and the Children

When Lasker was living in New York, years later, he became friendly with a lady of station who was having a good deal of trouble with her children; they were at a difficult age, and, with the best intentions in the world, she was spoiling them. Lasker watched this process for a while, and then protested. "Nobody," he told this good lady, "can *stand* as much love as you are giving those children. It makes them feel uncomfortable, and, worse, *guilty,* because they can't return as much love as you're giving them." He was speaking from experience. He had overwhelmed his own children with love, and in return yearned not merely for love from them, but for overt expressions of love, which children at a certain age are notoriously loath to give. Then, at times, he would go to the other extreme and be unexpectedly harsh.

Mary (before her marriage) had occasional difficulty in keeping beaux, because her father was so intimidating. He didn't mean to do so, but he scared suitors off. Mary protested about this when an extremely shy, well-brought-up young man was courting her. "*Please,* father," she begged, "be nice to Joe when he calls for me tomorrow night." Lasker determined to be on his very best behavior. He waited near the door. When the young man arrived, he threw his arms around him, stuffed a cigar in his mouth, and pushed him bodily indoors, booming such cries of welcome that the young man became even more frightened than before.

Mary was, and still is, a true chip off the old block; she has intensity, uncommon power of appreciation, a good hard business head, and the gift of heightening the sense of life in people. She was not at all afraid of her father; he subconsciously resented her habit of independence, and was often severe with her. She wanted to go to the Beaux Arts in Paris; but every Lasker woman had to go to Vassar these days, and to Vassar she duly went. Then she married Gerhard Foreman, and, as we shall see, put in a period of useful work later with Lord & Thomas. She and Foreman were divorced in 1942.

Edward in the middle 1930's was a tall handsome boy, sensitive as a spring, with his father's luminous dark eyes and a good deal of his temperament, including a capacity for defiance and unrest. Relations between father and son were not always smooth; Lasker took much hurt from him, and vice versa. Edward was graduated from Yale in 1933, got a job in London with the American Tobacco Company at £3 10s a week, and then returned to New York to fulfill his father's ardent dream and work for Lord & Thomas. He stayed with the company for eight years, mostly in the radio division of the New York office, but his heart was not in it. He was a restless as well as brilliant young man, and advertising bored him. In 1935 he married Caral Gimbel, the daughter of the Bernard Gimbels. Lasker père liked Caral, and became increasingly fond of her with the years, but he could not restrain a caustic little comment when he was informed of the engagement: "Never heard of getting a good omelet out of two spoiled eggs."

Francie, the youngest child, was particularly close to her father; he was extravagantly devoted to her, but could be firm as well. She had the habit, in her teens, of letting her eyes fill with tears when she was reproved. Albert said to her, "The blackmail of your tears does not touch me." This made a considerable impression on her, and she has rarely cried since. At about this time she had one beau (among many) who was persistent, and whom Lasker considered to be altogether unsatisfactory. At last, Francie broke off her relationship with this young man. "It is just as well," her father pronounced calmly. "I was going to give you enough money for a divorce as a wedding present."

Lasker saw no reason why his children should have to wait for his death before benefiting from his wealth. He did not want them to base their relations with him on the supposition that, in the future, they would be inheritors of his estate; he wanted them to establish their feeling about him absolutely without regard to the fact that they would gain by his death. He hoped, in a word, to be loved for love's sake alone, and one way to ensure this was to make all the children financially independent while he was still alive. So in December, 1931, and again early in 1932, he settled very large amounts on them—immediately before the new federal gift tax came into effect in May, 1932. Characteristically, he timed his benevolence to the moment.

*

Flora, often in ill health, would give way to irritation sometimes and nag Albert; one evening she tolled off petulantly some "mistakes" she thought he had made. He boiled over with sudden fury. He shouted, "Just a moment, Flora!" raced upstairs, and returned carrying with him an old blue suit, the oldest and shabbiest he could find in his wardrobe, and five ten-dollar bills. He brandished these at the astonished Flora, and then hurled them on the floor before her. Stamping with indignation and pointing to the suit and the fifty dollars, but now with an element of humor invading his voice, he intoned, "This, *this,* THIS, is all I started with!" Then he swung his arms around the room, pointing to examples of luxury and comfort visible in every nook and corner, and said, "Everything else we have is the result of my MISTAKES!"

Chapter 12

ZENITH

At about the time Lasker bought Mill Road Farm, in the middle 1920's, radio began to burst over the American scene as an overwhelming force. It was, of course, nothing new. David Sarnoff had worked out plans for "radio music boxes," to "bring music into the house by wireless," as far back as 1916, and Station KDKA in Pittsburgh (Westinghouse), the first broadcasting station in the country, was putting out regular programs by 1920. The first commercial broadcast for an advertiser came in 1922, over WEAF in New York (American Telegraph and Telephone Company), and the National Broadcasting Company, an offspring of RCA, was set up in 1926. The Columbia Broadcasting System began operations the next year.

But, obviously, radio was still in its infancy when Lasker became interested in it. Nobody knew that this magic instrument would soon transform the habits of a nation. Lasker was skeptical at first about its possibilities in advertising. He did not think people could take in advertising by ear. He was, however, close to Sarnoff, and he was much influenced by the fact that Bernard Gimbel seemed to be getting good results out of pioneer radio advertising. Lasker thought that he would experiment with a show or two. He said to Lou Hartman, in the Lord & Thomas office in New York, "You know what's going on, on Broadway—build up some kind of show for Palmolive." Hartman became a kind of one-man radio department, and, working with NBC closely, created an hour's musical entertainment for Palmolive, and then set up similar shows for RCA and Cities Service. Lasker was astounded by the response, and

Lord & Thomas, having put itself in the field first, placed nearly *half* of all national radio advertising on NBC in 1927-28.

The president of NBC at this time was Merlin H. Aylesworth. His theory was that there should be no formal, elaborate commercials; he wanted to introduce programs with some such simple statement as, "The following program comes to you through the courtesy of Lucky Strike," or whatever sponsor was involved. (The term "sponsor" had not yet been invented.) Lasker, still warily surveying this new arena, adopted quickly a diametrically opposite view. He foresaw how salesmanship in print could readily be expanded into a new dimension, salesmanship through space and by sound, and he insisted on full-dress, positive advertisements with the same "Reason Why" tone and spirit as those in newspapers and magazines. His view prevailed, and, for good or ill, the radio (and TV) commercial as we know it today was born. The torrent of dingy, vulgar, and obstreperous nonsense that has flooded most of the world ever since without intermission cannot be charged against Lasker because somebody else would have formulated the concept if he had not, but he was certainly a major actor in the origin of the process. In those days he was energetically proud of his contribution. He had devised a formidable new way of selling goods.

Next came Amos 'n' Andy. Lasker hired a man named Henry Salinger, who had been working for WGN, the Chicago *Tribune* station, as head of radio for Lord & Thomas. Salinger had on the air a pair of black-face comedians, Freeman Gosden and Charles Correll, who were known as Sam and Henry and who had a substantial local following. Salinger suggested that Lasker employ these two young men, and put them on the air for Pepsodent. Lasker was horrified. He thought that to advertise toothpaste, something applied to the mouth, by anybody with a black face, even if the black face was simulated, would be a disaster. But, in order not to discourage Salinger, he agreed to make a trial. WGN owned the name "Sam and Henry," and so, when Gosden and Correll duly came over to Lord & Thomas, it was necessary to rename the show.

Somebody thought up "Amos 'n' Andy," and the rest is history. Lasker did not invent the name himself. As usual he left such details to underlings on his staff. "Amos 'n' Andy" was the first big-time five-days-a-week show, and it knocked the country sideways. Its success was stupendous. Nothing like it has ever been known in American radio. Telephone calls throughout the nation dropped 50 per cent between 7 P.M. and 7:15, when Amos 'n' Andy were on the air, and movie theaters had "to stop their performances to pipe in the show."[1] Pepsodent sales tripled in a matter of weeks, and Lasker never had any doubt about the pulling power of radio thereafter.

Some years later Pepsodent sales began to fall off; Lasker sought to analyze the reasons, and came to the conclusion that the "Amos 'n' Andy" audience, which was almost tantamount to the population of the United States, consisted of three classes: (a) people who had already tried Pepsodent and were happily using it; (b) those who had tried it and did not use it; (c) stubborn incorrigibles who would never even try it. For the sake of his wounded honor as well as business, he proceeded to make a supreme, last-ditch effort to win over the latter two categories. Edward Lasker was now working in the radio department of Lord & Thomas in New York, and he came up with an idea, as his father flung himself about seeking inspiration. There was a comedian, Edward said, who had been a failure on several shows, but who was bright and who might do well if given another chance with better scripts. Lasker said to try him out for Pepsodent. His name: Bob Hope. So again history was made.

Meantime, the monstrous phenomenon known as the soap opera was born. Serial stories on the radio to amuse and captivate housewives were unknown until one of Lasker's men, Frank Hummert, developed them. The first major soap opera, "The Story of Mary Marlin," was originated for Kleenex, and was a fabulous success. For a time it had to be put on twice a day. It spawned hundreds

[1] *Time*, March 31, 1958. Gosden and Correll stayed with Lord & Thomas for a long period until, following a complicated deal, Lasker voluntarily released them and they went to a different sponsor. Recently they celebrated their thirtieth anniversary on the air.

—in fact thousands—of imitations, and the results are with us yet. Later "Mary Marlin" went to another sponsor, and Lord & Thomas turned out a profusion of substitutes.

Dozens of show-business people, little known then but nationally celebrated now, got their start with Lord & Thomas in these years, or, like Hope, were vastly improved in status. The list of Lasker discoveries is rich. One development was a staggering increase in the popularity of name bands, which became famous because they served Lucky Strike or other Lord & Thomas clients; this, in turn, gave a big boost to the talent agencies, like the Music Corporation of America, which had the job of providing the bands. There was a certain irony to all this as far as Lasker's active participation was concerned, because he was tone-deaf, and could not tell Paul Whiteman from Kay Kyser or "Dardanella" from "Silver Threads Among the Gold."

Agencies, like Lord & Thomas, played at that time more of a role in creating and assembling programs than they did later. Few programs were bought as a package. It was the job of the agency to make the package. Lord & Thomas, for instance, would get an idea for a show, find a man to write it, hire and pay the talent, order the necessary music, and, in short, act not only as agency but as producer. (Today, in TV, a strong trend has developed toward revival of this process.) Rehearsals were something of an adventure in the early Lasker days. For instance, B. A. Rolfe and his band went on the air every Saturday night for Lucky Strike. Each Saturday morning came a lot of commotion. The high brass of NBC, led by John Royal, together with George Washington Hill and his staff, Albert Lasker if he were in New York, and Edward Lasker, assembled in the studio. Hill insisted that members of this select group should, during the rehearsal, put the music to the test by dancing to it. Sedate executives were obliged to dance with secretaries, script girls, or whoever happened to be around, and the more extravagantly they performed, the better Hill was satisfied. He sometimes brought with him an old aunt, who was not quite,

but almost, deaf, and who kept time by beating with a pencil
on the back of a chair. For her to be able to hear at all the music
had to be abnormally loud. But if she stopped beating time at
any moment Hill would say that the program was no good, and
demand a change.

The late lamented "Information Please" was one of Lasker's
favorites; Lucky Strike was one of its first sponsors. Another im-
mensely successful show was "Mr. District Attorney" for Pepsodent.
"The Hit Parade" was an early Lord & Thomas invention, and
Judy Garland appeared on the "Bob Hope Show" for Pepsodent.
Bing Crosby got his first big audience in radio through Lord &
Thomas, and, later, Frank Sinatra was a star. "Lum & Abner" was
a Lasker show, as was "The Magic Carpet." Eddie Duchin, Hal
Kemp, Fred Astaire, Walter Winchell (in the very early days), Jack
Pearl, the Goldbergs, the Cavaliers, and the Revellers all had their
first national sponsorship through Lasker—an unprecedented record.

Lord & Thomas was the first agency to put on a daily radio
contest of national scope, the first to introduce a daily network
strip program, and the first to rebroadcast commercial programs, so
that West Coast listeners could hear what the East heard at the
same hour. It presented the first commercial broadcasts from the
Metropolitan Opera in New York, the first pick-ups of foreign dance
orchestras, the first "authentic" police and FBI dramatic shows,
the first chain sponsorship of football, and the first sustained commercial series of "spot" pick-ups, with performers brought in from
all over the country on the same name-band program. All of this—
naturally!—paid off, and Lord & Thomas had a new bonanza. Seemingly the only limitation on the size of the business was the amount
of energy Lasker was willing to give to it. In the first four years of
radio network operation, he purchased 30 per cent of all national
network time, an astonishing proportion. *All* other agencies in the
country, several thousand, shared the rest. In one peak year in the
1930's Lord & Thomas did an unprecedented $50,000,000 in total
billings, and resumed its position as the largest and most powerful
advertising agency in the world.

Frigidaire

One of the last great accounts to come to Lord & Thomas was Frigidaire, a division of General Motors and the biggest manufacturer of electric iceboxes in the world. A group of Frigidaire men, eager to impress Lasker, met him in conference and told him that they had spent $40,000 on research to be sure that they would appeal to women purchasers with the right "approach." Expensive research still made A.D. bristle. He glanced at the memorandum, slapped it down on the table, and said that he thought he could do better. Turning to his lieutenant, David Noyes, he commanded, "Send a stenographer, not a secretary, but a stenographer, to the Curtis Publishing Company office here, and have her look through all Frigidaire ads in the *Ladies' Home Journal* in the past ten years and have her write on a sheet of paper, just one sheet, a tabulation showing what the ads stressed most." The answer came—"Economy." Then occurred a second meeting with Frigidaire. Lasker announced that he had just spent $80, the cost of the stenographer's time, on research, not $40,000, and had everything he needed. He asked a single question, "What makes your icebox more economical than others?" The Frigidaire men replied, "We have a condenser, a compressor, which has only one moving part—it needs very little current." Lasker asked, "Have you ever mentioned this device in advertising?" "No," came the reply. Lasker had not lost his old Napoleonic magic. He turned to Noyes. "Name the device, and that will be the entire basis of our campaign."

The name chosen was Meter Miser (the man who invented it was not Noyes himself, but Ted Little, who later became head of a big advertising agency in Detroit), and a slogan was created to go with it—"CUTS CURRENT COSTS TO THE BONE." Lasker was delighted. He knew that almost all housewives resented public utility charges, and to emphasize that Frigidaire was a "miser" in respect to electricity bills was, he thought, a winning idea, which indeed it turned out to be.

In New York later A.D. took part in a staff conference discussing new advertising for Frigidaire. He glanced at the copy, sniffed, and, turning to Edward Lasker, at once launched into an interminably long anecdote. It had nothing to do with Frigidaire, housewives, advertising, Lord & Thomas, or, as far as anybody could gather, anything at all. But he kept right on. Nothing could stop him. Finally Edward, unable to restrain himself, asked, "May I interrupt, Father? What is the point of this story?" Lasker grinned. "That's just it. It has no point. Just like this copy here. It doesn't say anything, so throw it away and start over."[2]

Mary Foreman at Lord & Thomas

Mary Foreman, restless and feeling that she was not living up to her full capacity, wanted a job. When, however, she asked her father for a position with Lord & Thomas, he resisted her furiously. Edward was with the agency in New York, and to have two children in the business smacked too much, Lasker thought, of nepotism. Moreover, although he knew full well that Mary was a genuinely creative person, packed with energy and originality, he did not see quite how she would fit into Lord & Thomas. For months, he fought her off. Flora took Mary's side, and, to win Albert over, adopted a drastic technique; she woke her husband up several times in the course of every night, saying, "I won't let you sleep until you give Mary a job." Flora was still a most determined person.

Lasker summoned Mary at last. "Your mother won't let me sleep, so I have to submit to you." He added, "There is one requirement. Your handwriting is abominable. I won't give you a job until you go to school and learn to type." As a matter of fact, her handwriting was not abominable at all, but she went to a business college for

2 Frigidaire's general manager for many years was Elmer G. Biechler. The industrial designer Raymond Loewy, who was working on Frigidaire at the time, was witness to an encounter he has not forgotten. Lasker asked Biechler how many Frigidaires he would sell the next year, and the reply was, "Six hundred thousand." Lasker thought that this was too optimistic, and bet Biechler $10,000 that the figure would be less. Biechler won, and Lasker, torn between delight that business was so good and disappointment that his own judgment had been faulty enough to cost him $10,000, snorted once or twice and then dutifully paid up.

six months, and passed her examination with high marks. So, reluctantly, Lasker told her to report for work on Monday, and said that he would pay her $28 or $35 per week, whichever she preferred. Being given a choice of salary puzzled her, and her father explained. Years before he and Flora had a cook, who got $7 a week. She was a very good cook and the Laskers, fearing that they might lose her, raised her to $10. A few months later she quit. Indignant, Lasker asked her why, since she was getting such a mammoth wage. She replied, "Yes, I know that no other cooks get $10 a week, but it makes me nervous to live up to it!"

Lasker turned gravely to Mary, and said, frowning, "I don't want you to be in that position." He was quite serious. So she took $28 instead of $35.

On Monday morning she found her way to her office, which was a cubbyhole containing one chair, one desk, one typewriter, and no telephone. On the desk she found a longhand letter from her father, of which this is a paraphrase:

My Dear Mary—
    As you know you are starting work against my will. Nothing in your background warrants the opportunity I am giving you.
    May I therefore add that I have not assigned you to any specific job. You will have to make one for yourself. When you do, it will mean that you have proved yourself before the people in my organization.
    Our function is to be of service to others; nobody is here to serve you.
                                                    Your loving father,
                                                    Albert D. Lasker

For three months he did not speak to her.

He could not, however, resist some basic paternal impulses. One morning he burst out to Noyes, "What have you got against my daughter? Why isn't she getting ahead faster? Are you, hunh, *holding her back?*" Noyes was stupefied, since his orders had been to let her fend for herself.

Mary, as a matter of fact, made good quickly. The first thing she did was go up to the floor where the minor employees worked, saying, "I wish you would forget what my maiden name was, if you know. I want a right to be your equal. Give me a chance." Soon it became clear that, like her father, she had an exceptional eye for copy. She wrote the "Amos 'n' Andy" commercials, and was graduated to Kotex-Kleenex. Her immediate boss was Robert J. Koretz, one of the best copy writers of his day, who is now senior vice president of Foote, Cone, & Belding; at that time he was account executive for both Pepsodent and Kotex-Kleenex, and he taught her much. She worked on Frigidaire, Armour, Commonwealth Edison, and originated the idea for "The Hit Parade," which was first called "Lucky Strike Sweepstakes." Also, on her own, she brought in one big new account, Lady Esther (cosmetics), and at the end took over from Koretz as account executive for Pepsodent.

Mary stayed with Lord & Thomas for five and a half years, until 1938, when she was making $30,000 a year. Then came an office squabble. Lasker felt that, for reasons of office discipline, he had to support the executive with whom she was at odds, and, just like that, he fired her, loving her the while.

Another Gambling Episode

Lasker felt tired: his health was poor, and his doctors told him to give up business for a time. Holidaying in California, he played golf with a friend, the late Herbert Fleishhacker, a San Francisco civic leader and financier. They liked to play for high stakes—very high—and in one game Lasker lost $40,000. This shocked him a good deal, although he could amply afford the loss. But he had another typically Laskeresque reaction as well, that anybody who could lose that much money and not be prostrated must be fundamentally sound and so, cheerful, he prepared to go back to work.

Lasker instructed the art department of Lord & Thomas to prepare an elaborate engraved check, twenty inches by eight, which he duly put in the mails. No bank had ever seen a check of such stupendous dimensions before. After Fleishhacker cashed it several banks through which it passed wanted it as a souvenir, but, when it came back to Lasker, he had it framed and kept it on an office wall to remind himself that $40,000 was a lot of money to lose in an afternoon. He never gambled for high stakes again.

Farewell to Sollitt

Ralph V. Sollitt, the self-effacing factotum who was Lasker's indispensable right arm, and who had been elevated to the presidency of Lord & Thomas in 1931, decided to retire. He had never particularly liked advertising, and was tired of doing most of the dirty work. If Lasker decided to fire anybody, it was he who had to do the actual firing, and so on. Besides, he was utterly worn out.

But he did not know how to break the news to his chief. He was terrified. He fretted for weeks, and finally, in December, 1934, after talking the matter over with Will Hays, wrote Lasker a long letter announcing his determination to resign. Then, it took some days before he could nerve himself to deliver it. Silence. Lasker called him into his office at last, pointed inarticulately to the letter on the table, and then burst into tears. Sollitt, embarrassed, did not know what to do. A.D. simply stood there, with an arm on his shoulder, and kept on crying.

Finally Lasker said, "I refuse to talk about this now." Two or three days passed and he still said nothing. He then summoned a meeting of the senior staff, pulled Sollitt's letter out of his pocket, and said to him gruffly, without explanation to anybody, "Read this aloud." Half the letter consisted of declarations of his love for Lasker and heartbreak at leaving him.

Some Likes and Dislikes

Lasker liked tidiness, a challenge, people who made good, conversation including particularly his own, movies, shop windows, change of pace, practically anybody in the newspaper business, rich food, men who stood up to him, to learn, and, above all, to win.

He disliked pets (including cats in particular), trains or airplanes not on time, failures, to be alone, to be bored, anything badly done, anything false, bitchy women, and, above all, to be wrong.

What gave him his immense and radiant push, his drive? It was not desire to outstrip anybody, because he seldom paid the slightest attention to what other people were doing. Probably the answer lies in a combination of ego, natural energy, and a delight in perfectionism for its own sake.

Chapter 13

RUNNING THE OFFICE

We come now to the rare, the choice, the delicious theme of how Lasker ran an office. He was certainly not a conventional executive. His business never became institutionalized like J. Walter Thompson or Young & Rubicam. It was eccentrically run. Trying to find out exactly the sequence of officers in power during the 1930's, I asked one man who had been president of Lord & Thomas for a while who his successor was; he looked puzzled, scratched his head, and replied, "I don't think we had one." When Sollitt quit, A.D. insisted that he remain on the board of directors, but, years later, he testified that he had never attended a directors' meeting and did not think that any had ever been held.

Lasker hated committees as much as he hated graphs and charts. His definition of "administrator" was unusual—"somebody without brains." What he liked was stimulation, ideas, and originality. Lord & Thomas was not an organization at all, but a series of semi-autonomous pools, with Lasker, the dictator, way up on top. But this bothered him; he felt that he ought to decentralize, and continually sought men to run the business end of the business for him. Every six months or so after a period of trying to administer the whole shop directly, he would hire somebody to run a department and then, after a few months, fire him in disgust. In general, men got big promotions not necessarily because they were able, but because they had bright or creative ideas. He liked to give jobs on a personal basis. Miss Sachse, who had been Francie's governess for many years, became the office receptionist, and her brother became comptroller.

Lasker was always accessible to outsiders, and one of his favorite maxims was, "Everybody is a customer." Once he sat talking with "Babe" Meigs, and a caller was announced. He asked Meigs to step out—the caller, a minor executive in a soap company, wouldn't take a minute. When the interview was over Lasker summoned Meigs back, and said, "Of course, if that man had been *president* of his company, I might have kept him waiting." He felt that he must be particularly courteous to the caller if only because he was not an important man.

Meigs tells another story about Lasker's tactics. If he was utterly determined to win an argument, his manner would be disarmingly quiet, almost docile. "If you pound the table, the other fellow will too; he will get his back up, and you'll have a hard time winning." Instead he would say beguilingly to an antagonist, "I think you are probably right" (even when he knew the man to be altogether wrong) "but, if you don't mind, I'd like to put this thought to you. However, please give me your ideas first, and perhaps they will be better than mine." On the other hand, if he knew for certain that he was going to surrender on an issue, he talked stridently, blustered, and was defiant. Then, when he gave in at last, which he had intended to do all the time, his opponent would think that he had won a tremendous victory over the great Lasker after a strenuous battle.

He always got down to the office early; he was punctual, and demanded punctuality in others. His office in the Palmolive Building was separated from the rest of the establishment by a hall and a reception room; to get in or out, three sets of doors had to be passed. Lasker walked through these like a man in a trance, as if he were utterly oblivious of the barriers. On arrival, he spent an hour or two conscientiously reading his mail. On most letters he scrawled a notation in pencil—his handwriting was flowing, upright, and legible—directing what the answer should be. When he dictated, the little barks and hesitations in his speech disappeared. Then he went to the barbershop, which adjoined his office. Here he sometimes received clients, like an eighteenth-century monarch at a levee. One of his secretaries testifies that the main thing she remembers about him was that he could do nothing slowly. He was capricious and impatient. He crackled with energy and excitement. "With Mr. Lasker, you had to be alert all the time." Another girl says that she worked at Lord & Thomas for several months without ever having seen him, nor had his appearance been described to her. Then in a corridor she saw a group of men approaching swiftly. "I knew which was Mr. Lasker right away. Nobody had to point him out. He was neither first nor last and they were moving fast but you knew right away which man *he* was, all right."

He liked young people, and wanted a young staff. One house ad in the mid-thirties had the title, "TREES DIE FROM THE TOP—AND SO DO ADVERTISING AGENCIES"; he liked to boast that his business was conducted by men "who can still touch the floor without bending their knees." His oldest executive was fifty-five; the youngest, thirty. Average age was thirty-seven.

One of the brightest of his youngsters was William Benton, who worked for him twice. This was exceptional, because he seldom forgave a man who left him, and would almost never take a "deserter" back. Benton, during his second term with Lord & Thomas, was assigned to make a survey of the toothpaste–shaving cream–soap trade. Palmolive had just merged with Colgate, and Lasker wanted to impress the new executives there with his thorough knowledge of the business even if this meant going into the kind of research he detested. Benton asked, "What kind of survey should I make?" A.D. replied, "I don't care—just make it the *biggest* survey ever made by anybody." Most research was, in those days, market research; consumer research was still unborn. Agencies wanted to find out the number of drugstores in Des Moines, not why a consumer bought a certain product. Benton applied himself energetically to his task, sent out salesmen with long questionnaires, and put the results, which were voluminous, on paper and had them bound. He brought the shiny new books to the boss. Lasker said, "Magnificent!" The irreverent Benton said, "At least the bindings are as good as anything your money can buy." Lasker slammed his fist on the table.

"What—aren't the reports just as good inside as they look outside?" Benton said, "Let's see." They pored over the documentation together, and A.D. was fully satisfied.

This was the origin of the modern technique of polling in the United States, because Benton proceeded to do other surveys for Lord & Thomas which turned out to be brilliantly useful, and other agencies had to follow. For instance, to compete with him, Young & Rubicam decided to go into statistics in a big way, and hired a youthful sociologist at Northwestern University to organize their research; he was George Gallup. Within a few years, Gallup became a household name. So did the name Elmo Roper.[1] Now, of course, polling is so universal a phenomenon that it is hard to realize that it had such a casual beginning; polling not only decides the fate of products, but helps make national policies, politics and Presidents.

Despite all this, Lasker retained his old antipathy to elaborate statistical research. One day he came into Benton's office unannounced and found him on a stepladder, sticking pins into a large chart. The boss said, "What on earth are you doing?" Benton said, "I haven't the faintest idea, but the pins will tell me when every one is in."

Lasker growled, "Humph!" and walked out.

Once A.D. asked Benton how Lord & Thomas compared to the agency where he had worked before, and he replied, "There's a big difference. In the other agency, my boss hired second-rate men, and then gave them every opportunity to become first-rate. Here you hire first-rate men, browbeat them, humiliate them, refuse to give them parity, and drive them so hard they become second-rate." Of course Benton was exaggerating heavily, but sometimes it was necessary to exaggerate in order to seize Lasker's full attention.

After a time Benton sought new fields, and decided to leave Lord & Thomas. Lasker, who would go to almost any length to keep a valuable man, said he would double his salary if he would stay. Benton had risen from $9,000 to $25,000 in a few years, and now

[1] Lasker tried hard on one occasion to entice the estimable Roper into Lord & Thomas, but Roper would not succumb.

Lasker was offering him $50,000. There followed one of the few episodes in which A.D. was beaten in a tête-à-tête.

Benton said engagingly, "Why, Mr. Lasker, do you mean to say that I have been worth $50,000 a year during all this time that you have been paying me only $25,000? You've been taking *my* money!" Lasker was struck dumb with fury, but recognized that this artful way with words was closely akin to his own. After quitting Lord & Thomas, Benton founded Benton & Bowles in partnership with Chester Bowles, became publisher of the Encyclopaedia Britannica, and later rose to be Assistant Secretary of State and Senator from Connecticut, amongst much else. Lasker forgave him in time, and they became good friends. He was, in fact, the largest single contributor to Benton's campaign when he ran for Senator.

Lasker paid big salaries to big people, little salaries to little. He could be generous to the point of mania, and in the same breath stingy. He rewarded the man who first put him in touch with Mahler and the Kotex account by doubling his salary overnight, but a filing clerk could have a hard time climbing from $35 to $45 a week. During the booming years of Lucky Strike a copy writer came up with the descriptive line, "So round, so firm, so fully packed, so free and easy on the draw." Lasker was dizzy with delight at this, and on the spot gave the man a bonus of $10,000.[2] As a matter of fact he did not, except in the very highest echelons, have to pay abnormally large salaries, because young advertising men were so eager to be trained by Lord & Thomas that they would work for comparatively little. But he was always acutely conscious of his payroll. Returning once from a holiday in the South, he summoned a meeting of the staff in the Chicago office, and some two hundred men and women responded. "What!" exclaimed Lasker, aghast, "Do I pay salaries to *all* these people?"

There are countless stories, of the kind that cluster around eccentric executives, about Lasker and raises. A timid, nervous young man

[2] Similarly a writer got $5,000 for "an article, an adjective, a noun, and a period," when he devised the simple phrase "A light smoke" for Cremo cigars. *Advertising Age,* June 8, 1952.

who worked in the radio department mustered all his courage one day to confront the boss and demand a raise, and then lost his nerve; he stammered and stuttered. A.D. took pity on him. He said, "Mr. Goodman! If you are going to ask me for a raise, ask me! If you are trying to horse-trade with me, you'll lose the buttons off your vest!"

Some years later Emerson Foote entered the Lasker employ, and, in time, succeeded Coons as vice president in New York. His salary was modest at the time, and he thought that he would certainly get a raise—his post warranted it. Coons had got much more. But no raise was forthcoming. Months went by, and Lasker summoned him at last, saying, "Mr. Foote, you have never asked me for a raise! I will now ask you a direct question. Is this because you don't care about money, or because you think that *not* asking for a raise is the smartest way to handle me?"

Foote had to think quickly. (A man had to be fast on his feet with A.D. A second chance came seldom.) He replied, "The latter."

Lasker smiled his most winning smile: "I'm delighted."

However, Foote did not get the raise.

On the smallest level Lasker could be careful of the firm's money, i.e., his money. On the Century en route to New York he ran into Robert Koretz, one of his veterans. He was depressed, because an old friend had just died, and he sat down to have a drink with Koretz. This was unusual; the boss almost never had social relations with employees, even a casual drink on a train. Fraternization was taboo except among the viceroys at the very top. Koretz reached for the check with the words, "My pleasure, Mr. Lasker." A.D. said, "Very well, Mr. Koretz. When you get back to Chicago you may tell Mr. Sachse that you bought me this drink, and it is O.K. for your expense account. You are entitled to have a drink on the company's money once in a while." The bill was $1.80!

It pleased Lasker greatly that Lord & Thomas always did well— something exceptional—in depression years; this was because, as he himself put it, "sick advertisers came to us and did what we wanted." He was like a doctor, who made them well. Lord & Thomas placed one-third of all the advertising it did in its total life of sixty-nine years during the five depression years 1930-34. But in 1931, when his own personal profit was around three million dollars, he cut salaries straight across the board by 25 per cent, and on February 13, 1933, suddenly fired outright more than fifty men and women, some of whom were senior executives who had been with him for years.

He was, of course, sole owner; he could do what he liked. As a matter of fact, he was not, at this date, *quite* the sole owner, because he had given Flora a good deal of stock, and Edward and other members of the family had a little. Also he gave stock to a few important executives, like Don Francisco, and, to lure good men into the organization or to keep them, he had been obliged to scatter a little more around. Even so, he personally controlled between 90 and 95 per cent of all stock, and employees who were stockholders were obliged, by agreement, to surrender their holdings if they quit, were fired, or retired, at a price set unilaterally by him. However, several of his men have told me that he was generous in such contingencies.

When Lasker did not like a man he could not remember his name. He would mutter to his secretary, "Tell Serkin to come in—I mean Suffkin—no, Sufferman—oh, you know who I mean—Skinner!"

Turnover in personnel at Lord & Thomas was, of course, enormous; men quit to earn more money elsewhere, or because they could not endure the strain. Lasker, a virtuoso, created people, but sometimes could not hold them. He himself consumed most of the oxygen in the establishment; there was no air for anybody else to breathe. He trained his men, then let them go. One result of this was a phenomenon alluded to in an earlier chapter—the way Lord & Thomas sired other agencies. Lasker was like Ford in this respect: he was a kingmaker who populated an entire business. Dozens of his men, striking out for themselves, became sub-Laskers. The list is remarkable. Benton we have mentioned (he became the highest-paid commercial writer in the world); also Francisco, who went to J. Walter Thompson in his later years; also Frank Hummert, the specialist in soap operas. Charles R. Erwin and Louis Wasey, who founded Erwin, Wasey, were both associated with him for years; so was Walter O'Meara, who is probably the best paid copy writer in the world today; so was his friend and protégé Leonard M. Masius, who ran the London office; so was Mark O'Dea, one of Lasker's special favorites in the old Chicago days; so were men who became glittering potentates on their own, like J. Sterling Getchell, A.E. Aveyard (MacFarland-Aveyard), John Orr Young, Paul Faust (Mitchell-Faust), Jack Hurst (Henri, Hurst & McDonald), Hill Blackett (Blackett, Sample & Hummert), both Stuart Sherman and Arthur Marquette of Sherman-Marquette, to say nothing of Emerson Foote, Don Belding, and Fairfax Cone. Heads of other agencies, even rivals, often came to Lasker for advice. Lord & Thomas became a combination of incubator and Mayo Clinic; Lasker's own words for this phenomenon were, "I make my men so good that I can't keep 'em!"

Meantime, his attitude toward clients solidified. Probably no man in the whole history of advertising, not even the great Stanley Resor of J. Walter Thompson, whom Lasker admired, ever dared handle clients with the sinewy hand that A.D. used. He liked to say, "This is a wonderful business—except for the clients!"

He was quite capable of telephoning some exalted figure at General Motors, say, commanding him to come to see him at a certain hour, because he, Lasker, did not like the way things were going at Frigidaire, a General Motors company. He never had the faintest fear of any client, although there were some accounts, like Lucky Strike, that he would have disliked extremely to lose—as we shall see. Once he snorted cheerfully, "I have never felt secure with any client, whether he would stay with me or whether *I* would stay with him." If he felt that a client should spend a lot more money, he would say so; one of his best-known aphorisms was, "A little more is no more." Moreover, something unorthodox, he never hesitated to tell a client to spend *less* money, even if this cut into his own

212 TAKEN AT THE FLOOD

income. He felt keenly that a point could be reached in any account where the public, saturated, might become bored with a product, a fate worse than mayhem or sudden death.

✳

Lasker could be exasperating, infuriating, to work for, particularly when his nerves were on edge. He was continually *at* his men. He could not leave them alone. "Have you tried this? Why haven't you done *this?*" he would ask. He was quite capable of ordering an entire new campaign for a client on December 22, and demanding that it be ready on December 26, altogether forgetting Christmas; then forgetting that he had asked for it. His men had to work Sundays, if necessary, or all night. "Think when you're shaving!" he once exclaimed to Benton. He kept the staff on tenterhooks; one of his theories was never to tell anybody what he thought of him. His men became products. He baffled his senior executives by changing mood incessantly; one day he would talk about moving the whole plant out to Arizona, where everybody could meditate in peace; the next he would thunder at some underling about the glories of New York. Moreover, it was difficult even for his oldest associates to know what he was thinking when, at times, his flow of talk would overwhelm them. The only way to stop him was to interject some brief word sharply and repeatedly. David Noyes once reported that his principal job at Lord & Thomas was "to run softly, invisibly, behind the boss," picking up what dropped.

Lord & Thomas was certainly not an easy ride, but few of the veterans who survived have ever lamented being there; in fact, most look back to it as the most exciting adventure in their lives. Moreover, A. D.'s sheer winningness and his habit of always being scrupulously fair compensated for the stress and strain. He delivered; he kept his word.

Few have ever forgotten Lasker's persuasive power. A rising young man, adept and hard-working, was Fairfax Cone, the manager of the

San Francisco office. He had worked for Lord & Thomas for some years, but had never met Lasker. They had, however, corresponded a good deal, and the boss continually asked him if he would be interested in moving to New York. Cone said No. Peremptorily he was summoned to meet A.D. at a holiday resort in California, and was greeted with the words, "I imagine you think I have asked you to come here in order to talk to you about moving to New York. I just want to tell you—that is the last thing I want. Put your mind at rest. This is purely a social visit so that we can get acquainted." Cone returned to San Francisco, satisfied, but presently more letters came mentioning the urgent reorganization Lasker had in mind, which, if it went through, meant that Cone and others would have to move. But he did not *ask* him directly to change his mind. He felt (as Cone learned later) that transferring him to New York would be a fiasco unless he, Cone, was himself convinced that it was a good thing and volunteered of his own free will to make the change. So, with insidious subtlety, A.D. kept the issue alive. Before long, the tormented Cone became desperate. Lasker, he perceived, "had fallen in love with his own nobility" in not directly asking him to come, and was concentrating all his powers on the device of getting *him* to take the initiative. Cone could stand this game only a certain length of time, and, meeting Lasker again in Chicago, surrendered and said that he would move. "When?" A.D. demanded. "Whenever you want me," Cone replied. Lasker held up his hand solemnly. "Mr. Cone, I must have it understood that never, never, never have I *asked* you to move from California. I would not do such a thing." And, by this time, he really believed that he had not done so. A date was set. Lasker reached for the phone and called George Washington Hill in New York. Crooning with delight, he exclaimed, "George, I have good news for you. Mr. Cone, of our San Francisco office, has volunteered to come East. We need him, and he is coming of his own free will!"

Lasker could be thoughtless and temperamental; also he could be fabulously considerate—a benevolent father, a patriarch. The eagle and the dove were still imprisoned in the same man; Lasker A and Lasker B had not yet finished fighting it out. He was concerned beyond measure if anybody on the staff became ill. Once a Chicago girl who had been transferred to New York and who had a minor job came down with pneumonia. Lasker called in another young woman, the boss of her department, and said, "Do you love Miss X?" The reply was, "I'm very fond of her." He went on, "Yes, but do you *love* her?" "Yes." He thereupon ordered her to take Miss X to Chicago by the Century that night, so that she could be treated at the Michael Reese Hospital, one of the few hospitals in the country which he trusted. He explained, "You see, I don't want a young girl like that to go back to Chicago just with a nurse. I want her to have somebody with her who *loves* her." Years later, after he had liquidated Lord & Thomas, he passed through Chicago and dropped in to call on Fairfax Cone. Lasker took one look at him, and decided that he must be ill. He returned without warning the next day, and said, "You owe me much, Mr. Cone. But I am now going to say two words to you that will mean more to you all the rest of your life than any two words you have ever heard—*pernicious fatigue!* You are suffering from pernicious fatigue, Mr. Cone." Lasker then announced that he had made an appointment for him with his own doctor, and had him there in half an hour. Cone had indeed been suffering from a mysterious ailment, which caused inexplicable seizures of fatigue; the doctor diagnosed the disturbance correctly and treated it, and Cone has seldom had a day of ill health since.

Lasker craved perfection; he had wild enthusiasms for people, because he always looked for the best; if you were his friend, you were without fault, and he would back you to the limit. When men and women did not live up to his expectations, his disillusion was intense. He loved people too much for their own good; when his affection ebbed, they were left naked. But, even when this happened, he maintained an extraordinary generosity of spirit. For his friends he would bare himself to the bone, and tell anything about himself, if this would give them insight into their own troubles, succor, or encouragement.

A Bouquet of Anecdotes

Lasker loved to tell stories; one favorite had to do with an uncle of his, possibly mythical, named Heidenheimer who was a storekeeper on the old Texas frontier. Miners bought supplies from him, and then disappeared up into the hills for months at a time. One day an embittered prospector returned and confronted him with the words, "Heidenheimer, I ought to punch you right in the nose."

"Why, what's the matter, Zeke?"

"These matches you sold me don't light."

Heidenheimer took one, and struck it on the seat of his pants. It lit. "Nothing wrong with those matches, Zeke."

Zeke looked surly. "Maybe not. But I can't take a piece of your behind up in the hills with me."

Lasker's gift of association was swift, but circuitous. He liked to tell this story when he looked over copy and saw an ad which, in his opinion, needed clarification. Such advertising was, he drummed into his staff, just as worthless as Heidenheimer's matches which only lit under special circumstances. One of his maxims became, "If you have to explain an advertisement, it's no good."

He had a talk with Kenneth Smith of Pepsodent during a period when sales were falling off, and said urgently, "We must be more aggressive. We must *attack* the toothpaste market." Smith replied that Pepsodent was, after all, still well up and not doing too badly, whereupon Lasker said, "You remind me of the story of the man who jumped out of the thirtieth floor of a building. As he passed the fifteenth he called out, 'Nothing has happened to me yet!' "

No man could be said to have arrived in the Chicago of those days until he had been invited to lunch privately in the chambers of James Simpson, the venerable head of Marshall Field & Company, and this honor came to Lasker in due course. A letter from Simpson reached him the next day; the gist of it was:

The two hours we have just had with one another are among the most stimulating I have ever spent. I am most grateful. You strike me as the kind of person who would not mind a bit of forewarning from an older man. In any case, permit me to make an observation. You give a million dollars' worth of advice in every five cent situation. If you keep this up, you will soon discover that you will not be able to give five cents' worth of advice in a million dollar situation. Take care of yourself.

Very truly yours,
JAMES SIMPSON

Lasker paid attention to this warning. He had always assumed that he was inexhaustible, but now he sought not to spend himself exorbitantly.

Lasker, against his better judgment, lent a large sum of money to a friend who defaulted, but who would not concede that he was bankrupt, in which case the amount could have been written off and deducted against taxes. Negotiations, not altogether amicable, went on interminably and another man, who was a friend of both, finally offered himself as an intermediary. Lasker declined with the words, "When I sit on a hot stove I will wear my own, huh, blisters. Thank you very much."

The chairman of the board at Quaker Oats was a veteran named Crowell; he was past eighty, wrote letters in a splendid Spencerian longhand, and was a fervent churchman, much given to prostelytizing. He met with Lasker, as he had met with him for a decade, to work out the next Quaker Oats campaign; agreement was quick, and Albert was puzzled when he had a telephone call from him the next day, asking for another meeting. Crowell said, "I prayed to God all last night to give me the courage to say what I am now going to say to you. We have had an intimate association for many years. You have helped us prosper. You are a member of our family. One thing, and one thing only, separates us, the fact that you are a Jew. It is a great deal to ask, but would you consider renouncing your religion and joining ours?"

Lasker was astonished. But he replied quickly, "Mr. Crowell, I am so touched by your words that I could cry. You have paid me the greatest compliment I have ever had in my life. But, it so happens, my mother, and my mother's mother, and her mother's mother before that, all rise out of the same strain, and stem from the same tradition. I cannot break it. But I can tell you this: when it comes time for you to be taken from us here on earth, you will be welcome in *our* heaven."

Lasker's sense of fundamentals, his saltiness, could be expressed in several dimensions. One of his executives annoyed him by being extravagant. Admonition did no good. His wrath mounted and at last he strode into the man's office, high up in the Palmolive Building, and demanded, "Give me a quarter!" Bewildered, the man dug down into his pocket, and handed a quarter over to him. Swiftly Lasker yanked a window open and tossed the quarter out. "*That*," he barked, "is what *I* mean by wasting money!"

He had little patience with businessmen who complained about high taxes, and threw money away because advertising and other expenses were deductible. He liked to say, "Even if the government's cut is 80 per cent, the rest is yours. If you had a 20 per cent interest in an investment would you be careless about it just because it was a minority share?"

To be invited to play golf at Mill Road Farm was a big thing in the Chicago of those days. Harold Swift, the head of the great packing house and one of the most distinguished of local citizens, got one day a letter not merely inviting him to play on the following Sunday, but enclosing a permanent guest card to the course. Moreover, the card was conspicuously marked "Number One."

Not till years later did Mr. Swift learn that all other cards were similarly marked "Number One."

Once Lasker peeked into a conference room where a lot of people were chatting. He asked suspiciously what was going on, and the answer came, "It's a meeting about such-and-such." The boss wrinkled his nose scornfully: "I see some people in there who are supposed to be working, and if we're going to have *meetings*, unh, I suggest that we hire some *meetingers* and let the workers work!"

Lasker came back from Florida with a bright fresh tan, and ran into Robert Koretz in a corridor of the Lord & Thomas offices. Koretz said, "You look like a million dollars, Mr. Lasker."
Lasker said nothing, but strode on. Then he turned back abruptly. "Hey! Mr. Koretz! A million dollars? Huh!—New Deal money!"

Domestic Scenes

Lasker returned to Burton Place unexpectedly one afternoon; to his amazement Flora was on the doorstep, and a servant was putting her suitcases in a taxi. He demanded: "Where are you going?" She replied: "Back to my family in Buffalo!" He asked, thunderstruck, "Back to your *family*—for how long?" She answered, "Several months." Gently Lasker led her back into the house, and said, "Flora, so long as you are on *this* side of the threshold, you are the most important person in the world to me. The minute you cross it, I will forget that you ever lived."
She stayed.
Some time after this his three musketeers—Francisco, Noyes, and Coons—came to Mill Road Farm for a weekend. The day was for golf; the night for office problems and soul searching. Flora, at such gatherings, was a competent hostess; all the men liked and admired her, but she spoke little. Lasker was exhausted, and had a drink too many. He rose with the coffee, and, to the surprise of his guests, asked for speeches from everybody, including Flora, which should convey their opinion of *him*. An awkward silence followed. He called on Flora to speak first; she demurred but he insisted: then she rose and said, to everybody's astonishment, that she had found "peace" at last, but that he had not. Apparently what she meant was that she

had finally managed to adjust herself to their differences in temperament and incompatibilities, but that he was still—in this and other matters—in the grip of unresolved conflicts and rent by turmoil.

Albert was shocked. Visibly distressed, he sought to pull himself together. But worse was to come before this painful evening ran its course. Several of his men made speeches, as requested, but, instead of kowtowing to him and covering him with fulsome praise, which was what he had expected, they let loose with indignant criticism, particularly on the ground that he treated them as inferiors—slaves. Flora listened mutely, and Lasker became more and more embarrassed. Then, still white and shaken, struggling to control himself, almost tottering, he rose to reply. But he turned the tables on everybody and won them all back with a speech which, Noyes thinks in retrospect, was the most brilliant performance of the kind he ever heard. The key to it was that he was their "master" only because he constantly strove to make them live up to their potentialities and true capacity.

The next day he was sunny as a child; he had discovered something new and exciting to worry about. He tapped at the pages of the morning newspaper. "Look!" He pointed to frightening news about Hitler and Mussolini, who were now dominating the European scene. "You see what this Hitler business *means?*" His guests thought that he would allude to the danger of war and the possibility that America might be involved. Not at all. Lasker intoned, "We are facing a new kind of competition now. People are going to *read about Hitler and Mussolini instead of reading ads!*"

Advertising Pro and Con

In the 1920's and '30's Lasker seldom, if ever, questioned the basic ethical, cultural, or social implications of advertising. It never occurred to him to analyze the primary tenets of the instrument he had done so much to create. He had little interest in abstract thought, and in those days he still looked at himself as "a man climbing a mountain"—performing a beneficial and much needed service in helping to sell sound merchandise to the consumer at a reasonable price. It is not difficult to formulate roughly the answers he would have given to complaints. "Advertising made goods more expensive." His reply would have been that, on the contrary, it created a demand for goods which in turn led to mass production, prosperity, and a higher standard of living for all. "Advertising induced installment buying, which impoverished many." His answer would have been that it was good to be in debt; it made a person work harder. "Advertising debauched the public taste, and its use of hokum, idiotic slogans, ballyhoo, and sensational exaggeration tarnished the nation with unspeakable vulgarity." Not *his* advertising, Lasker would have replied. "Advertising helped to impose a deadly, sterile uniformity on America from the East Coast to the West; it made people puppets." Nonsense; it helped to create variety, and stimulated differences in tastes. "Advertising ate relentlessly into the editorial policy of publications, and was a sinister influence on the freedom of the press." Again nonsense; without advertising the best publications in America would go under. Also he had another and characteristically Laskeresque arrow in his quiver—that advertising was not his chosen work, but had been thrust on him—therefore its nature was not his responsibility! He often said that he would have left advertising in his youth and returned to what he really loved, the newspaper business, except for economic circumstances—first, the necessity to pay off the $500 he had lost in the crap game, and second, the cost of Flora's illness.

But he was becoming sharply disillusioned about advertising by the end of the 30's. Once he said with rancor, "Advertising has got lost in the advertising business!" Also, the sheer amount of power he could wield began to be discomfiting. Once he told Leonard Lyons that he could pick up an illiterate vagrant on Third Avenue, clean him up, take him to a tailor, set him up in his office behind a desk, and then parade him before his staff with the words, "I have just found this man. He is a genius." In twenty-four hours, Albert went on, the man would be accepted as a genius; in forty-eight, the man would think that he was a genius himself!

Many years after this Aldous Huxley said, referring to the powerful and sinister effect of ceaselessly repeated slogans in advertising, "What does a democracy depend on? A democracy depends on the individual voter making an intelligent and rational choice for what he regards as his enlightened self interest in any given circumstance. What these people are doing [the big advertising agencies] . . . is to try to bypass the rational side of man and appeal directly to the deep, unconscious forces below the surface. In a way they are making nonsense of democratic procedure, which is based on conscious choice on rational grounds."[3]

Probably Lasker would have agreed with most of Mr. Huxley's statement if he had lived into the late 1950's. He was already convinced, at the time of his death (1952), that advertising might wreck TV by reason of its own excesses, and what he would have thought of crooked disc jockeys and concealed commercials can be readily imagined. Lasker was not a cheat.

What would be his opinion of some written ads of the present day? One of his veteran associates thinks that he would have been appalled by the eyepatch on the Man in the Hathaway Shirt and perhaps by Commander Whitehead's beard (Schweppes) as well. I am not so sure. But Lasker, as we know, always detested tricky and "clever" ads. I do not think he would have liked the enormously oversize egg used recently by the Chase Manhattan Bank to denote the concept "nest egg," or the White Horse whisky ads showing a man on a blindingly white horse. On the other hand, I think he would have admired the institutional ads of the Container Corporation of America, which illustrate philosophical maxims, such ads as that of the Cessna Aircraft Corporation which has the headline, "In One Hour Your Top Men Will Be 220 Miles Ahead," and above all, a recent double-page ad for Rolls-Royce in *The New Yorker*. This, with its long persuasive text and engaging dead-pan air, might have come straight out of Lord & Thomas.

Several other contemporary automobile ads would probably not meet with Lasker's august approval. A recent example, for the "Lion-

[3] *Aldous Huxley, a Mike Wallace Interview.* Published by the Fund for the Republic, 1958.

hearted" Chrysler of 1959, uses such phrases as "True-Level Torsion-Aire Suspension"; another, for Chevrolet, contains gems like "Slimline Design," "Hi-Thrift 6," and "Easy-Ratio Steering." Lasker would have snorted. Nor can there be much doubt as to what his opinion would have been of a great deal of shoddy merchandise sold today which, in his view, would not have been fit to advertise—pens that drip blobs of ink, razor blades which keep an edge for all of two shaves, lamp bulbs that burn out every hour on the hour, and beer that tastes like soap.

Chapter 14

DEPRIVATION, DISCONTENT, DESPAIR

Albert and Flora were comfortably happy together and tranquil now. He told a friend, "It's a good thing that Flora and the children cut me down to size when I'm feeling too exalted." To accept one's family, he decided, was "the simplest way of living a life." Most of the strain and turbulence of the 1920's was gone; his early tenderness for his wife reblossomed. The Laskers went to New York and put up at the Ritz in December, 1936. Edward was there, and Frances came in from Vassar to join them on Saturday, December 19. They were all returning to Chicago on the Century late that afternoon, in order to be home in good time for Christmas. Flora had lost a good deal of weight, and looked prettier than in years; this delighted Albert, and he was proud of her. But she was not feeling particularly well. In fact she had had a series of minor embolisms, and a doctor had seen her that morning. Now, at noon, she was sitting up in bed, reading placidly. Albert and Edward had just left her, and were in the living room, talking about horses and the theater. They heard Flora's voice, cheerful, say, "Come in, you two, and talk to me—I feel like chatting." Edward walked through the door to the bedroom, and found that she was breathing heavily and had become suddenly unconscious. A cerebral thrombosis had struck her after her words, and she died a minute or two later.

This was the greatest shock of Lasker's life. Anguish overcame him. He was completely distraught. Riding home from the funeral, he stopped the car and demanded to see a movie!—any movie—and then the full weight of this irreparable loss hit him and he behaved

like a man bereft. He hung pictures of Flora everywhere and, recuperating with the Foremans in Miami Beach, kept his daughter
Mary up all night with unceasing affectionate talk of her. Sometimes
he had complained about how miserable Flora had made him, but
now he discovered what it was like to be alone. Since their marriage
in 1902, thirty-four years before, he had never, with the possible exception of some purely perfunctory contacts, had anything to do
with another woman. Now he found that he was utterly adrift.
Waves of guilt poured over him. He was inundated by remorse, although there was nothing substantial to be remorseful about. But he
remembered small disagreements that had become quarrels without
reason, and examples of thoughtlessness and neglect. He groaned
aloud at recollections of his lack of solicitude; and he began to realize
how much he owed her as well as how much he missed her. Too
late, too late! He bit on his pain, made it worse, and thought, quite
literally, that he would go insane.

His emotion took the most extravagant, grotesque forms. Having
undervalued her at times, he now overvalued her. He astonished a
company one night by moaning, "Until I met Flora I had never
even tasted a vegetable! I came from Texas, and the only things I
knew how to eat were chile con carne and hominy grits!"

Once the worst of his grief, his despair, had passed, Lasker faced
another problem. He was fifty-six now; he felt that he had to live
quickly. But how? He was a free man after a third of a century of
marriage; but what does a person his age, and of his peculiar temperament, do with freedom?

Around the World

First Lasker sought solace in his children, hospitality, and extension
of his friendships. He clung to the old Partridge crowd; cards went
out inviting—in fact, commanding—members to assemble at Burton Place, the farm, or the house in Miami which he had not yet
given up. At Mill Road Farm parties became more grandiose. At
one in June, 1937, he had 71 persons for golf, 107 for dinner. He
reached out for new people, and a variety of names appear in the

lists of guests—the late Dr. John O. LaGorce of the National Geographic Society; Niles Trammell of NBC; Daniel Mahoney, manager of the Miami *News;* Paul Patterson, president of the Baltimore *Sun;* Clem McCarthy, the horse race specialist; Walter Dill Scott, president of Northwestern University; the Roy Howards; the cartoonist John T. McCutcheon; Henry Horner, the governor of Illinois; and Chicago luminaries young or old, like James H. Douglas, Jr., of the Quaker Oats clan, who is now Deputy Secretary of Defense; General Robert E. Wood, later to become the head of America First; and the investment banker Charles Glore.

Something pleasant happened in August, 1937: he became a trustee of the University of Chicago. Most of his fellow trustees were, at this time, staid Baptists and conservative representatives of the peculiar amalgam which ran Chicago, the old packer aristocracy plus State Street (the merchants); Lasker puzzled and sometimes irritated them; usually he took Hutchins' side when disputes arose, and Hutchins was glad to have him on the board. A little later Hutchins took the unprecedented step of abolishing football at the University, for a variety of good reasons; this, as viewed by the alumni, was an appalling thing to do, and an unholy row broke out. Albert supported Hutchins firmly, and this meant a good deal because he was so prominently identified with sport. If *Lasker* said that football had to go, people reasoned, it had to go. Hutchins won him over to his side on the football issue with one word, when he somewhat hesitantly proffered the remark, "Football is what unifies a university—what will take its place?" The single word with which Hutchins answered him was, "Education!"

The University of Chicago had a nasty little Red scare about this time; several professors were accused of being subversive, and unpleasant incidents occurred—a foretaste of McCarthyism later. Lasker supported Hutchins and the so-called pink professors with the utmost vigor. No university, he said in a public address, could be worth supporting if its faculty was policed; even the most radical professors, he insisted, should have the right to speak freely on any subject. Once again, he was proving himself to be unusual—not at all the typical Chicago millionaire. Also in this period he began to be urgently interested in the Negro problem, and, until the end of his life, kept up an active interest in it. He was passionately pro-Negro on any issue having to do with segregation and civil rights. A utilitarian factor entered into this, because he felt that nothing could better assist the American economy in general, and his own business in particular, than a steady increase in the purchasing power of the Negro community, and this, he saw readily, could not come unless segregation patterns were broken down. Nobody would have applauded the great Supreme Court decision in March, 1954, more warmly than Lasker, if he had been alive.

*

In November (1937) Lasker set out for a nine months' trip around the world. With him went Frances, who was now sleek as a stalk of asparagus, fresh as an egg, and a glittering pearl of chicness; Gene Sarazen, the golfer, and Mrs. Sarazen; Legge, his valet, and Josephine, Flora's maid, who was now attached to Francie; and Francie's school friend Peggy James, now Mrs. Calvin Fulenwider. The party set out across the Pacific from San Francisco, and the itinerary included Japan, Manchuria, the Philippines, Bali, Java, India, Egypt, Italy, France, and England. The Sarazens dropped out after Singapore.

This trip was an important, broadening experience for Lasker; it opened his eyes to much. There was only one untoward experience —he became violently ill in Bali of some tropical complaint, which the local physician could not diagnose; a doctor and two nurses were summoned from Java by a chartered plane. Lasker lost eleven pounds in 120 hours. He records how panicky he was, partly because he thought he might die and also because, if he didn't, he was worried that his party might be stranded in the Dutch East Indies indefinitely, while he was convalescing. Bali had, he noted, a population of 1,500,000 "natives" and exactly thirty-seven whites; this made him alarmed and nervous, although no people in the

world are more placid than the Balinese, and Indonesian nationalism scarcely existed at this date. In any case, he recovered quickly,
and moved on to Singapore.

Lasker liked best the leisurely voyages between ports. He read a
good deal, and testified that he had time not merely to read but to
"digest" a book a day. A typhoon during a cruise off the Philippines
provided excitement. Ashore, he was apt to be disappointed, because
Tokyo, Bangkok and other oriental cities looked exactly as he expected them to look; there were no surprises, because he had seen
these cities too often in the movies. Moreover, it was too hot as a
rule to play golf, and he went all the way around the world without
having a round with Sarazen or anybody else. Climate aside, the
journey took place—needless to say—in considerable comfort. For
instance, the Frigidaire people arranged to have a brace of General
Motors cars at his disposal in every city the party visited.

Lasker wrote regularly to his children ("My Darling Children . . ."
"My Dear Ones . . .") and children-in-law back home, and to old
friends in the Partridges like Abe Selz; some of this correspondence
has survived, and is revealing. I have said before in this book that
Lasker, if he had stuck to journalism as a career, could have become
a really great reporter; these letters prove it. His intuition about the
political situation in the countries he visited, although they were
strange to him, was piercingly accurate, which is the more remarkable because, although he tried, he seldom met anybody except
American diplomats and businessmen who entertained him in each
community, and, as is notorious, most Americans living in Asia in
those days did not have the faintest knowledge of what was going
on underneath the surface. But Lasker got to the bottom of things
swiftly. Japan, he sensed, was irreversibly on the march; the Japanese
invasion of China was not an "incident," but a matter of life and
death for the entire nation; nothing would stop Japan except force.
The Dutch were good colonizers, but would lose everything if they
did not modify their "rigidity." India was important not merely
because it was so poor, but because it was *rich* as well. The genius of
the British colonial system was that the British were always willing

to give in when they had to. As to Europe, the rank and file of Italians detested Hitler, and *Anschluss* (union of Germany and Austria, which occurred while Lasker was en route) would end up by being a disaster for Italy, even though Mussolini gave it lip service. A general European war was inevitable, and would break out "in the spring of 1939 or 1940."

I met Lasker for the first time during this trip, when he was in India; the circumstances are curious. I had a friend in Delhi, Sir Aubrey Metcalfe, who was a member of the government; he was being given a trip up to Peshawar, on the North-West Frontier, and, because he was such an important official, he had a private car. He invited me to come along. Now, to have a private car (they were called "saloons") for a trip on the Indian railways was a serious distinction, which gave a man cachet and prestige; in the ordinary course of events, only the Viceroy and a few of the more resplendent maharajas had private cars at their disposal. Sir Aubrey picked me up at my hotel and we went to the station and stepped into his private car. Imagine, then, the consternation and well-bred chagrin felt by Sir Aubrey Metcalfe when he discovered that the train was carrying not merely one private car, his, but another as well; there were *two* private cars on the train! A grimace of exquisite pain creased his features. The other car was, of course, Lasker's. Sir Aubrey Metcalfe and Lasker, although they had adjoining cars on the same train on a journey that took two and a half days, never met or spoke. At each station when the long, noisy train ground to a slippery halt, I would see a straight-standing, silver-haired man and a beautiful young woman emerge from *their* private car and stroll along the platform. Stroll is the wrong word. Lasker never strolled. He darted. I did not have the faintest idea who he was, and my curiosity was aroused. But Metcalfe, although he was an extremely civilized and friendly man, not at all a Colonel Blimp, was a senior member of the Indian Civil Service and did not feel that it was incumbent upon him to make contact of any kind with a stranger. Lasker, I could see, was dying to meet Metcalfe, but, naturally, would not take the first step. So each pretended that the other did not exist. Finally, just before we reached Peshawar, I could stand this idiotic situation no longer, and went up to Lasker and introduced myself. He replied with the tense eagerness of a boy, "My name is Lasker." I exclaimed, "Not *Albert* Lasker?" because, of course, having lived many years in Chicago, the name was familiar to me. Instantly he asked me and the Metcalfe party to dinner in Peshawar that night, but we were going to Government House, and could not accept.

One of Lasker's letters to Edward contains this passage:

In three days is the anniversary of mother's going. She is, of course, every day and night in the forefront of my mind but during the past two weeks, as December 19 approaches nearer, I review more and more the last happy, happy days she and I spent together in New York, and the happier the memories the more poignant is my pain. I could not tell you why but somehow I realize more clearly than ever that the daily contact with my wife of thirty-five years is no more, and it leaves me with a feeling of almost helpless incompleteness. At the same time, I am determined . . . to find and lose myself in useful work when I come home. Until and unless I do, I know I will have no measure of contentment. Only in useful work, by being of aid to my fellows, can I keep mother alive with me.

The David Sarnoffs gave a party for Lasker and Frances when they landed in New York. Among the guests were several old friends, like the Paul Blocks, the Theodore Roosevelts, the Lenox Lohrs, the Samuel Chotzinoffs, and David Lawrence, the columnist; also Dorothy Thompson, who was at the height of her stormy fame as a commentator. Lasker made a little speech. It was about anti-Semitism around the world.

*

Lasker had met Franklin D. Roosevelt for the first time in the summer of 1937. Roosevelt, out of the blue, urgently summoned him from Chicago, and asked him to lunch at the White House. F.D.R. chatted amiably during lunch, scarcely asking a question and scarcely letting Albert say a word. Later, Lasker said that when he got to heaven, the first thing that he was going to ask St. Peter was why, *why*, WHY the President of the United States had asked him to lunch that day. The best theory to account for Roosevelt's behavior, unless it was based on pure caprice, was that he had intended to sound out Lasker about isolationist sentiment in the Middle West; then he changed his mind, but did not think that it would be courteous to call off the lunch. Lasker, as I say, scarcely got a word in; but there must have been an exchange of views on one topic at least, as the following letter proves.

December 12, 1938

Dear Mr. President:

Remembering most vividly the feeling and concerned interest you expressed to me regarding Anti-Semitism when I had the privilege of lunching with you last summer, I am taking the liberty—after considerable deliberation—of writing you on a matter that will not dismiss itself from my mind.

This letter is premised on two pieces of information, both or either of which may be erroneous. First, that Professor Felix Frankfurter is being considered by you for appointment to the vacancy on the Supreme Court. Second, that word has come to you from some fellow Jews that they feel the appointment of another Jew on the Supreme Court at this time would be unfortunate.

I know Professor Frankfurter but casually. I differ with him radically on many important concepts. I admire him for his knowledge, for his dedication to the public well-being and for his forthrightness. Even though I shall continue to oppose him in those things on which he and I cannot see eye to eye, I should fight with equal vigor for his right to project any thought he feels is in the interest of the country.

Even though I thought it would kindle the flame of Anti-Semitism for a Jew to be appointed to the Supreme Court at this time (which I do not) I would still feel that an infinitely greater hurt would be done that an American should be deprived of the privilege of serving America because he is a Jew.

I am not writing to endorse or urge Professor Frankfurter's appointment; I am simply stating as an American and as a Jew there can be no doubt of his overwhelming fitness for any Judicial responsibility which may come to him, and the fact that he is a Jew should not count for or against him.

I write you thus knowing in advance that you are in agreement with the thoughts expressed herein. My purpose is merely, as one who differs in many concepts with Professor Frankfurter, to record with you my protest against any Jewish protest which may have come to you. In that spirit please accept this letter.

Cordially,

Albert D. Lasker

Roosevelt wrote a friendly reply on December 27, but did not commit himself. On January 5 Frankfurter's appointment to the court was announced.

*

Lasker was becoming increasingly bored, fed up, with advertising now. For years he had felt that there was something creative about it, something adventurous and, to him, exhilarating, which made his efforts worth while; now it was frustrating, exhausting, shoddy, an endless struggle with unimaginative clients to get them to do what he thought they ought to do; worse, it had become mixed up with all manner of extraneous phenomena. The pioneering had gone out of it. He was fond of making an analogy between the Lord & Thomas of the early days and a contemporary agency by comparing an old-time pharmacy with a modern drugstore. In the 1900's, the man who ran a small pharmacy mixed the prescriptions himself, and prescriptions were the basis of his business; but in the 1930's the drugstore contained God knows what, from hamburgers to children's toys to water wings. So it was with advertising.

Voluntarily, Lasker "resigned" the cherished Quaker Oats account, which had been with him for more than thirty years, because he refused to submit his copy to a new kind of allegedly "scientific" system of checking. Then he similarly gave up both RCA and

General Electric because their officers dared to "evaluate" what he was doing for them by some "new fangled" method. More than this, his relations with the American Tobacco Company came under a peculiar cloud, as we shall see in a chapter following. But his disillusion ran deeper; it had little to do with anything personal, or any trouble with any particular account. He remarked to Bob Hutchins, "I am the most superficial man on earth, and yet I am dean of my profession. So there must be something wrong with the profession."

Abruptly, in July, 1938, he quit—that is, retired as president of Lord & Thomas, although he retained ownership of the firm. Don Francisco took office as his successor, with David Noyes and Sheldon Coons as executive vice presidents. But this retirement, like that of opera stars, proved to be short-lived.

Marriage to Doris Kenyon

That autumn Lasker went out to California for a few months; somebody asked him why, and he replied with irony, "For a much needed change of rest." Friends poured affection on him, but he was excruciatingly depressed and lonely. His great friend Will Hays, whom he had helped to make "czar" of the movie industry back in the twenties, and who still held this post, determined that something must be done to cheer him up, and thought that he might cure him of his misery by introducing him to some pleasant young woman whom he might marry. So a campaign to marry him off got under way. Hays held a series of dinner parties, and to each invited the most glamorous unattached women who could be found in Hollywood or adjacent areas, in the hope that Lasker would meet somebody he would like.

Almost at once, he did. She was Doris Kenyon, an actress of distinction, who was beautiful, a thoroughly nice person, companionable, and a good sport. Her first husband, who had died, was Milton Sills, a professor of philosophy in Illinois who changed his career in midstream to become an actor. Miss Kenyon starred in several well-known silent films, like *Valley of the Giants* and *Monsieur*

Beaucaire; also she wrote poems, and had experience as a concert singer.

Lasker, impetuous as always, irresistible, swept her off her feet. Apparently it never occurred to him that the fact that Will Hays thought he ought to get married was not a necessarily valid reason for doing so. He was convinced that he was in love with Miss Kenyon, and she with him, although they had known one another only a few weeks, and the marriage took place in the Waldorf-Astoria in New York on October 28, 1938. His wedding present to her was an exceedingly expensive sable coat.

They sailed on the *Ile de France* for a European honeymoon but, unfortunately, the marriage did not last for more than a very brief interval. Miss Kenyon had never met a man so easily upset by minor stresses, so prone to be hurt, so taut and sensitive. He exhausted her. Lasker, on his side, had never had a close association with a star; *he* had always been the star, and although she was tactful and unobtrusive, he was wounded when people paid more attention to her than to him. It soon became clear that no two people could be more incompatible. Lasker took the decision bluntly to end an impossible situation, and arrangements were made for immediate separation and a divorce. He was bitterly hurt that the marriage should fail so quickly, and felt agonized humiliation at his own shortcomings. Arriving back in New York, he called Gerhard Foreman in Glencoe from the dock and said, "I have made a mistake. Please come to New York and help me." Foreman brought him back to Chicago, and he lived with the Foremans that winter. During all this Miss Kenyon, who must have experienced her own share of disappointment and humiliation, behaved very well; she said that anything that Albert wanted was all right with her.

So she went to Reno, and a divorce was granted on June 8, 1939. Lasker settled a large sum on her—something fantastic considering that they had lived together as husband and wife hardly more than a week. She did not want to take it. Presently she resumed her movie career, and he helped find her a job on radio. Some years later she married Bronislav Mlynarsky, the brother-in-law of Artur Rubinstein, the pianist, and lives happily near Santa Monica to this day.

Now Lasker was on his own again, lonely again, desperate again. But he hadn't given up. He exclaimed doggedly to a friend, "I'm going to find the right woman if I have to marry *ten* of 'em!"

He did not have to marry ten, and he did not have long to wait.

Chapter 15

MARY

The most important event in Albert Lasker's life occurred at about 1:55 P.M. on April 1, 1939, in the New York restaurant "Twenty-One," when he met Mary Woodard Reinhardt for the first time. He was lunching with Colonel (later General) William J. Donovan, the illustrious "Wild Bill," who had won the Congressional Medal of Honor in World War I, and who was soon to become head of the Office of Strategic Services in World War II. Donovan was a lawyer, and for some years had been one of Lasker's friends. Blue-bland of eye, butter-soft in voice, and composed of equal parts of fire, iron, and pink leather, he had a strong appeal for him. Lasker even left him a small legacy.

"Twenty-One" had the atmosphere of a club, and almost everybody who went there regularly knew everybody else; particularly at lunch it swarmed with well-known people. Mrs. Reinhardt, whom it will be easier to call Mary from now on, was lunching at a nearby table with Rosita Winston. Donovan knew them both, nodded a greeting to them, and introduced Lasker to Mary. But Albert was concentrating on his conversation with Donovan, and paid no attention to her except to smile vaguely and mumble an acknowledgment of the introduction. Mary recalls that she said to herself, "That man is making a great mistake in not noticing me!"

Tables broke up toward the end of lunch, and groups of people coalesced. Mary was introduced to Lasker a second time, by Lewis Strauss, who later became head of the Atomic Energy Commission, and then a third time by Max Epstein, the Illinois industrialist and art collector. Lasker was still busy with his own thoughts and talk. At last he woke up, became acutely conscious of Mary, and exchanged a few words with her. Then she had to leave the restaurant. Lasker turned to Donovan, breathless, and said, "Tell me about that young woman. Who is she?" Donovan replied that, among other things, she was a successful businesswoman, and Albert listened attentively to his friend's account of her career.

The next day Lasker, who always did things with velocity, telephoned Mrs. Bernard Gimbel, and said that she must at once invite Mrs. Reinhardt to lunch on Sunday at the Gimbel country house, Chieftains, in Greenwich, where he was to be a guest. Next, Mary received an invitation to drop in and have a drink the following day with Max Epstein at the Ritz. She did not know Epstein well, but he had bought several pictures from the Reinhardt Galleries. She assumed that he was having a large cocktail party, and to her surprise found, when she arrived, that only one other guest was present— Albert Lasker. She was an hour late, and he was fuming with impatience. He was not accustomed to being kept waiting. Nor had Mary much experience of men who did not disguise it when they were cross. However, he immediately became tranquil, and a vivid conversation followed.

They discussed, among other things, holiday pleasures, business, gardens, theaters, and movies, and discovered that they had a strong community of interests. She said that she was fonder of flowers than almost anything, and he told her casually—but glowingly—about Mill Road Farm, where his quarter-mile of borders was one of the prettiest in the country. Then she said that she liked boating in the Sound, and he said that he would like to take her cruising with friends on Lake Michigan. Mary was startled by his directness—also by the continuing revelation that they had such a close identity of tastes and delight in the same pleasures. Once he said to her with boyish bravado, "Whatever you like, I have!"

*

And who was Mary Woodard Reinhardt? She had been one of the prettiest girls in her class at the University of Wisconsin, and

was now well known for her lustrous good looks and coloring—
she had dark hair, cheeks like peonies, and very large blue eyes the
color of cornflowers. She had been divorced from Paul Reinhardt,
the art dealer, five years before. Now she was associated with Condé
Nast in a pattern business she had created, and also with an industrial designer; between the two positions she earned $25,000 a
year. Her many friends admired not merely her beauty, but her
character and temperament. She was bland, unhurried, and good-
humored—also she had a serious mind. She was honest, practical,
and outgiving, and with these qualities went others; she was
decidedly feminine, and had a keen talent for the appreciation of
beauty and art.

Mary Woodard was born in Watertown, Wisconsin, of Puritan
Yankee and North Irish stock; her father, Frank E. Woodard, was a
local banker, and the family was quite well off. She was a frail child,
often ill; one of her early memories is of her mother and a friend
bending over her bed when she was convalescing from a mastoid
infection; they thought that she was asleep, and she heard the friend
say, "I don't think you'll ever raise her, Sarah." (Mary recalls that,
sick as she was, she said to herself, "She's wrong!") She was extremely
fond of her sister, who later became Mrs. Allmon Fordyce. Their
mother was full of public spirit. She had a passion about smoke
control; it was she who led a crusade in New York City forcing the
utility and other companies to install smoke consumers in their
chimneys, in order to abate the dirt caused by factory smoke. Robert
Moses, the Commissioner of Parks, was one of her heroes.[1] Mary's
family, like Albert's, always had a strong sense of civic duty and
good will. Public service was bred in her bones, as it was in his.

Her father was silent, scrupulous, and a model citizen. Handsome,
tall, he had a charming smile, but was extraordinarily uncom-
municative. He was much respected in the community, but had little
contact with his children. Frugality obsessed him. When Mary went

[1] Mrs. Woodard died in 1940. She was the founder of two public parks in
Watertown, Wisconsin, and is still remembered for her work for the Outdoor
Cleanliness Association of New York City.

to Radcliffe, where the winters are cold, she wanted—and needed
—a modest fur coat; her father replied, "Why don't you wear long
underwear?" (But she got the coat.) The pattern of her business
career was largely shaped by rebellion against her father's par-
simoniousness; she determined at an early age to learn about money,
become independent, and be responsible to no one for what she
spent. She also developed a healthy taste for luxury. She was
fascinated, when she met Lasker, to notice how different he was from
her father, although both were the quintessence of honesty, fairness,
and good citizenship. But whereas her father was profoundly cautious and reticent, Albert was articulate, vivacious, and bursting
with warmth and generosity. Above all, he understood the art of
living well, which her father thought was an invention of the devil.

Another influence in Mary's life, from the earliest years, was a
passionate interest in health—possibly because her own had been
so poor. She was very ill during the great influenza epidemic of
1917-18, as were several of her friends. She discovered that most
doctors, no matter how skillful, knew little about certain diseases;
that people in good health did not know, by and large, how to take
care of sick people; above all, that the rank and file of the population simply could not afford proper medical care. She knew men
and women whose life savings were wiped out by the cost of a
prolonged illness. Health insurance began to interest her. She demanded to know why more money was not available for systematic
research into medical problems—so that diseases could be studied
and controlled. When she was still in her teens she said to herself,
"I'm going to *do* something about all this, if it's the last thing I
ever do!"

She was graduated from the Donner Seminary in Milwaukee and
went to the University of Wisconsin for a year and a half, and after
that to Radcliffe, from which she was graduated *cum laude* in 1923
(at about the time Lasker left the Shipping Board); then she did post-
graduate work at Oxford. She was fond of art, and majored at
Radcliffe in the history of art. From her childhood, she had been
interested in paintings; she was almost painfully visual-minded,

with intense consciousness of design and color. She returned to New York, got a job in the Reinhardt Galleries, and married Paul Reinhardt in 1926. She was at that time the only American dealer on Fifty-seventh Street who had a degree in the history of art.

After her divorce she had a living to earn in earnest. The art business was a risky trade, and she needed something more secure. The depression was in full swing. She conceived the idea of having good inexpensive dress patterns made by *Vogue* and giving them sales appeal by decorating them with photographs of glamorous movie stars. She named the project "Hollywood Patterns," got releases from various movie companies, and set out. *Vogue* manufactured the patterns and she sold them for fifteen cents each, through the chain stores. The depression deepened, and more and more women were obliged to make their own dresses at home; Hollywood Patterns, after a slow start (the first pattern came out the day the banks closed in 1933), began to flourish. Mary got one-third of a cent on each pattern, and by the time she met Lasker she was comfortably established in her new business career. They enjoyed discussing business, and Albert admired her greatly for being a successful businesswoman. Mary now had the responsibility of investing the proceeds of her father's estate for her mother, her sister, and herself, and she enjoyed the company of men knowledgeable on business affairs.

But she had not forgotten about art—or medicine.

*

At this time Mary lived with her mother and her maid, Nancy Morris, in a small penthouse at 400 East Fifty-second Street. A Chirico painting of a white horse and a zebra hung over the mantel; in one corner stood a harp of exquisite workmanship; the terrace held a mass of flowers. Everywhere she lived, even on the top of a skyscraper, she had a garden. When Lasker saw her apartment for the first time he was astonished and charmed. He had no idea that a person could live so nicely on the amount of money she made, and he cried, "Why, you could support *me!*"

On Sunday he drove her out to the Gimbel place in Greenwich. Arriving, they took a walk on the property, and were an hour late for lunch. Not for a score of years had Lasker ever been late for anything. He was beside himself with excitement and delight. She asked him about Europe and the threat of war; he answered with extreme seriousness, and Mary thought that she had never encountered before a mind of such scope and comprehension. Moreover, he made everything seem simple, although he did not talk down. A long afternoon passed in two minutes, and before it was over both knew that they were deeply drawn to each other.

Mary had to go on to another engagement, and when she arrived home that evening her mother took one look at her and asked in alarm, "What's the matter?" She replied, "I'm exhausted—I've just had lunch with the most exciting man I ever met!"

Now Lasker began to see her frequently, but there were several obstacles. He was fifty-eight, and Mary's mother didn't like at all the idea of a possible romantic association between her daughter and a man so much older. One person in the household who, on the contrary, was delighted with him from the first minute was Nancy Morris, who had been Mary's maid for six or seven years. Nancy was, and is, a most special person—infinitely soothing, but with dash. She was British born, and, as a child, worked in the household of Mrs. Gladstone, no less. Eventually she found her way to America and Mary. Her devotion to Mary was utter and absolute, as it became to Albert later.

A few weeks after their first meeting Lasker asked Mary, "What do you want most out of life—what accomplishment?" She replied, "To push the idea of health insurance, because most people can't afford adequate medical care. And to help promote research in cancer, tuberculosis, and the major diseases."

This appealed to Albert strongly. He replied, "I'd like to help you, but for that kind of program my money is nothing. No private money, not even Rockefeller money, can be more than a drop in the bucket. You will need *federal* money." He added surprisingly,

"What's more, I'll show you how to get it." This from Albert
Lasker, a foremost apostle of private enterprise!

He had, of course, been interested in medical research all his
life, but only in a spasmodic, superficial way. He scarcely knew one
branch of medicine from another. Disease had always frightened
him, and although he appreciated the need of better medical facili-
ties, his general attitude had been, "I can supply money for research,
but after that it's not my business—leave it to God and the doctors."

Now Mary, who was erudite on these matters but not nearly as
erudite as she was presently to become, began to educate him, and
he, on his side, educated her. To work for really large sums of
money for medical research in the federal budget it would first be
necessary, he pointed out, to understand politics—that is, to make
friends with Senators and Congressmen and learn about the mysterious ways of Washington.

Albert and Mary complemented each other nicely. Their companionship was instinctive and fundamental. He represented everything she admired—good looks, business genius, power, vitality,
creative intelligence—and she was like no woman he had ever met
before. She looked like the loveliest of Renoirs, but could stand up
to him in any argument, maintain her own area of independence,
and hold her own with him. Above all, she appreciated him. His
eccentricities, his vagaries, did not irritate her; on the contrary, she
was entertained.

Business carried him back to Chicago; then he returned to New
York for his birthday, May 1. They had still known one another
for only a month. Now Lasker suddenly became aloof, diffident, and
constrained. He was deeply involved in Mary, but afraid. The
disaster of his previous marriage haunted him. He wondered if he
had any right to be paying court to a woman so much younger.
Self-doubt paralyzed him. He didn't want to do anything precipi-
tate. He was much more concerned about her happiness than his
own. In June Mary went to London, in fulfillment of plans made
long before. Lasker telephoned her once (a great concession—he

didn't like the transatlantic phone) , and sent her spectacular cargoes of orchids; then he telegraphed her that war was bound to break out by the end of August (he was wrong only by a day or two) and that she must return to New York by August 1.

She did so, but he became frightened again, and, to her great surprise, did not meet her boat. She became passionately sorry for him. He called her, and they met that evening; it was obvious that he was in profound distress. Presently she had to go to California on business; passing through Chicago she saw Mill Road Farm for the first time, and was enraptured. He telephoned her in San Francisco that his health had completely broken down, and he set out for a ranch in Arizona in company with a nurse. Here he stayed almost completely isolated for two months; the nearest telephone was ninety miles away. Once a week he drove this distance to telephone her (she was back in New York), and in the end he returned to New York. But he was still ill, although doctors disagreed about what ailed him. One in Arizona, whom he trusted, said that he was suffering from a malfunction of the adrenal glands; Mary set out doggedly to find who was the best physician in the world for this complaint, and came up with the name of Robert Loeb.

One night Albert and Mary went to the ballet. Salvador Dali had done the sets. Lasker was amused by these, but puzzled. Mary explained that, in a way, Dali's interest in the subconscious stemmed from Freud; he was depicting in color and form the world of dreams. His distortions were not accidental, but followed a subconscious logic of their own, in a pattern arising out of his own individual conception of the inner meaning of the ballet. Albert was interested, and Mary had a sudden idea. Several times she had tried to persuade him to go to a psychoanalyst, but he had merely scoffed. Now she pointed out a possible analogy, far-fetched as it might seem, between Dali's work and the suffering of a man like Lasker. Dali managed to put together totally unrelated images arising out of his subconscious, and could produce perfectly composed works of art. Similarly if Lasker's conflicts could somehow be brought to the surface he might find that his personality, relieved

of anxieties, would take on a new and harmonious pattern. Lasker
was startled. A window opened. For the first time in his life, he
accepted the possibility that psychoanalytic therapy might help
him.

Chapter 16

THE MANTON CASE

Something gnawing on Lasker's mind intermittently for several years was the so-called Manton case. Elements of this story are weird, it is intricate in the extreme, and its crisscross roots go far back into a network of deception. The easiest way to summarize it in a sentence is to say that Lasker was the innocent dupe of business associates— the only time in his life he was ever duped.

Lord & Thomas was, as we know, the advertising agency for Lucky Strike, and the American Tobacco Company was by far Lasker's most lucrative account. Moreover, one of Lasker's friends was Louis S. Levy, a well-known member of the New York bar, and Levy's firm—Chadbourne, Stanchfield, & Levy, one of the biggest and most successful law firms in Manhattan—was counsel for the tobacco company. Lasker, George Washington Hill of the tobacco company, and the law firm were all close.

Thomas L. Chadbourne, a famous figure in the New York of the day, was senior partner of Chadbourne, Stanchfield, & Levy, but he had little interest in the law as such. What occupied him was finance. He drew over a hundred thousand dollars a year from the firm, and Levy made even more. The third principal partner, John B. Stanchfield, had died some years before, but his name still appeared in the company's name. Both Chadbourne and Levy were continually on the lookout to make more money, out of the law or otherwise. They entered into all sorts of deals, and both were substantial stockholders in the American Tobacco Company.

So far so good. A younger man was another lawyer, Paul M. Hahn. He had been a member of the Levy firm, and as such had handled much of the tobacco company's legal business. Hill liked him and he moved over to American Tobacco as assistant to the president, at $50,000 a year, in 1931, and became a vice president in 1933. He did the tobacco company's legal work in its own offices, and at the same time naturally maintained contact with his former partners, Chadbourne and Levy, who were the company's counsel and who were of course consulted in regard to any important litigation involving the American Tobacco Company.

On October 5, 1931, Levy in New York telephoned Lasker in Chicago and asked him if he would lend him $150,000 in cash. Several men described as "minor" officers of the American Tobacco Company—they were not so minor—had been caught short in the stock market, and would be wiped out if their accounts were not promptly covered. Hill was fishing up in Canada, and was hard to reach by telephone. Levy, although he was not an official of the tobacco company but merely its counsel, stepped in and thought of turning to Lasker as a savior in the emergency. Lasker complied immediately. This was during the worst of the depression and, as has been mentioned earlier in this book, he had similarly rescued several friends and clients in similar situations. Lord & Thomas was doing $19,000,000 worth of business with the American Tobacco Company that year, which brought $2,850,000 in commissions (before expenses); compared to this huge sum $150,000 was a pittance. Lasker had no hesitation at all in accommodating Levy and the company officials who would otherwise have been ruined. It was a routine gesture. Since, however, the request had come from Levy and not from the company itself he insisted that he write him a formal letter as a memorandum of the transaction. This Levy did. No collateral or security was put up. Interest was 5 per cent.

Then Lasker completely forgot the matter. And as a matter of fact nothing untoward ever happened in regard to this loan. It was a perfectly legitimate loan, on the level, and it was repaid promptly. Levy recovered the money from the officials involved, and it was remitted to Lord & Thomas before the end of January, 1932.

Next came something much more complicated. On May 9, 1932,

Lasker came to New York for one of his regular conferences with Hill. At this time Ralph Sollitt was still president of Lord & Thomas, stationed in New York. Lasker and Sollitt called on Hill and Hahn. The meeting took place in the New York offices of the American Tobacco Company, which is a key point in the story. As Hill withdrew after the conference, Hahn asked Lasker to step into a room with him for a moment. Sollitt accompanied them. Hahn then said, according to Lasker's subsequent testimony when the matter reached court, "I want to speak to you on a matter that Mr. Hill is embarrassed to speak to you about. . . . You remember that loan you made at the request of Louis Levy last fall? An identical situation has arisen. This time it is for $250,000. Will you accommodate us?"[1]

Hahn later specifically denied that he made any reference to Hill in this conversation. His testimony was that he approached Lasker at the suggestion of his former partner, Chadbourne.

Lasker was somewhat startled. After all, a quarter of a million dollars is a lot of money. Still, the other loan had been repaid promptly, and there was no reason to assume that this would not be. His instantaneous if subconscious thought was that Hill himself must have lost heavily on the market, and, despite his enormous salary, needed salvaging. His testimony as to what happened next was the following. He said to Hahn, "Surely. But I don't want it [the loan] out indefinitely. When will it be paid back?" Hahn replied, "Oh, at the outside in a couple of months." Lasker said, "Let us define what you mean by a few months. Four months?" Hahn agreed to this, and Lasker agreed to accommodate him with the loan. Hahn then said that a "man" would give Lasker collateral and a note. Lasker said, "We don't want any note, we don't want any collateral. We are doing this for your accommodation." But Hahn insisted that the borrower should submit collateral, which would be in the form of stock or real estate. Lasker refused to entertain the idea of real estate, because this led to too much

[1] U.S. Circuit Court of Appeals, "In the Matter of Louis S. Levy," Transcript of Record, Vol. II, p. 908.

"detail." Then he complained that he was in a hurry, said impatiently that arrangements should be made with Sollitt, and walked out. He did not want to be bothered by the transaction, and left for Chicago the next day.

A man named James J. Sullivan appeared in Sollitt's office promptly. Levy had instructed him to go there, after learning that Lasker had agreed to lend the money. Nobody at Lord & Thomas had ever heard of Sullivan. Sollitt testified later that he telephoned Hahn to ask if this was the correct man to receive the money and Hahn said Yes. So Sollitt gave him, Sullivan, a check for $250,000; Sullivan signed a demand note, bearing interest at 5 per cent, and turned over 15,604 shares of something known as the National Cellulose Corporation as security—collateral—which Sollitt accepted and transmitted to the Chicago office of Lord & Thomas, although Lasker had not wanted any collateral at all.

The person of Judge Martin T. Manton now enters this tangled story. At just this time an important legal proceeding involving the American Tobacco Company was reaching climax. The company had put forward a bonus plan in 1931 whereby officers and employees were allowed to subscribe for shares of its common stock at $25 a share whereas the market value at the time was around $112 a share. About $10,000,000 was involved in all. Chadbourne and Levy, who were to be cut in on the transaction, stood to gain about $100,000 if it went through; so did Hill. But a stockholder's suit was initiated by a man named Rogers to prevent the bonus plan from being carried out, on the ground that it was grossly unfair to stockholders at large. The case dragged on, and was finally decided on June 13, 1932—a month, be it carefully noted, after the Lord & Thomas loan to Sullivan. Judge Manton, the senior judge of the United States Circuit Court of Appeals, rendered the decision. There were two other judges, who were divided; Manton cast the deciding vote, and wrote the majority opinion. And he ruled in favor of the tobacco company.

Judge Manton, aged fifty-two, was a powerful figure on the federal bench, and the tenth ranking judge in the country. He was a devout Catholic—a daily communicant—and prominent in lay Catholic circles. A fur of seeming respectability sheathed him, and only narrowly had he missed being appointed to the Supreme Court some years before. Now, however, his reputation was dubious among his colleagues on the bench. He owned a good deal of real estate, and was continually dabbling in shady businesses far removed from the law. He and Levy had been classmates at Columbia Law School. The brilliant Levy rose high at the bar, but Manton's early career as a lawyer was not distinguished. In fact, when he had been first appointed to a federal judgeship back in 1916, many members of the bar were shocked. The man largely responsible for his becoming a judge was none other than Louis Levy, who arranged it through his partner John Stanchfield, a man of much influence behind the scenes. Stanchfield was reluctant to press for Manton's appointment, but did so at Levy's urgent request.

Months passed in 1932, and the $250,000 loan was not repaid. Mr. Sachse, the comptroller of Lord & Thomas, reported this fact to Lasker, who cried indignantly, "Get Mr. Sollitt in New York on the telephone and tell him to go to Mr. Hahn. An agreement is an agreement." Sachse then asked Lasker to look at the collateral which Sullivan had given. Albert had never so much as glanced at this. He said that he did not want to bother with it (he was certain that the loan would now be repaid at once), but Sachse insisted. Lasker, grumbling, went through the papers, and had one of the cardinal shocks of his life.

The collateral, as stated above, was stock in the National Cellulose Corporation. Lasker had never even heard of this company. But, looking through its literature, he discovered that it manufactured an article named Puritas. Now Puritas had been an irritant to him for several years, because it had come into the market as a minor competitor of Kotex. Kotex was made by the International Cellucotton Products Company. Moreover, Puritas was a troublesome competitor, addicted to price-cutting and other unpleasant practices. Lasker was, of course, an important shareholder in International Cellucotton, he did its advertising and had helped build up its busi-

ness, and beyond this Kotex-Kleenex had for many years been dear
to his heart. Now he found that he held as collateral a large—in
fact controlling—interest in a company, National Cellulose, that
was his own worst competitor! He was dumbfounded. He was black
with anger. As he himself put it, he had advanced money "to destroy
himself" while he thought that he was merely doing a client, the
American Tobacco Company, a routine favor.

At once, in acute embarrassment, Lasker went to his old friend
Ernst Mahler of Kotex-Kleenex. He told him that, through an
extraordinary and indeed fantastic series of circumstances, he, Lasker,
was involved in the affairs of Puritas, which he hated, and which
was Mahler's bête noire as well. He even had the horrible thought
that Mahler might think that he was double-crossing him. Mahler
was much upset. The crazy situation was that Lasker, Mahler's
friend, now had $250,000 in a company which was trying to put
him, Mahler, out of business! Mahler set out to investigate. Except
for Mahler the story might never have been broken open. Mahler
found out that the president of National Cellulose, which made
Puritas, was none other than James J. Sullivan. All along Lasker had
assumed (as his subsequent testimony demonstrated) that Sullivan
was a minor employee of the tobacco company, a messenger for Hill.
He had no idea at all that he was a businessman, the president of a
company, much less the president of a competing company. Lasker,
fuming, kicked himself a thousand times for having been so careless
as never to have looked at the collateral. Then another curious fact
came out, although it was some time before its full sinister signifi-
cance was realized. Sullivan was the intimate friend and business
associate of a federal judge named Martin T. Manton!

To this day, it is not entirely clear why those involved in the loan
insisted that Lasker should accept collateral, particularly anything
so touchy as collateral of a company in the cellulose field. The most
reasonable supposition is that they thought that by offering collateral
they were "respectabilizing" the transaction, and making it easier
to get the money; also Manton had nothing else to "borrow" on,

and they were in a hurry.[2] Later it came out that Manton held 49 per cent of the common stock (and 80 per cent of the preferred) of National Cellulose, and that Chadbourne and Levy—through dummies—were stockholders to the extent of $37,500 each.

Lasker wanted his money back. That was all he cared about—at this time. Lord & Thomas billed Sullivan for the $250,000 several times in a routine way, but never even got the courtesy of a reply. Lasker was furious. He had always been free and easy with money, but he hated to be victimized. But Chadbourne kept insisting that the loan was as good as gold, and had not been repaid merely because Sullivan was suffering temporary embarrassment. Publicly, Judge Manton's name had not yet figured in the case.

Lasker was in a peculiar position. He might have taken the matter up with Hill directly, but never did so for what seemed to him a good reason. He was not sure that Hill had that much ready cash at the moment, and did not want to embarrass him or question a friend closely. Hill was, after all, his best client, and he did not want to prejudice his relations with the American Tobacco Company and lose a $19,000,000 account. He was torn between losing $250,000 and risking the commission on $19,000,000.

Why didn't he cash the collateral, since not a cent of capital or interest on the loan was ever repaid? One reason was that the stock dropped sharply in value, and in the end was worth only $2 a share. More important, he now firmly adopted and resolutely held to the line that Sullivan was no more than a front, a stooge, that he had lent the money in good faith on the assumption that it was an accommodation to officials of the American Tobacco Company, and that these officials, and nobody else, had the clear obligation to repay.

Lasker was caught in a trap. One result was something most paradoxical—he did his conscientious best to *ruin* National Cellulose, whose stock he held! He was delighted, not displeased, when its

[2] Another possibility is that Chadbourne, never dreaming that Lasker would not look at the collateral and not anticipating his reaction if he did, thought that the loan would be attractive to him because he was already involved in the cellulose business.

stock went down. He wanted Kotex-Kleenex to run it right out of business.

Why did not the American Tobacco officials repay? Because, as the case got muddier, they wanted at all costs to steer clear of any further involvement in it. They did not acknowledge that the loan was theirs at all.

Why did not Chadbourne and Levy repay? Because they did not want to part with that much money, or admit their part in the transaction. They agreed fully that Lasker should be repaid, but disclaimed responsibility.

Everybody evaded; everybody dodged; Lasker held the bag; the case was like a bizarre game of blind man's buff, or, as it was said by the judge in the court proceedings later, "a minuet danced by grandmothers" on tiptoes.

Then, in December, 1935, Sullivan died, and his estate was found to be insolvent. Judge Manton was the executor. Lasker now employed the celebrated criminal lawyer Max D. Steuer to attempt to collect the debt. This alarmed the A.T.C., and Steuer and Levy entered into negotiations. Levy's firm offered three indirect methods of settlement of the loan according to testimony in the subsequent court proceedings. First, the collateral would be sold for what it might bring. Then, to make up the deficiency, the following alternatives were put forward: (a) additional business might be given by the A.T.C. to Lord & Thomas to raise the sum necessary; (b) the rate of commission charged on accounts handled by Lord & Thomas for the tobacco company in England might be increased, to achieve the same result; (c) special additional commissions might go to Lord & Thomas out of the Lucky Strike Hit Parade show. But both Hill and Hahn testified later that these proposals were made without their authority.

Indignantly Lasker turned down these offers. He would accept nothing but full, direct, unequivocal payment because he felt that anything else would make him an ex post facto participant in events that were obviously shady in the extreme.

What were these events? A bombshell burst. Thomas E. Dewey,

at that time District Attorney of New York County, began early in 1938 to investigate Manton's activities, and a county grand jury examined various witnesses. No indictment was returned, but Dewey submitted details of the case to the chairman of the Judiciary Committe of the United States House of Representatives. The $250,000 loan was among items mentioned. At about the same time, the New York *World Telegram* printed a series of articles airing charges of corruption in the federal judiciary. Subsequently in the spring of 1939, a federal grand jury opened an exhaustive investigation, and Manton was indicted in April, after being forced to resign from the federal bench.

His trial, which lasted a month and was sensational in the extreme, opened in May, 1939, and on June 21, 1939, Manton was found guilty of "obstructing justice"—that is, he had accepted $186,146 in "loans and gifts" from eight different litigants—and was sentenced to a fine of $10,000 and two years in jail. No such scandal has ever defaced the federal judiciary before or since. In one case Manton got $10,000 from a banker for reversing a decision in which the banker himself had been convicted of bribery!

The $250,000 loan from Lord & Thomas played no role in Manton's trial, because of the statute of limitations. But as a result of the Dewey investigation the full story of what had happened to Lasker's money at last became known. There was good reason for people having tried to cover up. Manton got all the $250,000 except $32,000. Sullivan, from first to last, was no more than a "conduit," a pipe line, siphoning money into firms that Manton controlled. Some real estate largely owned by him, in particular the Esplanade Hotel in New York City, had gone sour, and the judge desperately needed money to retrieve his position. Taking a walk with Levy one morning, he told him—as if casually—that Sullivan, the head of National Cellulose, in which Levy and Chadbourne were stockholders, seemed to be in need of a loan; Levy said, "Send him to me." But the money, when Sullivan got the quarter-million from Lord & Thomas, never went to National Cellulose. It was not intended to go there. Almost all of it went at once (through Sullivan) into the Alamac-Esplanade Corporation, of which Manton owned 90 per cent of the stock, and other dingy little companies operated by him.

Of course the root point is that Manton got the money immediately before he was to give a decision in a court case in which the tobacco company had $10,000,000 at stake, and from which Chadbourne and Levy stood to gain $100,000. Nobody, even today, knows exactly what happened after Manton asked Levy to arrange a loan for Sullivan. But clearly Manton was, in effect, asking for a bribe, and, with the stockholder's suit pending, he was given one. It was as simple—and corrupt—as that. One problem remained—where to get the money? Someone came up with the thought that Lasker, who had been liberal in lending money before, would be an ideal source. Probably the conspirators intended to repay him in time, through the collateral or otherwise, when and if their affairs got straightened out. But they never did get straightened out, and he never got a cent of his money back.

Lasker became like a man haunted after the Dewey investigation began. It horrified him that a federal judge could have been corrupt. For years this case had given him black hours, but now it was no longer a matter of retrieving a quarter of a million dollars out of which he had been cheated, but something a great deal more important—his good name. The moral shock was profound. He was questioned by Dewey's office at length. This was an unpleasant experience. He was perfectly innocent of any wrongdoing; he had been a dupe, nothing more. But the highly embarrassing circumstance remained that he, Albert D. Lasker, had indirectly provided $250,000 with which a federal judge had been bribed.

Rage, worry, and humiliation possessed him. He was in a fantastically vulnerable position. After all, he was doing a very large amount of business with the American Tobacco Company, and the supposition might well be advanced in court by a hostile attorney that he, as well as Levy and Chadbourne, had been a party to the bribe. Why hadn't he ever directly pressed Hill for repayment? Why hadn't he even looked at the collateral? Why had he lent the money

in the first place? He decided that the only sensible procedure for
him was to tell the exact truth, and trust that, in spite of everything,
he would be believed. He employed the eminent jurist, Judge Joseph
M. Proskauer, as his attorney, who submitted his story to the
government. The government believed him, every word, and he was
saved.

Meantime, Levy had withdrawn from the Chadbourne firm,
and Chadbourne died. In subsequent proceedings Levy attempted,
in order to save his own skin, to throw as much blame as possible
on Chadbourne, who, if he had been living, would probably have
similarly tried to blame Levy.

The next act was a disbarment proceeding brought by the federal
government against Levy and Hahn. The hearings, which took place
in July and August, 1939, lasted for eight days, and provided
surpassing drama. One witness was Manton himself, whose own
sentence to jail was being appealed. Lasker was an important—in
fact, vital—witness for the government. He attended several of
the hearings; Mary, who had just returned from Europe, went with
him to one. His conscience was clear, but the experience was
painful beyond belief. He hated Levy now; detested him; but
Hill and Hahn were his friends as well as business associates, with
whom he had worked cordially for many years. Moreover, his
evidence was bound to throw an unpleasant light on certain activities of the tobacco company, his biggest client. The case was
heard by the senior United States District Judge of the Southern
District of New York, John C. Knox. The lawyers were a veritable
constellation. Prosecuting for the government was John T. Cahill,
the United States Attorney, who had prosecuted Manton; his
principal assistant was Mathias F. Correa.[3] Counsel for Levy were
John W. Davis, no less, who had been Democratic candidate for
President of the United States in 1924, and Harold R. Medina,
who was subsequently elevated to a judgeship and became nationally

[3] Cahill had left private practice temporarily, at the invitation of Attorney
General Frank Murphy, to investigate charges of corruption in the federal
judiciary.

famous for his patient handling of the Communist conspiracy cases in 1949. Hahn's attorney was a well-known veteran of the New York bar, George Z. Medalie.

The most dramatic evidence had to do with a letter dated April 26, 1932, purporting to have been written by Sullivan and addressed to Levy. It explained in detail why $250,000 was needed promptly to rescue Manton's investment in the Esplanade hotel. Actually, as a result of investigation by Cahill's staff, it was established that the letter was typed by Manton's secretary (she put Sullivan's name on it) on the same typewriter that the judge used for other correspondence, and that the paper (there was no letterhead) carried a United States government watermark. The most extraordinary efforts were made to conceal the fact that this letter existed, and the fact that it did exist did not become known to Cahill until July 19, 1939, a few days before the trial opened. Of course, this letter clinched the fact that Manton and Levy were bound together in the plot.

Lasker's position was completely vindicated by the trial, and he was absolved of any guilt. Cahill, indeed, paid tribute to his correctness, as did Judge Knox. Levy was found guilty and disbarred, which ended his career. Hahn was exonerated, and is now president of the American Tobacco Company.

*

This case is so convoluted as well as sordid that a recapitulation may be in order. Its gist may be stated in half a dozen paragraphs:

1. Lasker, in good faith, lent $250,000 to a man named Sullivan who he thought was a representative of the tobacco company.

2. This money secretly went to Judge Manton, who at about the same time rendered a judicial decision extremely important to the tobacco company.

3. Agents for this manipulation were members of the law firm which represented the American Tobacco Company.

4. Lasker lost every cent of his $250,000.

5. Manton went to jail (on other charges) and Levy, the principal attorney involved, was disgraced.

6. Lasker had no idea that he was contributing to the delinquency of a federal judge, but underwent grave embarrassment until he was cleared, and this was probably the most agonizing experience he ever had.

*

But now, at last, the whole ugly case was behind him, and he could resume free life.

Chapter 17

A NEW LIFE

One day in 1939 the telephone rang in the private office of Dr. Robert F. Loeb, director of medical services of the Columbia Presbyterian Medical Center in New York and one of the most distinguished physicians in the world. The nurse in the reception room downstairs said that a visitor wanted to see him. But Loeb takes no private patients; all his supple energies go into research, teaching, and administration.

He asked, "Does he want to see me as a patient?"

"Yes."

"Tell him that I don't take patients. It's the rule of the hospital."

"He says he knows that."

"Ask him the nature of his problem, and perhaps I can refer him to the proper doctor."

Pause. "No. He says he has to see you."

"I'm terribly sorry, but I can't see him."

"He says that he's come all the way from Chicago to see you."

"Tell him that he should have written first; he should have made inquiries."

Another pause. "He says that if he had written you, the reply would have been that you would not see him."

"I'm sorry, but you'll have to tell him again that I don't take private patients."

"He says that he's going to stay in New York and wait if it takes two weeks."

Loeb sighed. "I'll run downstairs and see him for a moment to get rid of him."

Lasker introduced himself—the name meant nothing at all to
Loeb—and said that he had an endocrine problem, which he
wanted him to treat because he understood that he was the best
doctor in America in this field (Mary had told him this); Loeb
repeated that the rules of the hospital forbade his doing any private
practice. Lasker still had all of his gift for original, dramatic salesmanship. He said, "Very well, Doctor. But do you realize what a
tremendous responsibility you are taking on yourself?"

"How so?" asked Loeb.

"You are sentencing me to death."

Loeb was so startled that he jumped. He said, "I can't take you
as a patient, but I'll give you fifteen minutes of my lunch hour.
Come on Thursday at 12:15."

This was Monday. Lasker said softly, "I'll stay right here till
Thursday."

So they had lunch; it lasted for an hour and a half, and one of
the great friendships of Lasker's life—also Loeb's—began. Loeb
turned him over to Dr. Dana Atchley and others of his expert
associates, and with them made a thorough study of his condition.
Nothing, it appeared, was seriously wrong with him physically, and
after some weeks Loeb suggested that he might do well to have a
brief bout of psychoanalysis. Loeb did not particularly believe in the
psychoanalytic method, but he thought that it would do his patient
good to talk himself out to a doctor if a doctor could be found who
was discerning and strong enough to stand up against his force of
personality.

Loeb fished a name out of his desk. He said, "Go to see George
Daniels."

Dr. Daniels, the Director of the Psychoanalytic Clinic for Training
and Research at the Columbia University College of Physicians and
Surgeons, is a tall man, who looks like a church elder, discreet, grave,
stable, and with a nice sense of humor. Lasker (despite Mary's talk
of Dali) still had strong resistance against psychoanalysis. But Loeb
and Mary talked him into calling on Daniels, and soon he began to
have sessions with him. Lasker went to him four or five times a

week for six or eight months, and in later years he occasionally dropped in to see him if some particular pressure or problem had emerged to bother him.

Daniels did not subject him to the full rigors of formal psychoanalysis; he was too old for that. He did not lie down on a couch; he and Daniels talked man to man. He did, however, go through the technique of free associations fully, and his dreams were analyzed. Daniels found him a fascinating patient; his dreams were voluminous and his fantasies dramatic.

Little by little, in the familiar way of a successful analysis, Lasker's inner conflicts and anxieties were explored and brought to light. His father played a large role in his memories. Once Morris Lasker had told him, "Whenever you are in doubt, do as I would do." Albert dutifully sought to follow this advice, but now it became clear that, while so doing, he had bitterly resented his father's domination. The real reason he left Galveston so long before was not merely desire to get ahead, or eagerness for adventure, but a fierce urge to remove himself from his father, with whom he wanted to compete, and whom he was determined to surpass.

Lasker had never understood this fully before. Patiently Dr. Daniels sought to explore and bring to the surface other episodes and experiences, secret humiliations and suppressed anxieties, in order to clear them up, and explain his current emotional tensions. Above all, Albert suffered because he felt that he had been a public success but a private failure. He knew that he had treated Flora badly sometimes, and had been difficult with his children; and he felt that in other personal relations (as well as in business) he had been inadequate and lacking in understanding on occasion. Why? No doubt to compensate for some hurt or cryptic frustration in his early life.

Most of his obsessive feelings of guilt, which pursued him like demons armed with pitchforks, derived from episodes almost childishly innocent or trivial. He was cursed, or blessed, with an extravagantly tender conscience; the least peccadillo, even if it had taken place years before, now took on exaggerated proportions. Some

things he felt guilty about were not only trivial, but actually sweet
—for instance, a minor lie told to save a child's feelings—but he
felt like a murderer. As an example he had been tortured for years
by the fact that, after Flora's death, he had finally revealed to one
of the children that she was older than he. So now he felt that he
had betrayed her.

Lasker, as the analysis proceeded, became detached enough to
be fascinated by the technique involved, and in some respects this
was the most exciting intellectual experience of his life; he was
learning who, what, and why he was, and moreover that his miseries
were not unique—he was like almost everybody. He respected
experthood, and Daniels, with his manner both dry and soothing,
was an expert. He had never realized before the importance of the
subconscious, and how much he would be relieved by having, as he
put it, some barnacles scraped off his soul. On the other hand, the
experience became so drastic and painful that he would have
called it off had it not been for the supreme end in view—to make
marriage to Mary a success.

One day, lunching with Richard Simon, the publisher, he said
abruptly, "I beg your pardon; I must run now—I'm late for my
psychoanalyst." Simon looked up astonished. Lasker went on, "I'm
not being analyzed for what you probably think. I'm doing it to
get rid of all the *hate* the advertising business put into me."

The analysis did Lasker a great deal of good, and opened up a
new world by explaining to him some of the inner motivations of
human behavior. His comment on it later was one of the most
penetrating ever made about psychoanalysis by anyone: "You
know what it did for me? *It taught me to forgive myself.*"

*

Meantime his friendship with Loeb flowered. Contrary to the
rules, Loeb became his personal physician, which he remained until
his death. A man of the most fastidious, intricate, and sophisticated
intelligence, Loeb found him altogether engrossing—he couldn't

resist him—and thought that he was probably the most intelligent man he had ever met. Not that he did not have defects. Loeb admired not merely his mind, but his sense of fun and *joie de vivre*. At sixty, he was still buoyant as a skiff, and he had the enlivening quality of always making everybody seem at his best. Loeb and his wife, who is also a doctor, were not social; they worked too hard; but they could never decline an invitation to dine with Albert Lasker. "He had communicability," Loeb says nowadays. "There was a bright cover on his book. He not only had faith in the capacity of man, but instinctive knowledge of man's limitations; he believed that people could surmount these, develop out of them; he had a marvelous instinct for concentrating on the valuable aspects of a human being, and sloughing off the rest. *Voilà un homme!*"

Loeb never sent him a bill, and this bothered Lasker deeply. One day he said, "I can't stand this any longer—I'm going to give you a Cadillac." Loeb replied, "What do I need with a Cadillac?—I have a Chevrolet." Albert persisted. The doctor said, "If you really want to do something for me, translate the Cadillac into $5,000 and give it to my research staff." Lasker wrote out the check at once, but felt that he owed Loeb much more. One night the dinner conversation turned to painting, and Dali, whose work Loeb liked, was mentioned. Like a flash, Albert asked him what his favorite country was, and Loeb replied, "Italy." Albert said, "I will get Dali to paint some Italian cities for you." Loeb protested and then dropped the subject, assuming that it would be forgotten.

A year later, he heard Lasker's voice on the phone. "The Italian Dalis have arrived." "What Dalis?" "*Your* Dalis." Albert had gone ahead and commissioned Dali to go to Italy and paint four cities for him—Venice, Rome, Como, Naples. The doctor said that he could not possibly accept so munificent a gift. Lasker said, "You can't decide whether or not you'll take them until you *see* them. But wait till I have them framed." Albert and Mary then sent them to Loeb's apartment, duly framed. "God bless my soul!" Loeb exclaimed. This was, he recognized, *force majeure,* and he had to succumb to it, which he did with grace and pleasure.

Lasker won another round, to which Loeb could not reply. He left him a tidy little legacy in his will.

End of Mill Road Farm

Lasker, who never had a delayed reaction in his life, decided late in 1939 to give up Mill Road Farm. Within a moment he telephoned Albert L. Hopkins, his principal lawyer in Chicago, to arrange the details. Hopkins thought that, if he sold it, he would get only a fraction of its value, and suggested that he give it away instead. Within another moment Lasker had Bob Hutchins on the telephone to ask if he would accept it, and in due course the $3,500,000 property was donated to the University of Chicago.[1]

Was this romantic, off-beat quixoticism—to give away a property so luxurious, so beloved, which he had lived in only twelve or thirteen years, and which he had always planned to keep forever? Hardly. First, he wanted a totally new life, and to achieve this he had to cut himself off from the past. Second, he felt that such a grandiose property had become an anachronism. These were new times; a new world was beckoning; and he hoped to march with it. He joked to one of his children, "Mill Road is the kind of place that's going to be surrounded by an angry mob someday. They'll say, 'Let's get the so-and-so who built this place!' When that happens I intend to be a member of the mob."

The University, after a time, came to the reluctant conclusion that the estate was a white elephant. First it was put in the hands of the botany department as a research center for horticulture, but it was too expensive to maintain; then Hutchins hoped to use it in the way that Columbia University uses Arden House near New York, as a place of assembly for men of affairs and scholars, but the idea was never carried through. So the whole property, including the golf course, was cut up and sold for building lots—what a waste! The house itself went for a pittance, $110,000.[2] *Sic transit gloria.*

---

[1] Lasker, however, rented it back from the University for brief periods in the summers of 1940 and 1941; after that he never saw it again.
[2] Chicago *Daily News*, October 12, 1943.

A Wedding, Politics, and Moving to New York

Albert and Mary were married on June 21, 1940, some fifteen months after they met, by Supreme Court Justice Floyd Church in the New York County Courthouse. The arrangements were made by their good friend, Judge Samuel Rosenman. Now, at last, Lasker was meeting Democrats. If anybody had been asked to the ceremony hundreds would have had to be asked, and so there were no guests at all—the only person present was a witness from the judge's chambers.[3]

The honeymoon was spent cruising on a yacht off Long Island; then the Laskers went to Philadelphia for the Republican National Convention. Albert had not missed a convention for years, and, as usual, was a delegate from Illinois. This was the convention which, as almost everybody will remember, upset the chances of both Robert A. Taft and Thomas E. Dewey for the presidency at this time, and confounded all the prophets by nominating a virtual unknown, Wendell Willkie, who had been a registered Democrat eighteen months before.

The Laskers knew Willkie quite well, but not nearly so well as they came to know him later. Mary had met him a year or so before, and he had impressed her greatly. In June, 1939, on Midsummer Night, she was a hostess at a gala evening party, and Willkie was an after-dinner guest. Mary thought that he had terrific appeal, political as well as personal, and after the party asked Albert if he did not think that he might make a good presidential candidate. Albert, shocked, said that this was sheer lunacy, and that a utilities magnate could no more be elected President than the man in the moon; he patted Mary condescendingly on the head and told her that she was a good girl but must learn not to be so naïve about politics.

[3] Immediately before the ceremony, at about 10:30 that morning, something odd happened. Herbert Hoover telephoned Lasker asking to see him at once. Incredibly enough, he thought that he had a chance for the Republican nomination for the presidency, and wanted Lasker to be one of his floor managers. Albert begged to be excused from calling on him on the ground that he had an engagement. Hoover said, "But this is important!" Lasker said, "So is my engagement—I'm getting married!"

Mary's own motive was quite simple. She scarcely (at this time) knew whether she was a Republican or a Democrat; all she knew was that it was good for the country to have two strong candidates.

Another event was a small dinner party arranged to set up a meeting between Willkie and Dorothy Thompson; it took place in a New York steak house, Christ Cella's, and at the bar Lasker saw a friend, Dan Golenpaul, who was owner of the radio program "Information Please." He said to Golenpaul, "Here is Wendell Willkie—he'd be wonderful on your show," which, at that time, was still sponsored by Lucky Strike. Willkie promptly went on "Information Please," and became a national figure overnight.

Now at the 1940 convention both Taft and Dewey sought Lasker's help, because he was such a powerful figure on the Illinois delegation. But Albert, whose political ideas were in full process of change, thought that Taft was far too isolationist, and he did not particularly like Dewey. He decided to go all out for Willkie, and, in a minor way, contributed to his nomination, because it was he who helped swing Illinois for him on the fourth ballot. Until the roll call reached Illinois Willkie was behind; when it became clear that Illinois would go for him, the deadlock was broken and state after state climbed on his bandwagon. He was nominated two ballots later.

*

The Laskers resumed their honeymoon, and cruised on Lake Michigan on a comfortable large yacht. There were movies on the open deck at night. Albert took a barber along, and Mary had Nancy. They visited Ernst Mahler in Wisconsin, and spent some weeks in Chicago and at Mill Road Farm, which Albert now rented from the University of Chicago at an extravagant price. He was happier than he had ever been in his life, and extracted from every hour a sense of joy, fulfillment, and well-being, He was famished for love, and, adoring him, Mary went to every length to please him.

That autumn Lasker left the Middle West for good, and established permanent residence in New York. (Mary would have liked to have kept Mill Road Farm, but he would not go back to the past.) They looked about for a place to live, and presently rented from William Paley of the Columbia Broadcasting System a seven-and-a-half-story house at 29 Beekman Place, overlooking the East River. This they proceeded to buy in 1944, and it became their principal residence. Mary did it over from top to bottom, in her own softly glowing taste, and filled it with mirrors, comfortable light-colored furniture and white rugs. The predominantly white walls were a backdrop for the pictures which came later, and in every corner flowers added a fresh note of color.

Another Ending

In the spring of 1942 Lasker resigned from the board of trustees of the University of Chicago. There were two reasons for this severance, which caused him much pain. First, he had turned full-wheel on international affairs. A principal factor in this evolution was, of course, Adolf Hitler. Long before Pearl Harbor Lasker gave up thinking of Hitler as a jackanapes competing with him for space in the newspapers. He knew that this monstrous Jew-killer was going to make a war, and that America was bound to be drawn into it. So Lasker, who had been an ardent isolationist since his youth, became an equally ardent interventionist of the Vandenberg-Willkie school. Moreover, he transferred his thoughts to action. He promoted and paid for an off-the-record conference at Mackinac Island where a group of leading Republicans met in an effort to organize Vandenberg-Willkie sentiment; he was a signatory to a famous manifesto, "You Can't Do Business With Hitler" (the other principal signers were Willkie, Matthew Woll of the American Federation of Labor, Mrs. Dwight Morrow, Carl Van Doren, John Kieran of "Information Please," and Raymond Clapper); he took a determined stand against America First, the isolationist lobby, even though this meant an irrevocable break with some of his oldest acquaintances, like Robert E. Wood of Sears Roebuck and Colonel

McCormick of the Chicago *Tribune;* above all, he made a sensation in orthodox Republican circles by coming out for Lend-Lease. When Lasker turned full circle, the turn was full indeed.

All this, naturally, served to bring him into conflict with Hutchins, who at that time was a leading isolationist. (One should add that, after Pearl Harbor, Hutchins at once turned the whole of the energies of the University to the war effort, and a little later changed his own views when the first chain reaction in history was achieved on the University of Chicago campus. In the atomic age, no man could be an isolationist.) But in the pre-Pearl Harbor period he still held views which Lasker, a whole-hogger if there ever was one, could not countenance, and Albert felt so deeply that Hutchins was wrong that he considered that he had no re-course but to resign his trusteeship at the University.

However, there was a second issue. The spark which set off the explosion was something else. In March, 1942, the *Saturday Evening Post* published an article called "The Case Against the Jew" by Milton Mayer, a part-time employee of the University who was one of Hutchins' best friends. Hutchins admired Mayer, a journalist with an exceptionally lively and original mind, and Mayer recipro-cated this emotion extravagantly. Mayer had done good work for the University. But his *Post* article (with which the University was not involved in any way) made Lasker angry, because he thought that it was anti-Semitic—although Mayer was, of course, a Jew— and would give succor to anti-Semites everywhere at a time when Jews the world over were suffering the most painful, dangerous persecution in their history. Certainly Mayer's article, whatever it said, came out at a most unpropitious moment. What angered Lasker particularly was the title. But this had not been Mayer's title. He had called his article "The Wondering Jew" and the *Post,* without his knowledge or consent, changed it to "The Case Against the Jew." But Lasker would not be mollified. He asked Hutchins to take issue with Mayer, which Hutchins refused to do. This con-firmed Albert in his resolution to leave the University, and, although Hutchins did his best to make him change his mind, he resigned as a trustee on June 11, 1942.

Meantime, in full indignation, he went after the *Post*. He summoned the principal *Post* executives to New York (they came hurriedly), threatened to withdraw all Lord & Thomas advertising from the magazine, and forced it to print a retraction and apology. A big shake-up on the *Post* staff followed. One small anecdote attends this fracas, which shows that, in spite of the fact that his most profound emotions were involved, Lasker had not lost all his sense of perspective. When the *Post* people arrived in New York he met them in the company of his associate Emerson Foote. "Mr. Foote," Lasker announced coldly, "is my *gentile* adviser on this unpleasant matter!" Foote had no idea that this was to be his function, but Albert wanted somebody not Jewish to hear him launch into the *Post* editors, and support his views.[4]

In spite of the break with the University Lasker and Hutchins remained friends, but they saw one another less as the years went on.

Family Affairs

Edward Lasker went into the Navy shortly after Pearl Harbor; he served first in Washington as an assistant to his father's friend, Frank Knox of the Chicago *Daily News*, who had become Roosevelt's Secretary of the Navy, and in 1942 went to sea. He spent most of his duty in the Pacific, set up a lively record, and rose to be a lieutenant commander. After the war he and Caral Gimbel were divorced.

---

[4] Subsequently he thought that the *Post's* apology did not go far enough. Still crackling with indignation, he called Foote in to ask his opinion of the statement. Foote thought, "Here goes—now I lose my job." But he told the truth, namely that he felt that the retraction did go far enough, and should be accepted. Lasker glared at him for a moment. Then he picked up the telephone to call a prominent Jewish businessman who had been as much exercised about the article as he was. He said, "Mr. Foote approves of the statement. I don't, but he is my adviser, and I thought I ought to tell you how he feels." This impressed Foote greatly. First he had crossed Lasker on a matter which affected him deeply, but A.D. showed no resentment; second, his sense of propriety was such that he wanted his Jewish friend to know how Foote felt.

Mary Foreman had also been divorced—in July, 1942—
after long unhappiness. She said to her father miserably, "I'm
thirty-eight—no one will ever take me out again." Lasker replied
amiably, "You're too conceited. You don't seem to realize that all
you're looking for is an audience of one." As a matter of fact, she
found her audience of one quite soon, and on October 21, 1942, she
married Leigh Block, an executive of the Inland Steel Company. For
avocation he collected rare books. He and Lasker got on at once,
almost like brothers. The Blocks moved into a large apartment in
Chicago not far from Burton Place, where Mary spent much of her
childhood, and soon (as will be told) started to collect paintings;
today they have a magnificent collection of modern art, one of the
most notable in the country.

Frances also married in 1942. Her husband, Sidney F. Brody, is
a California businessman who has specialized in building shopping
centers. The Brodys moved to California, and built in Los Angeles
an unusual, exciting, and distinguished modern house. Lasker to
the end of his life loved to visit them, and their children became
the apples of his eye.

Mary Lasker, by this time, was not merely Albert's wife, but
mother, daughter, sister, comrade, compass, and indispensable
collaborator and equal partner in every enterprise. Also, she loved
him madly. She widened his horizons, gave him direction, stimulated
him, soothed him, showed him new vistas of usefulness, supplied
answers to all his doubts, doted on him, admired him, petted him
and took infinite joy and pride in his happiness. In return, he gave
her a devotion almost stifling. "All she did," Lasker said to me once,
"was keep me from losing my mind."

His business affairs interested her keenly, and on every level she
was helpful. She introduced him to Raymond Loewy, who designed
the white package for Lucky Strike ("Lucky Strike Green Has Gone
to War"), and to André Meyer, a leading partner in Lazard Frères,
who presently took over his private financial affairs. The extraordinary thing was that, active as she was in his career, she also
managed to pursue an intensely busy and productive life of her

own. Albert demanded one thing only. This was that when he was in the room she should have no function whatever except to pay strict attention to what he was talking about, so that she could adore him more.

The End of Lord & Thomas

He came back from lunch one day late in 1942, and declared out of the blue, "Mary, I have decided to give up Lord & Thomas." Startled, she suggested that he think the matter over for forty-eight hours before taking any such irrevocable step. This he did dutifully, and then confirmed his decision to wind up the company, with which he had been associated for forty-four solid years, which represented his life work, and which was still providing him with an income of a million dollars a year.

There were several sound reasons for this seemingly quixotic step. First, he was only sixty-two but he was tired. Second, he was bored. Third, the new generation of executives with whom he had to deal seemed far beneath his standards. Fourth, he wanted to devote himself to public service. Fifth, he felt that shortages induced by the war effort were bound to curtail sales of consumer goods, on which his business largely depended. Sixth and above all, Edward had made it clear that he did not wish to succeed his father in the business, and would not return to advertising after the war. Lasker had been holding Lord & Thomas together largely because he wanted to pass it on to Edward. Now, as he wrote to one of his friends frankly, it dawned on him that this desire was simply a manifestation of his own ego, and that he had no right to force on Edward, or any of his children, a mode of life which they did not desire.[5]

Now the problem arose: how to make an end of Lord & Thomas? Several alternatives were possible. He could merge it with another agency. But this would mean delay, difficult negotiations, and haggling over price. He could sell it. But he had decided that, when he liquidated it, the name Lord & Thomas must disappear; obviously,

[5] Letter to Leonard Masius, December 19, 1942.

there could be no Lord & Thomas without Albert Lasker![6] This meant, however, that it would be difficult to sell the company, since the name was its biggest asset. Third, he might simply give it away. But this presented complicated legal problems, and might involve paying a large gift tax to the government. Moreover, even if he didn't wish the name Lord & Thomas to survive, he did want to feel that his old employees would be taken care of, that the business would be carried on by men who loved it, and that accounts some of which had been with the company for more than fifty years were not simply thrown out on the street.

The solution, which was not easy to work out, was to liquidate Lord & Thomas but at the same time set up a new company which would, if possible, carry on with the old accounts. The new company (at the beginning at least) amounted to Lord & Thomas under a different name, but with A.D. himself completely out.

If this astonishing liquidation had occurred a few years before, the new firm would have been Francisco, Coons, & Noyes. Lasker always regretted that Francisco was not there when the dissolution occurred. But he had left advertising soon after Pearl Harbor to go into war work and was now on the staff of Nelson Rockefeller's Office of Inter-American Affairs. Coons had also quit to go into business for himself, and the peppery and plausible Noyes, for reasons of health, had gone west and was devoting himself to ranching.

Consequently, the three senior executives now were Emerson Foote in New York, Fairfax Cone in Chicago, and Don Belding on the West Coast, and these duly became the successors. Lasker hardly knew Belding. But he had been close to Cone for some years and he liked and admired Foote. Most advertising men of the day had become stereotypes, with their Madison Avenue uniforms, ulcers, and somewhat prim glibness; but Foote was an individual. A tall, good-looking man, he was as respectable as an archbishop. Also he

[6] Also if he didn't abolish the name old clients would constantly think that they had the right to consult him.

was extraordinarily bright, and, what A.D. particularly admired, unselfishly devoted to public service.

Having made his decision Lasker summoned Cone to New York, on December 16, 1942, and met with him and Foote; Belding joined them later. Mary took part in all the conferences, which went on without interruption for two weeks. The first proposal was to form three new independent companies, one in New York, one in Chicago, one in California, but Mary made a suggestion which was at once adopted, that it would serve the same purpose and be much simpler if only one company, with three equal partners, were to be set up. Each partner would have his own area, but all would work together.

Lasker and Mary went to Chicago; here during Christmas week the last details were worked out. Charles Luckman, the head of Pepsodent at this time, sat in on some of the negotiations; the lawyer was the diligent Albert Hopkins. Lord & Thomas was duly dissolved and closed out its bank account. After outstanding debts were paid, et cetera, Lasker paid the correct capital gains tax on his share of this, and the rest was distributed to the other shareholders; he himself owned about 95 per cent of the company, and so this proportion of the proceeds went to him. Meantime, Foote, Cone, & Belding was set up. It paid a minor sum, about $150,000, for the furniture and equipment in the Lord & Thomas offices, and other arrangements were made so that the new company would have enough cash to start business. Three youngish men, who on Lasker terms did not have a nickel between them, and who had never worked in the same room before, were able to follow in the footsteps of a business that had done more than.$750,000,000 worth of advertising over almost seventy years. Moreover, Lasker at once sounded out the chief clients, informing them of the change, and urging them to stay on with the new company, even though he was not in it. Every important client but one chose to remain with Foote, Cone, & Belding and many are still there.[7]

[7] Among these are Sunkist, Kimberly-Clark, Armour, the First National Bank of Chicago, Pepsodent, Lockheed, Schenley, and Southern Pacific. Foote was first

On December 30 painters went to work taking down the Lord & Thomas signs in the Palmolive Building and putting up Foote, Cone, & Belding instead; on January 1 the new company set out on its own. So Lord & Thomas, with all its resplendent history and enormous prestige, came to its end.

After the liquidation Lasker never interfered in the new business in any way. But he was always available for consultation, and Foote in particular remained close to him until his death. Lasker was asked by somebody what he thought the future of the new company would be. He chuckled: "It is fails, people will say that it could not succeed without me. If it succeeds, they'll say that I trained my men so well that they couldn't fail."

*

Some years after this Lasker had a letter from Abe Selz, his old comrade in the Partridges. Selz asked him if he did not miss the crowded luster of the Lord & Thomas days. He replied, "The Lasker of the advertising business died in 1942. I never think of him, and I'm not sure I ever knew the man."

---

president of the new company, although the three partners had equal status; this was because he would be in New York and would be handling Lucky Strike, and it was thought wise to flatter George Washington Hill by giving him the president to work with. The Foote, Cone, & Belding triumvirs held together till 1950, when Foote left. Belding retired in 1957, and today Cone is the only partner remaining, although the firm name has never changed.

Chapter 18

MONEY

Many rich men are parsimonious, and perhaps that is why they get rich; what distinguished Lasker was his joy in money, the fun he had with it. He loved to do the work that brought it in, loved to spend it, and loved to give it away. Now for the remainder of his life he paid little attention to earning money, and most of his energies went into getting rid of large sums. Never, however, did he squander money recklessly, and his extravagances were not gross. He kept a prudent eye on his capital, and once told a friend, "Yes, I spend a lot but believe me I am going to be very, very careful of my last five million!" Then: "When I get down to two million, no one gets a damned cent!"

Actually, he was not as wealthy as some people made him out to be. When a newspaper article said that he was one of the ten richest men in America, a heavy exaggeration, he replied with his characteristic humor, "There are ten men on my street richer." Challenged to name these, he replied, "John D. Rockefeller, 3rd—that's six already."[1]

Nevertheless he was well aware of his financial standing. Until he met Mary he seldom took time out to do any shopping, and was unknown in most of the fashionable New York shops. One day he walked impetuously into Van Cleef & Arpels, the Fifth Avenue jewelers, with Mary, and asked to see a diamond and sapphire bracelet that had caught his eye in the window. It was expensive. It pleased him, and at once he put it in his pocket unwrapped, and started to walk out of the shop. Mary, somewhat startled, asked him if he had an account there and he replied, "No." The salesman,

[1] This anecdote comes from Lasker's good friend Leonard Lyons.

puzzled, did not know whether to stop him, and Mary whispered, "Don't you think you ought to tell them who you are?" Lasker did not interrupt his march toward the door and said calmly over his shoulder to the salesman, "My name is Albert Lasker. Call any bank."

Mary had never had much interest in old china or silver, but Albert loved it; he stimulated her feeling for it, and soon they were spending long hours together in antique shops. Also he had always been fond of fine linen, and he opened this world to her as well. His attitude in a shop, whether he was buying jewelry or a necktie, was almost always the reverse of the normal. He would say eagerly, "I'll take it—how much is it?"

Once Lasker offered to lend me some money when I was having difficulty finishing a book. But I said that, at the moment, I didn't need it, and anyway I could always borrow from my bank. He snorted, "Don't you think I'm as good as a bank?" Once a movie company offered me a large sum, $20,000, to work on a picture in California; Lasker disapproved of the project when I happened to mention it to him, and said that nothing but ill would come of it. I said that I could certainly use the money, and he replied earnestly with a phrase which I will never forget, *"Never pay too much for money!"* Then he added, still seeking to save my soul, "I will give you $20,000 *not* to go to California!" (I didn't accept his offer.)

Shortly after their marriage, Mary asked him, quite seriously, what budget they should live on. This amused him vastly, and he said that a budget didn't matter. She persisted. She declared, "I don't want to be mixed up with your money. You live on yours, and I'll live on mine." Albert, staggered, agreed that he would pay the rent and grocery bill but that she could pay for her own clothes and the like and, in particular, her own telephone bill; she was a formidable consumer of time on the long-distance telephone. She repeated, "I don't want to be taken over; I want to be able to spend what's mine in any way I like." He demurred at first, but respected her point of view; and this arrangement went on for some little time.

But one day a lady in search of funds for a charity came to Mary, and asked her for a considerable sum. She replied that she would like to contribute, but could not because she couldn't afford it. The lady—surveying the amenities of Beekman Place—was amazed, and did not think that she could be telling the truth; Mary went on to explain that, whereas Albert was rich, she was not. That evening she mentioned this story to Edward Lasker to amuse him. Edward, who didn't think it was amusing at all, went to his father without telling Mary, protesting that it was a scandal that she had no large capital. Albert said nothing. But he telephoned Mary from the office the next day, and told her to drop in and see him at 3 P.M. She did so, and he handed over to her a check for a million dollars. Since this was a gift, it cost Lasker about $350,000 in taxes on top of the million. He said, "There are no strings on this at all. Invest it as you will. It embarrasses me to think that you have no substantial money of your own."

Lasker was generous on almost every level, but he had two idiosyncrasies—about electric light and the telephone. He would pay $50,000 for a painting without a tremor but scream holy murder if the telephone bill was high. This had been one of his characteristics for many years. He loathed the telephone, particularly the long-distance telephone. In the old days he often called Bob Hutchins in Chicago from New York; sometimes, when his business was concluded, he would ask Hutchins to put in calls for him to half a dozen people in Chicago, transmitting messages so that he, Lasker, would not have to call them. As to electric lights, they were a positive obsession. He was like the thrifty father in Eugene O'Neill's *A Long Day's Journey into Night*. If he came back to Lord & Thomas by chance after hours and found any lights on, he would carefully switch them off one by one. When he arrived in Chicago to visit the Blocks he would notice that their pictures were lit up even by day; he would snap, "What's the matter—can't you see in the morning?"

*

Lasker had a marvelous mind for figures. He was a genius with a balance sheet. On the other hand he seldom followed the market closely, and in his later days never read the financial pages. He operated by flash, by instinct. That this was superlatively good may be demonstrated by the fact that, when he died, there was not a single bad investment in his entire estate. Of course, for some years he had had the advantage of counsel from André Meyer of Lazard Frères, whose financial acumen was (and is) unequaled. One detail is that both he and Meyer liked to put capital into things in the ground—basic resources rather than manufactured goods—although he had spent his whole life promoting manufactured goods. Another detail is that in 1950 Lasker raised the proportion of common stocks in his portfolio from 63 to 88 per cent. But this was not characteristic; it happened during the Korean War and was a brief, temporary hedge against inflation.

Basically, in spite of his large expenditures, he was quite conservative about money. He seldom carried much cash in his pocket because he thought he might lose it. He kept books to the last cent, and always knew exactly how he stood. Every two weeks his accountant briefed him with elaborate memoranda. Whenever he put money into a project which he thought might be even slightly adventurous, he would set up a reserve to cover any possible loss. He never put more than a certain sum—say a million—into any single investment, principally because he did not want to have to watch it too carefully.

Lasker liked money, yes, but he liked it for the enjoyment it gave him, the prestige and creative power. Once he said to me, "I love money, but I can't stand the rich." Most of his friends, however, were by no means paupers.

Meyer adored him. "It was such fun to see him operate," he recollects. "There are plenty of brilliant people but Albert was more than brilliant. Whenever he came downtown I would ask the best experts I knew to join us, to match his wits. We never could. How he exhausted us! And how he understood human nature!"

One more item in this field. At sixty-five he became eligible for

Social Security, and, with great satisfaction, carefully cashed his check each month and gave the proceeds to a favorite cause!

The Big Change

By the early 1940's the transformation in Lasker was so profound that old friends, seeing him after an interval, could scarcely believe that this was the same man. He gave up golf, seldom went to base-ball games except to the World Series (he remained faithful to movies, though, especially Westerns), and stopped gambling al-together except for baby stakes. He became more interested in the theater, and went enthusiastically to first nights. But these were superficial changes. What counted was a deep, pervasive alteration in his character. Not only did the range of his interests multiply, but his personality mellowed. He became much less egocentric. He decided that the world, not merely Lord & Thomas and its clients, was worth doing something about. He had always been a good citizen, but now he wanted to devote his whole life to good citizen-ship. Most of his life he had, in a curious way, been insular; now the blinkers were off. A clerestory at the top of his mind, hitherto closed, took in light. He had time enough, leisure enough, not merely to become benevolent, but—what is much more difficult—to become wise. A strong and essential sweetness broke through the sharp carapace of his former personality; he became silvery and shimmer-ing. Lasker B had won.

Paul Hoffman testifies, "I have never seen such a contrast in a man as between the pre-Mary and post-Mary Albert." One of his children testifies, with filial license, "You know, frankly, father simply was not well behaved until he met Mary."

It was not merely age that softened him, because he steadily seemed to become younger, not older, with the years; he was young till the day he died. The transformation was a process of growth, not of decay.

Some reasons for it—

First, the move from Chicago to New York. He was no longer suburban, no longer a commuter. He loved Chicago— its guts, sting, and brawn—but many of his Chicago friends were ultra-conservative businessmen, and his arc there was comparatively narrow. One of his secretaries told me that, in Chicago, if he left the office without saying where he was going, she could almost always track him down to one of three places; three telephone calls were enough. But in New York horizons were infinitely wider, higher, more various, and more complex. One irony is that Flora had begged him for years to move east, but he was crazy about Chicago and would not budge.

Second, the advertising business, with all it bark and screech, was behind him now. He had exhausted the joys of the chase, and could turn with full energy to new interests—art and science. He had a new and broader orientation altogether. Besides he was freed of the unpleasant dilemma of the Manton case. He was like a diver suddenly released from a caisson in deep water; he shot up bright with foam.

Third, Hitler.

Fourth, his analysis.

Fifth, and above all, Mary. Love conquers all, as the poets say, and it was both as simple and complex as that. He was starved for love, and blossomed when he had it; there is nothing like being in love to make a man want to be at his best. But it is relevant to note that he would never have fallen in love with Mary if something in his own character had not predisposed him to this kind of lucky choice.

Episode in a Theater

In a theater one evening Albert, in a mood when he was even more absent-minded about people than usual, excitedly clutched Mary's arm. He pointed. "I know that pretty woman. I *know* her. What's her name? Who is she?"

Momentarily he didn't realize that it was Doris Kenyon, his second wife.

Lasker's Jaw

One morning in New York I had a telephone call from my old friend and dentist, Dr. George K. Brazill. The estimable Dr. Brazill has had an interesting double career; he is not only an outstanding dental surgeon, but a military man, a general, who for many years was the commanding officer of New York's elite Seventh Regiment.

Dr. Brazill asked me, "Do you know a man named Lasker?"

"Albert Lasker? Yes, quite well."

"What kind of fellow is he?"

"Are you going to do dental work for him?" I asked.

"I think so."

"George," I replied, "he's the kind of man who, two weeks from now, will have you in the chair and he will be fixing *your* teeth."

This almost happened, but not quite.

Lasker had been put in touch with him by another dentist who wanted a consultation. Brazill discovered that several of his teeth were badly infected, but thought he could save them.

Albert was impressed. "How can you save them?" he demanded.

"By inlays."

"Do I have inlays now?"

"Oh, yes."

"Humph! How do you make an inlay? How do you put it in?"

"First, we make a casting. I'll show you," said Brazill.

"Do you do the mechanical work yourself?"

"Of course."

Brazill took him into his laboratory, where inlays for other patients were in process of manufacture. He showed him all the technical details—how the wax pattern was set in the mold, how an amalgam or metal die was made, how the gold was melted with a blowpipe—and Lasker was fascinated to the uttermost. Meantime, Brazill discovered that there were curious deep grooves in several of his teeth; he did not know what could have caused them. The explanation was that Lasker ground his teeth at night; for years, his nervousness, restlessness, and suppressed drive and tension had set him to gnashing his teeth while he slept. (Similarly, Morris Lasker many years before had clawed a carpet bare.)

Brazill and Lasker soon became devoted to one another. Albert made one condition for their association, which was that he must never be kept waiting for an appointment. Brazill dutifully sought to clear the decks for him, but this was not always possible and occasionally he had to spend a moment or two in the reception room.[2] He came usually at eleven in the morning. Then, dental work over, he would occasionally take the doctor for a ride in Central Park, and they would have lunch together. "What a man for ideas!" Brazill recollects nowadays. "He would watch children playing in the park and reminisce about baseball. He still knew the batting averages of players in the twenties. . . . He was a man who came out of the good book, all right. His good *rubbed off on you.*"

In time, Brazill constructed for Lasker a novel and startling object—an articulated model of his own jaw. Made of plastic, it was complete with teeth, and could open and shut like a real jaw. Its *raison d'être* was simple. Lasker had one tooth, an upper right incisor, which Brazill could not restore by an inlay; hence he capped it with a porcelain crown. This, however, might fall off, and so Brazill made a duplicate, which Albert kept in his toilet case. Any dentist anywhere, no matter how unskilled, could tell in an instant where this substitute crown should go, in case the original should be lost, by looking at the artificial jaw. Moreover, the jaw graphically told other dentists exactly what work had previously been done on Lasker's teeth, without the patient having even to bother to open his mouth.

This extraordinary device pleased Lasker no end, and one of the things I will always remember about him affectionately is the way he would set out on a trip with his own jaw tucked safely in his suitcase.

[2] To meet such a contingency Lasker took to arriving with a sheaf of newspapers; these were as a rule old papers, sometimes a month old or older; they were marked with a red pencil, and he had been hoarding them to read in an idle moment. That he should read *old* newspapers was a matter of unending amazement to Brazill's receptionist.

Chapter 19

NEW YORK, FUN, AND FRIENDS

Art and medicine largely filled Lasker's last decade, but other activities occupied him as well. Mary continually brought new people into their orbit; among these was Major Alexander P. ("Sasha") de Seversky with his concept, revolutionary at the time, of victory in World War II through air power. Lasker flung himself with full saturation and vigor into the Seversky crusade.

Oddly enough, Mary had been interested in the possibility that the fate of nations might be decided by warfare in the air ever since she read *The War in the Air* by H. G. Wells in her teens. In the spring of 1942 she picked up a book, *Victory Through Air Power*, by Major de Seversky, which had just been published. It excited her. But she knew little about these matters technically and was puzzled and upset, because an article by Winston Churchill, "Let the Criminal Tyrants Bomb," had impressed her greatly several years before. Churchill, drawing lessons from the Spanish Civil War, argued that air power, although important, could not be decisive, and that Britain would be able to hold out in the event of war no matter what havoc was wrought from the air. Now, reading Seversky who was convinced that air power was the absolute answer for victory, she decided that she must find out more. At this time, immediately after Pearl Harbor, the war was going badly for America and the Allies. The Japanese commanded the Pacific, and Hitler was at the zenith of his conquest. Mary knew many well-informed, influential people. She learned in Washington (a) that the United States was giving aircraft production only third place in manufacturing priorities, (b) that American airplanes, by and

large, were not a match for German planes in speed or range, and
(c) that the over-all commanders of the American war effort had
comparatively little interest in air power as such. For instance,
much of Roosevelt's strategical thinking was dominated by admirals
who scoffed at aviation. Mary had been stirred by Seversky's book;
then she went to hear him lecture, and became doubly stirred. She
told Albert that he must do something about all this at once, and
that the way to do it was through Frank Knox, his friend who was
Secretary of the Navy.

One day Richard Simon of Simon & Schuster, who had published
the book, asked Seversky if he knew Mary Lasker. "No," he replied.
Simon went on, "That's strange—she's just bought a hundred
copies of your book." A week later Simon asked the same question.
"You *must* know her—she's just bought another hundred." Apparently it was inconceivable to him that any reader would buy two
hundred copies of the work of an author and mail them to friends
all over the country without acquaintance. Then Norman Winston,
brought into the scene by Mary, telephoned Seversky and asked him
if he would go to the Lasker house for cocktails. Seversky had first
met Lasker at a social gathering in Florida years before, but for a
long time had been out of touch with him. He had never met Winston. The next day Seversky telephoned Simon and said that he had
been invited by a man he didn't know to have cocktails at a house
he had never been in—what should he do? Simon heard the magic
name Lasker, and said—"Go." Seversky did, and history was made.

Seversky was a contentious figure, a man possessed utterly by a
single cause. His absorption in his mission excluded every other
consideration. But, if only for this reason, he could be difficult to
deal with, and some people thought that he was a crank. Lasker,
however, recognized him at once for what he was: a genius. Seversky,
who was born in Russia, had a fascinating career as a pilot, aeronautical designer, and engineer. He was graduated in 1914 from the
Imperial Naval Academy, and, flying in the Baltic Sea area during
World War I, lost a leg on his first combat mission. Nevertheless he
returned to active duty, completed fifty-seven combat flights, shot

down thirteen German planes, and won the Russian equivalent of the Congressional Medal of Honor. He came to the United States after the Bolshevik Revolution, became a test pilot for the U.S. Army, the first one-legged test pilot in history, and in 1921 organized the Seversky Aero Corporation, which in time became the Republic Aviation Corporation; of this he was president, director, and chief engineer till 1940. He designed the prototype of the high-speed fighter of that era, invented the first fully automatic synchronous bombsight, and was a pioneer in the techniques which made it possible to refuel aircraft in flight.

Lasker liked Seversky, but strongly resisted his ideas at first. He thought that he must be exaggerating; he refused to believe that the United States could be as backward about aviation as Seversky said. He didn't want to believe it. He became cross, and even refused to read Seversky's book. But Mary won him over after a long and acrid argument, and presently they went with Seversky to Washington, where Albert arranged an overnight meeting with Knox and Donald Nelson, the head of the War Production Board, on the Secretary of the Navy's official yacht. Seversky stated his case. This —put briefly—was that long-range bombers were a more useful arm than battleships, and that the easiest way to win the war in the Pacific would be to increase enormously the striking power of aviation. Knox, who was very much a creature of the admirals, could not quite agree to this, and Nelson said that bombers of the immense range envisaged by Seversky did not exist. This was still 1942. Seversky said, "But aeronautical science has reached a stage where they could easily be produced." To this Knox replied, "We can't fight the war with weapons we haven't got." However, he proceeded to say that he would order *one* such aircraft—a prototype. Seversky said that he was not there to sell airplanes; all he wanted was to present his concept that long-range air power could defeat Japan. Later Nelson came around to supporting Seversky's view, and as a result the B-29, with its great range and shattering bomb load, was born.

Rival concepts in strategy continued, however, to split the Navy (the Army too) for months to come. Most admirals were still creatures of the sea, battleship-minded above all else. The battleship was king. They thought of aviation, not as a prime force, but as an auxiliary; planes were for "scouting." Of course, the Navy had carriers, and was using them brilliantly, but to a zealot like Seversky a carrier was little more than a floating garage. The Navy was thinking in terms of "mobility of the hangar," whereas Seversky wanted planes of longer range and superior speed. Without these, he felt, Japan could not be reached and beaten for a decade. He kept saying, "If we have twice the range, we will only have half as much fighting to do." Lasker, still the advertising man, transformed this into a more pungent slogan—"The longer the range, the shorter the war."

In other military circles, Seversky continued to meet severe, protracted opposition. Efforts were made to discredit him as an aeronautical authority. Still, the temper of the times was on his side. Obviously, the air age had begun in earnest. Soon the War Production Board promoted aircraft manufacture to first priority, and planes, big and small, poured off the assembly lines. Strategic thinking began to shift. It would not be an exaggeration to say that Seversky was responsible in large measure for all this. He was the originator of the strategic air power concept, and provided a vital spark. Finally he met by chance the late Judge Robert P. Patterson, Assistant Secretary of War. Lasker had a speaking acquaintance with Patterson, but did not arrange the meeting. Seversky skillfully, eloquently, stubbornly expounded to Patterson his thesis that air power should be regarded as the supreme, decisive instrument. Patterson brooded about this, and finally raised the Army's appropriation for B-29's from 3 to 100. And one of those who helped in all this was certainly Albert Lasker, who gave Seversky backing, confidence, and hope.

Late in 1942 Walt Disney conceived the idea of making a movie based on *Victory Through Air Power*. Seversky worked on the script. Then Lasker, lending his formidable experience in public relations to the project, set out to see that the film's message would reach circles which counted most. He operated practically like an engineer setting out to build a new Panama Canal. He was a man possessed. He arranged conferences with politicians and military folk, set up interviews with editors and organized a system whereby radio commentators and columnists saw the film in small, expertly chosen groups; he put all his friends in Hollywood to work, outlined what he thought would be the best publicity approach in movie houses, and went after the exhibitors. To cap it all, he gave a dinner at the Waldorf for no fewer than 1,700 guests, the cream of New York, with the enthusiastic co-operation of Miss Elsa Maxwell. Here the film was previewed. Lasker was so convinced by this time that the war would be won or lost by attention to Seversky's ideas that he even made a speech at the dinner, his first speech before a large gathering in many years, and was so excited that he would not let Seversky or Disney speak at all! And—of course—he paid the bill.

Several times Lasker tried to arrange a meeting between Roosevelt and Seversky, or at the least have *Victory Through Air Power* shown at the White House; he failed, largely because Admiral Leahy, who thought that Seversky was a crackpot, was now F.D.R.'s watchdog on such matters. Meantime, the film received wide attention in theaters in England. Lasker, through a British friend, got a print to Winston Churchill, and the Prime Minister was much impressed by it.

Came the Quebec Conference between Roosevelt and Churchill in the summer of 1943. Critical military decisions, preparatory to the invasion of Europe the next year, had to be made, but the conference was deadlocked. F.D.R. and General Marshall wanted to set a definite date for the operation, but Churchill, the RAF, and General Arnold felt that this should not be done until certain conditions were met, such as undisputed command of the air over the English Channel. In an effort to break through this impasse Churchill asked Roosevelt if he had ever seen *Victory Through Air Power*. F.D.R. said No, and a print was flown by fighter plane from New York to Quebec; the President and Prime Minister saw it together that night privately, and Roosevelt was much excited by the way Disney's aircraft masterfully wiped ships off the seas. It was run again the next day, and then F.D.R. invited the Joint Chiefs to have a look at it. This played an important role in the decision, which was then taken, to give the D-Day invasion sufficient air power.

A good many years later Lasker heard about the details of all this, and naturally he was pleased and impressed. He took no credit for himself but it moved him profoundly that Mary had prompted his interest in Seversky and that she had thus played an indirect role in saving many American lives. As to Seversky, he was completely vindicated. President Truman awarded him the Medal of Merit in December, 1946, with an appropriate and indeed highly eulogistic citation, and this delighted Albert too.

End of Lasker's Life with Pepsodent

Back in the mid-1930's Lasker hired Charles Luckman to be sales manager of Pepsodent. Luckman, born in 1909, was an architect by profession, but the depression, in full swing, cut off his career for the time being, and he got a job selling soap for Palmolive. He did extremely well, and Lasker, hearing of him, thought that he would be a promising person for the toothpaste business. Luckman was a brilliant success with Pepsodent, rose quickly to be president of the company, and acquired a block of its stock.

Lasker was still, in the 1940's, passionately interested in Pepsodent, which continued steadily to do a very large business. He no longer derived revenue from its advertising, since he had given up Lord & Thomas, but he was an important stockholder, and thought of his Pepsodent stock as an exceedingly fertile and lucrative nest egg which was not only his biggest single investment but which would, in time, benefit Mary and the children nicely.

But suddenly he was eliminated from Pepsodent. The circumstances are intricate. Lever Brothers, the great soap company, got interested in buying it. Luckman, although a minority stockholder in Pepsodent, had become increasingly powerful in its workings, and through his influence on Kenneth Smith (son of the original owner) , succeeded in negotiating the sale. Lasker, who was vacationing in Florida at the time, had little—if any—forewarning of any of this, and was confronted suddenly with a *fait accompli.* But he was helpless since he controlled no stock but his own, which was not a majority. The net result was that Pepsodent went over to Lever Brothers lock, stock and barrel for around $10,000,000 cash in June, 1944. Lasker was out—after almost thirty years with Pepsodent. He was paid a good price for his stock, but, even so, felt violently bitter about the transaction. On the other hand, he thoroughly respected the Lever Brothers management, and was gratified that Pepsodent should go into such competent hands.

The abrupt end of his connection with Pepsodent meant that Lasker was now cut off from his former business life altogether. He still maintained large investments in companies like International Cellucotton, but he no longer took active part in any business enterprise. At last, he was a totally free man.

George Washington Hill of the American Tobacco Company died in 1946, and this too was a major ending for Lasker. He and Hill maintained amicable—if intermittent—contact until the latter's death, but the cloud of the Manton case always lay between them. In 1948 Foote, Cone, & Belding, the successors to Lord & Thomas, voluntarily gave up the Lucky Strike account, and Lasker warmly applauded Foote's decision.

Among Friends

About 1940 Albert and Mary became permanently enriched by a new and sparkling friendship, when Anna Rosenberg entered their lives. She became equally close to them both. The circumstances of one of Albert's first meetings with her were exceptional. He and Mary had met her before, but only casually, and then one day they had lunch. She was ill, and was leaving that afternoon for a check-up in the Mayo Clinic. For some reason her effect on Lasker now became galvanic. He went through a procedure fantastic even for him. He acted as if he had known her all his life, and, moreover, was responsible for her. Exaggerating greatly the degree of her illness, he made elaborate arrangements for her when she arrived in Chicago the next morning, en route to Minnesota, without telling her. One can easily imagine Mrs. Rosenberg's stunned astonishment when, on getting off the Century in Chicago, she was met by a nurse, an attendant with a wheelchair, and, in person, the Commissioner of Health of the City of Chicago, Dr. Herman Bundeson. She was picked up bodily, placed firmly in the chair, and wheeled off. Nobody paid the slightest attention to her frantic protests, except to explain that this procedure had been ordered by Mr. Lasker. Whisked off to Dr. Bundeson's home, she was put to bed there until it was time for her to catch the train to the Mayos. From that day on, she never underestimated Albert Lasker.

Anna Rosenberg, whose maiden name was Lederer, was born in Budapest, and came to the United States at an early age. To describe her as a dynamo—the usual cliché—is to miss the point. "Dynamo" connotes mechanistic qualities, but one of Mrs. Rosenberg's chief characteristics is her intense warm humanness. She is a small, dark-haired woman, bright as a fragment of crystal, intuitive, and with an unerring eye for detecting the bogus. Lasker thought she had the best and fastest brain he ever met in a woman. After a remarkable career she became one of the foremost public relations counselors in the country, specializing in labor problems and settling strikes. She worked widely as a consultant in labor disputes for Studebaker and other corporations; also she represented Marshall Field, the Rockefeller Brothers, Macy's, and John Hay ("Jock") Whitney. Both sides, labor and capital, liked and trusted her. For years she did government work as well—on the NRA, the Social Security Board, and the office of Defense, Health and Welfare Services—and was the personal representative of President Roosevelt in Europe in 1944 to report on problems of returning G.I.'s. Later she served Mr. Truman in the same capacity. She was also head of the War Manpower Commission for the New York area. She became increasingly close to Roosevelt in his last days, and close to Eisenhower as well (it was she who arranged his speech to the CIO in Atlantic City in

1946, one of his first semipolitical appearances); above all she worked intimately with General Marshall and General Walter Bedell Smith, Eisenhower's wartime Chief of Staff and later head of the Central Intelligence Agency. In time, she became Assistant Secretary of Defense in charge of manpower, the first woman in history to hold such a post in the American military establishment.

Albert, Mary, and Mrs. Rosenberg saw one another constantly, and became devoted. She testifies that Lasker had a more profound influence on her than any man she ever met, even including Marshall and F.D.R.[1]

*

One friend in the early days at Beekman Place was the publicist Benjamin Sonnenberg, whom Albert met through Mary; Sonnenberg was (and is) an adroit and witty combination of imp, wizard, and fabulous man of affairs, with a marvelous knowledge of the byways of New York. But they parted company over the Pepsodent affair; Sonnenberg represented Luckman, and Lasker resented hotly an article about Luckman which he inspired. In retrospect today, Sonnenberg talks of Lasker with affection, and calls him "gargantuan."

Intimates in the Lasker circle were, of course, John Golden, Donovan, Sarnoff, the Bernard Gimbels, the André Meyers, and Mrs. Rosenberg. Other friendships proliferated. The names roll out—it is impossible to list more than a few—Jean and Robert Kintner (he presently became head of the American Broadcasting Company and then of NBC); the Gilbert Millers; the late Seymour Berkson, chief

---

[1] Often the Laskers and Anna took holidays together, which produced complicated hilarities. Sometimes Mary and Anna would try to slip away by themselves; Albert, a possessive creature, always managed to follow them. Once at Boca Raton he sat reading in the shade of a cabana, while Mary and Anna gossiped out in the sun. Furiously he demanded their attention, although it was he who had withdrawn from their company. "I'm not going to stand for this. You're deserting me!" he cried. He could not bear to miss anything. Of course, what he really wanted was both to read and hear all that they were saying at the same time.

of International News Service and later publisher of the New York *Journal American,* and his wife Eleanor Lambert, the fashion expert; the movie star Irene Dunne and her husband, Dr. Griffin; George M. Schlee and Valentina, the dress designer; John T. Cahill, who had resumed private practice and was now Albert's lawyer; Dorothy Draper, the interior decorator; Mary's intimate and highly valued friend, Florence Mahoney; Senator Murray of Montana; Margaret Sanger; Kay Swift; James Monahan and Lois Mattox Miller of *Reader's Digest*; James S. Adams of Lazard Frères; Gerald Van Der Kemp, curator of the palace at Versailles; Leonard Lyons, who appointed Lasker to a unique post, that of being *great*-godfather to his four sons; Greta Garbo; the Samuel Goldwyns; Dr. Alfred Frankfurter, editor and publisher of *Art News*; Sir Charles and Lady Mendl; Margaret Truman, whom the Laskers first met through Lyons; and many others. Later in the decade Albert met Barbara Ward (Lady Jackson), the British writer-editor-economist, and admired her greatly. Two other estimable ladies, quite different from one another, should be mentioned with a bow. One was the Hon. Mrs. Audrey Pleydell-Bouverie, one of the most romantically fascinating beauties of this or any day, who was (and is) a close friend of Queen Elizabeth—now the Queen Mother. The other was Mrs. Eleanor Roosevelt.

*

Lasker and Bernard M. Baruch were never close; they maintained good relations on the surface, but that was about all. Lasker never became a Baruch because, as one of his friends put it, he was rougher and too "diffuse"; but also Baruch never became a Lasker. Baruch was a bigger figure, but a smaller man. On the other hand, Lasker did not have his grace and incomparable, almost magical charm. Perhaps Albert thought the less of Baruch because he had made his great fortune partly through speculation, and was probably jealous of his position as elder statesman and perpetual adviser to Presidents. Also Lasker, who was partisan to the uttermost in everything he touched, resented it that Baruch always managed, in the midst of no matter what, to remain calm, detached, and balanced. One evening in 1944 a distinguished cavalcade set out from Lasker's house to the Roxy Theater, where the première of the movie *Woodrow Wilson* was to take place. In one car were Wendell Willkie, Josephus Daniels, Sr., David Noyes (who now had an important post at the White House), and the Laskers. Noyes had been to see Baruch that afternoon, and reported that, discussing politics, the old man said that Tom Dewey was a misunderstood character, whose capacity was much greater than generally realized. Dewey was, of course, an outstanding candidate for the presidency at this time. Lasker said in a flash, *"Bernie will always be for anybody who is President!"*

This wisecrack, which was no more than a wisecrack and was not maliciously intended, got into print in a Washington column, and Baruch was furious. Lasker went to extreme lengths to explain and apologize, but the remark was not forgiven.

*

One of Lasker's last friendships was with David E. Lilienthal, for many years chairman of the Tennessee Valley Authority and then of the Atomic Energy Commission. They met toward the end of the decade, at Mary's suggestion, when Lilienthal was on the point of leaving government. Lasker was impressed equally by his devotion to the public good, his elevation, and the constructive brilliance of his mind. Albert knew, too, that he had had some hard knocks and wanted to go into some private business. So Lasker approached André Meyer, pointing out that Lilienthal, with his vast experience in projects like TVA, was also an authority on atomic energy, which was bound to play an increasing role in industrial developments in the future, and would be a valuable man to have around. Meyer, who has a quick imagination, proceeded to create a position for Lilienthal, and a company was formed to work out projects having to do with long-range regional planning—irrigation, reclamation, et cetera—all over the world. So Lilienthal set out on a new career in Colombia, the Punjab, and particularly Iran, on developments wherein government and private enterprise co-operate. Once again, Lasker with his seminal mind provided the spark, the contact, which transferred idealism into reality, and helped produce good works.

*

The question may well be asked—how was it possible for Lasker to maintain such a wide range and variety of friendships? How could he, who had been a deep-dyed Republican under Harding, like a man like Lilienthal, the so-called advocate of "creeping socialism"? How could he have fondness both for Lilienthal and Wendell Willkie, who, representing the utilities, had been Lilienthal's chief antagonist at TVA? How, on another level, could Lasker be equally devoted to Gilbert Miller, the theatrical producer who would have liked to boil all Roosevelts in oil, and men as close to Roosevelt as Rosenman and David K. Niles, to say nothing of Anna Rosenberg? How could he, whose career had depended so much on advertising, admire De Witt Wallace, who founded *Reader's Digest* on the principle that advertising was wicked and taboo?

The answer is not that Lasker did not have convictions. He had plenty of convictions. He was never a mugwump, never a straddler. But he thought mostly in terms of people, not issues. A principal clue to his character was that he was almost exclusively "operational," and this was one of the factors that made him so accurate in reading the public pulse. His approach was inveterately personal; what counted was whether he liked a man or not no matter who or what he was. "*Every*thing in life is personal," he once told Mary. And, since he was interested in almost everybody who had talent and was willing to give almost anybody the benefit of the doubt and was fond of human nature, the wide crinkled net of his love brought in a very mixed bag indeed.

*

Admiral Lewis L. Strauss, a successor to Lilienthal as chairman of the Atomic Energy Commission, had been a good friend of Lasker's since the Shipping Board days. A striking example of Lasker's generosity, practical imagination, and desire to be useful occurred in connection with Strauss. In 1935 Strauss lost his mother, through cancer; in 1937, his father. At this time radium, which along with surgery and X-Ray was the only known therapy for cancer, was extremely scarce and expensive. Few hospitals had it. Strauss then came across two refugee physicists who told him about the possibility of transforming cobalt into its radioactive isotope, Cobalt 60, by bombarding it with "highly accelerated subatomic particles."[2] At once Strauss saw the possibility of making Cobalt 60 cheaply and being able to provide it to hospitals and research laboratories to replace radium. He said that he would build the necessary accelerator (which in those days was called a "surge generator") and distribute the isotope as a memorial to his parents. One day he mentioned this to Lasker. At once Albert became vehemently interested, and offered to contribute $100,000 to the project.

Work began at the California Institute of Technology. At this date, late in the 1930's, the most powerful tube to accelerate electrons against a target had a capacity of approximately one million electron volts. No one dreamed of anything bigger—not even in science fiction. The California team managed to build an apparatus capable of delivering eight to ten million electron volts. But then it became known that scientists in Germany, working on the fission of uranium, had produced infinitely more powerful devices, which made the California experiment obsolete. Then came the war and the Manhattan Project, and anything that had to do with atom splitting or nuclear energy became ultra-top secret. Lasker repeatedly called Strauss asking him to report on what was going on and to call on his money but Strauss could not, of course, say a word.

Not till some years later did Lasker hear the explanation which, needless to say, satisfied him fully. Nowadays Colbalt 60 is being

[2] Letter from Admiral Strauss to the author.

produced cheaply in large quantities, and serves hospitals all over the world.

Politics and the Full Circle

Lasker's metamorphosis on domestic politics now became as marked as on foreign affairs. He, who had once said that government intervention into business was "poison ivy in the garden of industry,"[3] now believed firmly in the necessity of a regulated economy. He felt that it was essential to protect the common man, and to "readjust the insecurities brought about by the industrialization of society."[4] Controls of business by government, he thought now, were as essential as traffic lights on Broadway, and the government, he declared, had the responsibility for maintaining full employment. In other words, he was now welcoming several major premises of the Welfare State.

In April, 1944, seven months before the presidential election of that year, I ran into Lasker at a party given by Margaret Case of *Vogue.* I had not seen him for some time. He grasped me. "I have been an ardent Republican all my life. I am going to vote for Franklin D. Roosevelt." This he did, and four years later, in 1948, he voted similarly for Mr. Truman. He even bet mildly on Truman although he was sure that he would lose. (The bets paid off handsomely, needless to say.) Lasker never became a registered Democrat —that would have been too much to ask—but he lived for the rest of his life in the atmosphere of the Democratic party.

One of Albert's old friends was Dr. Julius Klein, who had been Assistant Secretary of Commerce under Herbert Hoover, and who was now serving overseas, a colonel in the armed forces. Lasker wrote him a series of letters during the last stages of the war, excerpts from which show the progression of his thought:

July 3, 1944

I have never voted for a Democrat in my life and least of all did I ever think I would live to vote for Roosevelt but the platform adopted by the

[3] Chicago *Daily News,* May 18, 1922.
[4] Letter to Elmo Roper, May 12, 1943.

Republicans is so weasel-worded, I know I cannot vote Republican this time. You can imagine the distress that is mine to sever the ties with the party for which I voted all my life.

Aug. 2, 1944

There is no hope for any happiness in the United States unless we have an ordered world and there is no hope for an ordered world unless the United States in the 1940's takes the place its power demands, for power brings with it responsibilities.

Feeling as I do that there is no chance of domestic tranquillity without world tranquillity, I cannot, for my part, turn over the settlement of the world peace to a ticket, one of the members of which is an avowed Nationalist (sic) like Bricker. . . .

Lasker was shattered by Willkie's death:

October 17, 1944

After he [Willkie] had been in hospital a couple of days, he sent for me. I was hesitant to go but his secretary insisted. I was with him maybe half an hour and made an appointment to see him two days later. When his doctor heard of it, he was indignant that he had had anyone up and phoned me explaining the situation and, of course, I fully understood. I think from then until his death about three weeks later he only saw two or three outsiders for a short time.

November 24, 1944

Since last I wrote you, the elections have occurred and certainly they showed that Willkie's spirit goes marching on. I firmly believe his fight for "One World" brought understanding to millions. The tragedy is that maybe Willkie dead played a greater part in fashioning the minds of people to action than Willkie alive. . . . The victory for Liberalism as against narrow Nationalism, great as it was, is but winning the first battle. If we get 8,000,000 or 10,000,000 unemployed, nationalism will again assert itself. . . . To me the answer to all our problems is to have full employment, and no system that gives less will satisfy the people, nor should it.

January 19, 1945

I feel that somehow there should be organized a group . . . for coopera-
tion in the peace with our two great allies. I feel the kind of a treaty
the Senate will be willing to give us will be dependent on what the
Senators hear from the country. If they feel there is an overwhelming
sentiment in the country to back the type of peace the President proposes,
they will go forward with him in far greater measure than if they feel
the country is only casually behind the President. I am hoping some
such organization comes into being.

This from Albert Lasker, who a quarter of a century before had
organized a group with an aim exactly opposite!

*

Late in 1945, when I was doing research for my *Inside U.S.A.*,
I had a long lunch with Lasker. Someone had inquired of him the
night before, "Will it ever be 1929 again?" and he replied, "It never
was!" Then he was asked if he would defend the constitution, and
he had answered lightly, "Which constitution—the original, or
amendments that have come through legislation and judicial inter-
pretation?" These little sallies amused him in retrospect. He then
launched into a discourse on free enterprise that must have lasted
an hour. His main point was that enterprise had never been truly
free in this country; it was enterprise "licensed" by the big monop-
olies, railroads, et cetera. He saw the United States as a country torn
between economic needs and academic ideals. "How do you marry
these two, and still keep freedom?" Development of federal controls; a breakdown in states' rights; workers "putting their hours of
work," i.e., wages, to better use—all this contributed to the velocity
of change. "Even if Roosevelt had never lived we would have most
of the measures of the New Deal and Social Security." But "social
security" was an unhappy choice of words; nothing in nature is
"secure." "The only way the mass production–capitalist system can
justify itself and survive is to give everybody opportunity for employment, so that everybody shares in the process and has a stake in

the machine." "Freedom rests in essence on the fact that people have to eat." "Free enterprise must not be something which gives one section of the population the right to take economic freedom from another section." There must be controls. "But also we must control the controllers, and the only way to do that is to have a free press."

In September, 1947, I spent a weekend with the Laskers at André Meyer's summer house in Tarrytown; the other guests were Donovan and Norman K. Winston. It was pleasant to see that, after seven years of marriage, Albert and Mary were still wildly in love with one another. Two other things stick in my memory. One was that Winston, who liked delicatessen food as much as Lasker, brought with him a cargo of smoked sturgeon and kosher frankfurters; Albert was beside himself with joy. The other was a talk about presidential aspirants in 1948. Donovan favored MacArthur, but Lasker took a dim view of this. Somebody mentioned Eisenhower, and he bridled with irritation. This puzzled me until I found out the reason; Lasker was out of sympathy with Eisenhower because he was known to be cool to federal aid to medical education; this was unforgivable to Albert if only because Ike himself had been totally educated at the public's expense, right through to West Point and beyond. Also Lasker strongly opposed participation by military men in government.

Lasker's political shift brought some heavy brickbats, but he steadily became more and more liberal. One morning in 1950 he called me excitedly on the telephone. "I have defined what a liberal is," he spluttered. "A liberal is one who knows that, if he himself is to survive, all others must survive."

Domestic Scenes and Challenges

During the forties the Laskers continued to lead an extraordinarily full life. Mary plunged headlong into work on her consuming preoccupation, medical research, and this brought her into intimate association with government in Washington. Nor did she forget another of her passions, flowers. The cut flowers in Beekman Place continued to be a miracle of ravishing grace and color. But she thought that flowers should be something for everybody to enjoy, and that it was silly for cities to be plain when they might be beautiful; so she initiated an extraordinary series of projects to make the face of Manhattan bloom, and paid for some of these herself. University of Chicago botanists had, she learned, developed a hardy strain of winter chrysanthemums on the former Lasker property at Lake Forest. She bought two to three million seeds of these in 1941, and presented the plants to the City of New York as a memorial to her mother: they were placed in Central Park and elsewhere. Seldom has a more decorative and charmingly unusual gift been bestowed on any municipality, and the city government has carried it on.

But this was only the beginning. She conceived the idea that Park Avenue should have flowers, and in the late forties paid for planting forty thousand tulip bulbs, which she imported from Holland, between Thirty-fourth Street and Grand Central. The city authorities said that similar planting would be impossible north of Forty-second Street because of soot and grime. But Mary, in company with her sister, Mrs. Allmon Fordyce, determinedly kept on with the idea, and at last persuaded the city into making test plantings above Grand Central. These were successful, and now, thanks to co-operation from Mayor Wagner and Robert Moses, twenty-two blocks of the plaisance of Park Avenue are transformed into a glowing carpet of tulips every spring. Mary paid for the initial planting, but now the city does so, and other donors have planted additional blocks. Also Mary has donated chrysanthemum seeds to city parks in cities outside the United States, and has given one of the most charming of rose gardens to Magdelen College, Oxford. Finally in this realm, after Albert's death she and the three children planted 250 flowering cherry trees and 40,000-50,000 daffodils outside the United Nations Building as a donation in his memory.

But to return to Albert in the 1940's. He was busy with various enterprises. He was making his philanthropies, many of which were anonymous, systematic. Late in 1943 he gave $50,000 to the Planned

Parenthood Federation, the largest single gift it had ever received; planned parenthood was, of course, close to Mary's heart. Lasker, as has been mentioned in an earlier chapter, was a great believer in what he called "seed money"; in his own words, "he financed the financing." In principle, he still followed the habit of seldom giving money to any organization that asked for it, on the theory that such institutions, if deserving, could apply to the great foundations. What he enjoyed was something more adventurous: to scout out and discover for himself deserving new enterprises that were little known, and give them a lift unasked. Then too his political contributions remained considerable, but no longer did he finance candidates indiscriminately. He thought that it was a duty of good citizens to support deserving men, no matter of which party.

Albert was fond of his new offices on the thirty-third floor of the Chrysler Building. Running this establishment was child's play compared to Lord & Thomas; but he ran it in the same spirited way. Over the door was a framed motto, put there by Mary—a quotation from Maurice Maeterlinck which reads: "At every crossing on the road that leads to the future, each progressive spirit is opposed by a thousand men appointed to guard the past."

One of his major preoccupations for a time was a proposal for converting the Federal Security Agency into a full-scale Department of Welfare with cabinet status. The fight to effect this sensible reform took years, and Lasker deserves a good deal of credit for promoting it. He was almost as much interested in health matters as Mary, and his letters of the period contain phrases like, "I am certain that at this session of the Congress they will pass a very big bill for aid to hospital building." Meantime, he kept his eye on events everywhere, and, among other things, predicted an imminent period of "super-prosperity" for the United States.[5]

Also there was time for pleasure, and Lasker learned something of the art of innocent play. Traffic jams infuriated him; he took to

[5] He was always a good—or lucky—prophet. One of his letters early in 1945 predicted that the war in Europe would be over between April 15 and May 1. Actually V-E Day came on May 7.

walking around town instead of driving. Movies late in the afternoon; dinner parties formal or spontaneous; country weekends—
these were part of a rewarding pattern. He encouraged Mary to
back Broadway shows in a small way, more for fun than profit, and
persuaded Richard Rodgers to sell her a one per cent interest in
South Pacific before it opened in New York. Needless to say, this
was an investment which paid off. Once he said to Edward, "Please
take me to the races." He had not been to a horse race for fifteen
years, and his son was surprised; but Citation was running that
afternoon at Belmont Park, and Albert said, "Nothing in the world
interests me so much as a champion." Also the Laskers traveled a
good deal, and went to Europe every spring after 1949. Once in
London they had tea with King George VI and Queen Elizabeth in
Audrey Bouverie's flat on Berkeley Square, and this was a pleasing
experience although Albert had never been one to be much impressed by royalty.[6] Above all, there was art, as we shall see in the
chapter following. The Laskers spent innumerable hours in museums and art galleries, wandering along Fifty-seventh Street, arguing with dealers, and consulting connoisseurs.

Meantime, he never ceased doing things for people. A celebrated
movie star was unjustly accused of Communist affiliations by the
House Un-American Activities Committee; it was Lasker who found
him a lawyer and helped clear him. A well-known concert pianist
got into trouble with the immigration authorities; in a trice Albert
had a task force on the way to Washington to do its best to adjust
the matter.

With Mary, Albert's relationship became indissoluble. This did
not mean that they didn't have disagreements. He fussed over the
enormous amount of time she gave to medicine, because he thought
that this was wearing her out; he hated to come home in the evening
to find her still in conference with doctors. So the rule was set up

[6] The Duke and Duchess of Windsor attended a small birthday dinner given
for the Laskers in New York at about this time. Everything went well except
that Albert could not remember the title of the Duke's newly published book,
and kept referring to it not as *A King's Story* but as *The King and I.*

that she had to finish all business and household chores, even re-arranging the flowers, before he came home; after that her attention must go undividedly to him. She had, as a matter of fact, little time to devote to household affairs. A steward managed such details for her, and her contact with other members of the staff, except for Nancy and Celia, the faithful maids, was limited. In fact, for some months, she never met her own cook! This may seem extraordinary, but even Albert scarcely knew where the kitchen in Beekman Place was. But that Mary had never even *seen* the cook exasperated him beyond measure. They were about to set off for California. The bags were packed; the car was waiting. Weeks of preparation hung on the moment of departure. Albert stormed into Mary's room. She was still busy dictating a memorandum. He said, "We are NOT going to California until you meet the cook. The trip is CANCELED, unless you stop everything right now and MEET THE COOK!" She dropped her papers and raced downstairs while the steward, in a frenzy, dashed down into the bowels of the house to bring the submerged cook up to the surface. With a defiant and triumphant gesture, Lasker then paraded the cook before her, together with a kitchen maid whom *he* had never seen before.

Lasker had not lost his old acerbity. Once in New York he en-countered a taxi driver ruder than most. He gave him a dollar tip on the seventy-cent fare, and the driver gaped in astonishment. Lasker said, "If your manners had been better, I would give you my *usual* tip!" Once Albert had a sudden impulse to go to El Morocco, the night club. Only three times in his whole life had he ever been to a night club (although he loved to dance), and he had never been in El Morocco. He telephoned Edward, and asked him to get him a table, since it would embarrass him to enter a place where he was not known. Edward said, "It's not necessary. Just tell the head-waiter you're my father." Albert barked testily, "Listen, son, I am the Lasker that people are related to!"

Edward, it should be mentioned, had altogether settled down by now. Storms between himself and his father were less frequent. He married Jane Greer, the movie star, in 1947, and presently Albert had more grandchildren to adore. (After his father's death in 1952, interestingly enough, Edward gave up producing movies, the job that had occupied him for some years, went back to school, studied law, passed the California bar examination with flying colors, and set himself up as an attorney. He was successful almost at once, and this, if Albert had lived to see it, would have given him rich pride and pleasure.)

After Lasker gave away Mill Road Farm he promised Mary to buy her a small house somewhere in the country, but, for years, when-ever she mentioned this he avoided the subject. He was too old (so he said), too exhausted, to enter into any such ambitious project as a new house. Beekman Place was enough. Besides he must have felt that, subconsciously, he would always be comparing any new estab-lishment in the country to Mill Road Farm, and nothing could ever match the glories of Mill Road Farm. Mary persisted. She scouted around. One weekend in 1950 motoring in Dutchess County she came across a 410-acre property near Millbrook, called Heathcote Farm, which suited her. Immediately she saw how to fix it up. Albert was spending the weekend at White Sulphur Springs. She joined him there, and he said, "Well, if you like it, buy it. I won't bother to see it myself. Tell John Cahill to draw up the papers."

He wrote a friend, "I did not have energy enough to resist her." Then, on seeing the property, he fell in love with it. It was no more than a toy compared to Lake Forest, but it was a beautiful toy. The land grant derived from Revolution times, and the house was deli-cious. Green meadows lay freshly on sloping hills, and in the dis-tance could be seen the profile of the Berkshires; neither in Texas nor in Illinois had Lasker ever had hills, and he called them proudly his "mountains." He built a guest house, put in a swimming pool, and stuffed the farmers' cottages so full of TV sets and air-condition-ing units that they bristled like porcupines. He had not intended to spend a great deal of money; but the establishment cost a con-siderable sum before it was finished.[7] He smiled. "Do you know the

---

[7] He wrote Abe Selz, "The purchase price was just an admission ticket."

difference between a farmer and an agriculturist? A farmer makes money in the country, and loses it in the city. An agriculturist, which is what I am, is the opposite." But this did not interfere with his intense, appreciative love for Heathcote Farm. Shortly after moving in he wrote a friend, "What I have found here is peace—at last."

One evening Nancy, the maid, while busily putting his clothes in order, muttered to Mary with a smile both happy and matter-of-fact, "How long have *we* been married to Mr. Lasker?"

*

Lasker had been seriously ill in 1945 with a staphylococcus infection which resisted penicillin and which kept him in hospital intermittently for seven long months; and again in 1948 with a mild cardiac disturbance. Yet he still stood straight as a baton; he still had his alert, winning smile; his eyes shone and his step was taut and agile; he was immaculate, pink, and shining. In 1949 he had a group of doctors go over him, "to appraise him as a survival risk" as he put it, and demanded to know what they considered his life expectancy to be. He got an estimate which satisfied him, and proceeded to lay out a schedule. One day he mentioned this to David Noyes, who said, "The doctors are wrong. Put the estimate up by two and a half years. They may be all right about physiology, but they know nothing of your capacity to live psychologically on your reserves." But instead of taking solace from this, Albert was furious. If he *was* going to live longer than the doctors said, he would have to change his priorities and plans!

In 1941-42 and then after the war Albert and Mary had the habit of spending a month every winter at La Quinta, in the California desert near Palm Springs, to get some sunshine. After dinner each night it was Albert's custom to take a stroll along a circular path which led through a grapefruit grove. His companion one evening was Edwin Knopf, the movie producer, and it was a chilly night;

Albert was coatless, and as they passed the Lasker cottage Mary came out running, to hand him a topcoat solicitously. He gave her a light kiss and thanked her, then resumed his walk. He said, "You know, Eddie, I mustn't live too long. I must go while Mary is still young enough to have the life she deserves."

Chapter 20

NEW WORLDS IN ART ...

Now we must go back a bit, and interrupt chronological sequence to give an account of the two things that mattered most to Lasker in the last decade of his life, art and medicine.

For years, he had never had the slightest interest in painting, although as head of Lord & Thomas he was one of the largest purchasers of commercial art in the world.[1] As has already been related, he even resisted having an art department at all for a long time, because his conception of advertising was that copy should tell the story, with art as the merest auxiliary. Time and competition forced him to change, but his feeling about art didn't soften. Once Max Epstein told him that he had just bought a minor old master for $10,000. Albert replied, "I'd rather put that in cement to save my trees."

Back in 1940 Dr. Alfred Frankfurter, who became his intimate friend later, met him in the home of the late Maurice Wertheim, who had a well-chosen collection of modern art. Lasker and Frankfurter, the editor of *Art News*, looked together at some paintings, and the younger man was at once struck by (a) Lasker's complete naïveté; (b) his courage in admitting, even flaunting, his naïveté. He dared to ask questions—in public. He was willing to betray his ignorances in a way that no sophisticated New Yorker would dream of doing. He had humility and curiosity and when he asked a question he expected a good answer. He said to Frankfurter, "Now what does that painting *represent*? What are its affiliations to this other painting? Did the artist found a school?" Frankfurter mentioned

[1] "Personal Collector," by Aline B. Louchheim, *New York Times*, June 8, 1952.

casually that a Van Gogh they were inspecting was probably worth $45,000. Scoffing, Lasker replied, "I could get Norman Rockwell or Howard Chandler Christy to do it for $3,500." Frankfurter asked penetratingly with a smile, "But would you hang a Rockwell or a Christy in your house?" This adroit question amused Lasker, but it did not shake him as much as it might have because he was still totally unaware of the field of original works of art.

The dominating influence in the change that came was, of course, Mary. They talked about pictures a good deal. Mary pointed out that contemporary painting, even abstractions, had powerfully affected the modern trend in such things as industrial design and packaging, architecture, advertising posters and layouts, magazine make-up, and even the shapes of pots and pans. Why not, she suggested, be interested in the innovators of this style, the originators, not merely in those who copied from it or improvised on it? Albert was impressed. On the other hand, she never urged him to buy pictures. He would willingly have bought her almost anything in the world, but she knew that he must come to the decision to collect by himself. If he gave her paintings merely as an indulgence, then he would not be a real participant in the pleasure they induced. One day in 1944, after they moved into Beekman Place, she was delighted to hear him say that he thought they ought to buy some paintings to make the house more alive. He had begun to be interested at last, but his first purchase was extremely modest, an Eisendieck that cost $300.

The next step came when he and Mary dropped in one day at the Wildenstein Galleries, and he was not only entranced, but overwhelmed. This was the first time in his life that Albert had ever been in a dealer's showroom and the first time he had ever seen pictures handed about informally and cozily, instead of being displayed coldly on a wall. He asked about prices, and nearly fell dead. Dealers were getting fifty, sixty, seventy thousand dollars for a *picture!* He exclaimed in rapt horror, "How long has this been going on!"

Some time later Mary took him to an auction at Parke-Bernet. He had never been to an auction before, and did not want to go. He was fearful of the plunge. He didn't want to be involved. He was adamant. He told Mary, "I'll go with you as far as the door, but I won't go in." But, in the end, he could not resist following her inside. She had her eye on a Renoir. She started to bid, and was then astounded to hear Albert—he was standing behind her—beginning to bid as well. She dropped out early, but he was now caught firmly in the excitement of this game and went up to $25,000. Then, to their chagrin, the picture went to Paul Rosenberg, the eminent dealer, who was also bidding, for $26,000.

Another little story hangs on this Renoir, a glowing mass of red geraniums with two small kittens near a swatch of wool. Passionately eager for it was the impresario Billy Rose. But Rosenberg, meeting Rose at the auction, pleaded with him not to bid against him. "No matter what you bid," said Rosenberg, "I will outbid you. I want that picture." Rose demurred at first, but Rosenberg presented a good argument. He said, first, that he himself would go right up to the sky for it, which meant, second, that to recoup his expenditure he would have to add thousands of dollars to the price of every other picture in his inventory. Rose was buying heavily at this time, and naturally did not want to see prices go up. So he agreed not to bid, although he would certainly have been willing to go beyond $26,000. Later, Rosenberg handsomely rewarded Rose for this by letting him have another Renoir, priced at $20,000, for $11,000.

But now Lasker, zealous for the chase, determined to get for himself the red geranium Renoir which both he and Rose had missed. But Rosenberg had it now, and there was no way to get it except to buy it. Rosenberg's price was steep. Albert groaned. At last he did something characteristic— he bought not one Renoir from Rosenberg but two!—because Rosenberg shaved his price a trifle on the second picture, the radiantly lovely *Young Girl in a Boat*. Even so the two cost around $100,000, but by the time Albert got home he was so consumed with delight that he was convinced that he had made a tremendous bargain. And indeed he had, because the two Renoirs today are worth four times what he paid for them.

Now the Leigh Blocks enter the story. They were visiting New York and returned to Beekman Place one day to say that they had just seen an incomparable Van Gogh at Rosenberg's, but that the price was prohibitive, $55,000. It was the brilliant painting, one of the most celebrated in the world, which depicts the *mairie* (city hall) at the village of Auvers on the fourteenth of July, with holiday flags flying—the last picture the master completed before his suicide two weeks later. Lasker, without saying a word to anybody, went to Rosenberg's alone the next day to look the picture over. He liked it extremely and called Frankfurter, who reported that it was indeed a great picture but that the price seemed high. Albert said, "I am going to make a deal." He returned to Rosenberg's and, still without telling Mary or asking any further advice, worked out an agreement whereby the Blocks were able to buy the picture for $35,000. His argument to Rosenberg was that, if this picture could be had reasonably, the Blocks and other members of the family might start out to collect in a big way. The shrewd dealer saw the point. And, indeed, this Van Gogh did help to set the Blocks off on their long and rewarding chase. Mary Block had, at this time, only two or three pictures—a Dufy, a Franklin Watkins, and a Braque. Now the Blocks have 150 or more paintings including a score of indubitable glowing masterpieces, and have given eleven others to the Chicago Art Institute.

But to return to Lasker. The Renoirs, his first big acquisitions, made it clear that he was launched on his new career with a bang. He had several assets as a collector aside from enthusiasm—basic good taste, a strong interest in proportion and design, and love of color. Technically, he knew little at the beginning; few men have ever learned faster. He looked through books on art voraciously, and tramped for hours on end through museums. One of his companions was Emery Reves, a versatile character, not a professional art man, but an author and agent—Winston Churchill's agent, who arranged the transaction whereby Churchill's memoirs of World War II were bought simultaneously by *Life* and the *New York Times*. But he was fond of painting, knew where modern paintings not on the market were to be found in the chaotic days immediately following the war, and was beginning to collect himself. He and Lasker looked at pictures together, and became fast friends.

Not merely did painting in itself attract Lasker with passion; so did the technique of buying and selling paintings. The whole fabulous apparatus of the art business fascinated him. Beating somebody else to a prize, tracking down a lost masterpiece, hearing about something new about to appear in the market—all this sharpened his zest to buy. He became crazy about collecting as a game. Most dealers in impressionist and contemporary painting, he promptly discovered, had somewhat flexible ideas about price. He said one day to Dr. Brazill: "They are terrible—robbers. But if you are going to go into the collecting business, you have to make up your mind to like them and be amused, not angry." Once he observed ruefully, "I knew that I would have to pay the highest prices to get masterpieces but I did not know that I would have to pay even higher prices for the privilege of paying the highest prices."[2] Reves warned him about a renowned dealer in Paris, saying, "He'll overcharge you terrifically." Lasker grinned, "Why not? Don't be too hard on a man who's just a salesman!" Dealers, on their side, adored him. He was always fair, and he had a genuine understanding of their business, which was based on the trading instinct as much as on salesmanship. Moreover, some dealers, even the most blasé, at least do like painting, and it pleased them to find a man who never bought out of pedantry but for pleasure. Who but Lasker would have dared to say, "I want a Toulouse-Lautrec but it has to be a Toulouse-Lautrec with red in it!"

His appetite for pictures grew with the eating and, when he was almost seventy, he confided to Reves that he would like to try his hand at painting himself. Nothing ever came of this, however. He didn't quite want to risk taking lessons. Besides he took painting far too seriously. He told me once, "When I buy a picture, I'm

[2] This apothegm appears in *The Proud Possessors,* by Aline B. Saarinen, p. 107, and elsewhere. The first article ever to appear about the Lasker collection was "Color, Matisse, and the Personal Touch," by Alfred Frankfurter, *Art News,* March, 1951.

buying part of man's very, unh, life!" From every point of view his collection gave him extreme pleasure. He liked to murmur sagely, "Pictures have no upkeep except the insurance. They're not like horses or even grass. You have to feed horses and water grass. But pictures don't even eat!"

The Lasker Collection

Very few collections of modern French art in America can match Lasker's, although several may be bigger. The collection is divided between two houses—29 Beekman Place and Heathcote Farm. Albert started too late to compete with such collectors as the renowed Dr. Barnes in Pennsylvania. When Albert came into the scene prices were already fairly high—although nothing compared to what they are today—and he did not want to spend too much money. The main thing to say about his pictures, quite aside from the indisputable magnificence of many, is that they are joyous. They communicate, as he did himself. He didn't like pictures that had to be explained, although several of his Picassos are abstruse enough. He liked paintings that gave forth color, warmth, and drama. He bought for fun. What he liked best was to go into a gallery and see something unexpectedly and fall in love with it. Then, like as not, he would say without further ado, "I'll take it." Yet his taste was such that he bought very few canvases that were not masterpieces. His major determinant was not merely future value (although that certainly played a role); his criteria were personal, and he never bought anything he didn't like. Of course, on the other hand, the artist had to have a name. He was not adventurous among unknowns, but probably would have become so if he had lived.

After the two first Renoirs, sublime both, he bought variously, and then began to concentrate on Matisse. In the 1940's Matisse was neither as fashionable nor as academically accepted as he is today. Lasker plunged, and before he was finished bought nine, several of which are among the greatest examples in the world of Matisse's middle and late periods. Five of them, including the incomparable *Pineapple and Anemones* (the pineapple in a chrome yellow bowl on a salmon-colored table), went into the dining room at Beekman place; they are an unmatched constellation of blindingly effective line and color, which light up the oyster-white walls like fireworks. Probably nowhere else in the United States is there such a concentration of Matisse in his full, mature glory in so small a space.

Then Albert bought a radiant little Corot (he got it for a comparatively minor sum from a London dealer); a lovely Cézanne (*Large Vase in a Garden*), of deep blue flowers and grapes against an ocher background; four incomparable Braques (one is *The Pink Table*, a dramatic still life brilliant in its combination of pinks, red, and black); a stupendous Monet (*The Pool of Water Lilies*); and, on a different level, two horizontal arrangements, one of fruit, one of flowers, by André Bauchant which are miracles of deft originality. Altogether, in the end, he had about 170 oils, gouaches, and water colors of the first rank, among them no fewer than seventeen Picassos, including the classic *Woman in White Mantilla,* one of the most appealing of all Picassos, and *Still Life with Guitar,* an early example of cubism with a shining, enigmatic backdrop of violet-blue and hydrangea pink.

Other pictures Albert bought to give away, and his sisters, who lived together, got a superb Matisse. Once he astounded Alfred Frankfurter by asking him to help choose half a dozen Marie Laurencins water colors. "Half a *dozen?*" Frankfurter echoed, aghast. "For Christmas presents," Lasker explained calmly. Once he set out to buy an entire small museum, but the deal fell through.

Almost every picture he bought carries a story; every purchase was an adventure. By around 1949 his taste was fully formed; he didn't rely on experts, although he liked to consult with them. He said to one man who sought to help him, "Please let me make my own mistakes—it's the only way to learn." In this year in Paris he got two Rouaults and several of the Picassos; in 1950 came a small Miró. Occasionally he bought a picture Mary didn't like (notably a Bonnard, which she sold after his death) and sometimes, but not often, she bought something he didn't like. The most conspicuous in this latter category was a Picasso still life of fish on a table. For some reason Lasker, when at last he was able to figure out what it was, took a violent antipathy to it. He went at once to Anna Rosenberg with the words, "I am making you a witness to what I say. I think this is a terrible picture, and it is not mine." He had a card typed out and pasted on the back of the painting, "This belongs to Mary Lasker, and is not to be included in my collection." Mary, somewhat startled, tried to hide the picture by hanging it in a corridor on the sixth floor; every once in a while Albert would go up there, grunt with distaste, and turn it over to see if his notification was still there.

A meeting with the venerable Matisse at Nice in 1949 was one of the high points of Lasker's life. Matisse proudly showed him designs for the memorial chapel then being built at Vence; Albert said something to the effect that he wished he were a little younger. Matisse, who was eighty, patted his knee with the words, "You are still a child." Albert then asked him who was the best young painter in France, and Matisse replied calmly, "*Moi.*"[3] Also the Laskers had a friendly association with another hero, Raoul Dufy. Dufy was crippled by arthritis; he came to America, where the use of cortisone and ACTH in arthritis was just beginning (it was still unprocurable in France) ; Mary helped arrange to make these drugs available to him, and he became much improved in health as a result. Another friend was Salvador Dali, and the Lasker collection has no fewer than twenty-four of his water colors, including the *Lorelei* and the luminous *Dance with the Butterflies.*

The two greatest Lasker acquisitions, both Van Goghs, were among the last. One of these, the *Zouave,* has been reproduced so often that to see the original, with all its lustrous brilliance undimmed, comes almost as a shock—it is fresh beyond belief; the other is the upright *White Roses,* a canvas even more renowned. In Paris in 1950, Lasker was determined to buy at least one more really important picture, and heard through an agent that the *Zouave,*

---

[3] After Lasker's death Matisse did a design for a memorial window to him, but died before completing it. The sketch is in the Dallas Museum of Contemporary Art.

with its subject's flaring red pantaloons and tasseled cap, was available. But it was in Switzerland. Lasker refused to go to Switzerland. He heard, however, that a Brazilian millionaire coveted this painting hungrily, and this stirred him to special efforts. He contrived to get it shipped to Paris on approval, and went down to the customs shed at the railway station early in the morning to inspect it. It was not even framed. He asked permission of the customs authorities to carry it out into the sunlight to look at it more closely, and Mary asked him, "Do you like it?" The answer was Yes, and he bought it then and there out in the street for $85,000. An even more remarkable anecdote attends the purchase of the *White Roses*. Van Gogh painted his white roses twice. Averell Harriman has the horizontal one, and the whereabouts of the vertical twin was a mystery. Mary first got on its trail through an art book, and told Albert he must have it. It was discovered somewhere in Germany, and then found its way to America, where it was reposing placidly in a bank vault. Emery Reves, who was in New York at the time, got wind of this, and passed the news on to Lasker, who was in California. Albert in turn called Mary to go and see it, hoping that she would buy it at once. She, however, was en route to Washington to attend a meeting of the National Heart Council, and had an appointment with President Truman to boot. Lasker said, "You may be making a terrible mistake—get the picture first." She said, "I'm an old dealer and I know about these things; it's in a bank vault, nobody knows about it, and it can wait." She returned from Washington in due course, called Reves, and asked him to set an appointment for visiting the bank to see it. Reves said, "Wildenstein bought it yesterday for $100,000." Mary was thunderstruck. It had never occurred to her that a *dealer* might go after it in the vault. Albert was furious. Meantime, Leigh Block opened negotiations with Wildenstein to get the picture either for himself or for Albert. In the end Wildenstein let Albert have it for $135,000, which meant that Mary's engagement in Washington cost him $35,000, or approximately $7,000 an hour. He always told this story cheerfully, however; it was a good joke on Mary and proved that he could spend $35,000 too much

on something without blinking. Of course, the picture is worth two
or three times its purchase price now.

*

Since Lasker's death, his entire collection has been exhibited
twice (of course, individual pictures are out on loan often)—in
Dallas in 1953 and San Francisco the next year—for the benefit of
the American Cancer Society.[4] People fond of art who have not seen
the Lasker pictures can get a good view of them in a handsome book
recently published, *The Albert D. Lasker Collection, Renoir to
Matisse*, with an introduction by Dr. Frankfurter. This contains
color reproductions, expertly printed in Holland, of sixty of the 170
Lasker works of art. Included, aside from paintings I have already
mentioned, are one of the two Chagalls, all three of the exquisite
Fantin-Latours, ten Dufys (two of them oils), a Bernard Buffet, two
of the three romantic and beautiful Redons, two of the four Utrillos,
the Toulouse-Lautrec *Woman in Red*, a score of Foujitas, one en-
chanting little Sisley, one Degas, one Soutine, one Morisot (the
radiant *Young Girl in a Greenhouse*), one Modigliani, one superlative Manet portrait, and a Vuillard of mother and child, *The First
Steps*, of unsurpassable dexterousness, grace, and charm.

Certainly this gay and deliciously catholic collection is a fitting
memorial to Albert's taste. It was his collection, not Mary's. But it
is interesting that, of the sixty reproductions in the book, no fewer
than thirty-two contain flowers, her great love, and four more have
trees, shrubs, or other greenery.

[4] Several have been on loan at the Louvre recently, also at the Metropolitan.

Chapter 21

... AND MEDICINE

Art was fun. But Lasker, with his white-hot energy of soul, could not tolerate existence without something serious to bite into, and during his last decade his foremost preoccupation was not art at all, but medicine—the problem of life and death, no less. I have already stressed that, almost from the moment they met, he and Mary addressed themselves to medical problems, and their long, exhilarating, and exhausting struggle in the field of medical research and associated activities still goes on productively today in her capable hands. The Laskers worked concurrently or consecutively on at least four different fronts: (1) birth control; (2) medical research and care; (3) the American Cancer Society; and (4) the Lasker Foundation. Elements of the story overlap and intermingle, but I will do my best to deal with them one by one.

*

Mary, who admired Margaret Sanger greatly, had been active in the birth control movement for several years. Overpopulation was, she thought, a major world problem, as indeed it is; even today people at large have not even begun to consider the enormous economic, social, and political consequences that will face humanity in about 1980 when the population of the earth, if unchecked, will reach the appalling total of four billion, as against 2.7 billion today. Not only was she the sort of person to whom an abstraction like this was a serious reality; she thought of it in intimate human terms —the emotional distress which harasses parents of unwanted children, the hardship of maintaining large families on meager funds, and juvenile delinquency in overcrowded slum areas. She echoed the Sanger principle, that it was a human right to be born by choice rather than chance. Lasker knew about Mrs. Sanger long before he met Mary, and he and his sisters had given money to the movement in the thirties, but his interest had not been very direct or personal. Now Mary introduced him to Mrs. Sanger, and he was much struck by her. At once, in a typically Laskeresque way, he suggested that the name of her organization be changed. "Birth control," he said, was too negative a phrase; it connoted self-denial. He chose "Planned Parenthood" as a substitute from a list of names submitted to him, and presently the Birth Control Federation was reorganized and renamed the Planned Parenthood Association. Lasker supported it vigorously; he and Mary gave it $75,000 in its first three years.[1]

The planned parenthood campaign was important to the Laskers because it showed them, first, how extraordinarily dense was the web of prejudice, ignorance, and hypocrisy obscuring not merely the subject of birth control but much else in the realm of public health and hygiene, and, second, that any attempt to push forward, even with the mildest proposals for reform, would arouse the most implacable opposition from entrenched forces. The birth control fight led them to close inspection of related phenomena. It was certainly no news to Mary that American medical services were inadequate for people of modest means. Now it became clear to her that, with Albert's backing, she could try to put her ideas into practice, and their work for medicine and public health got actively under way.

In 1944, while vacationing in Palm Beach, she came across a book which described tellingly how malaria and typhus could be virtually eliminated in the armed forces by applying the results of recent research discoveries. Also it mentioned the work of the war-

[1] One ironic point: some time later one of the Lasker Foundation awards went to a Norwegian woman, Elise Ottesen-Jensen, an educator. The lady, it was discovered later, was the eighteenth of nineteen children born to her parents! If the Sanger principles had been fully applied to the Norwegian village where she was born, there would never have been an Elise Ottesen-Jensen to win a prize.

time Office of Scientific Research and Development, which, under the chairmanship of Dr. Vannevar Bush, was doing a good job but which had received only the minimum of public attention. Mary reasoned: "If federal money is available to eliminate malaria in wartime, why should it not be available in peacetime for work against cancer, heart disease, and mental illness, which, much more than malaria, damage and weaken our national economy?" She began to collect statistics—for example, to show the enormous cost of absenteeism, caused by illness, to American industry every year. The sum was staggering. Illness cost more than strikes. Albert taught Mary how to make dull figures come alive. Not for nothing had he spent nearly half a century in the advertising business. For instance, take the fact that the total amount spent in the United States for medical care in one year was $11,272,000,000; this may seem to be a very large sum, but it was only 3.53 per cent of the total national income. The problem was to dramatize such figures. They were important and disconcerting, yes. But who would listen? How were people to be reached? The message, the meaning, had to be grasped. Three and a half per cent of $11.2 billion conveys little. But it conveys a lot when translated into Lasker language—"TO KEEP OURSELVES FROM DYING, WE ONLY SPEND 3½ PER CENT OF WHAT WE SPEND ON EVERYTHING ELSE!"

In the early 1940's the federal government was not spending more than $560,000 a year, a pittance, on cancer research, and not one cent for research on the nation's biggest killer, heart disease. Yet millions upon millions of dollars were going into investigation of animal and plant diseases. The Laskers had no faintest objection to this; but, if the government was willing to pour in unending millions to save crops, like citrus and wheat, why not contribute something as well to save human beings, who are, after all, the basic crop of the nation? Meantime, they reached their first basic conviction, which never changed—that the key to everything had to be research. This, although it seems obvious now, was not accepted then. The emphasis in popular medical thought was on treatment, not prevention. Doctors worked more in terms of trying to treat arthritis, as an example, rather than to find out what caused it. But, manifestly, from a long-range point of view, research should have first priority because if it succeeded in producing the means of getting rid of a disease, the disease itself ceased to be a problem. The first task was to create a base. Soon the Laskers had to hand a perfect demonstration of their argument—the discovery of penicillin. Application of this drug and its allies has, as everybody knows, produced miracles beyond computation in the treatment and cure of various diseases. But before penicillin could do its magical work it had to be discovered.

Dr. Bush's wartime organization, the Office of Scientific Research and Development, which was attached directly to the presidency, contained a small unit devoted to medical research. Mary discovered that this, along with the parent organization, would be dissolved with the end of the war. It was purely a wartime agency. But, obviously, the end of the war was now in sight, and she was horrified that this good beginning, even though it was small, would be lost. She talked to Anna Rosenberg, who said, "Give me a memorandum, and I will take it to F.D.R." This set in motion a chain of important events, the results of which are with us yet. The issue was simple— would new mechanisms for research into illness financed by the federal government for war purposes be maintained when peace came? Or would this whole new promising apparatus have to be scrapped? Roosevelt turned the matter over to Judge Rosenman, who promptly wrote a letter in F.D.R.'s name to Dr. Bush, directing him to make a report. As a result, Bush prepared a document, *Science, the Endless Frontier,* which explored the whole subject and put on the table frankly the principal long-term issue, namely what the future relationship between government, science, and medical research was going to be.

The Laskers now came into close contact with Claude Pepper of Florida, who was chairman of a Senate subcommittee on Wartime Health and Education, through their close friends, Florence and Dan Mahoney, publisher of the Miami *News.* Pepper, with other Senators, had been shocked to find out that, in what was presumably the healthiest country in the world, rejections of draftees on medical grounds reached the enormous total of 40 per cent. Clearly, the United States was not as healthy a nation as it had thought itself to be. Pepper determined to hold hearings on this and related subjects. The U.S. Public Health Service maintained at this time a research instrument known as the National Institute of Health, but when the Pepper hearings began in 1944 the total federal budget for research in all illnesses was only $2,400,000 a year. Doctor after doctor testified that this sum was ridiculously, shamefully inadequate, but such was the tenor of thinking at the time that the Public Health Service itself had not even asked for an increase. The upshot was that Pepper introduced a bill to create a National Medical Research Foundation. At the same time two other Senators, Harley M. Kilgore of West Virginia and Warren G. Magnuson of Washington, inspired by the Bush report, introduced another bill to set up a National Science Foundation. Pepper agreed to merge his bill with theirs, but the science bill got into complex difficulties.[2] So the Laskers, the Mahoneys, and enlightened doctors began to think in terms of a different approach—namely, to work through the existing institutes of the Public Health Service (the National Institute of Health and the Cancer Institute) and look into the possibility of setting up other research institutes each with its own budget and devoted to specific disease problems. The work of the Laskers and others to this end was successful, and is a major and beneficent accomplishment.

Meantime, Albert and Mary went into other activity. One long fight had to do with better medical care through voluntary health insurance. The story behind this is abstruse. They were among the backers and incorporators of the Health Insurance Plan of Greater New York and Group Health Insurance, and Lasker became convinced that a national health insurance program was necessary and desirable for at least four reasons: (1) He hated to see people suffer. (2) In quick succession two of their servants, to whom they were devoted, died of cancer; both might have been saved if they

[2] It was not finally passed until 1950.

had received medical attention early enough. And, if people in *his* household could die a painful death because an illness was not diagnosed and treated promptly, he reasoned that there must be hundreds of thousands of others much more vulnerable. Citizens, he felt, did not go to doctors in time even if they knew the risk involved simply because they could not afford proper treatment, especially if this were prolonged. They concealed their illnesses from their employers out of fear of losing their jobs. At that time 97,000,000 Americans (those with incomes under $3,000 a year) could not, he calculated, afford to have a serious illness. American medicine was, he conceded, the best in the world, but, as he put it in his testimony to the Senate later, "There is a difference between the practice of medicine and the ability of the individual sufferer to take advantage of it." (3) Patients were deprived of satisfactory care because many doctors were not adequately trained. Medical knowledge was not disseminated quickly enough. (4) The cost of illness to American industry was almost immeasurable.

Hence, Albert Lasker became doubly convinced that the only solution was federal legislation to create a comprehensive national health insurance program, like unemployment insurance, to be paid for by employer and employees through payroll deduction, and with free choice of doctor. In July, 1947, he came down to Washington to testify to this end before a Senate subcommittee conducting hearings on the Wagner-Murray-Dingell bill for national health insurance. This bill had been prepared some years before, but had never reached the floor of either Senate or House. Lasker was a compelling witness, and Senators listened to him with great respect. From first to last he insisted that insurance would raise the earnings of individual doctors, not diminish them as enemies of the bill said, and added—a characteristic touch—that he didn't think that insurance, no matter of what type, was "socialistic" at all, but was as American as apple pie.

The bill was, however, beaten; in fact, it never even got out of committee, partly because of a massively effective campaign against it organized by the American Medical Association.[3]

The Laskers and the American Cancer Society

This was one of the most strenuous of all the Lasker efforts. We must go back to 1943. For a long time—ever since his brother Harry died of cancer in the 1930's—Albert and his sisters had been interested in lay education on the cancer problem.[4] The chief institution dealing with this was the American Society for the Control of Cancer, now known as the American Cancer Society. Mary lost a close friend through cancer, and every instinct she had was revolted by the suffering it caused. She was infuriated. She demanded of various doctors, without getting a satisfactory answer, "Why, why, cannot you *do* something about this horrible disease?" As always, her approach was personal.

It was also practical. The Laskers set about to find facts. They discovered that, as of this time, 1943, the Cancer Society, a private organization, was raising not more than $350,000 a year. They determined to help it get more, and Mary suggested a campaign on the radio to arouse citizens to the need for periodical medical examination and prompt attention to any symptom that might indicate cancer. The answer she got was that the word "cancer" could not even be mentioned on the radio. It was taboo. The word was not thought to be "proper" for dissemination on the air. Mary, as she herself tells the story, had a fit. Cancer was the second cause of

---

[3] But one paradoxical effect of this was to strengthen the voluntary health insurance plans. The Blue Cross and Blue Shield enlarged the scope of their services. The medical lobby couldn't quite afford to oppose all forms of medical insurance, and concentrated on the fight to stave off a national plan; hence, the voluntary plans flourished even though they are still inadequate and pay only a percentage of the total cost of care.

[4] Mention might be made here in passing of the grinding shock Lasker would have suffered if he had been alive during the contemporary controversy over cigarette smoking and lung cancer. Cigarettes were his baby. But the case against them as possible cancer-inducing agents is so strong that he would have felt a heavy sense of guilt and responsibility at having done so much to popularize them.

death in the United States, it led to anguish and terror and pain unmatched by any other disease, and yet it could not be mentioned on the air!

Also the Laskers discovered that, of the $350,000 raised by the Cancer Society in 1943, not one cent went to research. In fact, in its thirty years of existence, the society had never spent any money on research at all. The Laskers later made a proposal, namely, that they would help supply additional funds for a national drive on cancer, to be organized by the society, on the condition that one-quarter of all new funds should be devoted to research. The rest would go to public dissemination of knowledge about cancer—services, education, and allied purposes. The proposal was accepted, and at once the Laskers got to work. First, they supplied $80,000 from various sources, some of it contributed by Albert himself, to help pay for the campaign. As he sagely remarked in a little aphorism, *"To raise money you have to have it."* This was the beginning, and then other money flowed in.

Preparations began late in 1944, and the campaign, to last a month, was set for April 1, 1945. Eric Johnston was persuaded to be its head, and he enlisted the aid of prominent businessmen all over the country, like Elmer Bobst, now the head of a big drug company, and James Adams of Lazard Frères. Next, if the campaign was to be a success, the taboo against mention of cancer on the air had to be lifted. In this the indispensable Lasker ally and co-worker was Emerson Foote, who was still president of Foote, Cone, & Belding. Without Foote, results would have been much less than they were. On Mary's persuasion, he became an adviser to the society. Another valiant helper was Niles Trammell, the president of NBC; so were executives at CBS. A number of radio stars, like Bob Hope and Fibber and Molly McGee, lent their assistance freely, and at last the ban on mentioning cancer on the air was broken.

Another important contributor to the success of the campaign was Lois Mattox Miller of *Reader's Digest*. With Foote's assistance she wrote three articles appealing for money; these brought in a very considerable sum, which was used as a further instrument to finance the campaign. The De Witt Wallaces helped staunchly too by giving these appeals for funds a prominent place in the magazine.

The drive was a success beyond anybody's dream. No less than four million dollars was raised in a month, which meant that a million was now available for research. This may not seem to be a great deal in the light of today, but at that time it was a lot. In the entire United States in 1944 only $1,100,000 had gone to cancer research from all sources, governmental and private combined. So in their first campaign, the Laskers helped to raise funds almost equal to the total previous national effort.

One reason why research had been neglected before, even by the great foundations, and why so few contributions had been made specifically for research purposes, was that there were so few leads. The fight seemed to be against hopeless odds. But Mary said courageously, "If there are no leads, let us make them." Nowadays research institutions devoted to cancer are expanding; not only universities and foundations but the pharmaceutical companies devote large sums to research, and laboratories are hard at work; but this was not true in the early 1940's. By and large, attitudes were not only listless, but negative. The Laskers helped to change this—a considerable accomplishment. Another result of the campaign was that cancer became publicly mentionable, not merely on the radio but in the press. This was a vital advance. Ten years ago—to cite one example—the frankness with which the illness of John Foster Dulles was treated in the press and elsewhere would have been unthinkable. The Lasker theory was that to take the wraps off cancer, to make it less mysterious and terrifying, would help in the long uphill fight to conquer it.

Of course, the Laskers were by no means solely responsible for all these developments. They worked hard, but so did plenty of other people. The Damon Runyon Memorial Fund, established in 1947, brought in about a million a year; moreover, every cent of Runyon money went to research (and still does). Institutions like the Sloan-Kettering Institute in New York City were set up, which did admirable work.

A next step was to reorganize the American Cancer Society and

put it on a firmer basis. The motive was to ensure that the four
million raised by the campaign would be well spent. The Laskers
knew well that it was easier to raise money than to spend it wisely,
and they wanted the contribution to be real. Lasker became a member of the board of the Society, and sought at once to bring in more
new blood. Albert, Mary, and Foote felt that the organization
should be given a much broader base, and that membership on the
board should be divided half and half between doctors and lay
people. It would be pleasant to say that the medical men associated
with the society accepted this unconventional proposal with alacrity. They did not. Some fought it like tigers. On the other hand,
physicians like Dr. Frank Adair and the late Dr. Cornelius P.
Rhoads, both of Memorial Hospital, who had good will, devotion
to the ideal of research, and unflagging energy and imagination,
were powerful allies. The conflict exhausted Lasker. He found that
doctors had petty squabbles even as did businessmen, and were torn
by the same vanities and jealousies. Moreover, this was all voluntary activity and he could not direct the organization as if it were a
business. In the end the decision to make the board of the Society
half-medical, half-lay, as the Laskers wished, was taken. Recently a
prominent physician said, "The American Cancer Society and all
its beneficent work is no more than the shadow of one man—Albert
Lasker."

The next effort was to try to persuade the Cancer Society to support federal appropriations for research. The Society itself does not
accept money from the federal government; it is a voluntary group
which raises and distributes its own funds. But Lasker thought that
if the Society, with its great prestige and authority, would assist in
the task of getting increased funds for use by *federal* agencies, like
the National Cancer Institute of the U.S. Public Health Service,
this would serve a good purpose. At first he was vigorously opposed
by some physicians attached to the Society who hated and feared
federal money. In the end, however, representatives of the Society
duly went to Washington to testify, and their testimony had a pronounced effect on members of Congress. Figures tell the story. In

1946 the budget of the National Cancer Institute was under $600,000; by 1950 it had risen to not less than $18,900,000, partly as a result of testimony by members of the Society, and in fiscal 1960 reached the spectacular total of $92,000,000.

As to the Cancer Society itself, relying as it does purely on voluntary funds, the figures are even more remarkable. It raised no more than $350,000 in 1943; by 1946 the sum rose to $10,000,000 and the amount for 1959 was just over $30,000,000, close to being one hundred times more than the $350,000 raised in 1943. This money goes fruitfully to a multiplicity of hospitals, laboratories, institutions, and foundations all over the nation. Mary's homely words, "If there are no leads, let us make them," are still the slogan. With stubborn zeal day by day thousands of research scientists equipped with the Society's funds and funds from the National Cancer Institute are monitoring the frontiers of the unknown.

The Lasker Foundation and Its Awards

Back in 1942 the Laskers set up the Albert and Mary Lasker Foundation, and this organization, which is altogether independent of others described so far in this chapter, deserves a word. It has a wide charter; Albert was its first president, and Mary is president now.

When the Foundation was first created Lasker felt that he needed advice and Mary went to the late Dr. Alan Gregg of the Rockefeller Foundation for counsel. They did not have much money—nothing compared to what the Rockefeller organizations had—and, as Albert said frankly, he wanted "bargains," that is, to bestow funds to institutions or important causes which were neglected, or operated in fields not touched by the giant foundations. Gregg suggested a variety of leads. The Laskers gave funds toward the conquest of heart disease, arteriosclerosis in particular. Since that day the activities of the Albert and Mary Lasker Foundation have proliferated widely, and it works nowadays in many other areas.

Also the Foundation bestows the well-known Albert Lasker

Awards.[5] These, inaugurated in 1946, came about as a result of a casual conversation with a lawyer. Mary was making a will, and said that she wanted to work out a scheme whereby, after her death, part of her inheritance might go to awards for pioneers in medicine. Her purpose was to stimulate new discovery, make people alert to scientific advance, and thus save lives. Then the idea rose—why not begin right away? What was the point of waiting? Why not do this while she was still alive? Plenty of scientific and medical men were in need of recognition and encouragement right now. She talked the matter over with Albert, but he demurred at first because the publicity that might ensue would, he said, embarrass him. He had always sought to avoid the limelight, and to keep his benefactions as little known to the public as possible. But Mary won him over, and the awards were launched.

However, he continued to maintain a good deal of reserve about them; he avoided the ceremonies at which they were presented, and sometimes even refused to meet the winners. He was not being ungracious, but could not bear to be conspicuous as a donor. He still felt that he could operate best if he stayed behind the scenes. Then gradually as the awards became better appreciated he became prouder of them, and prouder still of Mary.

There are several awards each year. The Lasker Foundation provides funds for administrative expenses and supplies the prizes, but it does not choose the winners. Both Albert and Mary insisted on this. The winners are named by altogether independent juries, which change every year, and which are appointed by the American Public Health Association, the American Heart Association, and other organizations. Awards are given in the field of medical research ("for a major contribution to the struggle against killing or crippling diseases"), in the field of public health administration, and for the best medical journalism of the year and the best medical TV show. These awards, at first $1,000 each, are now $2,500, and

[5] Until his death these were called the "Lasker" Awards, indicating that both he and Mary were responsible for them; the name has been changed so that they are now a memorial to him, at Mary's request.

winners also receive a gold replica of the Victory of Samothrace. As is the case with Nobel prizes, the awards may go to co-workers as well as to a single person. Why awards in the field of administration? Because, the Laskers felt, research must be followed by execution. Why journalism? Because news of medical advance should be well reported. Also the Foundation gives a special award ($5,000) at unstated intervals for an outstanding continuing contribution in the field of public health. In addition various groups are cited, all the way from Alcoholics Anonymous to the International Health Division of the Rockefeller Foundation and the British Ministry of Health. Finally, a Lasker award is given from time to time by the Planned Parenthood Association for notable work in this special field; the last winner was Sir Julian Huxley.

About eighty Lasker awards have been bestowed in the last fourteen years, and they are recognized as being the equivalents in medicine of Pulitzer Prizes in letters, or, on a different level, the Oscars of the movie industry. There is no medical worker in the world who would not be flattered to win a Lasker award, and, year by year, the prestige associated with them mounts. One reason for this is that no fewer than ten Lasker winners won Nobel prizes later. In other words, the Lasker juries not only choose well, but do so before recognition becomes general.

One Lasker winner was Dr. Salk, the discoverer of polio vaccine. Another was Dr. Karl Paul Link of the University of Wisconsin, who found out that a substance named dicumarin killed cattle which ate spoiled hay, by unaccountably thinning out their blood; out of this discovery came the development of anticoagulants which have saved thousands of lives in attacks of coronary occlusion. Another group of winners, a four-man team at the University of Minnesota, invented a technique whereby the healthy heart of a donor can, so to speak, be hitched to the heart of a patient undergoing a severe cardiac or pulmonary operation, thus providing a living heart as a substitute pump. Another winner was Dr. Fred L. Soper, for his work on the natural history of mosquitoes and yellow fever; another, Dr. George Papanicolaou, for his discovery of a test, now used everywhere, for cancer of the cervix; others, a three-man team which found out the relation of the Rh blood factor to the death of newborn infants; still others, Drs. Edward H. Robitzek and Irving J. Selikoff, who were pioneers in the use of isoniazid in the treatment of tuberculosis. As a result, the death rate from this formidable killer has been cut 50 per cent since 1952.

The ten men who proceeded to win Nobel prizes for the same work for which they had already received Lasker awards are Carl Ferdinand Cori, M.D. (research on carbohydrate metabolism); Selman A. Waksman, Ph.D. (discovery of streptomycin); Vincent de Vigneaud, Ph.D. (discovery of new hormones of the posterior pituitary gland); Max Theiler, L.P.C.P. (yellow fever vaccine); Edward C. Kendall, Ph.D., and Philip S. Hench, M.D. (discovery of cortisone and its application to rheumatoid arthritis) ; André Cournand, M.D. (catheterization of the heart) ; Hans A. Krebs, Ph.D. (cellular metabolism) ; John F. Enders, Ph.D. (immunology and the polio virus) ; and George Beadle, Ph.D. (genetics) . A distinguished roster indeed—and more will come.

*

Activities in government, the American Cancer Society, and the Foundation did not exhaust the Laskers' interest in medicine by any means. They aided Dr. Howard W. Florey, the co-discoverer of penicillin, and urged federal funds for large-scale clinical trials of cortisone. When cortisone first came on the market it cost hundreds of dollars a gram, but as a result of federal purchases the price came down. Another important interest was psychosomatic medicine. Leigh Block, who was vice president of the Michael Reese Hospital in Chicago, told Albert about the need of a psychosomatic clinic there, and, following Block's suggestion, Albert and his children gave $225,000 to start a Psychoanalytic and Psychosomatic Institute for Training and Research, dedicated to the memory of Flora.

Mary Lasker was, incidentally, by no means a mere amateur in medical matters. She set out to learn about medicine technically, from the ground up, and learned a great deal. She slept with medical books four inches thick at her side, and has had close contact, on a serious level, with leading physicians in various specialties all over the United States. She knows far more about medicine than most laymen—more, I would even dare to say, than some doctors. Once in a telephone talk I mentioned casually that my doctor, after several days of being puzzled, had finally diagnosed a sore throat from which I was suffering as an exceptionally rare ailment known as Friedlander's Bacillus. She responded at once, "Of course—it's gram-negative—get some streptomycin."

Some Challenges and Pay-offs

The former are still with us; the latter cannot be predicted. But the extraordinary advances in medical knowledge and techniques which have taken place lately give good promise for the future, if research is maintained. The death rate from pneumonia has been cut 24 per cent between 1944 and 1957, largely because of antibiotics; syphilis, 74 per cent; acute rheumatic fever, 83 per cent. On the other hand, cancer deaths have risen menacingly from 118.3 per thousand in 1939 to 147.6 today. But, even in the realm of cancer, research provides hope. In hundreds of laboratories today thousands of chemicals are being steadily, meticulously screened, in the hope that a cancer-killing agent may be found or isolated. More than twenty-five compounds have already been discovered which cause temporary regressions with some types of cancer in human beings; more than fifteen compounds have been found which actually cure (at varying rates) transplantable animal cancers.

But, as Mary likes to point out, infinitely more needs to be done. The Lasker Foundation provides some relevant statistics. For instance, the federal government appropriated well over two *billion* dollars for roads and highways in 1957, but only $12.7 million for research against arteriosclerosis and hypertension, which caused more than 820,000 deaths. It spent $111 million for soil conservation, but only $4.26 million for research against arthritis and the metabolic diseases which cripple in varying degrees more than thirteen million Americans. It budgeted $157.8 million for agricultural research in 1959, but only $22.9 million for research against neurological diseases and blindness in human beings. Then consider cancer again. We plan to spend around $40 billion to defend ourselves against military attack in 1960, but only $92 million for research in cancer, which will kill one out of every seven living Americans.

The life expectancy of the American male (white) is now 67.3 years, a gain of 4.3 years since 1943; of women (white), it is now 73.7, a gain of 8.5 years. But the life expectancy of the Negro male is only 61.1 years, of the Negro female only 65.9 years. In other words, to have a black skin costs an American citizen 6.2 years of life if he is a man, 7.8 years if the citizen is a woman. We are doing well; but obviously there are important challenges ahead.

Zenith: The National Institutes

Back in 1944 Albert wrote to Senator Pepper:

The government collects and spends, in the course of time, billions in social insurance, veteran's aid to men stricken with postwar disabilities, and those who cannot take their place as producers in society (on account of illness or disability). A comparatively few millions spent [for medical research] annually over a period of a decade might make the need for such vast social security and veteran expenditures largely unneccessary.

This was his basic line from first to last.

Early in this chapter we reached the point where, in the mid-1940's, Albert and Mary became interested in the National Institute of Health[6] and the National Cancer Institute of the U.S. Public Health Service. Lasker always believed not merely in targets, but in precise targets. It was his theory that, if a series of semiautonomous organizations could be set up, an immense amount of waste and duplication of effort could be eliminated. He had no idea that the struggle to achieve this would entail such phenomenal effort. Most

[6] Now called General Research Services of the National Institutes of Health.

Senators and Congressmen, no matter what their good will, did not know the full facts. It had never been cogently brought to their attention that, for instance, only $1,100,000 was being spent annually on cancer research, from all sources, and nothing at all on heart or mental health. They had been so busy helping the nation to defend itself from external enemies that internal menaces in the realm of health were neglected; health matters had been inadvertently ignored in the total field of public spending, and many legislators thought that the foundations and private donors were supporting medical research on a larger scale than was the case. Now as a result of the impetus given by the Laskers to the collection and presentation of statistics they became more interested. In one year Mary went to Washington seventeen times. She, Albert, and their indispensable associate Florence Mahoney considered themselves to be "citizen petitioners." President Truman said later that Mary and Mrs. Mahoney were "the most tireless, consistent, and effective crusaders he had ever known."[7]

Lasker was a revolutionary among philanthropists, because he was the first to suggest putting *federal* money to work in a big way on health matters in addition to giving away a great deal of his own. Federal money is, of course, everybody's money, but he was convinced that, if the case were presented clearly enough and in terms of the common man's understanding, both legislators and voters would support tax-paid medical research. Nobody, he reasoned, wants to die before he has to die. Moreover, as he had written to Pepper, he was certain that spending a comparatively small amount of revenue now would save prodigiously in taxes later.

There exist today, partly as a result of encouragement given by the Laskers, as well as their work in presenting information, a group of National Institutes of Health, all at Bethesda, Maryland, which constitute what is probably the best integrated medical-*cum*-research

[7] Incidentally, Mr. Truman was the first President in American history to send a message to Congress asking specifically for legislation having to do with the national health. Part of his program went through; part did not. Once he told Edward R. Murrow in a TV program that the principal regret of his presidency was his failure to get a bill for national health insurance through Congress.

and training unit in the world. This development was made possible by the passage of three main bills—one setting up the National Institute for Mental Health (June, 1946), the National Heart Institute bill (1948), and an omnibus bill in 1950. Among senators who sponsored these bills were Pepper, Magnuson, Neely, Murray of Montana, Ives (New York), and Bridges (New Hampshire); later came peerless leadership by Lister Hill. Senators on both sides supported his effort to get adequate appropriations. Among Congressmen were Andrew Biemuller (Wisconsin), Javits of New York (now a Senator), Smathers of Florida (ditto), Wolverton of New Jersey, Keefe of Wisconsin, and, later, John E. Fogarty of Rhode Island,[8] who showed particular courage in this matter.

Once more, figures tell the story. Between 1946 and 1956 inclusive the American government spent more on medical research than any nation in history in an equivalent period. In 1945 the total research budget of the U.S. Public Health Service was a scant $2.4 million; by 1952 it had risen to $56 million, and in 1958 the figure for the operation of all eight institutes was $211 million, a hundredfold increase in thirteen years. For 1960 this figure, imposing as it is, was *doubled;* Congress ignored President Eisenhower's attempt to hold the line on the budget, and altogether the institutes got a record $400 million. So now the increase from 1945 is 2,000 per cent. For this the indefatigable pioneering of the Laskers and their many medical friends and crusading associates is responsible in part, and the farsighted legislators who put through the bills and favored adequate appropriations deserve well of the republic.

[8] Details of the work of the various institutes may be found in the Appendix.

Chapter 22

TERMINUS

Autumnal shadows were gathering now. "I tire easily," Lasker wrote to Abe Selz. "I can do only a fraction of what I once did, but I feel fine and I enjoy life." He asked to be remembered to the old Partridge crowd—"those who are still alive, or even fifty per cent so"—and flirted with the idea of inviting the surviving members to New York to celebrate his seventieth birthday. His plans changed, and he and Mary went to Paris instead. Here the birthday celebration did take place, on May 1, 1950, and it was a lively affair. Both his daughters and sons-in-law were present, and so was his good friend Danny Kaye. Kaye and his wife, Sylvia, found a gold coin minted in the year of Lasker's birth, 1880, and gave it to him; Albert always loved to have something unique, something that nobody else had, and this coin meant a great deal to him.

Leonard Lyons, the columnist, flew over to join the party; the Ritz was full up, with not a room available. Albert went to the Ritz manager, whom he had known for years.

"You are in trouble," he intoned, glowering. "You are in the worst trouble of any man I ever heard of."

The manager asked why.

"You say there is no room in this hotel, and I need one."

He got the room.[1]

On this trip Lasker, even if he was tired, behaved as friskily as a boy. One day he and Danny Kaye scrambled over the roof of the palace at Versailles, because the museum director said that this gave such a good view of the gardens—something of a feat for a man

[1] This anecdote has been told about other people in different circumstances, but the above is apparently its true origin.

333

of seventy. He rose early every morning, and, with unquenchable *joie de vivre,* set out to make full use of the day. He liked to stroll down the Champs Elysées, and then proceed cheerfully to the Plaza Athenée and rout the Brodys and Blocks out of bed. "Come on down! It's time for a drink! Let's see some pictures!"

Of a sudden he decided to visit Israel. With him went Emery Reves and his sisters, Loula Lasker and Mrs. Rosensohn. He still maintained the closest contact with his sisters, and adored them. Mary did not go with them. She did not like to fly, and perhaps in a peculiar way he wanted to be without her when he encountered the anguish and triumph of his people in Israel for the first time. Anna Rosenberg flew over to join Mary in Paris the night before he set out, and he told them to amuse themselves looking at pictures while he was away. (They did so, visited every good gallery in town, and tentatively picked out eight paintings which they thought he would like; of these they anticipated that he might buy one or two. When he returned eighteen days later he bought all eight! Several were Picassos.)

The Israel trip, although brief, was one of the most profound emotional experiences ever to come to Lasker. He called it seriously "the high spot" of his whole life.[2] Not only was the journey a challenging adventure in itself for a man now past seventy who was quite unused to rough travel; it was an intense, passionate episode in revelation. First, he was fascinated by the spectacle of a state, which had heroically set itself up as an independent country only two years before, seeking to create free institutions step by step against almost inconceivable obstacles, while beset by enemies on every side. A second reason for his exhilaration was that he, who had always felt a kinship for American and European Jews, now discovered that he was also part of a politically conscious Jewry that embraced men and women who seemed alien to him beyond speech—orthodox Jews with their hair in oily ringlets, Yemenite Jews, and Jews out of the gutters not merely of Warsaw and Poznań

[2] Letter to Dr. Eli Davis, director of the Hadassah Medical Organization, May 26, 1950.

but of Baghdad, Fez, and the deserts of Arabia. One afternoon he clambered up the hilltop (it was not graded then) leading to a church behind the King David Hotel. Part of the way he had to scramble on hands and knees. Around him were hundreds of newly arrived Yemenites—wretchedly backward, destitute, diseased, filthy, illiterate. He sat down to rest, and his face, as one of the sisters put it, started to "work" furiously. He conquered his emotion and said, "For the first time in my life, I know what the expression 'the Jewish people' means. These are my people, and I am part of them!"

Lasker's former attitude toward Zionism had been simple enough. He was neither pro- nor anti-Zionist; he was "non-Zionist." As a young man he had thought of Palestine not as a national home, but as a place of refuge; the Jews there were like poor relations. He had been willing to give money, but not to take part in the Zionist movement. His emotions were charitable, not political. He was American. Then came Hitler. Millions of Jewish refugees—those who managed to survive the Nazis—had to have a home somewhere. Nobody would take them in, in any number, and Lasker recognized the tragic desperateness of their situation. Mrs. Rosensohn, a dedicated Zionist, began to influence him. Suddenly in January, 1949, Albert called her and said that he and Mary wanted to give $50,000 to Hadassah, the Zionist medical organization. Mrs. Rosensohn suggested that this sum should be earmarked for building a children's clinic (no such thing existed in the new state) and he agreed that this would be a good idea. The clinic was promptly established in Jerusalem under the name Lasker Mental Hygiene and Child Guidance Center, and the ostensible purpose of his trip in 1950 was to see how this was getting on.[3]

So, here he was camping out in the King David Hotel with Reves

[3] Subsequently Lasker gave other substantial sums to Israeli projects, for instance to the Weizmann Institute at Rehoveth for assisting in experiments toward the extraction of chemicals from the Dead Sea water. Also he was instrumental in getting the first isoniazid, cortisone and ACTH into Israel. After his death Mary contributed money for cloud-seeding experiments by the Israeli government.

and his two sisters, grumbling a bit because the food wasn't good but otherwise exuberant. He was tireless. He covered practically every inch of the new state. He had long talks with Dr. Chaim Weizmann, the President of the republic, and David Ben-Gurion; he visited frontier settlements, citrus groves, and reclamation projects; and day by day his satisfaction mounted. On four separate scores he decided that Israel was a "miracle." First, this was the only community in the world where Jews never felt that they "had to keep looking back over their shoulders a little bit." Second, there was a feeling of "belonging to each other" on the part of citizens unmatched anywhere else on earth. Third, the country had absorbed 300,000 immigrants in two years, which was as if the United States had taken in sixty million; these came from fifty-seven countries and spoke forty-two languages; nobody was refused; immigrants became citizens at once, and were rehabilitated if necessary ("Even if you're a leper, you can come in"); the task of making the country homogeneous was going forward calmly and with complete confidence. Fourth, there had been a war and 800,000 Jews had beaten to a frazzle Arab forces representing thirty million people. How was this possible? Because the Jews had something real to believe in. "In the Israeli balance sheet," Lasker wrote, "you have to include the *spirit of man.*"

Also he made a neat little prediction—that if war came again, the tiny Israeli army could easily "take Cairo" in a week, which indeed it almost did in 1956.

*

In ten years Mary and Albert had never been separated for more than a day or two. These are excerpts from a longhand letter he wrote her from Israel immediately after his arrival.

April 8, 1950

Mary Beloved,

I have been gone a little over 60 hours but so much has transpired it might be 60 days. Besides I miss you greatly. It is good consolation being so far away for so long to confirm to myself how much your companionship means to me.

We arrived at Lydda at 5 A.M. your time. The flight was uneventful—one dramamine and I thought I slept fairly well. . . . We drove from Lydda here over biblical territory and thru which much fighting had been done in the war. The road was strewn with rusting war trucks—oh yes, we passed the stream where Samson courted Delilah!—sure makes the bible (sic) appear inaccurate.

Later Sat.

I spent 3 hours last night listening to Emery Reves niece, who with her mother (every other member of their family was killed) told of her 7 years wandering from country to country, village to village, camp to camp all during the war and thereafter. . . .

Darling, as to paintings, I wired you to use your own judgment, to buy what you thought we should and pay what is right. I count on you to bargain correctly. . . . I am amazed at Mr. X's Picasso being offered for 1.8 million francs. I thought 4 was ridiculous and therefore put him off 3 times. But I am still amazed. I hope you buy the Morisot. . . . But I am after the Degas. Don't hesitate to make decisions. . . . You can go up to $50,000—without the Degas, tho' if you are offered unimportant paintings I would suggest you spend only $25,000—until I get back. But darling, I leave it to you, knowing you will make only right decisions.

Several pages follow of detailed reflections and observations on things in Israel. Already he had seen a lot. Then:

Tell Nancy she is right—I am very lost without her taking care of my clothes. I don't know how I ever will pack without her. Have a good enough barber here ($4.20 one). Heaven knows what I will do in the weeks touring. Some days I will grow a beard and become Orthodox.

My love to her [Anna Rosenberg] and Nancy. And to you darling all the devotion and adoration and love of which I am capable. . . . I miss you.

Ever,

ALBERT

My sisters are lovely and congenial companions. I enjoy them much. They send all sorts of loving messages.

Some of Lasker's assessments of Israel still have point. He was quite conscious of demerits in the picture, for instance that the country would have to live for a long time on "charity money," i.e., its unfavorable balance of trade could be redressed only by private remittances from the United States and elsewhere. This, he thought, would put Israeli propagandists in a dilemma. Here was a country which—logically—should *not* put out any red carpet with which to impress visitors. It should, on the contrary, try to appear as poor as possible, in order to entice more "sustenance money." On the other hand, the country must contrive to give a note of firm hope, or funds might dry up altogether. The thing that impressed him most, after the signal austerity of the regime, was the absence of bias in social relationships. "Prejudice is practically non-existent, and it gives the visitor a feeling of serenity. . . . It's only when you come to this oasis of absence of bias that you realize what the pressure of bias is on people who live in it."[4]

Back in the United States

Vastly refreshed and happy Lasker returned to Paris and then to the United States. Almost at once, disaster struck. He felt liverish, but thought that this might be the result of too much rich food in Paris; then came a severe abdominal upset, and he went to the hospital for treatment.[5] It became apparent that something very grave indeed was the matter, and, under Dr. Loeb's supervision, an exploratory operation was performed. A second, much more serious operation followed. Lasker had cancer of the intestine. The surgeons did what they could, but it was impossible to know whether they had been able to remove all of the malignancy in time or not.

Lasker was never told that he had cancer. He hated and feared this disease so much that the shock of knowledge would have been

[4] Columbia, p. 76.
[5] Six months before this, in December, 1949, he had complained of stomach trouble and had a prolonged examination, including elaborate X-rays. This complaint must have been the first manifestation of the malignancy. But the doctors were unable to find evidence of cancer. If it had been possible to detect traces of the cancer at this time Lasker might still be alive today. This story illustrates unhappily one of the main points of his own work in pushing medical research. If we had better diagnostic methods and new and superior medical skills thousands of men and women could be saved from illness and death.

too much for him to bear. Once he said to a friend, "I would not thank anybody to tell me anything bad about myself." Probably he knew the truth subconsciously, but he did not want to live without hope. He wrote a cousin in Israel in October, "Early in July I had to undergo two operations for a tumor in my intestines. This is a very major operation and one from which recovery is a prolonged ordeal—the body seems to resent the insult. The doctors all tell me that if I am my own self within a year I will have done well."

If he did suspect a malignancy, he kept his mouth firmly shut. He did not want to increase the burden of his illness on those who loved him, and asked no questions; even if he did have cancer, he didn't want to know it. Only two people in the world aside from Mary and the physicians knew the truth, and they, too, kept silent. There was nothing to do but wait in agonizing suspense and hope desperately that the cancer had been totally removed.

*

Late in 1950 Anna M. Rosenberg, as has already been mentioned, became Assistant Secretary of Defense, the first woman ever to hold this post. The appointment was made on the suggestion of General Marshall, who was Secretary of Defense; Mr. Truman welcomed it warmly, and so did Robert Lovett, the Deputy Secretary. Previously Marshall, when he was Secretary of State, had sounded her out on the possibility of appointing her to be Ambassador to the Soviet Union, but she turned the proposal down because she felt there were people who could be appointed who were better qualified and who at the time could do a more effective job. But a year later she accepted the Assistant Secretaryship of Defense with alacrity although it interrupted her business career and entailed severe financial sacrifice. She could not resist her great friend Marshall, and, with the Korean War going on, felt that it was her duty to serve the country.

The appointment was announced on November 15, and Mrs. Rosenberg at once moved to Washington and plunged into work.

On November 29, after a hearing which lasted only an hour and a half, the Senate Armed Services Committee unanimously approved her. Then came an episode totally unexpected—and fantastic. Several persons came forward to accuse her of having been a Communist years before. On December 5, as a result, the committee voted to withdraw its approval, pending investigation of the charges, and hearings were held, under the chairmanship of Senator Richard B. Russell of Georgia, which lasted for ten tumultuous days.

Now it is important to note that, at just this time, Senator Joseph R. McCarthy's first smear campaigns were inflaming the country, and the Senator had become a national figure. He was looking ahead, and plotting to bag bigger game than the State Department "Communists" whom he had been attacking heretofore. Above all, he was hot after General Marshall (some months later he delivered his 72,000-word speech in the Senate accusing Marshall of being a traitor) and Marshall had, in fact, warned Mrs. Rosenberg when she took office that extremist reactionaries and crackpots might try to embarrass him through her. Whether McCarthy himself was an actual party to the conspiracy against Mrs. Rosenberg is unknown. But one of his investigators was involved in the case, and a subsequent witness against her testified that, on arriving in Washington, he had checked in at McCarthy's office.

Anyway Mrs. Rosenberg was vilified and calumniated; wildly irresponsible charges were put forward; the atmosphere was that of a crazy circus. But all the preposterousness had to be taken seriously, because her good name was at stake. She was not only one of the first conspicuous victims of the mass hysteria which defaced the nation until McCarthy's power was broken, but her case was a microcosm of much that came later. Guilt by association; reckless innuendo; charges advanced indiscriminately and never proved: the whole dreary performance had a rehearsal. Luckily the Rosenberg hearings took place before Senators who, after they recovered from their first shock, were courageous and fair-minded. The plotters against Mrs. Rosenberg drew support from two camps. First, professional Red hunters, ex-Communist riffraff, and last-ditch reactionaries, even including unsavory characters like Gerald L. K. Smith. Second, anti-Semites who were willing to go to any disreputable length "to keep a Jew out of the Pentagon," and who had close relations with lobbyists of the Arab League.

Of the many witnesses who were questioned, only two were against her—an admitted ex-Communist named Ralph De Sola, and Benjamin H. Freedman, a vociferous polemicist whose testimony, it soon became clear, was based on hearsay. The gist of De Sola's "evidence" was that he had known Mrs. Rosenberg as a member of the John Reed Club, a Communist front organization, early in the 1930's. She denied this utterly, and, in one dramatic scene, confronted De Sola with the words that she had never laid eyes on him in her life. Meantime, the FBI files revealed nothing in the slightest degree derogatory against her. Soon it became clear that the case might rest on mistaken identity. No fewer than six "Anna Rosenbergs" had signed a Communist election petition in New York in 1940, and more than forty different Anna Rosenbergs lived in Manhattan. Who was which? The people attacking the new Assistant Secretary, without the slightest justification or any serious attempt to investigate, simply assumed that the "Anna Rosenberg" who had been active in the John Reed Club and Anna M. Rosenberg, the candidate for important public office, must be the same.

When, early in December, the affair burst open, Albert Lasker could scarcely contain his wrath and indignation. Not for years had anything upset him so much. He was outraged not merely because he was devoted to Anna, but because, to his mind, this was an open-and-shut case of injustice—of evil trying to wreck good. As always, he had a considerable capacity to see the big in the small, the general in the particular. That a woman so impregnably loyal and patriotic as Anna M. Rosenberg should be submitted to this kind of monstrous ordeal was, he thought, not merely an ignoble demonstration of crackpotism but a cause for national humiliation and disgrace. It was a threat to the survival of decency in the United States. If Anna lost, the worst elements in the country won. "The people who are doing this thing," he exploded to me the night the story came out, "want to ruin the country. They stand against everything that is good. If they win, we will have fought the war in vain."

For some days Lasker scarcely ate or slept; he was a man possessed. He telephoned people in various parts of the country, consulted friends, and got prominent citizens to send telegrams of protest to members of the Senate Armed Services Committee. He told one acquaintance: "I have a substantial amount of money left. I am prepared to spend it all, every cent, to see that justice is done in this case." He meant it. Nor was he by any means alone in his efforts to give Mrs. Rosenberg aid. Dozens of leading citizens spontaneously came forward with testimonials on her behalf. Columnists ranging from Marquis Childs and the Alsops to Walter Winchell were vigorous in her defense. Political and other leaders, no matter of what party, took her side. Senator Ives of New York spoke up for her; so did Senator Lehman; so did James Byrnes, former Secretary of State; so did Clare Boothe Luce, Nelson Rockefeller, President Dodds of Princeton, Mrs. Oveta Culp Hobby, Lessing Rosenwald, John Hay Whitney, various labor leaders, Robert F. Wagner, and General Walter Bedell Smith; so did Bernard M. Baruch and Dwight D. Eisenhower.

Mrs. Rosenberg refused to have an attorney in the Senate committee hearings. She was confident that the facts alone would clear her. But Lasker, still boiling, went ahead on his own and enlisted the help of his good friend and attorney, John T. Cahill. Meantime, the FBI was scurrying all over the country to find, if possible, the Anna Rosenberg who *had* been a member of the John Reed Club, but the search was unsuccessful at first. Then several witnesses were produced who testified that they had known the other Anna in the old days and that the Anna now under investigation was *not* she. This was enough to satisfy the Senate Committee. Still, the Senators had to do their duty, and the whole idiotic and tawdry performance, which caused Mrs. Rosenberg agony beyond expression, dragged on day after day. At last on December 14 the hearings were concluded, and the committee voted unanimously to reapprove her appointment. Newspapers promptly described the case as "the smear that backfired," and Mrs. Rosenberg's friends were jubilant.

But she still had to be confirmed by the Senate as a whole. On December 20 she was informed that the FBI had at last discovered the identity and whereabouts of the other Anna, and could produce her. Mrs. Rosenberg said, "No. I will be confirmed on my own."

She was. Moreover, this came about not because sentiment had been mobilized on her behalf, but because her complete innocence was now incontrovertibly clear even without production of the other Anna, who, it turned out, was a Brooklyn housewife leading a perfectly respectable life; she had remarried and was living under her new name. Therefore, she had been reluctant to come forward to say that she was the Anna Rosenberg who had been a member of the John Reed Club. The "real" Anna was now triumphantly confirmed on the Senate floor with only two dissenting votes; even Senator McCarthy voted for her. Senator Russell said, "The charges against Mrs. Rosenberg have been demonstrated to be completely without foundation."

Lasker knew well that his own efforts and those of others for Anna had not directly affected the result, but he was proud of them and liked to think of the case as his last "crusade."

Nearing the End

Now 1950 gave way to 1951, and this year smiled on Lasker for its full course. He appeared to have recovered completely from his illness, and, with undimmed vitality, resumed his sunny enjoyment of life and bloomed in the light of Mary's boundless love. Mary, with Florence Mahoney as her staunch associate, kept eagerly on with their interest in medical research, and Albert bought the *White Roses,* a fitting cap to his career as a collector. They entertained widely and pleasantly in the country, gave lively parties at Beekman Place, and took several trips abroad; in London Albert enjoyed a cozy little chat with Winston Churchill that lasted four and a quarter hours.

I saw more of Albert in this year than in any other, and I never knew him to look better or have more bounce and fizz. There was a glow to everything he did. He was radiant with fulfillment. Moreover, he loved Heathcote Farm.

Yet . . . yet . . . there were indications that he was drawing a kind of invisible frontier around himself, drawing his lines in, as if to ward off dangers from the unknown. He clung closer to his oldest friends, and became more dependent on Mary than before. It was as if he were trying to contract the circle of life around him to a smaller dimension, so that, loving everything so intensely, he could continue to touch intimately every item in its circumference.

In plain fact, a life of extraordinary richness, usefulness, and variety was drawing to its close. Few men have ever traced such abundant patterns on so many sectors of the national scene. Baseball; golf; government; national politics; advertising; Jewish affairs; merchandising and the world of commerce; shipping; radio shows; philanthropy; public health and public welfare and social justice; a successful effort to increase both private and public funds to kill killers; art—all this and much else Lasker touched with magic fingers and powerful brain. And what a magnificent human being he was! To the last moment he was expanding, growing, bursting out, even if his physical horizons became circumscribed. The juice of life in him ran full to the very last.

If he feared that his illness was going to return, or suspected what it was, he never talked about it. But in January, 1952, he complained of abdominal pains and paid a routine visit to the hospital. I dropped in to see him; he was not even undressed or in bed; he was bristling with questions about the presidential campaign then about to begin. I had just had a long talk with General Eisenhower and he was avid to hear the details. He was funny, wise, practical, and gay. Also he predicted that Adlai Stevenson would be the Democratic nominee, and said that he would vote for him. After a few days the doctors let Albert return home. The next month, however, he felt suddenly ill again, with pain much sharper, and was obliged to return to the hospital. But the night before he was admitted—February 16—he felt well enough to have a small dinner party.

It became tragically clear now that the surgeons had not been able to get all of the cancer in the 1950 operation. Now, nineteen months later, a new drastic operation showed that the malignancy had spread elsewhere in the abdominal tract. There was nothing to be done. Lasker was told that he had a liver complaint which would necessitate prolonged treatment. If he had doubts about this he never let on or expressed them. Once he remarked to Loeb, "Don't let anybody *experiment* on me!" I saw him perhaps a dozen times in the next few months, and although this illness was obviously terminal and caused him the most appalling pain, he never looked seriously ill; he did not waste away, as do so many cancer patients; he did not lose his color; he was animated until the last few days; his incomparable love of life, his courage and superabundant vitality, sustained him to the end.

Mary moved into the hospital, and stayed there in a room next door for the next months. Edward and Frances flew in from California on alternate weekends, and the Blocks returned from a European trip; Mary Block stayed in New York from April 9 until the end. Meantime, Albert maintained as much of his normal activity as possible, consulted André Meyer about business, and even bought two pictures, a Fantin-Latour and a small Picasso. He asked callers what was going on on Fifty-seventh Street, summoned friends, gossiped, and never dropped his interest in world affairs. One thing that pleased him was a letter from Matisse, which the artist emblazoned with red-and-blue flowers. Dali sent him a water color of a dancing girl carrying a rose.

But nothing could be done to save him, and, after passing into a coma, he died at eight in the morning on Sunday, May 30, 1952, in the beginning of his seventy-third year. The funeral services were simple, with only members of the family and a handful of his oldest friends present, and he was buried at Sleepy Hollow on the Hudson not far from the Millbrook property he loved so well. Then Mary and the three children planted the cherry trees and daffodils at the UN Building in New York, a stone's throw from Beekman Place, as a memorial. I remember a quiet remark made by one of his friends at the funeral: "How we will need him!" And indeed there are hundreds of people who still think of Albert D. Lasker day by day with the most intimate and permanent emotion. I have never known anybody who has ever died less.

APPENDIX

Following is the briefest kind of sketch of the work of some of the National Institutes of Health mentioned in Chapter 21.

The National Cancer Institute. This was founded back in 1936 but it had no real funds to work with for many years. Its budget was $559,000 in 1945; this jumped to $13,998,000 in 1948. The advance came mainly because the American Cancer Society, under Lasker's persuasion, associated itself with the attempt to get federal funds for widespread research (it had never done so before), and several officers and board members of the Society were valuable witnesses before the Senate and House every year.

There followed other soaring jumps in the Cancer Institute budget to roughly $20 million in 1954 and not less than $92 million in fiscal 1960.

The National Heart Institute, founded in 1948. Its budget has sprung from around $1.6 million in that year to more than $62.2 million today; it administers the largest fund in the world, public or private, for the study of diseases of the heart.

The National Institute for Mental Health, established in 1946 with no funds at all. It got $34,000 in 1947, advanced to $18 million by 1956, and has $68 million now. It pursues, among many other activities, research in the properties of tranquilizing drugs and psychic energizers. One result of the use of these drugs has been to reduce the number of patients in mental hospitals; such patients fill no less than *one-half* of all hospital beds in the nation, and are an obvious drag on the national economy.

The National Institute for Arthritis and Metabolistic Diseases, founded in 1950, which conducts research in everything from obesity to asthma, from thyroid disorders to ulcers of the stomach. Its budget has gone up from $430,688 to more than $45 million. One person who worked for the establishment of this institute was Floyd Odlum, the financier, who is himself an arthritis sufferer; another was the New York physician, Dr. C.

H. Traeger. One pay-off has been the development of a diagnostic test for rheumatoid arthritis; another is the continuing exploration of the use of steroid hormones in the treatment of a galaxy of diseases.

The National Institute for Neurological Diseases and Blindness. This was established in 1950 but not one cent of federal money became available for research in these areas until two years later. Yet the country has 1,800,000 victims of cerebral vascular disease, between a million and a million and a half sufferers from Parkinsonism, about a million epileptics, 550,000 victims of cerebral palsy, half a million victims of multiple sclerosis, 200,000 suffers from muscular dystrophy, and 334,000 blind. Today the budget figure exceeds $40 million.

One of the most useful works of research done by this institute recently was discovery of the cause of retrolental fibroplasia, a form of blindness afflicting prematurely born babies, and the major cause of blindness in infants in the United States in the past decade; as a result this unpleasant disease is on the way to being wiped out.[1]

The National Institute of Allergy and Infectious Diseases. Here too the budget has gone up, and significant research in several fields is going on.

The National Institute of Dental Research, which was set up as a result of a rider on the Heart Bill.

[1] What caused it was overuse of oxygen in tents and incubators.

SOURCES AND ACKNOWLEDGMENTS

As I have already mentioned in Chapter One so many pages past, very little bibliography on Lasker exists. The only two primary sources, except a handful of speeches which do not have much interest, are *The Lasker Story*, published by *Advertising Age*, Chicago, in 1952-53, and *The Reminiscences of Albert Davis Lasker*, prepared by the Oral History Research Office at Columbia University. Both of these are in Lasker's own words, and, although brief, are invaluable. I have frequently quoted from them in my text, and I want to express my indebtedness to this indispensable material.

The full record of the disbarment proceedings against Louis S. Levy, including Lasker's testimony, is available in United States Circuit Court of Appeals for the Second Circuit, "In the Matter of Louis S. Levy, Respondent-Appellant," Transcript of Record, Volumes I and II. Lasker's testimony before the subcommittee of the Committee on Labor and Public Welfare, U.S. Senate, Eightieth Congress, in which he gives fully his views on health matters, may be found in Part 3 of the Hearings on S. 545 and S. 1320, National Health Program, July 9, 10, and 11, 1947.

Periodical literature on Lasker is scant in the extreme. A two-part profile by Norman Klein, "There Is No Mystery in Mastery," appeared in the *Chicagoan*, a magazine now extinct, on February 5 and March 1, 1930. *Country Life*, September 1941, carried a description of Mill Road Farm by Alice Fordyce, Mary's sister. *Advertising Age* published two revealing and appreciative obituaries, one of them by Sidney Bernstein, in June, 1952. Through the courtesy of Everett C. Norlander, Managing Editor of the Chicago *Daily News,* and my old friend Tom Sayer, its librarian, I had access to everything that appeared about Lasker in Chicago newspapers over a period of more than forty years, but there are only two or three hundred clippings in all.

Leonard Lyons published a column of anecdotes about Lasker in the New York *Post* a few days after his death in 1952; I have borrowed some of these, with Mr. Lyons' kind permission. Also Mr. Lyons courteously provided me with a round dozen more anecdotes by word of mouth, and many of these also make illuminating embellishments to my text at several points.

The Albert D. Lasker Collection, Renoir to Matisse, with commentaries by Wallace Brockway and introduction by Dr. Alfred Frankfurter (Simon & Schuster, New York, 1957), is, of course, with its sixty magnificent color plates, the definitive memorial to Lasker as an art collector.

The two books I used most in the field of advertising were *Madison Avenue, U.S.A.,* by Martin Mayer (Harper & Brothers, New York, 1958), and *The Story of Advertising,* by James Playsted Wood (Ronald Press, New York, 1958). Neither contains a great deal about Lasker, but both, particularly the latter, are valuable for background. Also, as is obvious from Chapter Five of my own book, I drew considerably from *My Life in Advertising,* by Claude C. Hopkins (Harper & Brothers, New York, 1927). Also I consulted a book (hard to come by) which I believe was written by John Kennedy, but not signed by him, *The Book of Advertising Tests,* published by Lord & Thomas in 1906. A sprightly vignette of Lasker is included in *Just Looking,* by Walter O'Meara, privately printed by Sullivan, Stauffer, Colwell, & Bayles in 1956.

On the Harding period in American politics the most interesting book is, to my mind, *Incredible Era,* by Samuel Hopkins Adams (Houghton Mifflin, Boston, 1939). It has a few references to Lasker and the Shipping Board, but not many. *Willkie,* by Joseph Barnes (Simon & Schuster, New York, 1952), similarly has a reference or two to Lasker—of course in connection with a later period. On general history of the era I used most two standard texts, the admirable *Recent America,* by Henry Bamford Parkes (Crowell, New York, 1941), and *Since 1900,* by Oscar Theodore Barck, Jr., and Nelson Manfred Blake (Macmillan, New York, 1947). *The Autobiography of a Curmudgeon,* by Harold L. Ickes (Reynal & Hitchcock, New York, 1943), contains several references to Lasker. Also I read or reread with pleasure such books as *Postscript to Yesterday* and *Not So Long Ago,* by Lloyd Morris (Random House, New York, 1947 and 1949); *The Good Old Days,* by David L. Cohn (Simon & Schuster, New York, 1940); and *Only Yesterday,* by Frederick Lewis Allen (Harper & Brothers, New

York, 1931), which still glistens as brightly as on the day it was written.

Finally in the realm of printed or written matter I should mention, first, that Robert Koretz, senior vice president of Foote, Cone, & Belding, kindly made available to me a substantial file of old Lord & Thomas advertisements and other material relating to Lasker's activity with the firm; second, Mary Lasker gave me access to all of Lasker's letters that have survived dating from about 1936. These were, of course, of the utmost value.

All this being said, I would like to add that, to an overwhelming degree, my principal sources about Lasker are personal, gathered by ear. Reading gave me comparatively little. But conversation with almost a hundred men and women who knew Lasker in one phase or other of his career provided me with an incomparable harvest of living memories. Among those who generously shared their broad knowledge with me or gave me intimate small details are these:

ALEXANDER, DR. FRANZ, *Psychiatrist*, and Mrs. Alexander, Los Angeles, Calif.

BENTON, WILLIAM, *Former Assistant Secretary of State, Former Senator* from Connecticut, *Publisher, Encyclopaedia Britannica*, New York City.

BERNAYS, EDWARD L., *Public Relations Counsel*, New York City.

BERNSTEIN, S. R., *Vice President and Director, Advertising Age*, Chicago, Ill.

BLOCK, LEIGH B., *Vice President*, Inland Steel Company, Chicago, Ill.

BLOCK, MRS. LEIGH B. (daughter), Chicago, Ill.

BRAZILL, DR. GEORGE K., *Former Commanding General, Seventh Regiment*, New York Guard. *Dental Surgeon*, New York City.

BRODY, SIDNEY, *Industrialist*, Los Angeles, Calif.

BRODY, MRS. SIDNEY (daughter), Los Angeles, Calif.

BROWN, EDWARD EAGLE, the late. *Chairman of the Board*, First National Bank, Chicago, Ill.

CAHILL, JOHN T., *Attorney at law*, New York City.

CERF, MR. AND MRS. BENNETT, Random House, *Publishers*, New York City.

CONE, FAIRFAX M., *Chairman of the Executive Committee*, Foote, Cone, & Belding, Chicago, Ill.

COONS, SHELDON R., *Former Executive Vice-President*, Lord & Thomas. *Business Counselor*, New York City.

CORREA, MATHIAS F., *Attorney at law*, New York City.

COWLES, GARDNER, *Editor, Look* Magazine, New York City.

DANIELS, GEORGE, M.D., *Psychiatrist*, New York City.

DONOVAN, GEN. WILLIAM J., the late, *Attorney and Diplomat. Director,* Office of Strategic Services, World War II, Washington, D.C.

DOYLE, JEROME, *Attorney at law,* New York City.

EPSTEIN, MRS. MAX, Chicago, Ill.

ERNST, MORRIS L., *Attorney at law* and *author,* New York City.

FOOTE, EMERSON, *Senior Vice President,* McCann-Erickson. *Former Executive Vice President,* Lord & Thomas, and *President,* Foote, Cone, & Belding, New York City.

FORDYCE, ALLMON, *Architect,* New York City.

FORDYCE, MRS. ALLMON (sister of Mary Lasker), National Committee Against Mental Illness, New York City.

FRANCISCO, DON, *Former President,* Lord & Thomas. Amagansett, New York.

FRANKFURTER, DR. ALFRED, *Editor and Publisher, Art News,* New York City.

GARBO, MISS GRETA, New York City.

GIMBEL, BERNARD, *Merchant* and *civic leader,* New York City, and MRS. GIMBEL.

GOLDBLATT, MAURICE, *Merchant. Member,* National Committee Against Mental Illness, Chicago, Ill.

GOLDWYN, SAMUEL, *Motion Picture Producer,* and Mrs. Goldwyn, Beverly Hills, Calif.

HARTMAN, LOU, *President,* L. H. Hartman Advertising Co., New York City.

HERTZ, JOHN D., *Financier and Business Leader. Former President,* Yellow Cab Co., Los Angeles, Calif.

HOFFMAN, PAUL G., *Former President,* Studebaker Corporation; *Former Chairman of the Board,* Committee for Economic Development, *Former Administrator,* E.C.A., *Former President,* Ford Foundation, United Nations, New York City.

HOPKINS, ALBERT L., *Attorney at law,* Chicago, Ill.

HORNBLOW, ARTHUR, JR., *Motion Picture Producer,* New York City.

HORNBLOW, LEONORA, *Novelist,* New York City.

HUTCHINS, ROBERT M., *Former President,* University of Chicago. *President,* Fund for the Republic, New York City.

JAVITS, JACOB K., *Senator from New York,* Washington, D.C.

KAYE, MRS. DANNY, Beverly Hills, Calif.

KERRIGAN, MISS ELEANOR (former secretary), New York City.

KINTNER, ROBERT, *President,* National Broadcasting Co., New York City.

KNOPF, EDWIN, *Motion Picture Producer*, Beverly Hills, Calif.

KORETZ, ROBERT, *Senior Vice President*, Foote, Cone, & Belding, Chicago, Ill.

LASKER, MRS. ALBERT D. (widow), New York City.

LASKER, EDWARD (son), *Attorney at law*, Beverly Hills, Calif.

LASKER, MRS. EDWARD (Jane Greer), *Actress*, Beverly Hills, Calif.

LASKER, MISS LOULA (sister), New York City.

LILIENTHAL, DAVID E., *Former Chairman*, Tennessee Valley Authority; *Former Chairman*, Atomic Energy Commission, New York City.

LOEB, DR. ROBERT F., *Professor of Medicine* and *Director of Medical Services*, Columbia Presbyterian Hospital, New York City.

LOEWY, RAYMOND F., *Industrial Designer*, New York City.

LOOS, ANITA, *Playwright*, New York City.

LUDGIN, EARLE, *Chairman of the Board*, Earle Ludgin, Inc., Advertising, Chicago, Ill.

LYONS, LEONARD, *Columnist*, New York *Post*, New York City.

MAHLER, ERNST, *Business Executive, Former President, Director*, Kimberly-Clark Corporation, Tryon, N.C.

MAHONEY, MRS. FLORENCE, *Member of the Board*, Lasker Foundation, Washington, D.C.

MARX, SAMUEL A., *Architect*, Chicago, Ill.

McPARTLAND, CECILIA J. (maid), New York City.

MEIGS, MERRILL C., *Publisher* and *Aviation Expert*, Chicago, Ill.

MEYER, ANDRÉ, *Banker*, Lazard Frères & Co., New York City.

MORRIS, MRS. NANCY (maid), New York City.

NOYES, DAVID M., *Financier, Former Executive Vice President*, Lord & Thomas, Beverly Hills, Calif.

ORAFTIK, EDWARD (chauffeur), New York City.

PLEYDELL-BOUVERIE, THE HON. MRS. AUDREY, London, England.

REIS, BERNARD, *Art Collector. Treasurer*, Lasker Foundation, New York City.

REVES, EMERY, *Author* of *The Anatomy of Peace, Agent* and *Art Collector*, Roquebrune, France.

ROOSEVELT, MRS. ELEANOR, New York City.

ROPER, ELMO B., *Marketing Consultant*, New York City.

ROSE, BILLY, *Theatrical Producer, Art Collector* and *Author*, New York City.

ROSENBERG, ANNA M., *Former Assistant Secretary of Defense. Public Relations Counselor,* New York City.

ROSENSOHN, MRS. SAMUEL (sister), New York City.

SARNOFF, GEN. DAVID, *Chairman of the Board,* Radio Corporation of America, New York City.

SCHLEE, MR. AND MRS. GEORGE, New York City.

SEVERSKY, MAJ. ALEXANDER P. DE, *Aviation Expert* and *Author,* New York City.

SIMON, RICHARD L., Simon & Schuster, *Publishers,* New York City.

SOLLITT, RALPH V., *Former President,* Lord & Thomas, Westport, Connecticut.

SOLLITT, MRS. RALPH V., Westport, Connecticut.

SONNENBERG, BENJAMIN, *Public Relations Counselor,* New York City.

STEIN, JULES, *Chairman of the Board,* Music Corporation of America, Beverly Hills, Calif.

STERN, DAVID B., *Broker.* A. G. Becker & Co., Chicago, Ill.

STRAUSS, ADMIRAL LEWIS L., *Former Chairman,* Atomic Energy Commission, Washington, D.C.

SWIFT, HAROLD H., *Former Chairman of the Board of Trustees,* University of Chicago, Chicago, Ill.

SWOPE, HERBERT BAYARD, the late, *Author, Editor* and *Publicist,* New York City.

TRAEGER, DR. C. H., *Physician,* New York City.

WARD, BARBARA (Lady Jackson), *Author* and *Editor,* London, England, and Accra, Ghana.

WHEELER, JOHN N., *General Manager,* North American Newspaper Alliance, New York City.

WINSTON, NORMAN K., *Financier* and *Housing Specialist,* New York City.

Never did I meet anybody who knew Lasker who did not have something to contribute, and it would be awkward for me to single out any of these warmly co-operative persons for special thanks, and not mention others. But I cannot resist making particular reference to Robert Koretz, who gave me a limitless treasury of glowing (or bristling) Lasker anecdotes; Edward L. Bernays, whose acumen opened much to my eyes; all the veteran associates at Lord & Thomas, like David M. Noyes, Ralph Sollitt, Don Francisco, Sheldon Coons, Fairfax M. Cone, Emerson Foote, and

William Benton; Anna Rosenberg; John T. Cahill; John N. Wheeler; and, above all, every surviving member of the Lasker family without exception. The whole family pitched in to help, in particular Edward Lasker whose zeal and candor were unbounded. Also I should mention that, many years before I had any thought of writing this book, I had the good fortune of uncounted fascinating hours with Albert Lasker himself. Back in 1942 I began taking and carefully keeping notes on his conversation, although I never knew what use I would make of them. Lest anyone think that Dr. Loeb, Dr. Daniels, or any physician mentioned in this book revealed to me medical details that belonged in the realm of their confidential relationship with Lasker, let me say that most of what I use about his illnesses came to me from Lasker himself before he died; he talked to me often about his medical experiences. Finally, I would like to add a special word of thanks to my good friend Alfred Frankfurter. Not only was he my indispensable guide on matters of art, but, more than anybody except members of the family, gave me pungent and revealing insight on Lasker's essential character.

Please also let me thank Mrs. Alice Furlaud, my secretary, who has assisted valiantly in typing, checking, and research on the manuscript. Also I want to acknowledge, with thanks, the friendly and efficient help of Jane E. McDonough, Executive Secretary of the National Health Education Committee, Inc., of New York, who was Lasker's last secretary. And, as always, I have my wife, Jane Perry Gunther, to thank warmly for her unceasing and scrupulous editorial attention as well as sympathy, stimulus, and encouragement.

A dozen or more friends and acquaintances helped me greatly by going through the considerable chore of reading the manuscript in whole or in part. They corrected me on various errors and infelicities, and gave me much new information. Yet none of them are to be held responsible if any errors or misinterpretations remain. For one reason or another I prefer not to mention these stoutly helpful friends by name, but let me say that I am grateful to them one and all.

Finally, this book could not have been written at all without the patient, generous, and objectively discerning help of Mary Woodard Lasker. It is not a subsidized undertaking in any way, not an "official" biography, but I want to express unalterably my profound appreciation of her assistance and hospitality, together with my affection, admiration, and esteem. Much of my material was gathered at La Quinta, California, in her company, and I wrote half a dozen chapters at Heathcote Farm, her house near Millbrook, New York. I should, though, in fairness to Mrs. Lasker, add that none of the responsibility for what I have written is hers, even though she assisted without stint in every phase of the undertaking.

J. G.

La Quinta, California, February, 1958
—New York City, March, 1960

INDEX